SOFTWARE ENGINEERING TECHNIQUES: DESIGN FOR QUALITY

T0137991

IFIP – The International Federation for Information Processing

IFIP was founded in 1960 under the auspices of UNESCO, following the First World Computer Congress held in Paris the previous year. An umbrella organization for societies working in information processing, IFIP's aim is two-fold: to support information processing within its member countries and to encourage technology transfer to developing nations. As its mission statement clearly states,

> IFIP's mission is to be the leading, truly international, apolitical organization which encourages and assists in the development, exploitation and application of information technology for the benefit of all people.

IFIP is a non-profitmaking organization, run almost solely by 2500 volunteers. It operates through a number of technical committees, which organize events and publications. IFIP's events range from an international congress to local seminars, but the most important are:

- The IFIP World Computer Congress, held every second year;
- Open conferences;
- Working conferences.

The flagship event is the IFIP World Computer Congress, at which both invited and contributed papers are presented. Contributed papers are rigorously refereed and the rejection rate is high.

As with the Congress, participation in the open conferences is open to all and papers may be invited or submitted. Again, submitted papers are stringently refereed.

The working conferences are structured differently. They are usually run by a working group and attendance is small and by invitation only. Their purpose is to create an atmosphere conducive to innovation and development. Refereeing is less rigorous and papers are subjected to extensive group discussion.

Publications arising from IFIP events vary. The papers presented at the IFIP World Computer Congress and at open conferences are published as conference proceedings, while the results of the working conferences are often published as collections of selected and edited papers.

Any national society whose primary activity is in information may apply to become a full member of IFIP, although full membership is restricted to one society per country. Full members are entitled to vote at the annual General Assembly. National societies preferring a less committed involvement may apply for associate or corresponding membership. Associate members enjoy the same benefits as full members, but without voting rights. Corresponding members are not represented in IFIP bodies. Affiliated membership is open to non-national societies, and individual and honorary membership schemes are also offered.

SOFTWARE ENGINEERING TECHNIQUES: DESIGN FOR QUALITY

Edited by

Krzysztof Sacha
Software Engineering Group
Institute of Control & Computation Engineering
Warsaw University of Technology
Warsaw, Poland

 Springer

Software Engineering Techniques: Design for Quality

Edited by K. Sacha

p. cm. (IFIP International Federation for Information Processing, a Springer Series in Computer Science)

ISSN: 1571-5736 / 1861-2288 (Internet)

ISBN: 13: 978-1-4419-4266-1
Printed on acid-free paper

eISBN: 10: 0-387-39388-9
eISBN: 13: 978-0-387-39388-9

9 8 7 6 5 4 3 2 1
springer.com

PREFACE

The aim of software engineering is to find methods for developing high quality software products at a reasonable cost. As more and more computers are being used in areas in which a malfunction of the system can be a source of serious losses or disturbances to the functioning of the society, the quality of software becomes more and more critical factor of business success, human security and safety. Examples of such application areas are enterprise management, public administration, social insurance or post delivery services. The quality of services offered to the society depends on the quality of software systems that support the functioning of the respective public or private organizations (service providers).

Software engineering consists of a selection of methods and techniques that vary from project to project and evolve in time. The purpose of this volume is to provide an overview of the current work in software development techniques that can help with enhancing the quality of software. The chapters of the volume, organized by key topic area, create an agenda for the IFIP Working Conference on Software Engineering Techniques SET 2006, held October 17–20, 2006 in Warsaw. The seven sections of the volume address the following areas and particular topics:

Software architectures. Methods for structuring the software in order to promote dependability and modifiability, component-based software development, aspect-oriented architectures, distributed and Internet applications.

Modeling. UML-based modeling of component systems, model transformation, semi-formal and formal modeling of software systems using of Petri nets, queuing network models and algebraic calculus.

Project management. Organization-wide process improvement, risk evaluation, modeling and management.

Software Quality. Quality specification and evaluation, user involvement in the quality improvement process, case study.

Analysis and verification methods. Test processes, test automation, test case development and test generation, mutation testing versus aspectoriented response injection, analysis and testing of Java programs, verification of UML state diagrams. headingsddfootoempty venfooteempty

Data management. Knowledge base system engineering, data warehouses and data quality monitoring and maintenance.

Software maintenance. Software refactoring, structuring of Java programs, legacy applications in Web based systems, security problems.

I would like to thank all authors and reviewers who, at the end of the day, create what this is all about.

Krzysztof Sacha   *Warsaw, July 2006*

Reviewers

Table of Contents

From Hubs Via Holons to an
Adaptive Meta-Architecture – the "AD-HOC" Approach

Leszek A. Maciaszek

Macquarie University, Department of Computing,
NSW 2109, Sydney, Australia
leszek@ics.mq.edu.au

Abstract. The ever increasing sophistication of software systems brings with it the ever increasing danger of humans losing control over their own creations. This situation, termed the 'software crisis', is said to have existed since the early days of software engineering and has been characterized by the inability of software developers to produce adaptive systems. This paper addresses the roots of the software crisis – the software cognitive and structural complexity and how it could be conquered through the imposition of a meta-architecture on software solutions. The meta-architecture, called PCBMER, epitomizes some important characteristics of holons and holarchies underpinning the structure and behavior of living systems.

1 Introduction

An *adaptive* system has an ability to change to suit different conditions; an ability to continue into the future by meeting existing functional and nonfunctional requirements and by adjusting to accommodate any new and changing requirements. *Adaptiveness* is an overriding software quality that consists of a triple of critically important sub qualities – understandability, maintainability, extensibility.

There are three principal underpinnings to achieving adaptive solutions [9]. The first underpinning is the prior existence of a *meta-architecture* (framework) to guide architects in doing their job of constructing architectural models for a particular software system. The second underpinning to achieving adaptive solutions is an enforcement of sound *engineering principles*. If the architectural design *defines* adaptiveness, the engineering principles *deliver* adaptiveness. The third underpinning to achieving adaptive solutions is an enforcement of sound *managerial practices*. Managerial practices *verify* adaptiveness.

This paper addresses the first underpinning to achieving adaptive software systems. The paper introduces and explains a meta-architecture called *PCBMER* that extends earlier meta-architectures proposed by the author, of which the last is known as the PCMEF framework (e.g. [10, 11]).

The acronym "AD-HOC" refers to our research aimed at modeling software systems on the image of living systems. This research started more than a decade ago with the papers [12, 13]. The research was then channeled to industry projects, elaborated in successive experiments and papers, applied in the textbooks [10, 11],

Please use the following format when citing this chapter:

Maciaszek, L.A., 2006, in IFIP International Federation for Information Processing, Volume 227, Software Engineering Techniques: Design for Quality, ed. K. Sacha, (Boston: Springer), pp. 1–13.

and it is now finding its way to a monograph still in writing during this manuscript preparation [9]. Originally, the "AD-HOC" acronym stood for Application Development – Holon-Object-Centric approach. The preferred meaning now is Application Development – Holons, Objects, Components.

2 Complexity in the wires

The *complexity* of modern enterprise and e-business systems is *in the wires* – in the linkages and communication paths between software modules rather than in the internal size of the modules. The communication paths create *dependencies* between distributed components that may be difficult to understand and manage (a software object A depends on an object B, if a change in B necessitates a change in A).

Software *adaptiveness* is a function of the software *cognitive and structural complexity* (e.g. [4]). It is a function of the ease with which we can understand the software flow of logic and any resulting dependencies.

2.1 Networks

Fig.1 shows a possible system in which objects in various packages (components, subsystems) communicate indiscriminately. This creates a network of intercommunicating objects. The complexity of such systems grows exponentially with the addition of new objects. Even if the complexity within packages can be controlled by limiting the size of the packages, the complexity created by inter-package communication links grows exponentially with the introduction of more packages. The growth is exponential not necessarily because of the *actual dependencies* between objects, but because the flat network structure (with no clearly defined restrictions on communication paths between objects) creates *potential dependencies* between any (all) objects in the system. A change in an object can potentially impact (can have a *"ripple effect"* on) any other object in the system.

Assuming unrestricted origin/destination communication links (i.e. allowing both-directional dependencies between objects), the cumulative measure of object dependencies is given by a simple formula:

$$_{net}CCD = n(n-1) \tag{1}$$

where n is the number of objects (nodes in the graph) and $_{net}CCD$ is a cumulative class dependency in a fully connected network (assuming that objects refer to classes).

The formula computes the worst *potential complexity*, where each object can potentially communicate with all other objects. For 17 classes in Fig.1, $_{net}CCD$ is equal to 272 (17*16). Although the worst scenario is unlikely in practice, it must be assumed in any dependency impact analysis conducted on the system (simply because real dependencies are not known beforehand). Systems permitting an indiscriminate network of intercommunicating objects are considered not adaptive.

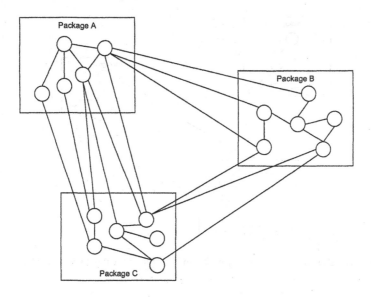

Fig. 1. Network of intercommunicating objects

2.2 Networks with hubs

The exponential growth of complexity in flat network structures is not acceptable. We need to have software architectural solutions that result in merely polynomial complexity growth when new objects/components are added. Such architectural solutions consist of meta-models, frameworks, principles, patterns, etc. At the most generic level, the reduction of complexity can be achieved through so called *hub structures* [3].

Fig.2 shows how the complexity of a system can be reduced by introducing hubs. Each package defines a *hub* – an interface object (this could be a Java-style interface or so called dominant class) through which all communication with the package is channeled. Despite the introduction of three extra hub objects, the complexity of the system in Fig.2 is visibly reduced in comparison with the same system in Fig.1.

More formally, the cumulative measure of object dependencies with hubs between packages but with still unrestricted origin/destination communication links within packages is given by the formula:

$$_{hubnet}CCD = \sum_{i=1}^{h}(n_i(n_i - 1)) + (h(h-1)) \tag{2}$$

where n is the number of objects in each package plus the hub object, h is the number of hubs (i.e. the number of packages) and $_{hubnet}CCD$ is a cumulative class dependency in a hub network. For 17 classes and 3 hubs, $_{hubnet}CCD$ is equal to 120.

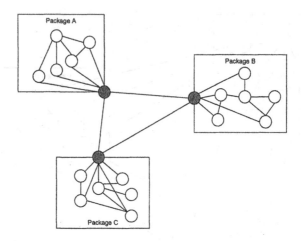

Fig. 2. Reduction of complexity owing to hubs (interfaces) between packages

2.3 Hierarchies with hubs

For the flat network structures, the best complexity values can be obtained in a *hub-spoke* structure, not discussed here [3]. However, in general, any network is a hopeless structure. All complex systems that are adaptive take the form of a *hierarchy*, or rather a *holarchy* (ref. Section 2). A hierarchy/holarchy consists of hierarchically organized layers of objects with one-way (asymmetrical) dependencies between the layers.

Fig.3 shows a *hierarchical structure with hubs* and downward only dependencies between subsystems. Objects are grouped into subsystems instead of packages (subsystems A-C mirror the structure of packages A-C in Fig.2). Subsystems are more appropriate here because the notion of the subsystem (at least in the UML sense) encapsulates some part of the intended system behavior, i.e. a client object must ask the subsystem itself (represented by a hub object) to fulfill the behavior. The notion of the package does not have such semantics [10].

The dependencies between subsystems are only downwards and the dependencies within subsystems have no cycles [11]. Any upward communication between subsystems is realized by a "dependency-less" loose coupling facilitated by interfaces placed in lower subsystems but implemented in higher-level subsystems and/or by event processing instead of message passing and/or by the use of XML-based meta-level technologies. Similarly, cycles within subsystems are eliminated by using interfaces, but also through refactoring techniques that extract circularly-dependent functionality into separate objects/components.

The complexity formula for hierarchies with hubs is:

$$_{hubhier}CCD = \sum_{i=1}^{root}\frac{o_i(o_i-1)}{2} + \sum_{j=1}^{root}p_{j+1} \tag{3}$$

where:

- o is the number of objects in each subsystem i including any hub objects,
- p_{j+1} is the number of objects in each directly adjacent subsystem above any leave subsystem minus any hub object (this computes the number of potential downward paths to all hub objects in the adjacent subsystems),
- and $_{hubhier}CCD$ is a cumulative class dependency in a hub hierarchy (and assuming as before that objects refer to classes).

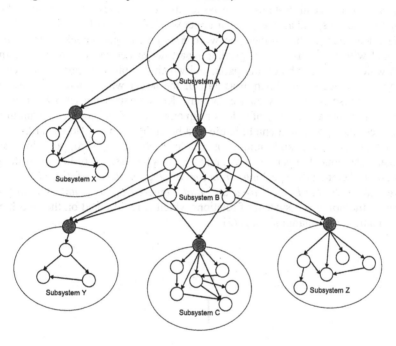

Fig. 3. Reduction of complexity in a hierarchy with hubs

Comparing between Fig.3 and Fig.2, $_{hubhier}CCD$ is equal 63 whereas $_{hubnet}CCD$ is equal 120. The overall $_{hubhier}CCD$ for the model in Fig.3 is equal 111 (63 for subsystems A-C plus 48 for the remaining subsystems).

3 Holons and holarchies

The complexity of living systems by far exceeds the complexity of any man-made system. This observation is easily validated by a simple fact that many intricacies of living organisms escape human understanding. Despite of, or rather owing to, this complexity – living systems are able to *adapt* to changing environments and evolve in the process. Therefore, it seems sensible to study the structure and behaviour of living organisms in search for paradigms of use in the construction of software solutions.

Living systems are organized to form multi-leveled structures, each level consisting of subsystems which are wholes in regard to their parts, and parts with respect to the larger wholes. Thus molecules combine to form organelles, which in turn combine to form cells. The cells form tissues and organs, which themselves form larger systems, like the digestive system or the nervous system. These, finally, combine to form the living person; and the 'stratified order' does not end there. People form families, tribes, societies, nations. All these entities - from molecules to human beings, and on to social systems - can be regarded as wholes in the sense of being integrated structures, and also as parts of larger wholes at higher levels of complexity.

Arthur Koestler [5] has coined the word *holon* (from the Greek word: *holos* = whole and with the suffix *on* suggesting a part, as in neutron or proton) for these entities which are both wholes and parts, and which exhibit two opposite tendencies: an integrative tendency to function as part of the larger whole, and a self assertive tendency to preserve its individual autonomy. Koestler uses the term *holarchy* (or *holocracy*) to name a hierarchy of holons from one point of development to another.

Fig.4 represents a possible mental picture of a holarchy. Looking downward, a holon is something complete and unique, a whole. Looking upward, a holon is an elementary component, a part. The diagram captures the essence of holons as defined by Koestler: "Generally speaking, *a holon on the /n/ level of the hierarchy is represented on the /n+1/ level as a unit and triggered off as a unit. Or, to put it differently: the holon is a system of relations which is represented on the next higher level as a unit, i.e., a relatum.*" [5, p.72].

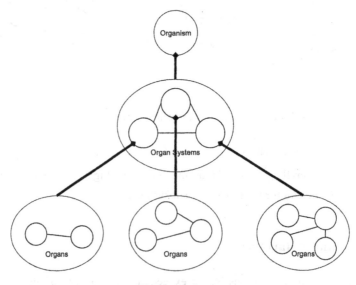

Fig. 4. A holarchy

Individual holons within a holarchy are represented by four main characteristics: (1) their internal charter (interactions between them can form unique patterns), (2) self-assertive aggregation of subordinate holons, (3) an integrative tendency with regard to superior holons, and (4) relationships with their peer holons.

Holarchies do not operate in isolation, but interact with others. "Thus the circulatory system controlled by the heart and the respiratory system controlled by the lungs function as quasi-autonomous, self-regulating hierarchies, but they interact on various levels." [7, p.463]. Koestler uses the term ***arborization*** for vertical structures and ***reticulation*** for horizontal net formations between holarchies.

Behavior of holarchies is defined by ***fixed rules*** and ***flexible strategies***. The rules are referred to as the system's *canon* that determines its invariant properties – its structural configuration and/or functional pattern. *"The canon represents the constraints imposed on any rule-governed process or behaviour.* But these constraints do not exhaust the system's degrees of freedom; they leave room for more or less *flexible strategies,* guided by the contingencies in the holon's local environment. ... In *acquired skills* like chess, the rules of the game define the permissible moves, but the strategic choice of the actual move depends on the environment – the distribution of the chessmen on the board." [6, pp.293-294].

Since the concept of holon was introduced by Koestler in [5], it has been used by various branches of science ranging from biology via communication theory to more practical uses for implementation of holonic manufacturing systems [16]. Holons and holarchies offer great architectural and other solution ideas for implementing software systems. Successful systems tend to resemble holarchies in many of their aspects, including the ability to hide complexity in successively lower layers, whilst providing greater levels of abstraction within the higher layers of their structures.

The space limitations do not allow us to discuss software technologies (some established, other emerging) that parallel various holon ideas [9]. Most interesting parallels seem to be:

1. Arborization → object composition (e.g. the GoF composite pattern).
2. Reticulation → weaving in aspect-oriented programming.
3. Fixed rules → meta-architectures.
4. Flexible strategies → autonomous agents in multi-agent systems.

4   Dependencies

Our goal is to minimize code dependencies through skillful architectural design. A necessary condition to understand a system behavior is to identify object dependencies and measure ripple effects that they may cause. A ***ripple effect*** of a dependency is a chain reaction that a change to a supplier object may cause on all client objects that directly or indirectly depend on the supplier.

In simple systems, the ripple effect can be determined by the analysis of ***actual dependencies*** in the code. But even in simple systems, finding all actual dependencies may be difficult if some suppliers of services are chosen dynamically at ***run-time*** and are, therefore, unknown at ***compile-time*** (i.e. not directly visible in the source code). It follows that the ripple effect, for all but very simple systems, needs to be determined by the analysis of all ***potential dependencies*** in the code, i.e. dependencies that are allowed by the architectural design of the system, whether or not they actually exist (and assuming that architectural design is adhered to in the implemented code). Fig.5 provides a classification of dependency relationships relevant to the discussion in this chapter.

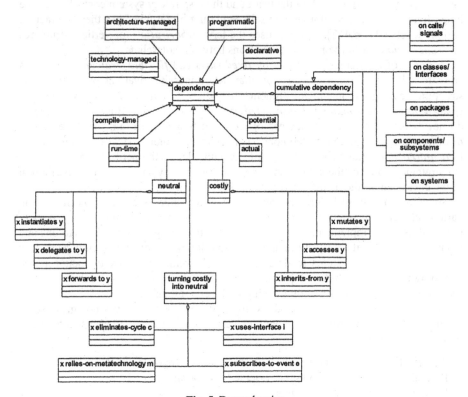

Fig. 5. Dependencies

A hierarchical architectural structure is undefined unless we determine precisely what dependencies are allowed between hierarchy layers and within the layers, and what their potential ripple effect is. These are ***architecture-managed*** dependencies that are under complete control of system developers.

However, *application software* is implemented using particular *system software* and applying particular development technology (application servers, databases, libraries, etc.). The system software takes then responsibility for some important functionality, which otherwise would have to be implemented in the application software. Clearly, application software *depends on* system software, but these are dependencies that cannot be really managed by application developers. These are meta-level ***technology-managed*** dependencies.

Ideally, the integration of application and system software should be based on ***declarative*** dependencies documented in various configuration files, preferably XML files. Configuration files act as agents able to determine actions to be taken (planners), selecting between different possible actions (decision makers), managing execution requests (mediators), etc.

Increasingly, XML-style declarative dependencies replace hard-coded **programmatic** dependencies not only in *integration development* (including integration of application and system software) but also within *application development*. As compared with declarative dependencies, programmatic dependencies introduce tight-coupling between client and supplier objects and are significantly more difficult to manage. Sometimes, programmatic dependencies are a sign of weaknesses in the technology applied, but in general they are just a way of making programming objects to communicate in order to make the application perform required tasks.

As mentioned, the main purpose of measuring dependencies is to define their ripple effects so that their impact on system complexity and adaptiveness can be quantified. However, not all dependencies are equally *costly*. Some categories of dependencies are relatively **neutral** in the calculations aiming at establishing cumulative dependencies for the system. There is also an important category of dependencies under the name *turning costly into neutral* – they can be used as a way of enforcing the agreed principles of the architecture so that the complexity of the system can be managed.

The notion of *object* can refer to a programming element of any granularity (call (message), signal (event), class, package, component, subsystem, or the entire system). Accordingly object dependencies can be specified on any of these object types. Object dependencies of lower granularity need to be then considered when determining dependencies of higher granularity. Because classes are the main programming modules in contemporary systems, *class dependencies* are the focal point of all modern complexity metrics, such as the CK metrics [2].

5 PCBMER meta-architecture

There is no one unique or best meta-architecture that could provide a framework for constructing adaptive complex system. Also, depending on the application domain, the system characteristics and the category of development/integration project, various variations of a particular meta-architecture can be determined and used. The *pivotal meta-architecture*, which we advocate, is called **PCBMER**. The *PCBMER* framework defines six hierarchical layers of software objects – *Presentation, Controller, Bean, Mediator, Entity* and *Resource*.

5.1 PCBMER layers

Fig.6 illustrates the *Core PCBMER* architectural framework. The framework borrows the names of the external tiers (the Client tier and the EIS tier) from the Core J2EE framework [1]. The tiers are represented as UML nodes. The dotted arrowed lines are *dependency relationships*. Hence, for example, Presentation depends on Controller and on Bean, and Controller depends on Bean. Note that the *PCBMER* hierarchy is not strictly linear and a higher-layer can have more than one adjacent layer below (and that adjacent layer may be an *intra-leaf*, i.e. it may have no layers below it).

Fig.6 presents two variants of the *Core PCBMER* framework – one defined on UML packages and the other on UML subsystems. As opposed to the variant with packages, the services that components/subsystems provide are fully encapsulated and exposed as a set of *ports* that define the provided and required *interfaces*.

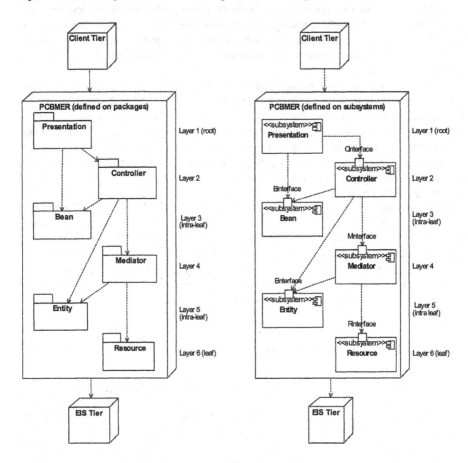

Fig. 6. The Core PCBMER meta-architecture

The emphasis that the notion of component places on encapsulation, ports and interfaces makes components directly applicable for modeling hub structures. Therefore, architectural frameworks presented in the context of subsystems may imply lower cumulative class complexity than those presented with the notion of package.

The **Bean** *subsystem* represents the data classes and value objects that are destined for rendering on user interface. Unless entered by the user, the bean data is built up from the entity objects (the Entity subsystem). The *Core PCBMER* framework does not specify or endorse if access to Bean objects is via message passing or event processing as long as the Bean subsystem does not depend on other subsystems.

The *Presentation subsystem* represents the screen and UI objects on which the beans can be rendered. It is responsible for maintaining consistency in its presentation when the beans change. So, it depends on the Bean subsystem. This dependency can be realized in one of two ways – by direct calls to methods (message passing) using the *pull model* or by event processing followed by message passing using the *push model* (or rather *push-and-pull* model)

The *Controller subsystem* represents the application logic. Controller objects respond to the UI requests that originate from Presentation and that are results of user interactions with the system. In a programmable GUI client, UI requests may be menu or button selections. In a web browser client, UI requests appear as HTTP Get or Post requests.

The *Entity* subsystem responds to Controller and Mediator. It contains classes representing "business objects". They store (in the program's memory) objects retrieved from the database or created in order to be stored in the database. Many entity classes are container classes.

The *Mediator* subsystem establishes a channel of communication that mediates between Entity and Resource classes. This layer manages business transactions, enforces business rules, instantiates business objects in the Entity subsystem, and in general manages the memory cache of the application. Architecturally, Mediator serves two main purposes. Firstly, to isolate the Entity and Resource subsystems so that changes in any one of them can be introduced independently. Secondly, to mediate between the Controller and Entity/Resource subsystems when Controller requests data but it does not know if the data has been loaded to memory or it is only available in the database.

The *Resource* subsystem is responsible for all communications with external persistent data sources (databases, web services, etc.). This is where the connections to the database and SOA servers are established, queries to persistent data are constructed, and the database transactions are instigated.

The *Core PCBMER* framework has a number of immediately visible advantages resulting in minimization of dependencies. One noticeable advantage is the *separation of concerns* between subsystems allowing modifications within one subsystem without affecting the other (independent) subsystems or with a predictable and manageable effect on the other (dependable) subsystems. For example, the Presentation subsystem that provides a Java application UI could be switched to a mobile phone interface and still use the existing implementation of Controller and Bean subsystems. That is, the same pair of Controller and Bean subsystems can support more than one Presentation UI at the same time.

The second important advantage is the *elimination of cycles* between dependency relationships and the resultant six-layer hierarchy with downward only dependencies. Cycles would degenerate a hierarchy into a network structure. Cycles are disallowed both between *PCBMER* layers and within each *PCBMER* layer.

The third advantage is that the framework ensures a significant degree of *stability*. Higher layers depend on lower layers. Therefore, as long as the lower layers are stable (i.e. do not change significantly, in particular in interfaces), the changes to the higher layers are relatively painless. Recall also that lower layers can be extended with new functionality (as opposed to changes to existing functionality), and such extensions should not impact on the existing functionality of the higher layers.

5.2 PCBMER structural complexity

To compute *cumulative dependencies* between program's objects we use *structural complexity* metrics and apply them to a particular design and to a resulting implementation. The metrics can apply to objects of various granularities, from methods in classes to subsystems and systems. However, in the structural complexity argument, the most indicative is a cumulative dependency computed on classes.

In traditional software engineering sense, structural complexity metrics reveal the classic tension between cohesion and coupling of objects (e.g. [15]). *Coupling* is really another name for dependency between objects. Two objects are coupled if they collaborate with one another. In good designs, coupling is minimized so that collaboration is just enough to perform required tasks. As opposed to our stance on dependencies, coupling allows both-ways collaboration, i.e. cycles are permitted.

If coupling is a relationship between objects, *cohesion* defines the internal responsibilities of each object. "A class with low (bad) cohesion has a set of features that don't belong together. A class with high (good) cohesion has a set of features that all contribute to the type abstraction implemented by the class." [14, p.246].

The objective is to have low coupling and high cohesion, but unfortunately these two concepts contradict each other. For any system, the challenge is to define a right balance between coupling and cohesion. The best known strategy to balance coupling and cohesion in object-oriented designs is known as the *Law of Demeter (LoD)* (Lieberherr and Holland, 1989). The LoD is known in the popular formulation as "talk only to your friends" principle. It aims at minimizing coupling by prescribing what targets are allowed for messages within class methods. Note that the LoD has a direct counterpart in the *PCBMER*'s NCP principle.

We believe that a starting point to achieve proper balance between the system-wide cohesion and coupling is to ensure that the initial definition of each class is determined alone on the basis of its cohesiveness. We, therefore, assume that – for comparisons of structural complexities in various designs for the same system – the cohesion of classes is constant (with reason, of course; i.e. classes cannot be grouped together to achieve lower coupling, but extra classes may be created to ensure architectural conformance or to take advantage of a particular technology).

With the above in mind, the generic *cumulative class dependency* formula for the *Core PCBMER* defined *on subsystems* is the same as Formula 3 for hierarchies with hubs (this is a *generic* formula and other formulas may apply to specific *PCBMER* architectures derived from the *Core* framework). Strictly speaking, there is a difference in the way the formula is applied because the *PCBMER* framework permits a lower-layer subsystem to be communicated from more than one higher-layer subsystem. However, these higher-layer subsystems are considered to be "directly adjacent", thus the formula applies as stands. Note that because only downward dependencies are allowed, the communication from higher-layer subsystems retains the hierarchical properties of the *PCBMER* framework.

Formula 3 ensures *polynomial* growth of dependencies between architectural layers represented as subsystems, while allowing *exponential* growth of class dependencies within layers. However, the exponential growth can be controlled by grouping classes within a layer into *nested subsystems* (as subsystems can contain other subsystems). The communication between nested subsystems can then be performed using hubs.

6 Summary

In this paper we: (1) explained the interplay between software complexity and adaptiveness, (2) showed that hierarchical structures with hubs minimize complexity in the wires (and mentioned, but not elaborated, that hub-spoke structures can provide further minimization), (3) talked about the structure and behaviour of living systems in terms of holons and holarchies and linked these concepts to software systems, (4) provided an elaborated classification of object dependencies, (5) introduced the *PCBMER* meta-architecture and defined its layering structure, architectural principles, and structural complexity.

The lack of space did not permit to address software engineering practices and technologies that could guarantee the compliance of an implemented software system with the *PCBMER* meta-architecture and its principles. Similarly, no reverse-engineering verification procedures were defined to substantiate in metrics the level of compliance in the implemented system. Many of these issues have been addressed in other "AD-HOC" papers and are being compiled into a book [9].

References

1. Alur, D. Crupi, J. and Malks, D.: Core J2EE Patterns: Best Practices and Design Strategies. 2nd edn. Prentice Hall (2003)
2. Chidamber, S.R. and Kemerer, C.F. A Metrics Suite for Object Oriented Design. IEEE Tran. od Soft. Eng. 6 (1994) 476-493
3. Daskin, M.S.: Network and Discrete Location. Models, Algorithms and Applications John Wiley & Sons (1995)
4. Fenton, N.E. and Pfleeger, S.L.: Software Metrics. A Rigorous and Practical Approach. PWS Publ. Comp. (1997)
5. Koestler, A.: The Ghost in the Machine. Hutchinson (1967)
6. Koestler, A.: Janus. A Summing Up. Hutchinson (1978)
7. Koestler, A.: Bricks to Babel. Random House (1980)
8. Lieberherr, K.J. and Holland, I.M.: Assuring Good Style for Object-Oriented Programs. IEEE Soft. 9 (1989) 38-48
9. Maciaszek, L.A.: Development and Integration of Adaptive Complex Enterprise and E-business Systems. Pearson Education (2007) (in preparation)
10. Maciaszek, L.A.: Requirements Analysis and System Design. 2nd edn. Addison-Wesley, Harlow England (2005)
11. Maciaszek, L.A. and Liong, B.L.: Practical Software Engineering. A Case-Study Approach. Addison-Wesley, Harlow England (2005)
12. Maciaszek, L.A. De Troyer, O.M.F Getta J.R. and Bosdriesz, J: Generalization versus Aggregation in Object Application Development - the "AD-HOC" Approach. Proc. 7th Australasian Conf. on Inf. Syst. ACIS'96., Hobart, Tasmania, Australia (1996) 431-442
13. Maciaszek, L.A. Getta, J.R. and Bosdriesz, J.: Restraining Complexity in Object System Development - the "AD-HOC" Approach. Proc. 5th Int. Conf. on Inf. Syst. Development ISD'96, Gdansk, Poland (1996) 425-435
14. Page-Jones, M.: Fundamentals of Object-Oriented Design in UML. Addison-Wesley (2000)
15. Pressman, R.S.: Software Engineering. A Practitioner's Approach, 6th edn. McGraw-Hill (2005)
16. Tharumarajah, A. Wells, A.J. and Nemes, L.: Comparison of the Bionic, Fractal and Holonic Manufacturing System Concepts. Int. J. Comp. Integr. Manufact. 3 (1996) 217-226

A C++ Workbench with Accurate Non-Blocking Garbage Collector for Server Side Internet Applications

Piotr Kołaczkowski and Ilona Bluemke
{P.Kolaczkowski, I.Bluemke}@ii.pw.edu.pl

Institute of Computer Science, Warsaw University of Technology,
Nowowiejska 15/19, 00-665 Warsaw, Poland

Abstract. At the Institute of Computer Science Warsaw University of Technology a workbench for building server-side, dependable, Internet applications was designed and implemented. This workbench is a collection of C++ classes. The design and implementation of these classes are briefly described. The most important part of the workbench is the web server, implemented as a C++ class that can be used in a standalone application. To implement the web server a precise, concurrent garbage collector was designed. Our garbage collector is based on the concurrent mark-and-sweep algorithm and smart pointer pattern. It makes the risk of memory access faults or memory leaks much lower than in standard C/C++ applications. The advantages of our workbench are shown in some experiments. We have measured the overhead of our garbage collector and the performance of the workbench. A comparison with other systems is also given.

1 Introduction

Automatic memory management techniques have been successfully employed for years. Existence of a garbage collector increases the dependability of applications and makes programming easier. A garbage collector is a core component of many programming environments e.g. for languages like Java or C#. On the contrary, originally designed without automatic memory management, uncooperative environments are still used. The C++ language belongs to such environments. Although conservative garbage collection techniques are quite popular [1], the design of an accurate, non-blocking garbage collectors is a very complex task and those collectors are rather uncommon. In the paper we show, how the accurate, non-blocking garbage collector designed and implemented at the Institute of Computer Science Warsaw University of Technology [2, 3] was employed in a C++ workbench for dependable server side Internet applications. A very important issue is to provide the high quality and the dependability of such applications. Although there are many techniques for building an Internet application [4], it is not easy to develop it in widely used C++ programming language. A C++ programmer can use only few techniques: CGI [5], FastCGI [6] or .NET environment. One of the problems that has to be solved by the programmer in C++ programs is the memory management. Errors in the memory management are often the source of defects and security holes.

The paper is organized as follows. In the next section some general memory management approaches in C++ applications are briefly described and their usability for building Internet applications is discussed. In Section 3 the implemented workbench is

Please use the following format when citing this chapter:

Kołaczkowski, P., Bluemke, I., 2006, in IFIP International Federation for Information Processing, Volume 227, Software Engineering Techniques: Design for Quality, ed. K. Sacha, (Boston: Springer), pp. 15–24.

presented. The following aspects of the web server are mentioned: memory management, application interface, concurrency support, session handling. In Section 4 some experiments are described. The throughput and the response time of sample C++ applications, prepared with the workbench, were measured. The overheads of the garbage collector are examined. The final section contains conclusions.

2 Related work

Boehm and Weiser have developed a good and widely used conservative garbage collector for C and C++ languages [1, 7]. This garbage collector can work in one of the two modes: blocking or incremental. The blocking mode uses the *mark-and-sweep* algorithm. The incremental mode uses the *train* algorithm [8], which is much slower, but reduces the execution delays. In both modes the collector does not guarantee that all *dead* (inaccessible) data are removed, so some small memory leaks are possible. The probability of such leaks is higher for applications with larger heaps e.g. extensively caching webservers. Memory leaks can be disastrous in long-running applications.

Barlett proposed a generational, mostly-copying, conservative garbage collector for C++ [9], which according to the benchmarks presented in [10] performs better than the Boehm-Weiser's collector. It is also more accurate, because the programmer provides special procedures enabling the garbage collector to find pointers in objects. On the other hand, some parts of memory are still treated conservatively, so the problem of possible memory leaks remains. Additionally, the programmer can give erroneous relative pointer locations and mislead the garbage collector. This can be a cause of severe memory management failures.

Detlefs studied the possibility of using the C++ template metaprogramming techniques to achieve the garbage collector's accuracy [11]. *Smart pointers* can be used to track references between objects. This allows for the accurate garbage collection without the need to manually specify the relative pointer locations. Detlefs used this technique in a reference counting collector. His measurements show that reference counting can impose a time overhead of over 50% which is probably too high for being successfully used in a high performance web application.

In spite of some small programming inconveniences introduced by smart pointers (their usage differs a little from the C++ built-in pointers) [12], we proposed how to use them with a concurrent *mark-and-sweep* algorithm to get an accurate, non-blocking garbage collector [3]. Our research did not show how the garbage collector performs in a real-world application. Only benchmarks for single memory operations were done. Some interesting recent benchmarks can be found in [13], but these don't cover real-world server side applications, too.

Henderson designed a different technique for building an accurate garbage collector based on the code preprocessing approach [14]. The preprocessor inserts additional instructions into the original C code. These instructions enable the garbage collector to find exact pointer locations. Although Henderson didn't implement a multithreaded garbage collector, he proposed how to do it using his approach. He also performed some simple benchmarks and obtained promising results.

While garbage collection techniques were being improved, engineers and researchers were independently creating new ways of building internet server side applications. The latters can be divided into two main categories: scripts and applications servers. Scripts may be used for small applications. Severs are dedicated for more complex ones, even distributed. An overview of techniques for Internet applications can be found in [4].

The script is a file containing some instructions. By processing these instructions a WWW server is able to generate the Internet page. There are many kinds of scripts e.g.: CGI [5, 6], PHP [15], Cold Fusion [16], iHTML [17], ASP [18]. The script is invoked for each request by the WWW server. The script technique is simple but it can be used to build applications like portals or Internet shops. Some script languages e.g. PHP contain special constructs useful in such applications like: data exchange, access to data bases, interfaces based on MVC (Model View Controller) patterns. Due to the short time of living of the script process, scripts don't take much advantage of garbage collectors.

Application servers can be used for building complex, multilayered, distributed applications. Such applications may communicate with users by Internet browsers. The application is active all the time and receives HTTP requests from the browser. Java servlets and JSP [19, 20] operate this way. In application servers some optimization techniques can be included e.g. caching data or keeping a pool of open database connections. Servers often provide advanced services e.g. load balancing, distributed transactions, message queuing. Components for MVC model are also available. Application servers usually run on virtual machines. These environments need a lot of memory but the execution of the application is more efficient than in script interpreters. Due to longer run times, this approach usually requires employing a good garbage collector. Virtual machines like JVM or CLR often contain more than one built-in garbage collector implementation.

3 The C++ workbench

The C++ workbench designed and implemented at the Institute of Computer Science is dedicated to small and medium size Internet applications. A very important issue is to provide the dependability and the high quality of applications prepared with this workbench. Efficiency and good memory management had also high priorities in the design process.

Main functions required were sending/receiving text and binary data to/from Internet browsers, sending and receiving HTTP cookies, session handling. A set of C++ classes was implemented. These classes constitute two components: the WWW server and the garbage collector. The garbage collector enables the programmer to create software of higher quality than using standard, manual memory management schemes. Automatic memory manager would never deallocate the same memory region twice or deallocate memory being used, causing a memory access error or a potential leak. Although it is possible to avoid these errors without a garbage collector, using it can significantly reduce the total software production time. The garbage collector finds inaccessible objects by analysing references among objects. This collector is accurate and is able to find all inaccessible objects. Objects created with the functions provided by our collector are destroyed automatically. Our collector does not influence any code that manages memory

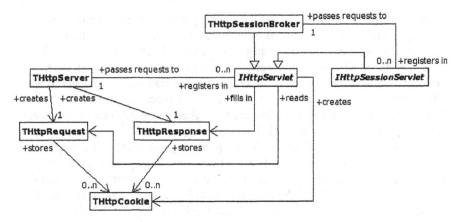

Fig. 1. Class diagram of the WWW server

manually. Objects created by built-in *new* operator should be destroyed manually. Automatic garbage collection introduces some overhead compared to manual memory management. Our garbage collector works concurrently with the application. Execution of application's threads is interrupted for a predictable, limited amount of time. This time does not depend on the number of objects and is so short, that will not be noticed by a user waiting for an Internet page. The implementation details of this garbage collector are given in [2]. Automatic memory management by this collector was used in other components of the C++ workbench i.e. the WWW server. The WWW server is a very important part of the C++ workbench. It is implemented by the class THttpServer presented in Fig. 1. This class interacts with the browser by the HTTP protocol. A programmer has to create an object of this class, set some attributes and call the Run method. As the server is one class only, several servers listening on different ports can be created. In Fig. 1 some other classes are also shown. These classes are used to improve functionality of the embedded WWW server and are described in sections 3.1 – 3.4.

3.1   Servlets

Servlets are objects registered in the server handling HTTP requests. Servlets are created by the programmer. Each servlet implements the IHttpServlet interface. The application programming interface of the workbench never uses raw C++ pointers to pass data to or from the class methods, instead it uses smart pointers provided by the garbage collector component. Hence, to register the servlet, a smart pointer to it must be passed to the server. The server with registered servlets, handles a request in the following manner:

1. The WWW server receives a request and checks its correctness. If it is incorrect, an appropriate error message is returned to the browser.
2. During the registration process the servlet receives an identifier. Basing on the URI identifier included in the request, the server identifies the servlet responsible for handling it. If the servlet can not be found, an error message with a HTTP 404 code is sent to the browser.

3. The server creates an object of the THttpRequest class and fills it with the data send by the browser. The object contains identifier of a resource requested by the client, HTTP headers and a pointer to the opened input stream.
4. The server creates an object of THttpResponse class.
5. The objects created in steps 3. and 4. are given to the servlet. The server waits for the next request.
6. The servlet reads data from the THttpRequest object and generates a response by writing appropriate data into the THttpResponse object.
7. The server closes the connection.

3.2 Receiving and sending data

When a HTTP request comes, the data sent by the Internet browser are written into the THttpRequest object, which is then passed to the servlet. This object has methods returning e.g.: the requested HTTP method (GET, POST or others), the identifier of the requested resource (URI), the HTTP cookies, the text and binary data sent in the 'body' of the request. The servlet receives also a THttpResponse object. This object is used to send a response to the web browser. The following methods in this object are available:

– setting a status code of the HTTP message,
– setting a header,
– setting, modifying or deleting HTTP cookies,
– setting content-type MIME of the sent document,
– opening a buffered output stream and sending the body of the response.

All arguments are passed either by value, by reference or by smart pointer. The raw C++ pointers are not used. This allowed to achieve an easy programming interface. Objects allocated on the heap inside the methods of the THttpRequest and THttpResponse classes are always created by the garbage collector.

3.3 Threads

At its start the server initialises a pool of threads. These threads are waiting on a semaphore for HTTP requests. The main thread listens on a local port (initially 80) and passes requests to one of the waiting threads. If the pool of waiting threads is empty, the main thread stops receiving new requests. The user can set the total number of threads in the pool. Handling concurrent request may cause some problems with common data accessed or modified by several threads at once. To alleviate this problem some simple mutex based synchronization is provided by the servlet container. There is no distributed transaction monitor.

3.4 Session

The class THttpSessionBroker is a session manager. It is responsible for recognizing clients, assigning session identifiers and directing requests to an appropriate session servlet. The session servlet is an object implementing the IHttpSessionServlet interface.

This interface provides methods for passing information to the session manager about opening or closing a session. There is a separate session servlet created for each session. The manager opens a session for each new client. The session can also be opened explicitly by calling an appropriate method from the manager. The session manager also closes inactive sessions. The session identifier is 128 bits long and is randomly generated. The association between the session identifier and the servlet is made in an associative table. The session identifier is stored implicitly in a HTTP cookie. The session manager is able to find the session identifier as an argument of the GET request or inside the WWW page.

4   Experiments

Below some experiments with the C++ workbench are presented. The goal of these experiments was to measure how the garbage collector influences the performance and response times of the system.

4.1   Performance experiments

In the experiments described below a gratis program http_load [21] prepared in ACME was used. ACME produced also a very powerful Internet server *thttpd* [22]. In our experiments two simple applications were used:

application A Displays a page containing simple text of parameterized length.
application B At the start allocates some permanently reachable objects and produces a constant memory leak per each request.

All the tests were run on a Celeron 2.4 GHz / 256 MB RAM computer. Results of throughput measurements are shown in Fig. 2.

Each server running application A was sequentially sent 10000 requests by the test client residing on the same machine. The length of the response was set to 10 bytes, so that the time of transmitting the data was negligible. The experiment was conducted 10 times. The mean values were calculated and are presented in Fig. 2. Our workbench performed not worse than well known enterprise-level webservers. Response times were also typical (Fig. 3). Under heavy load (Fig. 4), when more users tried to access the servlet at the same time, the performance dropped slightly after exceeding 25 concurrent requests, but was still better than that of Tomcat, running on a JIT enabled Java Virtual Machine 1.4.2. The experiment described above shows, that the implemented garbage collector can be effectively used in Internet interactive applications.

4.2   Overhead of the garbage collector

The overhead was measured using the GPROF profiler from the GCC 3.3.4 package and is presented in Fig. 6. The application B was queried 100,000 times at an average rate of 400 requests/second. It allocated 6 MB at the start and produced 2,5 kB memory leak per request. The measurements show, that it spent most of the time serving requests or waiting for them to come. The total garbage collector overhead was less

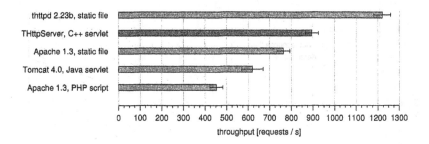

Fig. 2. Comparison of performance of various WWW servers serving application A

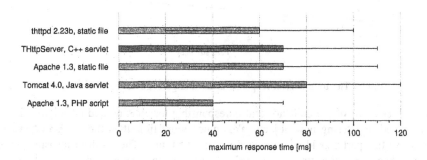

Fig. 3. Comparison of maximum response times of various WWW servers

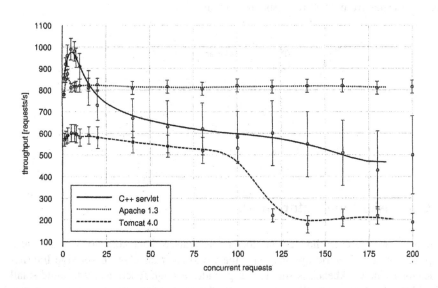

Fig. 4. Performance of the server under heavy load

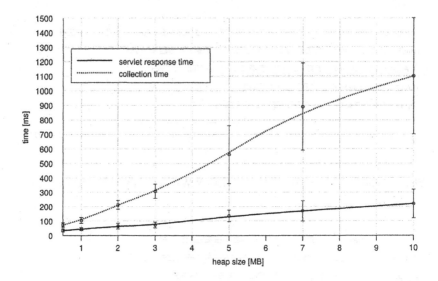

Fig. 5. The total servlet response times and garbage collection times.

than 5%. The part of the collector that is responsible for creating and destroying smart pointers and registering new objects takes much more time than the mark-and-sweep process, so this part should be optimized in the near future. The result of measurements of the garbage collection time (given in Fig. 5.) proves that the garbage collector works concurrently. The requests were handled successfully while the garbage collector was running. The requests were sent at a rate of 100 per second to the Application B. Maximum times from 1500 requests are shown.

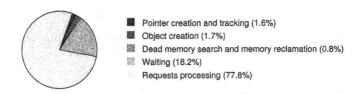

Fig. 6. CPU overhead in the garbage collector

5   Conclusions and future work

In the paper we presented how a non-blocking accurate garbage collector was used as a component in a real-world application – the workbench for C++ server side Internet applications. The workbench is simple, but provides enough functionality to build small and middle size Internet applications. The performance of our www server, as shown in section 4.1 is also pretty good.

The smart pointer pattern used in the garbage collector resulted in simplicity of the interface. The lack of manual memory management routines in the servlet container and user's servlets enables to achieve high dependability of applications. As was experimentally proved these features neither severely diminish the system performance, nor make response times too long to annoy the user. There was also no significant difference in the performance of the presented system and systems not using the garbage collector at all, or systems running on virtual machines with advanced, generational, copying garbage collectors. This shows that usage of a non-conservative, non-blocking garbage collector in an uncooperative environment like C++ is reasonable and practical.

The garbage collector used in our workbench can be further refined. The object architecture of it makes such modifications easy. So far our workbench was used in rather simple applications. A generational version of the garbage collector is possible and can be a subject of the future research. There is evidence that generational garbage collectors perform better than the non-generational ones [13].

References

1. Boehm, H.J., Weiser, M.: Garbage collection in an uncooperative environment. Softw. Pract. Exper. **18**(9) (1988) 807–820
2. Kołaczkowski, P., Bluemke, I.: A soft real time precise tracing garbage collector for c++. Pro Dialog (20) (2005) 1–11
3. Kołaczkowski, P., Bluemke, I.: A soft-real time precise garbage collector for multimedia applications. In: V International Conference Multimedia in Business and Education, Multimedia w Biznesie i Edukacji. Volume 2., Częstochowa, Poland, Fundacja Współczesne Zarządzanie Białystok (2005) 172–178
4. Kołaczkowski, P.: Techniques for building server side internet applications. Pro Dialog (18) (2005) 31–59
5. Colburn, R.: Teach Yourself CGI Programming in a Week. Sams Publishing, Indianapolis, Indiana, USA (1998)
6. Open Market, Inc.: FastCGI homepage (2006) http://www.fastcgi.com/.
7. Boehm, H.J.: Space efficient conservative garbage collection. In: PLDI '93: Proceedings of the ACM SIGPLAN 1993 conference on Programming language design and implementation, New York, NY, USA, ACM Press (1993) 197–206
8. Seligmann, J., Grarup, S.: Incremental mature garbage collection using the train algorithm. In: ECOOP '95: Proceedings of the 9th European Conference on Object-Oriented Programming, London, UK, Springer-Verlag (1995) 235–252
9. Bartlett, J.F.: Mostly copying garbage collection picks up generations and c++. Technical Report TN-12, Digital Equipment Corporation Western Research Laboratory (1989)
10. Smith, F., Morrisett, G.: Comparing mostly-copying and mark-sweep conservative collection. In: ISMM '98: Proceedings of the 1st international symposium on Memory management, New York, NY, USA, ACM Press (1998) 68–78
11. Detlefs, D.: Garbage collection and run-time typing as a C++ library. In: C++ Conference. (1992) 37–56
12. Edelson, D.R.: Smart pointers: They're smart, but they're not pointers. Technical report, University of California at Santa Cruz, Santa Cruz, CA, USA (1992)
13. Blackburn, S.M., Cheng, P., McKinley, K.S.: Myths and realities: the performance impact of garbage collection. SIGMETRICS Perform. Eval. Rev. **32**(1) (2004) 25–36

14. Henderson, F.: Accurate garbage collection in an uncooperative environment. In: ISMM '02: Proceedings of the 3rd international symposium on Memory management, New York, NY, USA, ACM Press (2002) 150–156
15. The PHP Group: PHP documentation (2006) http://www.php.net/docs.php.
16. Adobe Systems, Inc.: ColdFusion documentation (2006) http://www.macromedia.com/support/documentation/en/coldfusion/.
17. Inline Internet Systems, Inc.: User's guide to iHTML extensions version 2.20 (2001)
18. Mitchell, S.: Teach Yourself Active Server Pages 3.0 in 21 Days. Helion, Gliwice, Poland (2003)
19. Goodwill, J.: Pure JSP: Java Server Pages. Helion, Warszawa, Poland (2001)
20. Damon Houghland, A.T.: Essential JSP for Web Professionals. RM, Warszawa, Poland (2002)
21. ACME Labs: Multiprocessing HTTP test client (2005) http://www.acme.com/software/http load/.
22. ACME Labs: Tiny/turbo/throttling HTTP server (2005) http://www.acme.com/software/thttpd/.

Scenario-based Component Behavior Filtration*

Yan Zhang, Xiaofeng Yu, Tian Zhang, Xuandong Li, and Guoliang Zheng

State Key Laboratory of Novel Software Technology
Department of Computer Science and Technology
Nanjing University, Nanjing, P. R. China 210093
zhangyan@seg.nju.edu.cn, lxd@nju.edu.cn

Abstract. Components with undesired behavior could not be used properly by users. Therefore, the *scenario-based behavior filtration* of components is a significant problem to be solved, where the scenarios specify what behavior is undesired and what is desired. We propose an approach for filtering out the undesired behavior specified by a scenario specification from components. The main idea of our approach is that by constructing a special environment, i.e., *conditional exclusive environment*, for a component, all undesired behavior specified by one scenario specification can be filtered out and all desired behavior specified by another scenario specification can be preserved when the component works in the environment. We use interface automata to model the behavior of components and a set of action sequences to abstract the scenario specification in message sequence charts. The composition of components is modelled by the product of interface automata. We give the relevant algorithm in our approach and illustrate it by an example.

1 Introduction

Component-based software development (CBSD) is a good approach to attain reliable, flexible, extensible and evolvable systems. By the reuse of existing software components and the plug-and-play mechanisms, complex systems can be developed more rapidly and economically. In CBSD, users retrieve desired components from repositories and composite them to build a new system.

When an existing component could not meet the requirement of users exactly, we can compose several available components to perform the given task [1, 2]. Although components composition can repair inadequate behavior of sole component, it is insufficient to tackle the undesired behavior in available components. The behavior of a component that could obstruct the use of the component in some scenario may be undesired for specific users. Retrieved components with undesired behavior are frequently encountered by users, because users' requirements are various and it is difficult to find an exact match in repositories.

Usually, users give their requirements by a description of scenarios, which is called the *scenario specification*. The scenario specification can describe either the

---

* This paper is supported by the National Grand Fundamental Research 973 Program of China (No. 2002CB312001), the National Natural Science Foundation of China (No. 60425204, No. 60233020), and by Jiangsu Province Research Foundation (No. BK2004080).

Please use the following format when citing this chapter:

Zhang, Y., Yu, X., Zhang, T., Li, X., Zheng, G., 2006, in IFIP International Federation for Information Processing, Volume 227, Software Engineering Techniques: Design for Quality, ed. K. Sacha, (Boston: Springer), pp. 25–36.

user's desired or undesired behavior of a component when it interacts with other. The *scenario-based behavior filtration* of a component is to discard the undesired behavior and preserve desired behavior of the component in terms of the scenario specifications given by a user.

In this paper, we propose an approach to filtering the behavior for a component based on scenarios. By constructing an environment (i.e., another component) for a component, filter out all undesired behavior and preserve all desired behavior of the component when the component works in the environment. The undesired and desired behavior of the component are specified by scenario specifications. Interface automata [3] are used to model the behavior of components. Scenarios are specified by message sequence charts (MSCs) [4] and a MSC is abstracted as a set of action sequences further. The composition of components is modelled by the product of interface automata. We extend the concept of environment in the interface automata theory and introduce *conditional exclusive environment* (CXE). By constructing a CXE E for a given interface automaton R under two known sets $\mathcal{L}^+, \mathcal{L}^-$ of action sequences, make all behavior represented by some element in $\mathcal{L}^-$ to be discarded in $R \otimes E$. At the same time, all behavior represented by any element in $\mathcal{L}^+$, if it is also the behavior of R, is preserved in $R \otimes E$.

The remainder of this paper is organized as follows. Section 2 gives a brief introduction on interface automata and message sequence charts. Section 3 introduces some relevant concepts about our proposal. Section 4 describes the approach to scenario-based behavior filtration of components in detail and shows the constructive algorithm of CXE. Finally, in section 5 we discuss the related works and conclude this paper. Additionally, an example is used to illustrate our approach throughout the paper.

2 Background

In the section, interface automata and MSCs are introduced briefly. The most of concepts about interface automata and MSCs refer to [3] and [4] respectively.

2.1 Interface Automata

Definition 1 (interface automaton, IA). *An* interface automaton $P = \langle V_P, V_P^{init}, \mathcal{A}_P^I, \mathcal{A}_P^O, \mathcal{A}_P^H, \mathcal{T}_P \rangle$ *is a 6-tuple, where*

- V_P *is a finite set of* states.
- $V_P^{init} \subseteq V_P$ *is a set of* initial states. *If* $V_P^{init} = \emptyset$ *then* P *is called* empty.
- $\mathcal{A}_P^I$, $\mathcal{A}_P^O$ *and* $\mathcal{A}_P^H$ *are mutually disjoint sets of* input, output *and* internal *actions*. $\mathcal{A}_P$ *denotes the set of all* actions, *i.e.,* $\mathcal{A}_P = \mathcal{A}_P^I \cup \mathcal{A}_P^O \cup \mathcal{A}_P^H$.
- $\mathcal{T}_P \subseteq V_P \times \mathcal{A}_P \times V_P$ *is a set of* steps. *If* $\tau = (v, a, u) \in \mathcal{T}_P$, *then write* $label(\tau) = a$, $head(\tau) = v$, $tail(\tau) = u$.

If $a \in \mathcal{A}_P^I$ (resp. $a \in \mathcal{A}_P^O$, $a \in \mathcal{A}_P^H$), then (v, a, v') is called an input (resp. output, internal) step. If there is a step $(v, a, v') \in \mathcal{T}_P$ for some $v, v' \in V_P$, $a \in \mathcal{A}_P$, then we say that action a is *enabled* at state v. For $v \in V_P$, let $\mathcal{A}_P^I(v) = \{a \in \mathcal{A}_P^I \,|\, \exists v' \in$

$V_P \cdot (v, a, v') \in \mathcal{T}_P\}$, $\mathcal{A}_P^O(v) = \{a \in \mathcal{A}_P^O \mid \exists v' \in V_P \cdot (v, a, v') \in \mathcal{T}_P\}$ and $\mathcal{A}_P^H(v) = \{a \in \mathcal{A}_P^H \mid \exists v' \in V_P \cdot (v, a, v') \in \mathcal{T}_P\}$ be respectively the subset of input, output and internal actions that are enabled at the state v. Let $\mathcal{A}_P(v) = \mathcal{A}_P^I(v) \cup \mathcal{A}_P^O(v) \cup \mathcal{A}_P^H(v)$.

If IA P satisfies $\left|V_P^{init}\right| = 1$ and $\forall (v, a, u), (v, a, u') \in \mathcal{T}_P \cdot u = u'$, then P is *deterministic*, otherwise P is *non-deterministic*. For simplicity, we make a convention that all interface automata referred in this paper are deterministic.

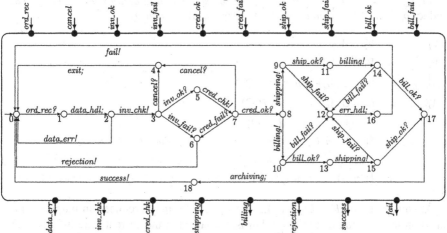

Fig. 1. Interface automaton *Seller*. The symbol "?" (resp. "!", ";") appended to the name of actions denotes that the action is an input (resp. output, internal) action. An arrow without source denotes the initial state of the interface automaton

Example 1. The IA *Seller* (see Fig. 1) specifies the behavior of a component when it interacts with other. The component stands for a seller in a business to business system. The seller receives an order (*ord_rec*) from a customer and handles data in the order (*data_hdl*), e.g., transform of data format. If there is some error in the order, it will report the error (*data_err*) to the customer, otherwise it continues to check the inventory (*inv_chk*) from the supplier and the customer credit (*cred_chk*) from the bank. Contingent on availability of inventory (*inv_ok*) and valid credit (*cred_ok*), the seller will inform the shipper to ship product (*shipping*) and the bank to bill the customer for the order (*billing*). Either unavailability of inventory (*inv_fail*) or invalid credit (*cred_fail*) will lead to reject the order (*rejection*). The seller can receive some information (*cancel*) from the customer to terminate (*exit*) the order. If shipping and billing finish successfully (*ship_ok* and *bill_ok*), the seller will make archive (*archiving*) and give the notification (*success*) to the customer. Otherwise the negative notification (*fail*) will be given after processing the exception (*err_hdl*).

An *execution fragment* of IA P is a finite alternating sequence of states and actions $v_0 a_0 v_1 a_1 \cdots a_{n-1} v_n$, where $(v_i, a_i, v_{i+1}) \in \mathcal{T}_P$, for all $0 \le i < n$. Given two states $v, u \in V_P$, we say that u is *reachable from* v if there is an execution fragment with v as the first state and u as the last state. The state u is *reachable in* P if there is an initial state $v \in V_P^{init}$ such that u is reachable from v.

Let Γ_P denote the set of all execution fragments in IA P. For every $\eta \in \Gamma_P$, write the first state of η as $first(\eta)$, the last state of η as $last(\eta)$ and the set of all states of η as $V(\eta)$.

Definition 2 (interface automata product). *Two IAs P and Q are* composable *if* $A_P^H \cap A_Q = \emptyset$, $A_Q^H \cap A_P = \emptyset$, $A_P^I \cap A_Q^I = \emptyset$ *and* $A_P^O \cap A_Q^O = \emptyset$. *Let* $shared(P,Q) = A_P \cap A_Q = (A_P^I \cap A_Q^O) \cup (A_P^O \cap A_Q^I)$ *be the set of shared actions of P and Q. The* product *of P and Q, denoted by $P \otimes Q$, is the IA defined by*

$$
\begin{aligned}
V_{P \otimes Q} &= V_P \times V_Q \\
V_{P \otimes Q}^{init} &= V_P^{init} \times V_Q^{init} \\
A_{P \otimes Q}^{I} &= (A_P^I \cup A_Q^I) \setminus shared(P,Q) \\
A_{P \otimes Q}^{O} &= (A_P^O \cup A_Q^O) \setminus shared(P,Q) \\
A_{P \otimes Q}^{H} &= A_P^H \cup A_Q^H \cup shared(P,Q) \\
T_{P \otimes Q} &= \{((v,u), a, (v', u)) \mid (v, a, v') \in T_P \wedge a \notin shared(P,Q) \wedge u \in V_Q\} \\
&\cup \{((v,u), a, (v, u')) \mid (u, a, u') \in T_Q \wedge a \notin shared(P,Q) \wedge v \in V_P\} \\
&\cup \{((v,u), a, (v', u')) \mid (v, a, v') \in T_P \wedge (u, a, u') \in T_Q \wedge a \in shared(P,Q)\}.
\end{aligned}
$$

At some state of $P \otimes Q$, one IA, say P (or Q), may produces an output action that is an input action of Q (or P), but isn't enabled at the current state in Q (or P). Such state is an *illegal states* of $P \otimes Q$. For two composable IAs P and Q, the set of illegal states of $P \otimes Q$ is denoted by $Illegal(P,Q) \subseteq V_P \times V_Q$,

$$
\begin{aligned}
Illegal(P,Q) = \{(v, \quad u) \in V_P \times V_Q \mid \exists a \in shared(P,Q)\,. \\
((a \in A_P^O(v) \wedge a \notin A_Q^I(u)) \vee (a \in A_Q^O(u) \wedge a \notin A_P^I(v)))\}.
\end{aligned}
$$

Definition 3 (environment). *An IA E is an* environment *for an IA R if: (1) E and R are composable, (2) E is not empty, (3) $A_E^I = A_R^O$, and (4) if $Illegal(R,E) \neq \emptyset$, then no state in $Illegal(R,E)$ is reachable in $R \otimes E$.*

2.2 Message Sequence Charts

MSC [4] is a trace description language for visualization of selected system runs. It concentrates on message interchange by communicating entities and their environment. Every MSC specification has an equivalent graphical and textual representation. Especially the graphical representation of MSCs gives an intuitive understanding of the described system behavior. Therefore, MSC is a widely used language for scenario specifications.

The fundamental language constructs of MSCs are component and message flow. Vertical time lines with a named heading represent components. Along these time lines, MSC events (i.e., message send or receive events) are arranged that gives an order to the events connected to this component. A message is depicted by an arrow from the send to the receive event. The fact that a message must be sent before it can be received imposes a total order on the send and receive event of a message and, furthermore, a partial order on all events in a MSC. An example of MSCs is shown in Fig. 2.

Definition 4 (message sequence chart, MSC). *A message sequence chart* $Ch = \langle C, \mathcal{E}, \mathcal{M}, \mathcal{F}, \mathcal{O} \rangle$ *is a 5-tuple, where*

- C *is a finite set of* components.
- $\mathcal{E}$ *is a finite set of* events *corresponding to sending or receiving a message.*
- $\mathcal{M}$ *is a finite set of* messages. *For any* $m \in \mathcal{M}$, *let* $s(m)$ *and* $r(m)$ *to denote the events that correspond to sending and receiving message* m *respectively.*
- $\mathcal{F} : \mathcal{E} \rightarrow C$ *is a* labelling function *which maps each event to a component.*
- $\mathcal{O} \subseteq \mathcal{E} \times \mathcal{E}$ *is a partial order relation* over the set of events. *For every* $(e, e') \in \mathcal{O}$, *there is* $e \neq e'$. (e, e') *represents a visual order displayed in* Ch.

Each MSC describes a set of message sequences. A *message sequence* of one MSC must be composed of all messages of the MSC and any message occurs only once in the sequence. For any two messages in the sequence, if one precedes the other then their send events and receive events should not violate the partial order relation over the set of events. Observe that messages in MSCs correspond to actions in IA. Hence, we call a message sequence of MSC as an *action sequence* derived from the MSC and write it as $\varrho = \varrho(0)\varrho(1) \cdots \varrho(n)$, where $\varrho(i)$ is a message in the message sequence for all $0 \leq i \leq n$.

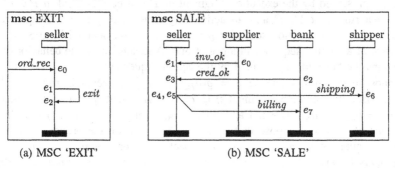

(a) MSC 'EXIT'　　　　　　　　(b) MSC 'SALE'

Fig. 2. MSCs specifying scenarios about the interaction among the seller component, consumers and other components

Example 2. The MSCs 'EXIT' and 'SALE' (see Fig. 2(a) and 2(b) respectively) show two scenario specifications about the seller component (in Example 1) interacting with consumers and other components. The MSC 'EXIT' describes a scenario: the seller interrupts the process of ordering and exits after it receives an order from a customer. From the MSC 'EXIT' we can derive a set of action sequences, $\mathcal{L}_E = \{ ord\_rec \hat{\ } exit \}$. For legibility, we use the symbol "$\hat{\ }$" to separate two adjacent actions in an action sequence. The MSC 'SALE' describes a scenario: if the seller receives inv_ok and $cred\_ok$ it should produce $shipping$ to the shipper and $billing$ to the bank. From the MSC 'SALE' we can derive a set of action sequences, $\mathcal{L}_S = \{ inv\_ok \hat{\ } cred\_ok \hat{\ } shipping \hat{\ } billing,\ cred\_ok \hat{\ } inv\_ok \hat{\ } shipping \hat{\ } billing,\ inv\_ok \hat{\ } cred\_ok \hat{\ } billing \hat{\ } shipping,\ cred\_ok \hat{\ } inv\_ok \hat{\ } billing \hat{\ } shipping \}$.

3 Conditional Exclusive Environment

For any execution fragment $\eta = v_i a_i v_{i+1} a_{i+1} \cdots a_{j-1} v_j$ $(i < j)$ of IA P, where $v_i \in V_P^{init}$, if $v_i = v_j$ or $\mathcal{A}_P(v_j) = \emptyset$, then η is called a *run* in P. Let Σ_P denote the set of all runs in IA P. For any execution fragment $\eta = v_i a_i v_{i+1} a_{i+1} \cdots a_{j-1} v_j \in \Gamma_P$ $(i < j)$, we say that execution fragment $\eta' = v_s a_s v_{s+1} a_{s+1} \cdots a_{t-1} v_t$ $(i \leq s < t \leq j)$ is in η, denoted by $\eta' \sqsubseteq \eta$. Specifically, if $\eta' = v_s a_s v_{s+1}$ $(i \leq s < j)$, then we say that the step $\tau = (v_s, a_s, v_{s+1}) \in \mathcal{T}_P$ is *in* the execution fragment η, denoted by $\tau \sqsubseteq \eta$.

The *trace* of an execution fragment $\eta = v_0 a_0 v_1 a_1 \cdots a_{n-1} v_n$ is a subsequence of η, which consists of all actions in η. We write $trace(\eta) = a_0 a_1 \cdots a_{n-1}$. Given an execution fragment $\eta \in \Gamma_{P \otimes Q}$ and $trace(\eta) = a_0 a_1 \cdots a_{n-1}$, the *projection* of η on IA P, denoted by $\pi_P(trace(\eta))$, is a subsequence of $trace(\eta)$, which is obtained by deleting all actions $a_i \in \mathcal{A}_Q \setminus shared(P, Q)$, $0 \leq i \leq n-1$ from $trace(\eta)$.

Given two composable IAs P and Q, there are $\eta = v_0 a_0 v_1 a_1 \cdots a_{n-1} v_n \in \Gamma_P$ and $\alpha \in \Sigma_{P \otimes Q}$. If there exists an execution fragment $\zeta \sqsubseteq \alpha$ satisfying $\pi_P(trace(\zeta)) = trace(\eta)$ and for any $v_i a_i v_{i+1} \sqsubseteq \eta$ there is $(v_i, u_i) a_i (v_{i+1}, u_{i+1}) \sqsubseteq \zeta$, where $u_i, u_{i+1} \in V_Q$ and $0 \leq i < n$, then we say that η is *covered* by α. At the same time, (u_i, a_i, u_{i+1}) is called the *corresponding step* of (v_i, a_i, v_{i+1}) if $a_i \in shared(P, Q)$, and u_i, u_{i+1} is called the *corresponding state* of v_i, v_{i+1} respectively. If an execution fragment of IA P can be covered by a run of IA $P \otimes Q$, then it means that the behavior represented by the execution fragment of P can be preserved in $P \otimes Q$.

Given a run α of IA P and an action sequence ϱ, if ϱ is a subsequence of $trace(\alpha)$, then we say action sequence ϱ *occurs* in run α, denoted by $\varrho \propto \alpha$. The occurrence of an action sequence in a run of one IA means that some behavior of the IA contains the behavior represented by the action sequence.

Suppose that action sequence $\varrho = \varrho(0)\varrho(1) \cdots \varrho(m)$ occurs in run $\alpha \in \Sigma_P$. If there exists an execution fragment $\eta \sqsubseteq \alpha$ satisfying that ϱ is a subsequence of $trace(\eta) = a_0 a_1 \cdots a_n$ $(n \geq m)$ and $\varrho(0) = a_0$, $\varrho(m) = a_n$, then η is a *proper occurrence* of ϱ in α. Suppose that $\eta_0, \eta_1, \ldots, \eta_n \sqsubseteq \alpha$ are the proper occurrences of action sequences $\varrho_0, \varrho_1, \ldots, \varrho_n$ in α respectively. For any $\eta \sqsubseteq \alpha$, if $(V(\eta) \setminus \{first(\eta), last(\eta)\}) \cap V(\eta_i) = \emptyset$, $i = 0, 1, \ldots, n$, then η is a *proper inoccurrence* of $\varrho_0, \varrho_1, \ldots, \varrho_n$ in α.

Given a set $\mathcal{L}$ of action sequences, for any IA P, Σ_P can be partitioned as two subsets: $\phi_{\mathcal{L}}(\Sigma_P) = \{\alpha \in \Sigma_P \mid \exists \varrho \in \mathcal{L}. \varrho \propto \alpha\}$ and $\overline{\phi_{\mathcal{L}}(\Sigma_P)} = \Sigma_P \setminus \phi_{\mathcal{L}}(\Sigma_P)$. For every run in $\phi_{\mathcal{L}}(\Sigma_P)$, there exists at least one action sequence in $\mathcal{L}$ that occurs in it. For any run in $\overline{\phi_{\mathcal{L}}(\Sigma_P)}$, no action sequence in $\mathcal{L}$ occurs in it.

Definition 5 (conditional exclusive environment, CXE). *Given an IA R and a set $\mathcal{L}^-$ of action sequences, the* exclusive environment *of R under $\mathcal{L}^-$ is an environment E of R such that for any $\varrho \in \mathcal{L}^-$, if ϱ occurs in a run α of R, then the proper occurrence of ϱ in α must be not covered by any run of $R \otimes E$. If an exclusive environment E of R under $\mathcal{L}^-$ satisfies that for any $\varrho \in \mathcal{L}^+$, if ϱ occurs in a run α of R then α must be covered by some run of $R \otimes E$, where $\mathcal{L}^+$ is a set of action sequences and $\mathcal{L}^+ \cap \mathcal{L}^- = \emptyset$, then E is a* conditional exclusive environment *of R under exclusion condition $\mathcal{L}^-$ and inclusion condition $\mathcal{L}^+$.*

Let $CXE\,(R:\mathcal{L}^-,\mathcal{L}^+)$ denote the set of conditional exclusive environments of R under exclusion condition $\mathcal{L}^-$ and inclusion condition $\mathcal{L}^+$. If we consider $\mathcal{L}^+$ and $\mathcal{L}^-$ as the representation of two sets of behavior, then all behavior of R which contain any behavior in $\mathcal{L}^-$ isn't preserved in $R \otimes E$, at the same time, all behavior of R which contain any behavior in $\mathcal{L}^+$ is preserved in $R \otimes E$, where $E \in CXE\,(R:\mathcal{L}^-,\mathcal{L}^+)$. For arbitrary IA R and two sets $\mathcal{L}^-,\mathcal{L}^+$ of action sequences, it is possible that $CXE\,(R:\mathcal{L}^-,\mathcal{L}^+) = \emptyset$. It means that a CXE of R under exclusion condition $\mathcal{L}^-$ and inclusion condition $\mathcal{L}^+$ may not always exist.

4 Construction of Conditional Exclusive Environment

We can use an IA, say R, to specify the behavior of a component, say COMP. An user can give his or her undesired and desired behavior about COMP by two scenario specifications in MSC, say 'SCENE$^-$' and 'SCENE$^+$' respectively. Filtering out the user's undesired behavior from COMP and preserving the desired behavior amounts to constructing a CXE for R under exclusion condition $\mathcal{L}^-$ and inclusion condition $\mathcal{L}^+$, where $\mathcal{L}^-,\mathcal{L}^+$ are the sets of action sequences derived from MSCs 'SCENE$^-$', 'SCENE$^+$' respectively. If there exists $E \in CXE\,(R:\mathcal{L}^-,\mathcal{L}^+)$ and we can construct it, then all of the user's undesired behavior in R do not exist in $R \otimes E$, at the same time, all of the user's desired behavior in R are preserved in $R \otimes E$.

In this section, we will discuss how to construct a CXE $E \in CXE\,(R:\mathcal{L}^-,\mathcal{L}^+)$ for known IA R and two sets $\mathcal{L}^-,\mathcal{L}^+$ of action sequences in detail, and give the algorithm for constructing CXE.

4.1 Basic Approach to Constructing CXE

An environment of one IA, say R, can affect the runs of R only by the input actions of R. For arbitrary input step τ on arbitrary run of R, if the label of τ is a shared action of R and its environment and the environment does not provide the input action for R when R needs it, then R cannot go on along the run. For example, if the environment does not provide input action *cancel* for IA *Seller* (see Fig. 1) when *Seller* stays at state 3, then *Seller* cannot run along execution fragment "3 *cancel* 4 *exit* 0" back to initial state. That the environment does not provide input action $label(\tau)$ for R, when R needs it, amounts to no corresponding step of τ in the environment.

Suppose that η is a proper occurrence of some action sequence in $\mathcal{L}^-$. Only by not constructing the corresponding step in E for any input step τ of R, where $first(\eta)$ is reachable from $tail(\tau)$, the CXE E can make η not to be covered by any run of $R \otimes E$. For ensuring all runs in $\phi_{\mathcal{L}^+}(\Sigma_R)$ to be covered by runs of $R \otimes E$, the input step τ should not be in any run in $\phi_{\mathcal{L}^+}(\Sigma_R)$. We can find all such input steps in R by traversing all runs in $\phi_{\mathcal{L}^-}(\Sigma_R)$. But, if there exists a loop (i.e., execution fragment η with $first(\eta) = last(\eta)$) in some run, then Σ_R is an infinite set and the lengths of some runs in Σ_R, i.e., the number of steps in a run, may be also infinite. Accordingly, $\phi_{\mathcal{L}^-}(\Sigma_R)$, $\phi_{\mathcal{L}^+}(\Sigma_R)$ and the lengths of some runs in them may be infinite. Thus, it is unfeasible to traverse all runs in $\phi_{\mathcal{L}^-}(\Sigma_R)$ directly. For getting a feasible approach, we introduce the concepts of the simple run and simple loop.

Given an IA R and a set $\mathcal{L}$ of action sequences, a run $\alpha = v_0 a_0 v_1 a_1 \cdots a_{n-1} v_n$ of R is a *simple run* when it satisfies the following conditions:

1. if $\alpha \in \overline{\phi_{\mathcal{L}}(\Sigma_R)}$, then there is $v_i \neq v_j$ $(0 < i < n, 0 < j < n, i \neq j)$;
2. if $\alpha \in \phi_{\mathcal{L}}(\Sigma_R)$, then (a) for any proper inoccurrence $\eta = v_i a_i v_{i+1} \cdots a_{j-1} v_j$ $(0 \leq i < j \leq n)$ in α, there is $v_s \neq v_t$ $(i \leq s \leq j, i \leq t \leq j, s \neq t)$; and (b) for any proper occurrence ζ of $\varrho = \varrho(0)\varrho(1) \cdots \varrho(m) \in \mathcal{L}$ in α, if there is $\zeta' = v_i a_i v_{i+1} a_{i+1} \cdots a_{j-1} v_j \sqsubseteq \zeta$ $(0 \leq i < j \leq n)$, and $a_i = \varrho(k)$, $a_{j-1} = \varrho(k+1)$, $0 \leq k < m$, then there is $v_s \neq v_t$ $(i < s < j, i < t < j, s \neq t)$.

We put some constrains on runs to get the definition of the simple run. The meaning of the condition 1. is that there is not any loop in a simple run without occurrence of action sequences in $\mathcal{L}$. The meaning of the condition 2a is that there is not any loop in a proper inoccurrence of action sequences in a simple run. The meaning of the condition 2b is that in a proper occurrence of an action sequence in a simple run, there is not any loop between the occurrence of two neighbor actions in the action sequence. The set of all simple runs of IA R under $\mathcal{L}$ is denoted by $\Omega_R^{\mathcal{L}}$. Similarly, $\Omega_R^{\mathcal{L}}$ can be partitioned as $\phi_{\mathcal{L}}\left(\Omega_R^{\mathcal{L}}\right)$ and $\overline{\phi_{\mathcal{L}}\left(\Omega_R^{\mathcal{L}}\right)}$.

Given an IA R and a set $\mathcal{L}$ of action sequences, an execution fragment $\eta = v_i a_i v_{i+1} a_{i+1} \cdots a_{j-1} v_j \in \Gamma_R$ $(i < j)$ is a *simple loop* if: (1) $v_i = v_j$, $v_i, v_j \notin V_R^{init}$, (2) $v_s \neq v_t$ $(i \leq s < j, i \leq t < j, s \neq t)$ and (3) $\forall \alpha \in \phi_{\mathcal{L}}\left(\Omega_R^{\mathcal{L}}\right) . \eta \not\sqsubseteq \alpha$.

The first and second conditions ensure that except the first and the last states, there aren't duplicate states in a simple loop. The third condition ensures that a simple loop isn't the loop in a proper occurrence of some action sequence in $\mathcal{L}$. For given IA R and set $\mathcal{L}$ of action sequences, $\Theta_R^{\mathcal{L}}$ denotes the set of all simple loops of R. We say that simple loop $\eta \in \Theta_R^{\mathcal{L}}$ *associates* with simple run $\alpha \in \Omega_R^{\mathcal{L}}$ if $V(\eta) \cap V(\alpha) \neq \emptyset$ or $V(\eta) \cap V(\eta') \neq \emptyset$, where $\eta' \in \Theta_R^{\mathcal{L}}$ associates with α. Let $\psi_{\mathcal{L}}\left(\Theta_R^{\mathcal{L}}\right) = \left\{\eta \in \Theta_R^{\mathcal{L}} \mid \exists \alpha \in \phi_{\mathcal{L}}\left(\Omega_R^{\mathcal{L}}\right) . \eta \text{ associates with } \alpha\right\}$ be the set of all simple loops associated with simple runs in $\phi_{\mathcal{L}}\left(\Omega_R^{\mathcal{L}}\right)$.

Notice that every step in any run in Σ_R corresponds to a step in some simple run in $\Omega_R^{\mathcal{L}}$ or in some simple loop in $\Theta_R^{\mathcal{L}}$. However, $\Omega_R^{\mathcal{L}}$ and $\Theta_R^{\mathcal{L}}$ are finite sets and the lengths of all simple runs and simple loops are finite. Furthermore, $\phi_{\mathcal{L}}\left(\Omega_R^{\mathcal{L}}\right)$ and $\psi_{\mathcal{L}}\left(\Theta_R^{\mathcal{L}}\right)$ are finite sets.

Additionally, we also notice that it is impossible to eliminate the undesired behavior represented by $\varrho \in \mathcal{L}^-$ from $R \otimes E$ by not constructing the corresponding step in E for any step in R "after" the proper occurrence of ϱ. A step τ "after" a proper occurrence η means that $head(\tau) = last(\eta)$ or $head(\tau)$ is reachable from $last(\eta)$.

Suppose that ζ is a proper occurrence of $\varrho \in \mathcal{L}^-$ in a simple run α of IA R. We call a prefix η of α as the *minimal simple prefix* about ζ if ζ is a suffix of η, where a prefix of α is an execution fragment η in α and $first(\eta) = first(\alpha)$; a suffix of α is an execution fragment η in α and $last(\eta) = last(\alpha)$. Let $\lambda_{\mathcal{L}^-}\left(\Omega_R^{\mathcal{L}^-}\right)$ denote the set of all minimal simple prefixes about all proper occurrences of any action sequence in $\mathcal{L}^-$ in any simple run of R, i.e.,

$$\lambda_{\mathcal{L}^-}\left(\Omega_R^{\mathcal{L}^-}\right) = \Big\{\eta \mid \exists \varrho \in \mathcal{L}^- . \exists \alpha \in \Omega_R^{\mathcal{L}^-} . (\zeta \text{ is a proper occurrence of } \varrho \text{ in } \alpha) \wedge$$

$$(\eta \text{ is the minimal simple prefix about } \zeta \text{ in } \alpha)\Big\}.$$

For any $\eta \in \lambda_{\mathcal{L}-}\left(\Omega_R^{\mathcal{L}^-}\right)$, there must be a proper occurrence of some $\varrho \in \mathcal{L}^-$ in η, and there is not any step "after" the proper occurrence in η.

Theorem 1. *For arbitrary IA R and sets $\mathcal{L}^-, \mathcal{L}^+$ of action sequences, if there exist $\eta \in \lambda_{\mathcal{L}-}\left(\Omega_R^{\mathcal{L}^-}\right)$ such that $\forall \tau \sqsubseteq \eta . \; label(\tau) \notin \mathcal{A}_R^I$, then $CXE\left(R:\mathcal{L}^-,\mathcal{L}^+\right) = \emptyset$.*

In [5], we prove that there maybe exist some kind of execution fragments in one IA, say P, which cannot be covered by any run of $P \otimes E$, for any environment E of P. Accordingly, we have the theorem as follows.

Theorem 2. *For arbitrary IA R and sets $\mathcal{L}^-, \mathcal{L}^+$ of action sequences, there does not exist any $E \in CXE\left(R:\mathcal{L}^-,\mathcal{L}^+\right)$ if there are $\eta_1, \eta_2 \in \Gamma_R$, $\eta_1 \sqsubseteq \alpha$ and $\eta_2 \sqsubseteq \beta$, for some $\alpha \in \left(\Omega_R^{\mathcal{L}^+} \cup \Theta_R^{\mathcal{L}^+}\right)$ and $\beta \in \left(\phi_{\mathcal{L}+}\left(\Omega_R^{\mathcal{L}^+}\right) \cup \psi_{\mathcal{L}+}\left(\Theta_R^{\mathcal{L}^+}\right)\right)$, which satisfy any of the following conditions: (1) $\eta_1 = v_i a v_j$ and $\eta_2 = v_j b v_k$, where $i \neq j \neq k$, $a \notin shared(R,E)$, $b \in \mathcal{A}_R^I \cap shared(R,E)$ and $b \notin \mathcal{A}_R(v_i)$. (2) $\eta_1 = v_i a v_j$ and $\eta_2 = v_i b v_k$, where $i \neq j \neq k$, $a \notin shared(R,E)$, $b \in \mathcal{A}_R^I \cap shared(R,E)$ and $b \notin \mathcal{A}_R(v_j)$. (3) $\eta_1 = v_i a_i v_{i+1} a_{i+1} \cdots a_{j-1} v_j$ and $\eta_2 = v_i b v_i'$, where $i < j$, $v_i' \notin V(\eta_1)$, $a_k \notin shared(R,E)$, $k = i, i+1, \ldots, j-1$, $b \in \mathcal{A}_R^I \cap shared(R,E)$ and $\exists v \in V(\eta_1) . \, b \notin \mathcal{A}_R(v)$.*

4.2 Algorithm of Constructing CXE

The skeleton of the constructive algorithm for CXE is described as follows. Step one, for every minimal simple prefix about the proper occurrence of any action sequence in $\mathcal{L}^-$ in some simple run of R, traverse it from the first state and find the first input step in it, which is not in any simple run with occurrence of action sequences in $\mathcal{L}^+$ or any simple loop associated with it. Step two, remove these input steps from R and all unreachable states after the removal. Step three, construct corresponding steps in one IA for all residual steps in R.

Make the convention of $\mathcal{A}_E^H = \emptyset$ and $\mathcal{A}_E^O = \mathcal{A}_R^I$ [5]. Let $R \downarrow T$ to denote the IA obtained by removing all steps in $T \subset T_R$ from R and all unreachable states in R after the removal. The algorithm of constructing CXE $E \in CXE\left(R:\mathcal{L}^-,\mathcal{L}^+\right)$ is shown in Algorithm 1.

We can prove that the return (in line 24) of Algorithm 1 is a CXE of R under exclusion condition $\mathcal{L}^-$ and inclusion condition $\mathcal{L}^+$ since it is consistent to Definition 5. Thus, Algorithm 1 is correct.

About line 1 in Algorithm 1, we had given an algorithm to find which simple run in an IA has the occurrence of a given action sequence in [6] and we can obtain those sets in line 1 based on the algorithm. About line 22 in Algorithm 1, we had given a method of constructing corresponding steps in [5].

Suppose that the maximal length of all elements in the set $\Omega_R^{\mathcal{L}^-} \cup \Omega_R^{\mathcal{L}^+} \cup \Theta_R^{\mathcal{L}^+}$ is $n = \max\left\{length(\eta) \mid \eta \in \left(\Omega_R^{\mathcal{L}^-} \cup \Omega_R^{\mathcal{L}^+} \cup \Theta_R^{\mathcal{L}^+}\right)\right\}$, where $length(\eta)$ is the number of steps in η. Suppose that $m_1 = \left|\phi_{\mathcal{L}-}\left(\Omega_R^{\mathcal{L}^-}\right)\right|, m_2 = \left|\phi_{\mathcal{L}+}\left(\Omega_R^{\mathcal{L}^+}\right)\right|$ are the number

---

Algorithm 1 Constructing CXE E of IA R under exclusion condition $\mathcal{L}^-$ and inclusion condition $\mathcal{L}^+$

Input: Interface automaton R and sets $\mathcal{L}^-$, $\mathcal{L}^+$ of action sequences, $\mathcal{L}^- \cap \mathcal{L}^+ = \emptyset$.
Output: CXE $E \in CXE\left(R : \mathcal{L}^-, \mathcal{L}^+\right)$.
Variables: $T \subset T_R$, step τ, IA R' and boolean found
1: Traverse R to get $\lambda_{\mathcal{L}^-}\left(\Omega_R^{\mathcal{L}^-}\right)$, $\phi_{\mathcal{L}^+}\left(\Omega_R^{\mathcal{L}^+}\right)$ and $\psi_{\mathcal{L}^+}\left(\Theta_R^{\mathcal{L}^+}\right)$.
2: **if** some execution fragment satisfies the conditions of Theorem 2 **then**
3:     **return** E doesn't exist   // by Theorem 2
4: **else**
5:     $T \longleftarrow \emptyset$
6:     **for all** $\eta \in \lambda_{\mathcal{L}^-}\left(\Omega_R^{\mathcal{L}^-}\right)$ **do**
7:         found$\longleftarrow$ **true**
8:         $\tau \longleftarrow$ the first step in η // $head(\tau) = first(\eta) \wedge \tau \sqsubseteq \eta$
9:         **while** $\left(label(\tau) \notin A_R^I \vee \exists \zeta \in \left(\phi_{\mathcal{L}^+}\left(\Omega_R^{\mathcal{L}^+}\right) \cup \psi_{\mathcal{L}^+}\left(\Theta_R^{\mathcal{L}^+}\right)\right) \cdot \tau \sqsubseteq \zeta\right) \wedge$ found **do**
10:             **if** τ is not the last step in η **then**   // $tail(\tau) \neq last(\eta) \wedge \tau \sqsubseteq \eta$
11:                 $\tau \longleftarrow$ the next step in η
12:             **else** found$\longleftarrow$ **false**
13:             **end if**
14:         **end while**
15:         **if** found **then** $T \longleftarrow T \cup \{\tau\}$
16:         **else return** E doesn't exist   // by Theorem 1
17:         **end if**
18:     **end for**
19:     $R' \longleftarrow R \mid T$
20:     Initialize E: $V_E \longleftarrow \{u_0\}$, $V_E^{init} \longleftarrow \{u_0\}$
21:     **for all** $\tau \in T_{R'}$ **do**
22:         Construct the corresponding step of τ in E
23:     **end for**
24:     **return** E
25: **end if**

---

of simple runs in $\phi_{\mathcal{L}^-}\left(\Omega_R^{\mathcal{L}^-}\right)$, $\phi_{\mathcal{L}^+}\left(\Omega_R^{\mathcal{L}^+}\right)$ respectively, and $k = \left|\psi_{\mathcal{L}^+}\left(\Theta_R^{\mathcal{L}^+}\right)\right|$ are the number of simple loops in $\psi_{\mathcal{L}^+}\left(\Theta_R^{\mathcal{L}^+}\right)$. In the worst case, line 6 to 18 in Algorithm 1 can be done in $O\left((m_2 + k)m_1 n^2\right)$ time. According to [6] and [5], line 1 and line 22 in Algorithm 1 need $O((m_1 + m_2)n)$ and $O\left(|V_{R'}|\right)$ time respectively, where $|V_{R'}|$ is the number of states of IA R'. In general, there are $length(\eta) \ll length(\alpha)$ for $\eta \in \Theta_R^{\mathcal{L}^+}$ and $\alpha \in \Omega_R^{\mathcal{L}^+}$ and $|V_{R'}| \ll (m_1 + m_2)n$. Hence, the complexity of Algorithm 1 is $O\left(m_1 m_2 n^2\right)$.

Example 3. Suppose that MSCs 'EXIT' (Fig. 2(a)) and 'SALE' (Fig. 2(b)) describe a user's undesired and desired behavior about IA *Seller* (Fig. 1) respectively. That is, the user does not want the process of ordering to be terminated by cancellation. By Algorithm 1, we can obtain a CXE E (Fig. 4) of the IA *Seller* under exclusion condition $\mathcal{L}_E$ and inclusion condition $\mathcal{L}_S$, which are two sets of action sequences derived from MSCs 'EXIT' and 'SALE' respectively (see Example 2). The intermediate result R' (see line 19 of Algorithm 1) is shown in Fig. 3. It can be found that the user's undesired behavior of *Seller* is discarded in the composition of *Seller* and E, i.e., *Seller* $\otimes E$ (Fig. 5). At the same time, the user's desired behavior of *Seller* is preserved in *Seller* $\otimes E$.

5   Related Works and Conclusion

In this paper, we give an approach for filtering the undesired behavior and preserving the desired behavior of components based on scenario specifications.

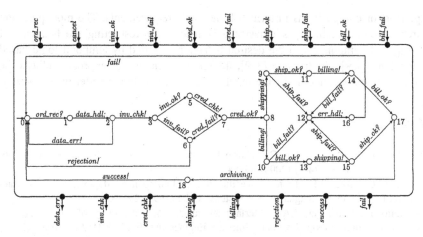

Fig. 3. IA R'. The intermediate result of Algorithm 1 with inputs *Seller*, $\mathcal{L}_E$ and $\mathcal{L}_S$

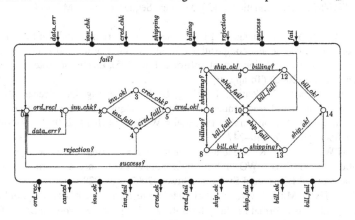

Fig. 4. The CXE E of *Seller* under exclusion condition $\mathcal{L}_E$ and inclusion condition $\mathcal{L}_S$

In [1, 2, 7], the authors mainly solve the behavioral compatibility of components composition, but do not concern whether all behavior of the composition are the needs of users. By using environment, our approach can filter out undesired behavior from

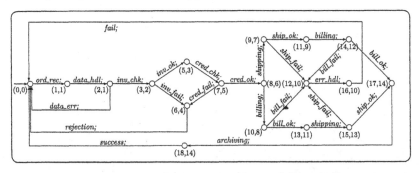

Fig. 5. *Seller* $\otimes$ E. The composition of *Seller* and E

components or compositions in terms of the user's requirements. The most pertinent research is to automatically synthesize a connector for restricting the behavior of the composed components to the desired behavior specified by temporal logic based specifications [8, 9]. Contrary to [8, 9], the environment in our approach adjusts the behavior of components only by the inputs, and our algorithm is better in complexity.

References

1. Bracciali, A., Brogi, A., Canal, C.: A formal approach to component adaptation. Journal of Systems and Software **74**(1) (2004) 45–54
2. Yellin, D.M., Strom, R.E.: Protocol specifications and component adaptors. ACM Transactions on Programming Languages and Systems **19**(2) (1997) 292–333
3. de Alfaro, L., Henzinger, T.A.: Interface automata. In: Proceedings of the 9th Annual ACM Symposium on Foundations of Software Engineering (FSE 2001), ACM Press (2001) 109–120
4. ITU-TS: ITU-TS recommendation Z.120: Message Sequence Chart (MSC). ITU-TS, Geneva (1999)
5. Zhang, Y., Hu, J., Yu, X., Zhang, T., Li, X., Zheng, G.: Deriving available behavior all out from incompatible component compositions. In: Proceedings of the 2nd International Workshop on Formal Aspects of Component Software (FACS'05), Electronic Notes in Theoretical Computer Science (2006) (To appear).
6. Hu, J., Yu, X., Zhang, Y., Zhang, T., Wang, L., Li, X., Zheng, G.: Scenario-based verification for component-based embedded software designs. In: Proceedings of the 34th International Conference on Parallel Processing Workshops (ICPP 2005 Workshop), IEEE Computer Society (2005) 240–247
7. Schmidt, H.W., Reussner, R.: Generating adapters for concurrent component protocol synchronisation. In: IFIP TC6/WG6.1 Fifth International Conference on Formal Methods for Open Object-Based Distributed Systems, Kluwer (2002) 213–229
8. Inverardi, P., Tivoli, M.: Software architecture for correct components assembly. In Bernardo, M., Inverardi, P., eds.: Formal Methods for Software Architectures. Volume 2804 of Lecture Notes in Computer Science. Springer-Verlag (2003) 92–121
9. Tivoli, M., Autili, M.: SYNTHESIS: a tool for synthesizing "correct" and protocol-enhanced adaptors. L'Object Journal **12**(1) (2005)

Mobile Ambients in Aspect-Oriented Software Architectures

Nour Ali, Jennifer Pérez, Cristóbal Costa, Isidro Ramos, Jose A. Carsí

Department of Information Systems and Computation
Polytechnic University of Valencia
Camino de Vera s/n
E-46022 Valencia, Spain
{ nourali, jeperez, ccosta, iramos, pcarsi }@dsic.upv.es

Abstract. Nowadays, distributed and mobile systems are acquiring importance and becoming widely extended for supporting ubiquitous computing. In order to develop such systems in a technology-independent way, it is important to have a formalism that describes distribution and mobility at a high abstraction level. Ambient Calculus is a formalism that allows the representation of boundaries where computation occurs. Also, distributed and mobile systems are usually difficult to develop as they need to take into account functional and non-functional requirements and reusability and adaptability mechanisms. In order to achieve these needs it is necessary to separate the distribution and mobility concerns from the rest of the concerns. PRISMA is an approach that integrates the advantages of Component-Based Software Development and Aspect-Oriented Software Development for specifying software architectures. In this paper, we describe how our work combines Ambient Calculus with PRISMA to develop distributed and mobile systems gaining their advantages.

1 Introduction

In the last few decades, the information society has undergone important changes. New technologies have become part of our daily life and the Internet has been established as a framework for global knowledge. For these reasons, two important ideas have been arisen: the world is considered as a whole unit with no boundaries, and people work in a collaborative way without meeting physically. These ideas have created the need for current software development processes to deal with complex structures, new non-functional requirements, dynamic adaptation, and new technologies. In addition, most software systems require the capability to work with different devices (PCs, laptops, PDAs, smart phones, etc) through communication networks in a distributed and secure way. As a result, software development processes must also take into account the distributed, ubiquitous and mobile nature of software systems.

The development of distributed, ubiquitous and mobile software systems is a difficult task, especially if these characteristics are to be considered from the beginning of the software life cycle. Currently, decisions about these characteristics are usually postponed to late stages of the software life cycle (design and implementation). As a

Please use the following format when citing this chapter:

Ali, N., Pérez, J., Costa, C., Ramos, I., Carsí, J.A., 2006, in IFIP International Federation for Information Processing, Volume 227, Software Engineering Techniques: Design for Quality, ed. K. Sacha, (Boston: Springer), pp. 37–48.

result, there is a loss of traceability, and the system is subject to a specific technological platform (such as CORBA [1] or .NET Remoting [2]). As a result, the development of systems of this kind introduces important challenges such as: how to specify distribution and mobility features in a technology-independent way, how to consistently manage a distributed state, how to support non-functional requirements such as security or fault tolerance.

Software Architecture is considered to be the bridge between the requirements and implementation phases of the software life cycle. Software Architectures describe the structure of software systems in terms of computational (components) and coordination (connectors) units of software. Architecture Description Languages (ADLs) specify the functional and coordination properties of these software units in a formal way. However, current ADLs do not provide constructs for describing distribution or mobility features in an abstract way.

A formalism that provides mechanisms to describe distribution and mobility properties is Ambient Calculus (AC) [3]. AC introduces the concept of ambient, which represents boundaries where computation occurs. Ambients can model the location hierarchy encountered in distributed systems and model the mobility as the crossing of the locations boundaries.

PRISMA [4] is an approach that integrates the advantages of Component-Based Software Development (CBSD) [5] and Aspect-Oriented Software Development (AOSD) [6] to specify software architectures. This approach has a meta-model [4], formal Aspect-Oriented Architecture Description Language (AOADL) [7], and a framework [8].

In this paper, we combine the PRISMA approach and the AC in order to deal with the specification of distributed and mobile features from the beginning of the software life cycle in a technology-independent way. In this work, ambients are specified as architectural elements that use separation of concerns (aspects) to describe their functionalities.

The paper is structured as follows: Section 2 presents related works performed in the area of distribution at an architectural level. Section 3 presents the PRISMA approach and the motivation for the work presented in this paper. Section 4, gives an overview of AC. Section 5, introduces how the PRISMA approach combines ambients. Finally, Section 6 presents conclusions and further works.

2 Related Work

One of the reasons why software architectures emerged was to simplify the construction of dynamic distributed systems. However, at the present time, few ADLs support the specification of distributed systems properties. The first research that provided significant results in distributed software architectures was carried out in the Darwin ADL [9]. Darwin uses π-calculus [10] to define the semantics of distributed message-passing. It builds architectures by defining composite components that are bound and given locations at instantiation time. Darwin has also been used in the CORBA environment to specify the overall architecture of component-based applications [11]. However, in the literature, we have not found new advances to Darwin in constructing software architectures with mobile and replicable components. As Darwin is based on π-calculus only, mobility can only be simulated by the movement of channels. It lacks primitives to express the movement of crossing boundaries.

The work in [12] states that an ADL should consider features such as composition, reusability, and configuration in order to specify dynamic distributed software architectures. It presents a configuration language that describes a method for a reconfiguration model at run-time. However, the reconfiguration model is not formal. Moreover, it neglects a distribution model for specifying distributed message-passing among components and connectors.

The works of Mascolo and Ciancarini [13,14] introduce MobiS, which is a specification language that is based on a tuple-space model that specifies coordination by multiset rewriting. MobiS can also be used to specify architectures containing mobile components. However, it does not specify the mobility concern separately from the rest of the functionalities of the software architectures, reducing reusability and adaptability to changes.

The ADL C2Sadel has adapted a style to support both distribution and mobility. The style [15] provides software connectors that are able to move components. It also has an implementation infrastructure to support this architectural style. However, this approach has the drawback that there is no separation between coordination and distribution. Therefore, the components are the only architectural elements that are mobile while the connectors are static.

The work of Lopes in [16] describes the semantics of externalizing a distribution dimension in order to support distribution and mobility for software architectures. This distribution dimension is very similar to a connector, but instead of containing the business logic, it controls the rules for mobility and location. In this way, a separation between computation, coordination and distribution is achieved. A difference between our work and Lopes's work is that our work defines the semantics of distribution and mobility by using Ambient Calculus. This allows our approach to have an explicit primitive to represent a location with boundaries allowing the specification of security and authentication.

3 PRISMA Distribution and Mobile Model

The PRISMA model [4] allows the definition of software architectures of complex software systems by integrating the AOSD and the CBSD. PRISMA uses the AOSD to separate the crosscutting concerns (distribution, security, context-aware, coordination, etc.) of architectures in aspects. The PRISMA architectural elements are specified using aspects that define their behaviour. As a result, an architectural element (components and connectors) can be viewed as a prism where each side of the prism is an aspect (*white box view*). In addition, an architectural element encapsulates its functionality and publishes a set of services that it offers to the rest of the architectural elements (*black box view*) (see Figure 1).

There are two kinds of architectural elements: components and connectors. A component is an architectural element that captures the functionality of software systems and a connector is an architectural element that acts as a coordinator among other architectural elements. Components and connectors are formed by a set of aspects, the weaving relationships among these aspects, and the ports that offer and request services.

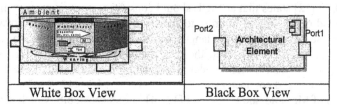

| White Box View | Black Box View |

Fig. 1. Views of an Architectural Element

Weavings indicate that the execution of an aspect service can trigger the execution of services in other aspects. Weavings are the glue of the aspects of an architectural element. This glue is defined using temporal operations called weaving operators. Initially, the weaving operators that PRISMA provides are *after, before, around, afterif, beforeif, and insteadif.* For example, if a weaving with the *after* operator is specified between service s1 of aspect A1 and service s2 of aspect A2, this means that s2 of A2 is executed after s1 of A1.

It is important to emphasize that connectors do not have the references of the components that they connect and vice versa. Thus, architectural elements are reusable and unaware of each other. This is possible due to the fact that the channels (*attachments*) defined between components and connectors have their references, instead of architectural elements. Attachments are the channels that enable the communication between components and connectors. Each attachment is defined by attaching a component port with a connector port (represented as lines in Figure 2).

However, when we applied PRISMA to a real case study such as the tele-operated *TeachMover* robot local communication was a limitation. Tele-operation systems are control systems that depend on software to perform their operations. They are usually robots that perform high-risk activities. For this reason, they must be controlled by operators from safe areas. As a result, the need to locate components in different places (nodes) as well as to communicate the distributed software components of the operator and the robot emerged.

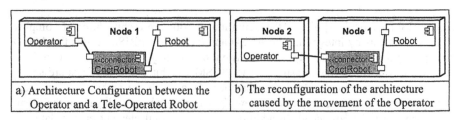

| a) Architecture Configuration between the Operator and a Tele-Operated Robot | b) The reconfiguration of the architecture caused by the movement of the Operator |

Fig. 2. Mobility of the Operator in a Tele-Operated System

Mobility is also a characteristic that is fundamental in distributed and dynamic systems, where the topology of the architecture can change at run-time. For example, in the tele-operated system, the mobility requirement emerges to be able to move the operator to different places (nodes). This mobility is necessary to allow the operator send commands to the robot from different places, maintaining the information of the operator component consistent (see Figure 2).

As Figure 2 illustrates, mobility is the process of transferring a component instance from one node to another one. Moreover, the transfer process must ensure that the transferred component instance continues its execution at the target node, conserving its state and maintaining the same execution point.

PRISMA has been adapted to support distribution and mobility properties [17] in order to be applied to real case studies. Distribution is supported in PRISMA by introducing the following properties into the model:

1. The use of attachments: Attachments store, not only the references of the architectural elements that they are connecting, but also the locations of these architectural elements (nodes). In this way, the reusability of architectural elements is preserved, and distributed communication is enabled. As a result, architectural elements are unaware of the distributed or local nature of the others.
2. The use of a Distribution Aspect: The distribution aspect specifies the features and strategies that are related to the distributed behaviour of a PRISMA architectural element. It specifies the site where the architectural element is located and indicates when an element needs to be moved.

This distribution model was initially implemented in the PRISMANET middleware [8] and has been validated using case studies where distribution properties are required. However, a model that includes an explicit primitive for supporting locations as boundaries, describes the location hierarchies and supports the mobility of elements by the crossing of boundaries is richer. Therefore, we have combined the PRISMA model and AC.

4 Ambient Calculus

Ambient Calculus [3] (AC) is a process algebra that extends π-calculus [11] in order to introduce the concept of ambient. An ambient is a bounded place where computation occurs. Thus, an ambient can be anything with a boundary such as a laptop, a web page, a folder, etc. Each ambient has a set of running computations that can control it. These are responsible for moving an ambient. In addition, an ambient can contain other subambients that have running computations.

Thus, mobility is performed at an ambient level, i.e. ambients are mobile. Also, mobility is performed by crossing boundaries of ambients. AC provides mobility and local communication primitives. These primitives can be expressed in a textual syntax and in a graphical syntax which is called Folder Calculus [20] (see Figure 3). Folder Calculus is a graphical metaphor for AC where ambients are visually represented as folders.

AC uses some of the constructs inherited from π-calculus such as naming, restriction, parallel processes, inactive process and replication. However, the names in AC are names of ambients instead of names of channels as in π-calculus. Therefore, in order to syntactically write that an ambient with name n has process P, it is written as $n[P]$.

Textual Syntax	Visual Syntax	Comments	Textual Syntax	Visual Syntax	Comments
(νn)P		New name n in a scope P.	0	O	Inactive process (often omitted).
			!P		Replication of P.
n[P]		Folder (ambient) of name n and contents P.	⟨M⟩		Output M.
M.P		Action M followed by P.	(n).P		Input n followed by P.
P¦Q	P Q	Two processes in parallel. (Visually: contiguously placed in 2D.)	(P)		Grouping

Fig. 3. The Textual and Visual Syntax of Ambient Calculus constructs

Some of the primitives that AC provides are called capabilities. Capabilities are actions that can be performed on ambients. There are three main types of capabilities: enter, exit and open capabilities. The enter capability orders an ambient to enter another ambient on its same hierarchy level (see Figure 4). The exit capability orders an ambient to exit its parent ambient. The open capability dissolves an ambient leaving the processes that were in it.

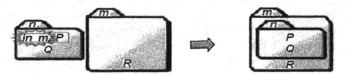

Fig. 4. Applying the enter capability to the ambient n

4   AMBIENT-PRISMA: Combining Ambient Calculus and the PRISMA Approach

This section presents how the AC concepts are integrated to the PRISMA approach in order to describe distributed and mobile systems. To allow PRISMA architectural elements to make use of the ambient concept of AC, the ambient construct must be included in the PRISMA meta-model. Therefore, some mappings between the AC meta-model and the PRISMA meta-model have been identified.

In [18], it is discussed that an ambient can be seen as a software component that offers mobility and that it has a proper identity at run-time so that it can be maintainable. In our model, this corresponds to a PRISMA architectural element. Since PRISMA architectural elements are components and connectors, an ambient cannot be a PRISMA Component because a PRISMA component performs the computations. Nor can the ambient be a PRISMA Connector because a PRISMA Connector coordinates computations. Therefore, in the PRISMA meta-model an ambient is introduced as a new type of architectural element (see Figure 5) that is responsible for providing mobility sevices to distributed architectural elements. As a result, an ambient inherits all the characteristics of a PRISMA architectural element (its CBSD view and its AOSD view) and provides its proper semantics. Figure 6 shows the graphical representation of a PRISMA ambient. The graphical representation preserves the folder calculus representation of an ambient. The Ambient CBSD view describes it as a black box where it communicates with others by using ports that send and receive invocations of services.

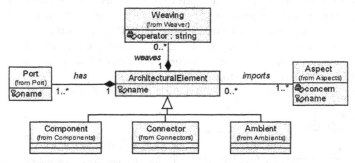

Fig. 5. Including the Ambient as another architectural element

An ambient has a collection of local agents and can also have other subambients [18]. In PRISMA, the local agents correspond to components that are coordinated using connectors. Ambients in PRISMA are complex architectural elements that represent the places where components, connectors and other ambients are located. In addition, by allowing an ambient to have other ambients inside it, the hierarchy of distributed and mobile systems can be modelled in PRISMA.

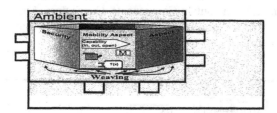

Fig. 6 A PRISMA Ambient with CBSD and AOSD views

The AOSD view describes the PRISMA ambient with a set of aspects that can be weaved. The ambient uses different aspects to specify the services it offers and requests. As ambients are responsible for the mobility concern, all ambients must have the Mobility Aspect to provide mobility services to their local architectural elements.

The Mobility Aspect specifies the following ambient functionalities:

- It allows an ambient to offer the exit service to its subambients that need to exit from it. (The specification of the AC exit capability).
- It allows an ambient to offer the enter service to its subambients that need to enter other subambients. (The specification of the AC enter capability).
- It allows an ambient to create subambients. (The specification of the AC restriction).
- It allows an ambient to accept a new ambient in it from external ambients.
- It allows an ambient to execute the open service. The open service allows a subambient to be destroyed a local ambient without destroying its local architec-

tural elements. As a result, the architectural elements of the destroyed subambient become to form part of the ambient. (The specification of the AC open capability)

The separation of the Mobility Aspect concern from the rest of concerns provides a better maintainability of these functionalities because they are not scattered through the ambient specification. In addition, this is a generic aspect that must be reused by all PRISMA ambients. As a result, ambients are defined by importing the generic mobility aspect and adapting it to the software system needs through weavings. For example, a LAN ambient may need some security policies that are different from a PC ambient inside of the LAN. Therefore, both the LAN and PC ambient import the same Mobility Aspect, but the Mobility Aspect is weaved with different security aspects.

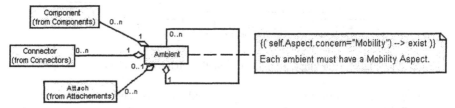

Fig. 7. The Ambient Package in the PRISMA meta-model

In order to introduce the concepts that describe a PRISMA ambient, an Ambient Package has been defined in the PRISMA meta-model(see Figure 7). This package contains the relationships and constraints that an ambient has with other meta-model concepts. An Ambient can contain Components, Connectors, Attachments, and other ambients. A constraint is specified in the Object Constraint Language in order to indicate that an Ambient must have a Mobility Aspect.

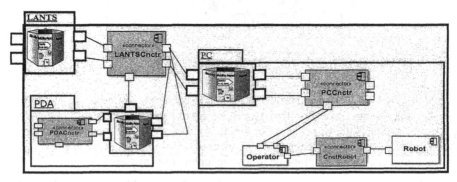

Fig. 8. The Initial Configuration of the Robot software architecture modeled with Ambients.

We are going to use the tele-operation system example to illustrate how a distributed and mobile system is specified in PRISMA after introducing the ambient architectural element. In the example, the operator is a mobile component that can move from a PC to a PDA to be closer to the robot. Figure 8 shows the distributed hierarchy of the tele-operation software architecture. It shows that the *LANTS* ambient (the LAN of the Tele-operation System) consists of a *PDA* ambient and a *PC* ambient. The *Operator* component, *Robot* component and their connector (*CnctrRobot*) are initially located in the *PC* ambient. Using the ambient calculus syntax, this is written as *LANTS[PDA[]\ PC[Operator[out PC, in PDA] , CnctRobot, Robot].*

Every ambient has services that are offered to its local architectural elements and services that are offered to the exterior. As a result, some of the ambient ports in Fig. 8 are only internally connected through attachments to a connector (e.g. the *PCCnctr* of the *PC*) that synchronizes the ambient with its local architectural elements.

Figure 9 (b) shows how the *Operator* Component is specified in the PRISMA ADL. As the *Operator* is a distributed component, it imports a predefined Distribution Aspect *OpDistribution*, specified in Figure 9(a), which defines a distributed behaviour. The *Operator* has three ports: *ExitingPort* to request an *exit*, *EnteringPort* to request an *enter*, and *FunctPort* to send commands to the robot. The *OpDistribution* specifies the *move*. *Move* indicates that the movement of the element that imports this aspect needs to *exit* from its parent ambient and then *enter* to another ambient. For this reason, requests for *enter* and *exit* are made to other architectural elements (*out* = client behaviour). For example in Figure 8, to move the *Operator* from the *PC* to the PDA, the Operator makes a request to *exit* the *PC* from the *PC*. Figure 8 also shows that the ports *ExitigPort* and *EnteringPort* are connected to the *PCCnctr* in order to be synchronized with the *PC* ambient. *FunctPort* is connected to *CnctRobot* to be synchronized with the *Robot*.

Distribution Aspect OpDistribution
        using IExiting, IEntering
Services
... ...
  out exit (MyName: **String**);
  out enter (MyName: **String**, NewAmbient: **loc**);
 	
Transactions move(NewAmbient: **loc**)
  Exiting= **out** exit(MyName).Entering;
  Entering= **out** enter(MyName, NewAmbient);
... ...
End Distribution Aspect OpDistribution
	Component_type Operator
	  Import Distribution Aspect OpDistribution;
	  Import Functional Aspect OpFunct;
	  Port
	    ExitingPort: IExiting;
	    EnteringPort: IEntering;
	    FunctPort: IRobotCommands,;
	  End_Port
	End Component_type Operator;

(a)	(b)

Fig. 9. The Operator Distribution Aspect and Component specified in the ADL

Mobility Aspect Mobile
      using IExiting, IEntering, IAccepting
... .
Transactions in exit(Requested: **String**, NewAmbient: **loc**):
  EXIT ::= **out** isSon(**input** Requested, **output** isSonOK)→
    EXIT1;
  EXIT1::= {isSonOK==true} **out** checkTypeAmbient(**input**
    Requested, **output** isTypeAmbient) →
    EXIT2;
  EXIT2::= **if**(isTypeAmbient==false)**then**
    createAmbientFor (**input**
    Requested, **output** RequestedAmbient →
    EXIT3 **else** EXIT3 ;
  EXIT3::= **out** movingInf(**input** RequestedAmbient, **output** Type,
    output MobileInstance, **output** AttachmentList[])→
    EXIT4;
  EXIT4::= **out** accept(**input** Type, **input** MobileIntstance, **input**
    AttachmentsList, **output** Acceptance)→ EXIT5;
  EXIT5::= {Acceptance==true} **out** modifyAttachment(Requested)→
    EXIT6;
  EXIT6::= **out** destroy(RequestedAmbient)→EXIT7;
  EXIT7::= **out** removeAttachments(requestedAmbient);
 	
... ...
End_Mobility Aspect Mobile
	Ambient_type PC
	  Import Mobility Aspect Mobile;
	  Import Security Aspect Sec;
	  Weavings
	    Sec.CheckSecurity() **before**
	      Moile.exit(Requested, Ne-
	  wAmbient);
	  End_Weavings
	
	  Ports
	    AccceptancePort: IAccept;
	    DistServicesPort: ICall;
	    ServicesPort: ICall;
	    CapabilitiesPort: ICapability
	  End_Ports
	
	End Ambient_type PC ;
	
	(b)

(a)	

Fig. 10. The Mobility Aspect and the PC Ambient specified in the ADL

Figure 10(a) shows a fragment of the Mobility Aspect *Mobile* that all ambients import. It shows how the *exit* capability is mapped in PRISMA. Figure 10(b) shows the specification of the *PC* ambient. It shows that the *PC* imports the behavior that the *Mobile* aspect defines. It also shows that it imports a Security Aspect *Sec*. In the **Weavings** section, a weaving is specified to indicate that a security rule must be checked in the *Sec* aspect *before* the exit is executed in the *Mobile* aspect.

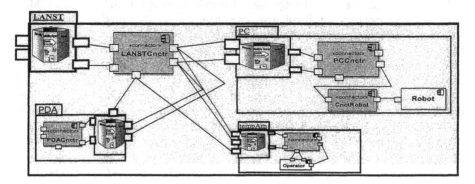

Fig. 11. The new configuration of Figure 8 after the execution of the *exit*

The *exit* in Figure 10(a) is specified as a transaction in the **Transactions** section. The *exit* has a server behaviour in the ambient that imports the aspect, that is, other architectural elements are going to request it (*in*=server behaviour). Using the example in Figure 8, the *Operator* would be the element that makes an *exit* request to the ambient. Then the *exit* **Transaction** consists of a set of services. First, it checks if the requested element (*Operator*) is one of the PCs children (is one of its local elements). If it is, then the *exit* checks if the requester is an ambient or not. If it is not an ambient, then an ambient is created to encapsulate the element. The creation of an ambient is necessary due to the fact that ambients are the only architectural elements that can be mobile. Then the information needed for the exit of the *Operator* is collected: the state of the *Operator* and its attachments. The *exit* transaction then asks the parent ambient (*LANTS*) if it can accept the *Operator's* ambient (*tempAm*) and sends the needed information. If *LANTS* accepts the *tempAm*, for each attachment between the *Operator* and other architectural elements, a new attachment is created between the *PCCnctr* and those local architectural elements that are connected to *Operator*. Figure 11 shows the new attachment that is created between *CnctRobot* and *PCCnctr* in place of the attachment between *CnctRobot* and *Operator*. Then the *PC* ambient deletes the *Operator* and all its attachments. Figure 11 shows the result of the software architecture configuration after executing the *exit* transaction.

Finally, Figure 12 shows the *Operator* component in the *PDA*. This is possible after the *Operator* in *tempAm* in Figure 11 requests the *LANTS* to enter PDA. Then, the *LANTS* checks if the PDA is local to it and requests the PDA to accept the *tempAm*. The *PDA* accepts *tempAm* and opens it, leaving the *Operator* in *PDA*.

The tele-operation system specification shows how its distributed and mobile properties can be described. The previous specification benefits from the concepts introduced in AC; thus the mobility of the *Operator* is specified in a formal way thanks to the AC capabilities. Also, the AC primitives can be completely specified by the PRISMA ADL in a technology-independent way. In this way, the ambient functionalities can benefit from the reusability and maintainability that the AOSD and CBSD provide.

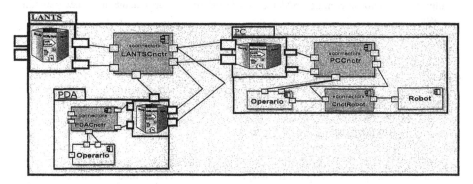

Fig. 12. The configuration of the architecture when the *Operator* reaches *PDA*.

5. Conclusions and Further Work

In this work, we have presented an approach to represent complex, distributed and mobile systems in a technology-independent. Our model combines the PRISMA approach with the AC formalism, which provides the following advantages: 1) It can describe a complex system in terms of computational, coordination and distribution and mobility units on different levels of abstraction. In this way, a system is built by reusing and adapting these separated units achieving a higher level of maintainability. 2) It can also describe the specific issues of current distributed systems such as the network topology and security.

We have introduced the ambient concept in the PRISMA meta-model as a new architectural element that can contain several computation and coordination processes (components and connectors) or other subambients. The capabilities provided by an AC ambient are offered in PRISMA by an ambient-specific aspect called the Mobility Aspect. Another aspect, the Distribution Aspect, manages the location of an architectural element and defines how and when ambient capabilities can be executed. A Security Aspect can be added to an ambient in order to provide security mechanisms. Mobility, distribution and security concerns are specified separately from other functional and non-functional requirements, thereby increasing reusability and adaptability to changes.

In the near future, we are going to introduce these concepts into the PRISMA tool to be able to model and execute mobile distributed software architectures. This will be done in three stages: first, ambients will be introduced in the PRISMANET middleware [8] to execute these concepts; second, ambient graphical metaphor and code templates will be introduced in the modelling framework; third, the implementation will be validated by modelling and executing a complex, distributed, and mobile case study.

References

1. CORBA Official Web Site of the OMG Group, http://www.corba.org/
2. Microsoft .Net Remoting: A Technical Overview, http://msdn.microsoft.com/library/default.asp?url=/library/enus/dndotnet/html/hawkremotin g.asp
3. Cardelli, L., Gordon, A. D. "Mobile Ambients", Foundations of Software Science and Computational Structures: First International Conference, FOSSACS '98, LNCS 1378, Springer, 1998, pp. 140-155.
4. Perez, J., Ali, N., Carsí, J.A., Ramos, I. "Dynamic Evolution in Aspect-Oriented Architectural Models", European Workshop on Software Architecture, Pisa, June 2005 © Springer LNCS vol n.3527.
5. Szyperski, C., *Component Software: Beyond Object Oriented programming*, ACM Press and Addison Wesley, New York, USA, 2002.
6. Aspect-Oriented Software Development, http://aosd.net
7. Pérez, J., Ali, N., Carsí, J.A., Ramos, I. "Designing Software Architectures with an Aspect-Oriented Architecture Description Language", 9th International Symposium on Component-Based Software Engineering (CBSE 2006), Mälardalen University, Västerås near Stockholm, Sweden, June 29th -1st July 2006 (accepted to appear)
8. Perez, J., Ali, N., Costa, C., Carsí, J.A., Ramos, I. "Executing Aspect-Oriented Component-Based Software Architectures on .NET Technology",3rd International Conference on .NET Technologies, Pilsen, Czech Republic, May-June 2005 , 2005
9. Magee, J., Dulay, N., Eisenbach, S., Krammer, J. "Specifying Distributed Software Architectures". 5th European Software Engineering Conference (ESEC 95), Sitges, Spain, 1995, pp 137-153.
10. Milner, R., Parrow, J., Walker, D. "A calculus of mobile processes", Parts 1-2. Information and Computation, 100(1), 1992, pp. 1-77.
11. Magee, J., Tseng, A, Kramer, J. "Composing Distributed Objects in CORBA", Third International Symposium on Autonomous Decentralized Systems, Berlin Germany, 1997, pp 257-263.
12. Virginia C. de Paula, G.R., Justo, Cunha, Ribeiro, P. R. F. "Specifying Dynamic Distributed Software Architectures", XII Brazilian Symposium on Software Engineering, BCS Press, October, 1998.
13. Ciancarini, P., Mascolo, C. "Software Architecture and Mobility", 3rd Int. Software Architecture Workshop (ISAW-3), November, 1998.
14. Mascolo, C. "MobiS: A Specification Language for Mobile Systems". 3rd International Conference on Coordination Models and Languages, 1999.
15. Medvidovic, N., Rakic, M. "Exploiting Software Architecture Implementation Infrastructure in Facilitating Component Mobility". Software Engineering and Mobility Workshop, Toronto, Canada, May 2001.
16. Lopes, A. Fiadeiro, J.L., Wermelinger, M. "Architectural Primitives for Distribution and Mobility", 10th Symposium on Foundations of Software Engineering, SIGSOFT FSE 2002, pp. 41-50.
17. Ali, N., Ramos, I., Carsi, J.A. "A Conceptual Model for Distributed Aspect Oriented Software Architectures", International Conference on Information Technology (ITCC 2005), IEEE Computer Society, ISBN 0-7695-2315-3, April 2005, pp 422-427.
18. Cardelli, L. "Abstractions for Mobile Computation." In Vitek, J. and (Eds.), C. J., editors, Secure Internet Programming: Security Issues for Distributed and Mobile Objects, volume 1603 of LNCS, Springer Verlag, pp. 51-94.

The architecture of distributed systems driven by autonomic patterns

Marcin Wolski, Cezary Mazurek, Paweł Spychała, Aleksander Sumowski

Poznań Supercomputing and Networking Center,
ul. Noskowskiego 12/14 Poznań, Poland
{maw, mazurek, spychala, sumek}@man.poznan.pl

Abstract. The autonomic computing notion has introduced the concept of self-optimizing, self-healing and auto-diagnosis applications. In this article we would like to present how this idea affects the building of distributed systems. As a reference base, we take advantage of the Data Management System (DMS), which has been developed within the scope of the PROGRESS project. DMS enables the creation of a grid environment capable of storing large amounts of data. The complex architecture of this system, which constitutes a model of loosely coupled components, involves a special approach to its maintenance and management. To address these problems, we have applied the autonomic computing patterns in the DMS architecture. Our solution was designed to be reused in any project dealing with the same issues. It can also act as an autonomic service for any other applications and services.

1 Introduction

Data grid systems have been designed to be up to complex data processing in a geographically distributed environment and exact performance demands. Over the years this class of systems has matured and at present they are offering a wide range of functionality related to the management, collaborative sharing, publication, and preservation of distributed data collections. This wealth of capabilities, however, complicates the managing of such large systems, increases its complexity as more heterogeneous components are added, and makes it more difficult to find and solve any technical problems. They constitute a typical example of an environment where administrators spend too much time doing repetitive tasks, monitoring the system burden, reacting when problems with performance arise or continuously blocking the hackers' attacks.

The concept of the Service Oriented Architecture (SOA) [9,13], which common implementation is based on existing Web services standards and specifications, helps to deal with these inconveniences. The notion of a service is nothing new, but the concept of the SOA has evolved over the past couple of years. It is an architectural style of building software applications that promotes loose coupling between components so that you can reuse them. SOA makes it possible to construct architectures where client applications can simply register, discover, and use the services deployed over the grid.

Please use the following format when citing this chapter:

Wolski, M., Mazurek, C., Spychała, P., Sumowski, A., 2006, in IFIP International Federation for Information Processing, Volume 227, Software Engineering Techniques: Design for Quality, ed. K. Sacha, (Boston: Springer), pp. 49–60.

SOA itself narrows the focus on the overall system maintenance and management but it does not cope with many problems derived from the complexity of distributed systems. We need a solution which enables the system to automatically configure its components, discover and correct faults, monitor and control resources and proactive identify and protect from arbitrary attacks. Autonomic computing (AC) researches offer the most promising approach to addressing such challenges.

The conjecture of AC was inspired by IBM's autonomic computing initiative to deal with the main problem in large and distributed systems - increasing complexity. Autonomic means able to operate without conscious control of a human – similarly to our heart or lungs controlled by our autonomic nervous system. AC generally has two main goals: to reduce the work and complexity associated with a large system and be able to better respond to rapid changes in the system.

In this paper we would like to present how the autonomic computing notion affects the building of distributed systems. Moreover, the solution that we provided can also act as an autonomic service for any other applications and services. As a reference base, we take advantage of the Data Management Suite (DMSuite) [3,4] – a platform of integrated services supporting data management processes in the grid environments. DMSuite has been designed and developed in the scope of the PROGRESS project [2] – an initiative undertaken within the PIONIER National Program [1] and funded by the State Committee for Scientific Research and Sun Microsystems Poland. Currently the Data Management Suite is a part of the Gridge (Grid Enterprise Solutions) [5], which covers the whole grid architecture, from tools and portals down to core middleware.

The remainder of this paper is organized as follows: Section 2 introduces the background and technical aspects of the AC model. Section 3 details the current implementation of DMSuite and indicates its advancement in terms of autonomic computing. Section 4 demonstrates some case studies taken from various projects using the DMSuite software and presents a definition of autonomic patterns and its relationship with the system architecture. Section 5 summarizes the paper with our conclusions about building distributed systems on the basis of the SOA model and AC patterns. It also indicates what will be held in the upcoming release of DMSSuite.

2 Autonomic computing design

Autonomic computing was introduced by IBM as a response to overwhelmingly increasing complexity of novel systems [12]. The process of growing complexity threatened that at some future point of time computer systems would become a burden, covering its initial use.

The autonomic computing vision is based on an autonomic nervous system. Autonomic computer systems are supposed to be able to operate without human attention. They are supposed to automatically interoperate between each other without the need to tweak large amounts of switches and XML configuration files.

The system architecture built according to autonomic computing principles should limit the hands-on intervention to uncommon cases which occur during the system's regular work. This postulate could be fulfilled by applying predefined policies for administrative operations which can take decisions leading to the system reconfiguration, basing on gathered knowledge during the system work. Such vision of the fully self-managed system seems to be hard to realize, but it allows to determine the aim, an ideal system architecture which uses different technologies and solutions for achieving the assumed autonomic computing level. The autonomic computing architecture can be understood as a continuum for a system.

2.1 Self-CHOP paradigm

There are four components that comprise the autonomic computing vision [11]:

- Self-configuring – means the ability to dynamically adapt to changing environments. Self-configuring components use policies provided by the professional staff to perform self-configure procedures. Such changes could include the deployment of new components or the removal of the existing ones, or even remarkable changes in the system characteristics.
- Self-healing – means the ability to discover, diagnose and react to malfunctions. Self-healing components can detect system disruptions and initiate policy-based repair procedures without any influence on the rest of the environment. Corrective action could involve a product altering its own state or effecting changes in other components.
- Self-optimizing – means the ability to monitor and tune resources automatically. The tuning actions could imply, for example, reallocating resources (such as in reaction to dynamically changing workloads), improvement of the overall utilization, or ensuring that particular transactions can be completed in a timely fashion.
- Self-protecting – means the ability to anticipate, detect, identify and protect against threats from anywhere. Self-protecting components can identify hostile behaviors as they occur and take appropriate actions to make themselves more resistant. The hostile behaviors can include unauthorized access and use, virus infection and denial-of-service attacks.

Those four ideas together form a self-CHOP paradigm which, in short, stands for configuration, healing, optimization and protection.

2.2 Maturity levels

The autonomic computing architecture ideas could be realized in the developed system in a different way, in a different scope and on a different level. Following the [14], there are five levels of maturity that refers to the state of implementation of the autonomic computing recommendations. These levels are: basic, managed, predictive, adaptive and autonomic. Although the distributed applications constantly evolve along these stages, the general state of the novel system remains at the basic and managed levels. These two base levels do not allow the application to be aware of the system environment state.

The basic level defines an architecture which still requires human intervention and expertise basing on their knowledge. The managed level is achieved when the environment is equipped with some scripting and logging tools, allowing to automate routine execution and reporting. The plans and taken decisions are based on this gathered information; however, it still needs an individual specialists review.

Systems at a predictive level of autonomic computing maturity have a basic intelligence, which bases on predetermined thresholds and knowledge base, suggesting solutions according to the set of events stored at a centralized base and their common occurrences and experience. The adaptive level defines environments that allow them to take action themselves basing on predictive system capabilities according to the arising situations.

The highest level of the autonomic computing system architecture is defined as autonomic, which is understood as a policy-driven system, which is able to e.g. allocate resources according to priorities.

It is worth underlining that the system maturity levels evolve and there is no approach to make a self-optimizing, self-protecting, self-configuring and self-healing system.

3 Data Management Suite

DMSuite is a middleware platform providing a uniform interface for connecting heterogeneous data sources over a network. It may stand for the backbone on which a computational grid would perform its operations. The following figure depicts the main components belonging to this integrated platform.

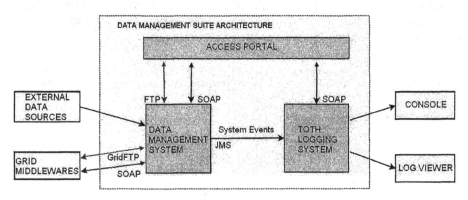

Fig. 1. Data Management Suite architecture

The Data Management System and Toth constitute a base for our architecture that combines autonomic and data grid technologies. The Data Management System is the main part of Data Management Suite solutions. It is a middleware application based on the SOA model that determines loose coupling between reusable components. Similarly to computing and network resources, DMS provides services to manage and retrieve data files in order to support grid jobs. The computational resources managed by DMS can be described by metadata schemas which allow the creation of an abstract, semantic and explorable layer of resources.

The Toth Logging System simplifies the system administration process by gathering all events incoming from distributed components of the DMSuite. It is based on the JMS technology [15], which assures simple exchange of binary messages in the asynchronous way.

3.1 Autonomic design

DMSuite has been built using some autonomic computing principles, such as self-management, fault detection and self-configuration. The Data Management System (DMS) - the key element of DMSuite - contains three logically distinguished modules: Data Broker, Metadata Repository and Data Container [16]. Together they create the basic layer of the data management environment, the so-called DMS core. DMS architecture is comprised of distributed modules, each of them can be treated as a separate service using XML messages to communicate with other applications.

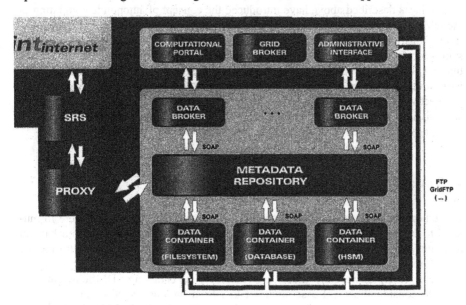

Fig. 2. Data Management System

Metadata Repository stores various type of information about resources managed by the system. Data Broker is a distributed entry point to the system. Data Container is a storage element, which arranges data on various types of media. Proxy provides an uniform interface to external data sources with a diversified structure. Within the PROGRESS installation Proxy enables access to biological databanks managed by SRS (Sequence Retrieval System) [19]. All modules belonging to the DMS middleware automatically register themselves in the Metadata Repository.

According to the five-degree maturity levels of autonomic computing (section 2.2), DMSuite currently comes in the second (managed) level. The first (basic) level of maturity is assured by the presence of the Toth Logging System. The Toth is responsible for gathering all events that occur in the monitored system. It stores the messages in the internal structures and provides an interface to explore them. But it is not enough to achieve the second level of maturity, which ensures that systems management technologies can be used to collect details from managed resources, helping to reduce the time it takes the administrator to collect and synthesize information. Therefore Toth has been equipped with additional functionality related to the messages processing. It performs advanced parsing on each of the received events, constructs a set of metadata on their base, and exposes an interface for searching the collected events, according to the specified criteria.

Our initial solution aimed to fulfill the basic AC principles is completed by a single access interface to the whole data components. It allows the end users (professional staff, administrators, researches) to manage the entire data grid infrastructure as easily as managing one application running on one computer. This interface has been developed in a form of a Web portal which offers a single and efficient tool to simplify the management of the distributed components.

The ideas described above have introduced the concept of autonomic computing in the DMSuite environment. This includes self-configuration, that is automatic registration of distributed components in the Metadata Repository, and self-healing, which stands for restoring coherency in the distributed file system. But these features constitute only a part of the autonomic computing model and are appropriate to achieve the basic level of AC implementation. On the basis of some scenarios taken from various perspectives (users, developer, administrators), we will point out which features are still missing, and describe some extensions to the DMS architecture which will take advantage of advanced capabilities from the autonomic computing area.

4 Toward the concept of autonomic patterns

In the beginning we would like to recall a few general principles which were formulated to design the data grid architectures (following the [6]). These are: mechanism neutrality, policy neutrality, compatibility with grid infrastructure, and uniformity of the information infrastructure.

These principles were the underlying reason for the creation of DMSuite. But taking into consideration real case studies taken from various projects using our software, we noticed a lack of AC capabilities which are necessary to fulfill the enterprise requirements. These are:

- Self-configuration: self-discovery and self-configuring of the system components. For example: providing and maintaining the current information about active Data Brokers and their hierarchy, automatic detection of inactive Data Containers.
- Self-healing: automatic discovery of errors and their corrections. For example: searching for files with stale properties[1] and their automatic refreshing, system recovery after Metadata Repository failure.

---

[1] In case of internal failure the file properties may become invalid. Dealing with this problem requires hands-on reaction. This is an internal DMS feature.

- Self-optimization: continuous monitoring and control of resource usage, which assures their optimal utilization, for example, automatic file replication, file transfer optimization in terms of speed and bandwidth.
- Self-protection: proactive identification and protection against the attacks. For example: active detection of incoming threats, response to the specific events in a form of a system message (mail, log journal etc.).

Owing to the above assumptions, we perceive a necessity to define two additional guidelines, pointing at directions of the building of novel data grid systems (generally distributed systems). These are:

- The component model – instead of building a monolith architecture and thus assigning all resources to a specific application, the software should be treated as a set of logical, reusable services that can dynamically utilize (and share) the underlying hardware resources. These services should be platform-, language-, and operating system-independent;
- Autonomic patterns – system design patterns should lead to building self-management service architectures, being able to runtime adaptation to the changing environment conditions. It indicates the presence of the event services, capture and sharing of state information between sub-systems, integrity and autonomy of self-management systems. This idea will be revealed further in the next sections.

With regard to the first notion (the component model), in the previous section we introduced the Data Management System as an example of a distributed system based on loosely coupled components. The implementation on the second assumption - autonomic patterns - involves an extension in the present DMS architecture. This topic will be described more precisely in the next section.

4.1 AC principles implementation

Before we get down to the autonomic computing implementation, we discuss the initial principles that lay down at the basis of the autonomic patterns. We base this list on the well-known CHOP model (section 2.1):

Self-configuration – distributed components configure themselves without any human intervention in the form of configuration dialogs or external files. We can assume that each element possesses a high-level description of its behavior in a standardized form and the address of the central information repository. This repository stores all information about the services and resources belonging to the distributed environment. A new element retrieves the appropriate information that it needs to function, configures itself on this base and then registers itself in the repository.

The Web Services platform (WSDL, UDDI, WS-Addressing and more) [17] seems to be the most viable option to implement self-configuration patterns.

Self-healing – we assume that the distributed environment should be capable of dealing with the failure of any of its components. It is important, however, to distinguish between the local and the global approach. The former is related to the creation of a reliable and robust single entity, which involves using the appropriate architectural techniques or hardware protection. The latter, which remains our interest, assumes the presence of a monitoring element responsible for determining if the distributed components are performing properly, according to their desired behavior. If the monitoring element detects any inconsistent service, then it reacts, possibly terminating the failure element or updating appropriate records in the information repository.

Self-optimization – similarly to the previous case, we should also distinguish between local and global tuning aspects. It is obvious that each element must utilize the underlying resources efficiently but it does not assure that the whole environment will work properly. Therefore we assume that on the global level we will take advantage of the policy-based management [18]. It involves the presence of an autonomic manager which will perform the self-optimize actions according to the desired policy. The policy should be expressed in an abstract language, for example "On average, users will not wait more than 5 seconds for the response", and the autonomic element will translate it into the system commands (or workflow) and execute in the environment.

Self-protection – the self-protection aspects cover two distinct issues: undesirable system behavior due to bugs or other unexpected conditions and unauthorized access by attackers. Regarding the former issue, some of the self-healing or self-optimize patterns are suitable for protection from this type of event. For example, self-regenerative clusters may be useful when a single node is down because of internal failure. It is also recommended to take advantage of the intrusion detection system which is responsible for preventing from any unauthorized access. Similarly to the other computing systems, the autonomic environment requires strong security control. It can be realized by defining the security policies which are a part of the self-tuning policies described in the previous paragraph.

Event service. As a base for our autonomic architecture we will use the central log repository gathered events from the distributed components. The Toth Logging System, which is ready to use in various environments and accommodated to cooperate with different kinds of applications, perfectly fits our needs.

The main functionality, which is storing events coming from many wide-spread modules, fulfills only one basic assumption – a central message gathering. It does not treat the statistical analysis of this data. This feature is particularly important in reference to AC patterns when we must distinguish between many types of events which may occur in the distributed system. These can be, for example, situations in which:

- The user waits for data transfer longer than the expected value.
- The user failed to logon into the system.
- The amount of data transferred daily for one user exceeded a given value.

To handle these issues Toth provides a context analysis mechanism of collected messages. It is based on a set of attributes which are passed in the event body in a form of the key-value pairs. The sequence of operations, comprising the message processing and drilling for the attributes according to the specified criteria, is realized on the database level. These criteria may be a type of operation, name of the file, preferred file pr transfer protocol.

In this paragraph we have outlined the general concept of Toth architecture, and the next sections provide a detailed description of its main components with reference to the autonomic computing.

Predictive level. To achieve level 3 (predictive) of autonomic computation, Toth has been equipped with two specialized modules. First of all, it is the Knowledge Base built on the basis of recent activities of managed resources. This part of the application acts as a foundation of further actions and defines the global environment state. It is very important to note that this knowledge does not comprise only log messages from the registered modules, variables values or states and measurements. It has to be considered as a real knowledge, which is a base set of conclusions that are drawn from the collected data. To accomplish this assumption we have introduced the System Diagnostic Monitor – a separate Toth module characterized by the following features:

- It analyzes the gathered logs, monitors the system components and creates recommendations.
- It generates alerts on the basis of several thresholds. It assures proactive monitoring, which means reaction to problems before they may appear.
- It runs at regular intervals (autonomic control loop).

On the basis of the CHOP model (section 2.1), we can present a few examples of system rules which act as a rationale to create recommendations. These are:

- Self-optimization: if a file is accessed frequently, then it can be spread among different nodes.
- Self-configuring: if a request passed to distributed component finishes with a network error, then it may indicate its failure.
- Self-healing: if a file is locked more than reservation time, then it is probably stale[2].
- Self-protection: if the administrator tried to log in from the machine outside the secure zone, then it may indicate an attempt to break in.

The rules are encoded according to XML methodology and apply to the form of IF(condition) THEN (action). Additionally, we define a set of alerts in the system, which are triggered when a certain condition (threshold) takes place. It can be, for example, "low free space" which raises an alarm when the space usage at the Data Container is higher than 90 percent. By default, the alert notifications will be sent to the console, but Toth will also support the email or SMS notifications.

The predictive level ensures faster and better decision making providing appropriate recommendations for the professional staff members. But the realization of the autonomic computing vision involves to automate the processes of self-* procedures, which stands for the adaptive level.

Adaptive level. At level 4 (adaptive), the distributed environment can automatically take actions based on the available knowledge. The decisions are taken on the basis of the knowledge base and have to fulfill the assumed policy and defined base rules.

To provide a consistent view of this level of AC, we have to firstly define a term of a policy with reference to autonomic computing methodology. The anatomy of the

---

[2] File management within DMS is based on the reservation of physical storage on a specific amount of time

policy defines the system ability for high-level, broadly scope directives, which are translated into the specific actions to be taken by the elements. Policy-based management is an active research topic among the scientists. In the autonomic computing approach this refers to the policy-based self-management.

System rules introduced in the previous section actually constitute a basic form of policy (based on actions IF-THEN). In order to satisfy the requirements of AC level 4 we define a goal policy which describes the conditions to be attained without specifying how to achieve this (for example, the time of a file restoration after the failure must not exceed 60 seconds). This notion is much more flexible than system rules, because the human or autonomic element can perform specific actions in the monitored components without knowing of its inner behavior.

This set of rules and policies allows to define the demanded system characteristics and it is a base for performing self-* procedures. Actions that are taken during self-healing or self-tuning operations are performed by individual components. Thus it is necessary to equip these components in manageability interfaces which provide various ways to gather details and change the behavior of the managed resources.

The service-oriented architecture defines a number of standard interfaces, but in order to fulfill the autonomic computing requirements we need to provide the additional interfaces as well. Because our idea concerns the SOA model and grid technologies, we plan to base the final solution on the OGSA [10] architecture. In terms of the Web Services Description Language (WSDL), OGSA defines interfaces and associated conventions, mechanisms required for creating and composing sophisticated distributed systems, including lifetime management, change management, and notification.

We also define an additional Toth module which will take desired actions on distributed components. This module – the so-called Change Manager – will be responsible for two main actions:

- Planning – generating the appropriate change plan according to the assumed policy and recommendations (made by the system diagnostic monitor). The plan function can take on many forms, from a single command to a complex workflow.
- Executing – scheduling and performing the necessary changes to the monitored system. We must consider that part of the execution of the change plan involves updating the Toth knowledge base. It is necessary to indicate the actions that were taken as a result of the analysis and planning and how these actions affected the managed resources.

Autonomic level. Level 5 (autonomic) is closely defined with the business and industry demands. It is characterized by a closed loop with the business processes level, business policies and objectives governing the whole infrastructure operation. Users interact with the autonomic technology tools to monitor business processes, alter the objectives, or both.

At the highest level of autonomic computing we need to extend the meaning of the goal policy (see the previous section) and provide a way to automatic determination of the most valuable goal in any given situation. To achieve this intention we define the utility policy which makes use of an additional attribute – a value expressing the relative priority of a policy.

Now it is very complicated to create a system which would be 100 percent compliant with the highest AC level. We notice the fact that there is still a need for research in this area. Our team performed some effort in this direction and as a possible solution we see the combination of the SOA capabilities (service workflow, service bus, BPEL) and autonomic computing concepts. A detailed presentation of our visions, however, is beyond the scope of this article (it involves providing a solid background of the Service Oriented Architecture), so we shall outline only a brief description of this idea.

Let us suppose that we have an environment built according to the SOA principles. It means that the services and processes can be decomposed into workflows of activities and tasks that are used to realize them. According to one of the main SOA assumptions, these workflows are created, managed and monitored by professional staff which has specialized tools to perform these operations. Having such an environment, we can take advantage of the SOA concept and combine it with the AC model. It means, in short, that the recommendation performed by the system diagnostic monitor can be translated into the SOA-specific workflow in order to perform the desired activity in the system. This workflow may be automatically deployed on a specialized runtime engine and executed. Thanks to the existing tools designed to manage the SOA, professional staff have a possibility to analyze, check, redefine or monitor these autonomic activities.

5 Conclusions

In this paper we have described an approach to creating a distributed environment composed of loosely coupled components and capable of performing self-managing actions. This solution may constitute an example of a novel application (data grid system), which faces the problem of increasingly complex systems.

We have provided a step-by-step solution describing how to achieve the desired goal. We have started from the basic level of autonomic computing implementation and finished with the most advanced issues, referring to the business processes level and business policies. The DMSuite platform served us as a reference base for implementing autonomic patterns. As it was mentioned, the current release of this software supports the basic level of the AC model. But we are currently working on the extensions which were described in this article, and will implement a part of advanced autonomic computing technology. It will include the proactive reactions to some well-defined situations, detections of any "unusual" events, generating recommendations for administrators and many more.

There is still much to be done within the scope of the self-aware environments. This is not only because of the scale of distributed applications and systems, but also because QoS (Quality of Service) support needs to be specific to the requirements of individual end-users. In our opinion, in the near future much of research work will pursue the full vision of autonomic computing systems, and this will rely on aggregated grid resources and autonomic computing software platforms. This may be a crucial step to pass from the academic to the enterprise environment.

References

1. Rychlewski, J., Weglarz, J., Starzak, S., Stroinski, M., Nakonieczny, M.: PIONIER: Polish Optical Internet. Proceedings of ISThmus 2000 Research and Development for the Information Society conference. Poznan Poland (2000) 19-28
2. Bogdański M., Kosiedowski M., Mazurek C., Stroiński M.: Facilitating the process of enabling applications within grid portals. Grid and Cooperative Computing (GCC 2004) ed Jianhua Sun et all Proceedings of Third International Conference, Wuhan, Chiny, October 2004, Springer, Lecture Notes in Computer Science, 3251, pp.175-182
3. Kosiedowski, M., Malecki, M., Mazurek, C., Spychala, P., Wolski, M.: Integration of the Biological Databases into Grid-Portal Environments, Workshop on Database Issues in Bioological Databases DBiBD. Edinburgh UK (2005)
4. Grzybowski P., Mazurek C., Spychała P., Wolski M.: Data Management System for grid and portal services. Submitted to Grid Computing: Infrastructure and Applications special issue of The International Journal of High Performance Computing Applications (IJHPCA), Cardiff University, UK, http://progress.psnc.pl/English/DMS.pdf
5. Journal of Computational Methods For Science and Technology no. 12 vol. 1 – Grid Applications - New Challenges For Computational Methods
6. Chervenak, A., Foster, I., Kesselman, C., Salisbury, C. and Tuecke, S.: The Data Grid: Towards an Architecture for the Distributed Management and Analysis of Large Scientific Data Sets. J. Network and Computer Applications, 2000
7. Kephart J.O, Chess D.M., "The Vision of Autonomic Computing," Computer, vol. 36, no. 1, 2003, pp. 41–50
8. Steve R. White, James E. Hanson, Ian Whalley, David M. Chess, Jeffrey O. Kephart,: An Architectural Approach to Autonomic Computing", International Conference on Autonomic Computing (ICAC'04), May 17 - 18, 2004.
9. Foster, I., Kesselman C., Tuecke S.: The Anatomy of the Grid: Enabling Scalable Virtual Organizations. International Journal of High Performance Computing Applications, 2001. 15(3): p. 200-222
10. Foster I., Kesselman C, Nick J.M., Tuecke S: The Physiology of the Grid: An Open Grid Services Architecture for Distributed Systems Integration," a research paper, Globus Project; http://www.globus.org/alliance/publications/papers/ogsa.pdf
11. An architectural blueprint for autonomic computing, a white paper, IBM corporation, http://www-03.ibm.com/autonomic/pdfs/ACBP2_2004-10-04.pdf, June 2005, third edition
12. Automating problem determination: A first step toward self-healing computing systems", a white paper, IBM corporation, http://www-03.ibm.com/autonomic/pdfs/Problem_Determination_WP_Final_100703.pdf, October 2003
13. Erl, T.: Service-Oriented Architecture: A Field Guide to Integrating XML and Web Services, Prentice Hall, Upper Saddle River, NJ, USA (2004)
14. Ganak A. G., Corbi A. T.: The dawning of the autonomic computing era. IBM Systems Journal, 42(1):5–18, 2003
15. JMS, the Java Message Service, http://java.sun.com/products/jms/index.jsp
16. Data Management System Portal, http://dms.progress.psnc.pl
17. Weerawarana S., Curbera F., Leymann F., Storey T., Ferguson D. F.: Web Services Platform Architecture : SOAP, WSDL, WS-Policy, WS-Addressing, WS-BPEL, WS-Reliable Messaging, and More, Prentice Hall, Upper Saddle River, NJ, USA (2005)
18. Sloman M.: Policy Driven Management for Distributed Systems, Journal of Network and Systems Management, Vol.2 (1994)
19. SRS, the Sequence Retrieval System, http://www.biowisdom.com/solutions_srs.htm

An optimizing OCL Compiler for Metamodeling and Model Transformation Environments

Gergely Mezei, Tihamér Levendovszky, Hassan Charaf

Budapest University of Technology and Economics
Goldmann György tér 3., 1111 Budapest, Hungary

Abstract. Constraint specification and validation lie at the heart of modeling and model transformation. The Object Constraint Language (OCL) is a wide-spread formalism to express constraints in modeling environments. There are several interpreters and compilers that handle OCL constraints in modeling, but these tools do not support constraint optimization, therefore, the model validation can be slow. This paper presents algorithms to optimize OCL compilers to reduce the number of database queries during the validation process by eliminating the unnecessary traversing steps and caching the database queries. Proofs are also given to show that the optimized and the unoptimized code are functionally equivalent. The optimized compiler has been integrated into the Visual Modeling and Transformation System tool and applied to constraints appearing in both metamodels and graph rewriting-based model transformation rules.

1 Introduction

The information conveyed by a model created by a traditionally generic modeling language has a tendency to be imprecise [1]. For example, if a UML Class diagram [2] expresses a relation of type association between vehicles and the passengers traveling in the vehicle, the multiplicity between the two classes is 0..*, representing that several passengers can travel on a single vehicle. This multiplicity expresses that there is no upper limit to the number of passengers in general, because the limit depends on the type of the vehicle. Without additional techniques it is not possible to define that the maximum number of passengers equals the number of seats plus the number of standing rooms on the vehicle. Even if the generic modeling languages are extended with constraint handling, they cannot always describe the special attributes of the target domains. Thus, customizable models, modeling techniques, and model transformation algorithms are required by model-based software development. Domain Specific Modeling Languages (DSMLs) are a means to create customized models for domains where generic modeling languages would fail. Metamodeling is a proven solution for modeling DSMLs. The metamodel acts as a set of rules for the model level: it defines the available model elements, its attributes, and the possible connections between them. Metamodel definitions can usually define simple, topology-based rules, but they cannot express constraints for attribute values or other sophisticated requirements. Thus, sometimes the metamodeling rules are also incomplete. For example, if there is a resource editor domain for mobile phones, it is useful to define the valid range for slider controls. Specifying constraints in both generic and domain-specific models is

Please use the following format when citing this chapter:

Mezei, G., Levendovszky, T., Charaf, H., 2006, in IFIP International Federation for Information Processing, Volume 227, Software Engineering Techniques: Design for Quality, ed. K. Sacha, (Boston: Springer), pp. 61–71.

crucial to create precise and verifiable models. Constraint definitions are not only useful in modeling, but in model transformations as well. To define the transformation steps, beyond the topology of the visual models, additional constraints must be specified, which ensures, for example, value checking of the attributes. Dealing with constraints means a solution to several unsolved model transformation issue [3]. For example if the model transformation executes a search algorithm for non-abstract classes in a class diagram, then it is useful to express this condition. Constraint-based model transformation is very popular, it is used for example in QVT [4].

One of the most wide-spread approaches to constraint handling is the Object Constraint Language (OCL) [1]. OCL is a flexible, user-friendly yet formal language. Although it was created to extend the capabilities of UML [2], it can also be used in metamodeling environments to validate the models, or to define constraints in metamodel-based model transformations.

Visual Modeling and Transformation Systems (VMTS) [5] is an n-layer metamodeling and model transformation tool. VMTS uses OCL constraints in both model validation and in the graph rewriting-based model transformation [3]. VMTS contains an OCL 2.0 compliant constraint compiler to generate code for constraint validation. The constraints contained by both the rewriting rules and metamodel diagrams are attached to the metamodel, thus they can be handled with the same algorithms.

The primary aim of this paper is to give an overview on the optimizing algorithms used in the OCL compiler of VMTS. Previous work [6] has presented two efficient algorithms to reduce the navigation steps in the constraints by relocating the constraints and separating clauses based on Boolean operands. These algorithms are introduced in short, and they are extended with a third algorithm that can accelerate the database queries by an efficient caching technique. The paper also gives a concise description in which compilation step the optimization algorithms can be used and how the three algorithms can cooperate. Novel, detailed proofs are also discussed that the optimized and the unoptimized code are functionally equivalent.

The main advantage of the presented algorithms is that they do not rely on system-specific features, thus they can be easily implemented in any other modeling or model transformation framework. The algorithms do not require a specific implementation language, or database to store the models. The presented approach does not even need an environment based on a DBMS, it can be applied to all model repositories, such as MOF 1.4 repositories.

The paper is organized as follows: firstly, Section 2 elaborates some of the popular tools that support constraint checking. Section 3 introduces the previous work in short, while Section 4 presents the new results. Finally, Section 5 summarizes the presented work.

2 Related work

There are several modeling frameworks and extension tools for frameworks that support OCL constraints in a more or less efficient way. This section deals with the most typical compilers only.

Object Constraint Language Environment (OCLE) [7] is a UML CASE Tool. OCLE helps the users to realize both static and dynamic checking at the user model level. The tool also has a user-friendly graphical GUI. Although the tool supports model checking, it does not use compiling techniques.

The Dresden OCL Toolkit (DOT) [8][9] generates Java code from OCL expressions, and then instruments the system in five steps. (i) OCL expressions are parsed using a LALR(1) parser generated with SableCC [10]. The result of the step is an Abstract Syntax Tree (AST). (ii) A limited semantic analysis is performed on the AST to find errors. (iii) The AST is simplified in order to make the further processing simpler. (iv) The code generator traverses the simplified AST and builds Java expressions. (v) The generated code is inserted into the system that contains the constraint source code, thus, the contracts can be tested at runtime. DOT does not support metamodeling, or optimized constraint-checking.

Kent Modeling Framework [11] is a set of tools that supports model driven software development. One of these tools is KMFStudio a tool to generate modeling tools from metamodels. KMFStudio supports dynamic evaluation of OCL constraints. It enables the language to be bridged to other modeling frameworks. The tool was integrated into the Eclipse tool set. The Kent Modeling Framework does not use optimizing algorithms to improve the efficiency of the constraint validation.

Open Source Library for OCL (OSLO) [12] is a new tool and it is a further development of Kent OCL Library. OSLO is based on the Eclipse framework. OSLO supports OCL 2.0 functions for arbitrary metamodels based on EMF, and constraint checking for UML2 models (Eclipse UML2). OSLO supports therefore constraint checking for metamodeling system, but it cannot cooperate with model transformation systems. Since it is a recent project, only a few publications are available, and not all of the supported features are introduced in depth.

3 Backgrounds

3.1 VMTS OCL 2.0 Compiler

The OCL Compiler realized in VMTS consists of several parts (Fig. 1). This section gives a short description of the architecture of the compiler, more detailed information on the compiler can be found in [13] and [3].

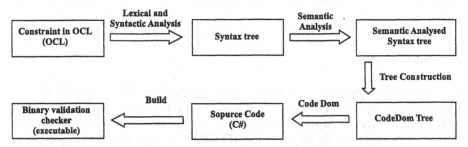

Fig. 1. VMTS OCL Compiler 2.0 Architecture

The user defines the constraints in OCL, then the constraint definitions are tokenized and syntactically analyzed. The lexical analysis reads the constraint definition as a text, and creates a sequence of token, such as the keywords of the language. Syntactic analysis builds a syntax tree using the grammar rules of OCL specified in EBNF format [1]. To accommodate the ambiguities in the specification, the grammar rules are simplified. The information missing because of the simplification is reconstructed in the later compilation steps, where the analysis has more information (e.g. about available types and defined variables). Since the syntax tree does not contain all the necessary information, it should be extended e.g. with type information, and implicit self references. This amendment is performed in the semantic analysis phase, and it produces a semantically analyzed syntax tree. The semantic analysis also reconstructs the mentioned simplification made in the grammar. In the next step, the constructed and semantically analyzed tree is transformed to a CodeDOM tree. CodeDOM [14] is a .NET-based technology that describes programs using abstract trees, and it can use this tree representation to generate code to any languages that is supported by the .NET CLR (like C#, or Visual Basic). The compiler transforms the CodeDOM tree to C# source code. To support the base types available in OCL, a class library has been developed. The constraint classes inherit from the base classes implemented in this class library. The output of the OCL compiler is a binary assembly (a .dll file) that implements the validation method.

Since the constraints are compiled only once, not each time when the constraints are evaluated, the validation process is fast and efficient. The compiled OCL validation assembly can be used either in model validation, or in graph transformation. There are no differences between the two cases in handling the constraints: the editing framework (VMTS Presentation Framework) collects the appropriate model items and invokes the validation method for them.

The evaluation of the OCL constraint consists of two parts: (i) Selecting the object and its properties that we need to check against the constraint, and (ii) executing the validation method. Although the execution of the validation method can use several optimization methods, in this paper the presented algorithms focus on the first step. There are two reasons for this: (i) Since the efficiency of the validation depends on the realization of the OCL types and expressions, optimizing the validation process is usually more implementation-specific. (ii) In general, the first step has more serious computational complexity, because the model items are matched in the underlying model. If the model is stored in a DBMS, then each navigation step means a database query.

3.2 Normalization

If the constraint does not contain any unnecessary navigation steps, then it is in *Canonical Constraint Form*, or simply it is *normalized*. The normalization, namely reducing the navigation steps can accelerate constraint evaluation. The aim of the first introduced optimization algorithm, called RELOCATECONSTRAINT is to provide a method to normalize the OCL constraints if it is possible. The algorithm is shown in Fig. 2. The algorithm processes the OCL constraints propagated to the transformation step. The main *foreach* loop examines the navigation paths of the actual constraint and relocates the constraint to the node with the smallest navigation cost.

```
RELOCATECONSTRAINT (Model M)
foreach InvariatConstraint C in M
  minNumberOfSteps = CALCULATESTEPS (CurrentNode in C)
  optimalNode = CurrentNode of the C
  foreach Node N in C
    numberOjSteps = CALCULATESTEPS(N)
    if(numberOJSteps < minNumberOfSteps) then
      minNumberOfSteps = numberOnSteps
      optimalNode = N
    endif
  end foreach
  if(optimalNode != CurrentNode of the C) then
    UPDATENAVIGATIONS of the C
    RELOCATE C to optimalNode
  endif
end foreach
```

Fig. 2. The Relocate Constraint algorithm

Using constraint relocation, the RELOCATECONSTRAINT algorithm eliminates all unnecessary navigation steps to produce non-decomposable (atomic) expressions. The proof of this statement, and the algorithm in more detail is discussed in [6].

3.3 Invariant decomposition

The goal of the constraint normalization is to achieve the pure canonical form, which does not contain navigation steps. Using the RELOCATECONSTRAINT algorithm, it is not possible in all cases, because constraints are often built from sub-terms and linked with operators ($self.age = 18$ *and* $self.name =' Jay'$), or require property values from different nodes ($self.age = self.teacher.age$).

Although subterms are not decomposable in general, they can be partitioned to clauses if they are linked with Boolean operators. A clause can contain two expressions (OCL expression, or other clauses) and one operation (AND/OR/XOR/ IMPLIES) between them. Separating the clauses, we can reduce the number of the navigation steps contained by the OCL expressions and the complexity of the constraint evaluation during the constraint validation process. It is simpler to evaluate the logical operations between the members of a clause than to traverse the navigation paths contained by the constraints.

The ANALYZECLAUSES algorithm (Fig. 3) is invoked for the outermost OCL expression of each invariant. The algorithm recursively searches the constraint for possible clause expressions and creates the clauses.

Applying the ANALYZECLAUSES algorithm, the number of the navigation steps in the constraints contained by the output model is minimal (supposing that only the logical relations can be decomposed) [6].

```
ANALYZECLAUSES (Expression Exp)
    if (Exp is LogicalRelationExpression) then
        Clause=CreateClause(Exp.RelationType);
        Clause.ADDEXPRESSION(ANALYZECLAUSES (Exp.Operand1)),
        Clause.ADDEXPRESSION(ANALYZECLAUSES (Exp.Operand2));
        return Clause;
    else
        if (Exp is ExpressionInParantheses) then
            return ANALYZECLAUSES (Exp.InnerExpression);
        else
            if(Exp is OnlyExpressionInConstraint) then
                Clause=CreateClause(SpecialClause);
                Clause.ADDEXPRESSION(RELOCATECONSTRAINT(Exp));
                return Clause;
            else
                return RELOCATECONSTRAINT(Exp);
            endif
        endif
    endif
```

Fig. 3. The Analyze Constraint algorithm

4   Contribution

4.1   Caching algorithm

Since the relocation and constraint decomposition algorithms can eliminate the *unnecessary* navigation steps only, the compiler cannot reach the pure canonical form in all cases. The clauses can also contain navigation steps, the validation still requires queries to obtain the model elements, and their attributes.

In compiler optimization, an occurrence of the expression E is called a *common subexpression* if the value of E has previously been computed, and it has not changed since then [15]. In these cases recomputing this expression can be avoided, because the value of the expression is already known.

Proposition 1. *In OCL constraints navigation steps and attribute references are always* common subexpression*s if they are used more than once* .

Proof. OCL specification defines the constraints as restrictions on one or more values, but these restrictions cannot have any side-effects. This means that the model cannot change during the validation, thus the computed values can be reused.

The presented idea is the basis of the third optimization algorithm. On one side, caching the model items can eliminate the redundant database queries in the constraint expressions. On the other side, the more attribute or navigation is cached, the more memory the cache requires. Thus, only those expressions are cached that are referenced more than once. Therefore the optimization algorithm (the REFERENCECACHING algorithm) has two main steps: (i) getting statistical information about the model references (GETCOMMONREFERENCES algorithm), and (ii) caching the evaluation expressions (CACHINGMANAGEMENT algorithm).

Collecting the statistical information set from the whole constraint expression is not straightforward, because sometimes only partial validation is required on a model. Thus, the caching algorithms are used at the context level, the statistical information of the different contexts are separated.

The GETCOMMONREFERENCES algorithm is shown in Fig. 4. The algorithm uses a breadth-first search to traverse the syntax tree recursively. It processes the attributes, the navigations, and the *control flow expressions*. The attributes and navigation expressions increment the statistic of their path reference (*IncReferencePath* method). To minimize the number of queries, the algorithm increments not only the reference of the full path, but also the references of the path steps. For example the expression $self.employee.wife.Name$ will increase the statistics with four entries: $self$, $self.employee$, $self.employee.wife$ and $self.employee.wife.Name$. The statistics contains even the $self$ element, because it is not cached always, if there is only one reference to it. This solution is useful if two expression have a common subset in the navigation steps, for example, in the expression $self.employee.wife.Name = 'Mrs.' + self.employee.Name$, the path self.employee is used twice.

```
GET COMMON REFERENCES (CurrentNode)
switch(CurrentNode.Type)
    case AttributeDefinition:
        if(CurrentMode.HasOneChild) then
            IncReferencePath(SelfExpression, null)
        else
            IncReferencePath(Attribute,
                GETCOMMONREFERENCES(CurrentNode.Children))
        endif
        return
    case NavigationStep:
        IncReferencePath(ModelItem,
            GETCOMMONREFERENCES(CurrentNode.Children))
        return
    case ControlFlowExpression:
        GetMinimumReferencesForEveryExecutionPath()
        UpdateCurrentGlobalReferences()
        return
endswitch
if(CurrentNode.HasChildren) then
    GETCOMMONRENCES(CurrentNode.Children)
endif
```

Fig. 4. The Get Common References algorithm

The *control flow expressions* are complex expressions that have several execution paths, thus, they can affect the number of the references, for example conditional expression, or loops. In this case the algorithm should obtain the minimum number of the references for each referenced objects for each execution paths. For example in case of the conditional expressions this means that both branches are processed, statistical information is collected for both branches, and then the results are compared. For each model reference path (attribute, or navigation reference), the minimum number is obtained and placed into the global statistical information set.

As the result of GETCOMMONREFERENCES algorithm, the compiler has reliable statistical information. CACHINGMANAGEMENT algorithm uses this information to handle caching. CACHINGMANAGEMENT algorithm differs from the previously presented algorithms, because it affects the generated source code directly instead of the syntax tree. Each time the compiler generates a navigation step or an attribute query, the statistics are checked, and a cache (a local variable) is created if required. This variable obtains the appropriate value from the database if it has not been read before, or returns the value from the cache if it is not the first reference. If the model reference is not cached, the code generator will create a conventional source code for it.

Proposition 2. *Using the REFERENCECACHING algorithm to evaluate the constraint the number of the applied queries is equal or less than that without optimization.*

Proof. The GETCOMMONREFERENCES references algorithm is applied in design-time, it does not raise the number of the queries during the evaluation. The CACHINGMANAGEMENT algorithm handles two types of model references: the cached, and the uncached references. The source code and thus, the number of database queries of uncached model references is the same as in the unoptimized code. The cached references execute the appropriate database query only if the required value is not in the cache, i.e. it has not been not read before. Therefore, neither the uncached nor cached references increase the number of the database queries.

Proposition 3. *Each attribute or navigation cached by the algorithm reduce the number of the database queries, namely no unnecessary caching is applied.*

Proof. The GETCOMMONREFERENCES algorithm is executed for each referenced context. If the context contains an expression that has several possible execution paths, then every path is examined, and for every model attribute and navigation the smallest number of references is stored. The sequential execution paths are examined step-by step, and the statistics is increased if required. As result the statistics contains the minimum number of the references in the context for every model item (attribute, or navigation). The CACHINGMANAGEMENT algorithm creates caching code only for the model references that have greater statistical index, than one. Since the statistics contains the minimum number of the references of the current item, thus, no unnecessary caching is performed.

4.2   An optimizing OCL compiler

In order to create the optimizing OCL compiler, the presented algorithms (i) have to be placed in the compiler control flow, (ii) a proper order of execution should be set, and (iii) proofs should show that the results of the optimized and unoptimized compiler are always the same.

The optimization algorithms require a semantically analyzed syntax tree, since, for example, the caching algorithms would not work without proper type-information.

Thus, the optimization algorithms are used after the semantic analysis. The constraint decomposition, relocation, and the statistical information retrieval algorithms are executed before the code generation phase, because they affect the syntax tree from which the code is generated. The CACHINGMANAGEMENT algorithm affects the code generation directly, it is used during the generation phase.

The next step is to set the order of execution of the optimization algorithms. Since the CACHINGMANAGEMENT algorithm is used in code generation compilation step it is executed as the last of the optimization algorithms. The constraint relocation algorithm is optimal only in case of non-decomposable constraints, hence the constraint decomposition should be processed firstly, and then the relocation, and obviously, the processing order cannot be changed [6]. The GETCOMMONREFERENCES algorithm uses the syntax tree only, thus, it can be used both for processing clauses and normal constraints. At the same time the caching algorithm handles the contexts separated from each other. Since the constraint decomposition can change the contexts, for example it can divide them into several clauses, the GETCOMMONREFERENCES algorithm should be used after the decomposition. The relocation algorithm can also affect the context definitions by relocating the expressions into other contexts, thus, the execution order of the optimization algorithms is the following: (1) ANALYZECLAUSES, (2) RELOCATECONSTRAINT, (3) GETCOMMONREFERENCES, (4) CACHINGMANAGEMENT.

The last step to create the optimizing compiler is to prove that the optimization does not change the result of the validation.

Proposition 4. *Applying the optimization algorithms for an optional input model does not modify the result of the constraint evaluation.*

Proof. Let *H* be an optional input model, and let H' be the result model of the optimization executed by the ANALYZECLAUSES, RELOCATECONSTRAINT and REFERENCECACHING (GETCOMMONREFERENCES and CACHINGMANAGE-MENT) algorithms. We prove that evaluating the constraints contained by *H'* produces always the evaluation in *H*.

Suppose that a constraint processed by the algorithm conflicts with the original constraint definition, because the cached references created and used by the REFER-ENCECACHING algorithm are not up-to-date. This contradicts Proposition 1.

In the RELOCATECONSTRAINT algorithm *UpdateNavigation*, and the *Relocate* function calls can modify the result, because other steps examine the existing constraints only. *UpdateNavigation* step replaces the existing context references with the new ones. The function *Relocate* does not modify the constraint but relocates it to a new model item. The functions together do not affect the result of the constraint according their definition.

The algorithm ANALYZECLAUSES can be divided into three main cases: (i) the examined expression is a complex (non-atomic) expression with Boolean operators; (ii) the examined expression is an expression between parentheses; (iii) or the expression is an atomic expression. The simplest case to examine is (ii), where the inner expression (the expression between the parentheses) is recursively processed. The evaluation order of the subexpressions is the same as that of the original expression, and since no further modification is made, therefore case (ii) does not affect the result of the constraints. Case (iii) has two subcases. If the examined expression is the only expression in the constraint, then a special clause is created, and the relocated constraint is placed into it. The special clause type is required only because of the uniformity. The inner expression (the normalized constraint) is processed when it is validated as if it were not contained in any clauses. The second subcase applies when the examined expression is a part of the constraint. In this case the relocated expression is returned. In both subcases the result of the constraint is not modified. Case (i) is used only if the constraint consists of two subparts linked with Boolean operators. A clause is created that preserves the Boolean operator, and the subexpressions are recursively processed. The subexpression is processed individually when validating the constraint, and their results are connected using the operator (the order of the subexpressions are the same as in the original constraint). Therefore the result of the validation is modified only if the subexpressions cannot be processed independently. The independency is not true only if the first subexpression has an effect on the second subexpression, this means that the first expression modifies one or more value used in the second expression. These modified values can be either model attributes, or variables defined in the current scope. The constraints used in validation cannot modify the model according to the specification of OCL [1]. Local variables can be defined for example in *Iterate*, and *Let* expressions, but using any variable definition expression would mean that the outermost expression cannot be an expression linked with Boolean expressions. This means that the subexpressions of the clauses are independent, thus the result of the validation cannot be modified.

To summarize, the algorithms - if they are executed separately - relocate the constraint without changing its meaning, thus, the only way in which H' and H can have different results is that the algorithms affect each other, and thus their composition changes the meaning of the constraint. The algorithm REFERENCECACHING is executed independently from the other algorithms, and the proven correct output of the ANALYZECLAUSES is the input of the RELOCATECONSTRAINT algorithm. Thus, the result created by the composition of the algorithms is always correct.

5   Conclusions

This paper has presented the main concepts of an optimizing OCL Compiler in an n-layer metamodeling and model transformation system. The primary aim of the optimization was to reduce the number of database queries by normalizing and caching the constraints. Constraint relocating, constraint decomposition and caching techniques have been proposed. The correctness and the efficiency of the algorithms have been proven.

Optimizing OCL constraints is a rather new idea; none of the existing tools supports constraint optimization. This means that these tools can only use external optimization algorithms offered by the underlying applications, such as the query optimization in the underlying database system, or the code optimization of the executing environment. Although these external optimization algorithms are optimal in general, they (i) require system-specific (tool-specific) solutions and (ii) cannot use particular OCL-specific algorithms. For example, the executing environment that executes the validation code cannot recognize automatically that attributes are always common subexpressions. In contrast, the presented optimizing OCL compiler can use OCL-specific, but implementation- independent optimization algorithms. These algorithms can be based on the characteristics of the OCL, which means a higher level of optimization. Furthermore optimizing compilers can also take the advantages of the underlying tools. We have accomplished several simplified performance tests, and we have found that the optimization can speed up the validation by 10-15% according to the circumstances. Since only basic tests were applied, further testing is required to give a detailed overview about the efficiency of the algorithms against the optimization supported by the external tools.

Although three efficient optimization algorithms have been presented, processing the OCL constraints is not optimal. The decomposition and the normalization of the atomic expressions have reduced the navigation steps to the minimum, and the caching algorithm has reduced the number of queries, but further research is required to extend the scope of the optimization algorithms and accelerate the process. The validation process can be optimized by rewriting the constraint and avoiding time consuming expressions, such as *AllInstances*.

6 Acknowledgements

The found of "Mobile Innovation Centre" has supported, in part, the activities described in this paper.

References

1. Jos Warmer, Anneke Kleppe, Object Constraint Language, The: Getting Your Models Ready for MDA, Second Edition, Addison Wesley, 2003
2. UML 2.0 Specification homepage, http://www.omg.org/uml/
3. László Lengyel, Tihamér Levendovszky, Hassan Charaf, Compiling and Validating OCL Constraints in Metamodeling Environments and Visual Model Compilers, IASTED 2004, Innsbruck
4. MOF QVT Specification, http://www.omg.org/docs/ptc/05-11-01.pdf
5. VMTS Web Site, http://avalon.aut.bme.hu/~tihamer/research/vmts
6. G. Mezei, L. Lengyel, T. Levendovszky, H. Charaf, Minimizing the Traversing Steps in the Code Generated by OCL 2.0 Compilers, Issue 4, Volume 3, February 2006, ISSN 1109-0832, pp. 818-824.
7. Object Constraint Language Environment, http://lci.cs.ubbcluj.ro/ocle/
8. Ali Hamie, John Howse, Stuart Kent, Interpreting the Object Constraint Language, Proceedings 5th Asia Pacific Software Engineering Conference (APSEC '98), December 2-4, 1998, Taipei, Taiwan, 1998
9. Dresden OCL Toolkit, http://dresden-ocl.sourceforge.net/index.html
10. SableCC, http://sablecc.org/
11. David Akehurst, Peter Linington, and Octavian Patrascoiu, OCL 2.0: Implementing the Standard, Technical report, Computer Laboratory, University of Kent, November 2003.
12. Open Source Library for OCL,http://oslo-project.berlios.de/
13. Gergely Mezei, Tihamér Levendovszky, Hassan Charaf, Implementing an OCL 2.0 Compiler for Metamodeling Environments, 4th Slovakian-Hungarian Joint Symposium on Applied Machine Intelligence
14. Thuan, T.,Hoang, L.: .NET Framework Essential", O'Reilly,2003.
15. Alfred V. Aho, Ravi Sethi, Jeffrey D. Ullman, Compilers Principles, Techniques, and Tools, Addison - Wesley, 1988

Crossing the Borderline –
From Formal to Semi-Formal Specifications

Andreas Bollin

Institute for Informatics-Systems
University of Klagenfurt, Austria
Andreas.Bollin@uni-klu.ac.at

Abstract. Being part of the systems' documentation state-based formal specifications can play a crucial role in the software development process. However, besides dense mathematical expressions, their semantical compactness and lack in visually appealing notations impede their use and comprehensibility among different stakeholders. One solution to this problem is to enrich the specification by a semi-formal view, in most cases diagrams with a sufficiently understood semantic meaning. However, as control- and data-dependencies within declarative specifications are hard to detect, existing approaches only cover statics-bearing diagrams. As a way out this paper presents an approach for control- and data dependency analysis within declarative formal specifications. Based on these dependencies, UML diagrams showing static and dynamic properties of the specification are generated.

1 Introduction

Formal software specifications are usually recommended as means to produce high-quality software. They can solve the verification problem ("do the system right"). But, even if the system has been refined correctly, there is another problem to be solved: the validation problem ("do the right system").

What sounds like a requirements elicitation problem also has to do with the problem of choosing a suitable notation. The risky part is that the stakeholders of the project (developers, customers, authorities) have to agree upon the meaning of the formal specification. Here, unclear requirements and specifications lead to futile validations easily. And this, in consequence, leads to a "buggy" system. So, the problem is not the formal notation, as its semantics is well-defined. The problem is the likely misinterpretation of concepts – due to the different habits of the stakeholders.

So why not just combining formal specifications and wide-spread semi-formal approaches? Such a combination would have several advantages. Different views (either of graphical or textual/mathematical nature) convey the concepts much better between different stakeholders. The approaches are not meant to replace each other, but they extend the possibilities of concept description: properties of semi-formal descriptions get deducible (by stepping into the formal world) and formal specifications can be described at an even more abstract level.

Several research teams are working on the issue of mapping graphical approaches (e.g. UML) to formal specification languages. The generated specification is then

Please use the following format when citing this chapter:

Bollin, A., 2006, in IFIP International Federation for Information Processing, Volume 227, Software Engineering Techniques: Design for Quality, ed. K. Sacha, (Boston: Springer), pp. 73–84.

used for consistency checking and test-data generation [1, 2]. Moving the other way round still has its limitations [3]. The reasons are the superficial analysis of state-based specification and missing flow of control. As a result only static class diagrams (that represent state variables of the specification) are generated so far.

With the reconstruction of control- and data- dependencies (via specification transformations [4]) much more gets possible: slices and chunks allow to excerpt pieces of the specification text with well-defined semantics, and cluster generation allows for carving out higher level specification concepts [5]. Finally, and as demonstrated in this contribution, by making use of control dependencies it gets feasible to visualize dynamic behavior of specifications the first time.

The contribution is structured as follows. Section 2 explains the need for bridging the gaps in more detail and presents the state-of-the-art of transforming UML diagrams to formal specifications and vice-versa. It gives special attention to some limitations of existing approaches: the scaling problem, and missing dynamics. Section 3 discusses ways to identify relevant elements within Z specifications [6] which will then be the basis for control- and data-dependency reconstruction. Section 4 then presents rules for the transformation (based on these dependencies). It explains the approach by making use of a small Z specification. The paper concludes with a short summary and an outlook.

2   Bridging the Gap

It would be the dream of every maintenance personnel, but neither does a SW-system, in general, adapt itself to changing situations or domains (retaining or even improving its quality), nor is it just straight-forward to produce new software products of high quality. As Glass [7, p.122] points out, comprehending the requirements and valid (and consistent) documentation is essential, but rarely all documents are available or are of suitable quality. This is one of the main problems during software comprehension[1]. A situation that should be improved whenever possible.

2.1   Comprehension Challenges

There are several models describing how to maintain software systems [8, 9], but all of them stress that it is necessary to first comprehend the requirements *and* the relevant parts of the underlying system. Starting from scratch and stepping through the code is very time-consuming. Banker et. al. point out the fact that the time needed to comprehend a system on the basis of software code alone is about 3.5 times longer than comprehending the system by additionally studying its documentation [10]. Thus making use of design documents and specifications helps in saving time. But where are the problems?

Well, formal specifications are closer to the requirements – but comprehension needs special skills, and so stakeholders seem to shy away from them. The problems are manifold and are the result of the following gaps between the two worlds:

P1 Formal specifications are said to be of high perceived complexity.

---

[1] According to Glass it is second only. The main cause for software comprehension problem is staff turnover.

P2 Not all stakeholders that are forced to comprehend the systems (and then to decide) are able to read and understand the underlying documents.

P3 Relating formal specifications with well defined semantics to less formal notations is a loss in precision.

P4 Creating formal specifications from less formal documents is impeded due to information deficiencies. It needs effort to fill the gaps.

What is easily overseen is that comprehending a system means the reconstruction of the missing documentation anyway. Concerning problem P1, the overall (and inherent) complexity cannot be reduced. But there are approaches to deal with the density of specifications [11]. And the remaining challenges P2 to P4 (understandability and formality) can be dealt with by consciously mapping the relevant representations to each other. The gaps can be bridged.

2.2 Impediments

The statements so far lead to one observation: the better and more extensive the documentation the easier the comprehension process. A less formal or less mathematical document can also serve its purpose. And a further improvement to the situation is to combine the formal and semi-formal documentation, to reconstruct parts of the documentation, and to be able to switch between different types of notation as needed.

As explained below, complexity (problem P1) does not make difficulties. In fact it is in the nature of formal specifications, and it concerns two aspects:

1. Usually there are too few clues for reconstructing the original structure. Putting too much structure into a formal specification is understood to be a hint towards implementation, something that is avoided at the time of writing the specification.
2. The declarative nature also impedes the reconstruction of the behavior. There is no execution-sequence, which is known from programming languages.

Above all, the latter aspect is crucial. As there is no execution order and, in general, there are no control statements, control- and data-dependency are not predominant concepts. Well-known techniques from the field of program comprehension cannot be applied directly. A state-based specification focuses on, naturally, states, and alternative forms of representation are then restricted to just static information, too.

2.3 Related Work

For the reasons mentioned in Section 2.2 the mapping between formal specifications and less formal approaches is limited to static information. Besides formal extensions to existing notations (e.g. VDM-link to UML [12], or Petri-nets with Z extensions [13]), two directions of the mapping are possible.

Firstly, there is a mapping between some graphical notations to formal specifications. As UML is wide-spread, most of them take static UML diagrams and generate formal state descriptions of it (e.g. UML to Z [14, 15], or UML to Z++ [16, 17]). The approaches have in common that formal specification skeletons are generated which then have to be completed by the designer. As a second step the resulting predicates are simplified, leading, finally, to a full and compact formal specification. This means that semantics has to be added by the designer, but when dealt with it carefully, the specification can be taken to prove properties of the system. Results can then be mapped back to the design documents and deficiencies eliminated.

The other way round is the mapping of formal specification to some graphical notation. An early approach is the Z visualization of Kim [18], who makes use of constraint diagrams (a notation formally defined by Kent [19]). The notation is able to express predicate logic, but there is no integration into existing frameworks. And it is not UML, which does not really ease the understanding among some stakeholders.

However, not all the time the full content has to be imparted, and UML, keeping on spreading, is a good target for the transformation. The approach of Fekih et.al maps B specifications to UML [20]. It takes the state space of the specification and creates an UML class for every abstract set that is element in the domain of relations. The transformation rules are simple but lead to incomplete class diagrams as operations are not regarded. In addition to that the generated classes are not associated. Idani and Ledru improve the approach by mapping occurring relations to UML associations [3]. Furthermore they take operations into account and provide an algorithm for mapping an operation as a method to the most suitable class. Altogether this leads to a more complete static UML diagram.

Contributions mapping formal specifications to UML diagrams follow a pragmatic approach: sets do correspond to classes and relations do correspond to associations. However, as also noted in [3], the resulting diagrams provide less information than the formal specification, and dynamics is not touched at all.

3   Theoretical Background

The reconstruction of dependencies within declarative specification languages is not straight-forward. When looking for control constructs (which will then be the basis for the reconstruction of dynamic behavior), one has to be careful about the basic elements the control is defined about.

3.1   Specification Primes

Specifications are constructed from basic (atomic) units, called specification literals. They can be identified by looking at the grammar of the specification language. As an example, the Z predicate *"assigned ⊆ Permitted"* contains the specification literals *"Assigned"*, *"⊆"*, and *"Permitted"*. Specification literals are not very expressive when standing alone. It is the combination of literals that makes them rich in content. By aggregating specification literals, *prime objects* of a specification are built.

Definition 1 *A specification prime object represents the basic entity of a specification. It is built out of specification literals and forms logic, syntactic, or semantic units.*

Schema	Approximation via Conditions	Related Primes
S	$post\ S \Rrightarrow_c\ pre\ S$	$po_S \Rrightarrow_c pr_S$
$\neg\ S$	$post_s(\neg\ S) \Rrightarrow_c\ pre_w(\neg\ S)$	$po_S \Rrightarrow_c pr_S$
$S \vee T$	$post(S \vee T) \Rrightarrow_c\ pre(S \vee T)$	$(po_S \cup po_T) \Rrightarrow_c (pr_S \cup pr_T)$
$S \Rightarrow T$	$post_s(S \Rightarrow T) \Rrightarrow_c\ pre_w(S \Rightarrow T)$	$(po_S \cup po_T) \Rrightarrow_c (pr_S \cup pr_T)$
$S \wedge T$	$post(S \wedge T) \Rrightarrow_c\ pre_w(S \wedge T)$	$(po_S \cup po_T) \Rrightarrow_c (pr_S \cup pr_T)$
$S \Leftrightarrow T$	$post_s(S \Leftrightarrow T) \Rrightarrow_c\ pre_w(S \Leftrightarrow T)$	$(po_S \cup po_T) \Rrightarrow_c (pr_S \cup pr_T)$
$S \upharpoonright T$	$post(S \upharpoonright T) \Rrightarrow_c\ pre_w(S \upharpoonright T)$	$(po_S \cup po_T) \Rrightarrow_c (pr_S \cup pr_T)$
$S \mathbin{\raise.3ex\hbox{$\fatsemi$}} T$	$post_s(S \mathbin{\raise.3ex\hbox{$\fatsemi$}} T) \Rrightarrow_c\ pre(S \mathbin{\raise.3ex\hbox{$\fatsemi$}} T)$	$(po_S \cup po_T) \Rrightarrow_c pr_S$
$S \gg T$	$post_s(S \gg T) \Rrightarrow_c\ pre(S \gg T)$	$(po_S \cup po_T) \Rrightarrow_c pr_S$

Tab. 1. The table summarizes the control dependencies occurring between pre- and postcondition primes in Z schema operations.

In specification languages prime objects can be expressions or predicates, but they can also be generic type or schema type definitions. When looking at the decoration of identifiers ($'$ or $!$ for after-states), post condition primes can easily be identified.

Definition 2 *A Z-specification prime p is considered a post-condition prime, if prime p contains an after state identifier. Otherwise it is considered a pre-condition prime.*

The following two predicates of the *AssignResource* operation schema in the *AccessControl* Z Specification (see App. A) can be assigned to one pre- and one post-condition prime,

$user? \notin \mathrm{dom}\ Assigned$ %Precondition Prime

$Assigned' = Assigned \cup \{user? \mapsto resource?\}$ %Postcondition Prime

as the second prime contains an after-state identifier ($Assigned'$). The identification of control-dependencies is then based on these definitions.

3.2 Dependencies

The approach is based on the following simple idea: Preconditions determine whether predicates in the postcondition part are evaluated or not. Thus in specifications post-conditions are control dependent on pre-conditions, and the problem of the identification of control dependencies is reduced to the problem of the identification of pre- and post-conditions.

Not all specification languages do make pre- and post-conditions explicit. Additionally, when schema operations are used, pre- and post-conditions have to be calculated by performing a semantic analysis, a time- and resource-consuming task which cannot be fully automated. In [11] a syntactic approximation to the semantic analysis (see Tab. 1) is suggested and it is formally shown that this approximation yields suitable results.

Definition 3 *Let S be a schema of a Z specification. Furthermore, let pr_S be the set of pre-condition primes of S and po_S the set of post-condition primes of S. There is control dependency ($po_S \Rrightarrow_c pr_S$) within schema S, if pr_S and po_S are not empty.*

Type	Symbol	A	B	Type	Symbol	A	B
Relation	$A \leftrightarrow B$	*	*	Part. Surj.	$A \twoheadrightarrow B$	1..*	0..1
Partial	$A \nrightarrow B$	*	0..1	Total Surj.	$A \twoheadrightarrow B$	1..*	1
Total	$A \rightarrow B$	*	1	Total Bij.	$A \rightarrowtail B$	1	1
Part. Inj.	$A \rightarrowtail B$	0..1	0..1	Total Inj.	$A \rightarrowtail B$	0..1	1

Fig. 1. According to [3], relations between sets A and B are mapped to associations with given multiplicities.

Table 1 summarizes the dependencies among the predicates in the schemata. When there is flow of control, data-dependencies are easily detected:

Definition 4 *A specification prime p is data dependent on a specification prime q (p $\rightrightarrows_d$ q) if (i) there exists at least one identifier v (literal denoting a data element) that occurs in both p and q, and (ii) v is defined in q and used in p, and (iii) either p and q are in the same scope, or p is control dependent on q.*

4   Semi-Formal Transformation

With the reconstruction of dependencies within declarative specifications it gets possible to exploit both, static *and* dynamic diagrams of UML. In the following the Access Control system (see App. A) is taken to illustrate the transformation process.

4.1   Static Diagrams

The mapping to static class diagrams is based on the idea of looking for global type definitions. It follows mainly the approach of Idani et. al. [3], but omits assigning the operations to derived (and hard to find pertinent) classes. Instead it introduces a system class and assigns the operations to it.

Rule 1 *Every state schema corresponds to a root class with the stereotype <<system>> and the name of the schema.*

Rule 2 *In a Z specification "given sets" correspond to classes in the UML specification. They are connected to the system class by using a "use" association.*

Typically this exactly is the view of a specification's designer: having a state and relevant operations. Abstract types are mapped to classes, and these classes are associated to the system class.

A specification also consists of several identifiers holding the state. When they describe relations between given sets, then they are resolved as associations. Subset relations ($\subset$ or $\subseteq$) are made explicitly. Finally, operation names are added, and for the description of the diagram unique names for the associations are introduced:

Rule 3 *Every variable representing relationships between entities in the state schema is translated to associations. It holds that (i) multiplicity is resolved by the mapping rules presented in Fig. 1, and (ii) subsets between relations are resolved by a subset constraint.*

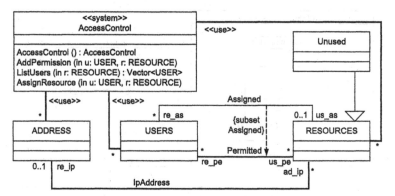

Fig. 2. Applying Rules 1 to 6 leads to a static UML Diagram for the Access Control system specification (see Appendix A).

Rule 4 *Every variable representing a subset of entities in the state schema is translated to a specialization class and connected to its root class.*

Rule 5 *Associations do get role-names. They are built by combining the first characters of the source class and association name.*

Rule 6 *Every operation schema is added as a method to those system root class, which has been included in the operations' declaration part. The initialization schema is mapped as a constructor to this class.*

Fig. 2 presents the result of the transformation. The system class contains the operations. As there are three given set definitions (Users, Resources, Addresses), three classes are introduced and connected to the system class. *Unused* is modelled as a subset of *Resources*, and *Assigned* and *Permitted* are enriched by a subset constraint.

In fact, the above algorithm leads to class/attribute candidates. Still some problems with the transformation remain. It works well when there is only a small set of given sets. With larger specifications the approach of taking given sets as classes leads to a huge static UML diagram. Carving out higher-level concepts [5] and grouping them into extra diagrams might be a way out.

4.2   Dynamics

UML also allows for dynamic diagrams, and as there is also some sort of dynamics within specifications it should be represented in a convenient way. The approach makes use of UML's activity diagrams and focusses on the above defined notion of control and data dependencies.

Rule 7 *Every schema operation is represented by an activity diagram. Logical operations are resolved as boolean expressions. Sequential operations are transformed to sequential control arcs.*

(a)

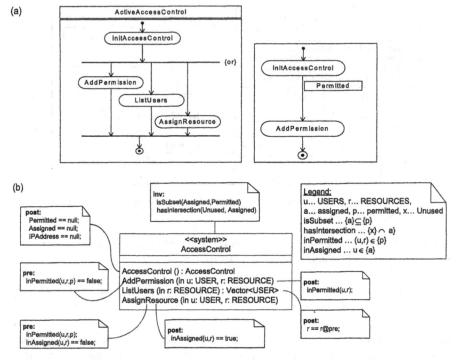

(b)

Fig. 3. (a) Applying rules 7 and 8 leads to two UML Activity Diagrams, (b) applying rule 9 leads to an annotated static UML Diagram that makes use of OCL-like annotations.

Rule 8 *Control dependencies between two operations are mapped to activity diagrams with control flow vertices. Data dependencies are mapped to activity diagrams by using object flow nodes with the label of the relevant identifier(s).*

The specification has one schema operation called *ActiveAccessControl*. It contains a sequential schema operation and the logical combination of the remaining operation schemata. Fig. 3(a), left side, presents the result of rule 7. It puts the initialization in sequence to the operations, which are logically combined by an OR-operation.

According to the definition of control dependency and the rules in Tab. 1 there is, e.g., control dependency between the two schemata *AccessControl* and *AddPermission* (as *AddPermission* includes the state schema and has post-condition primes which get dependent on the *AddPermission*'s pre-condition primes). Another diagram is added and thus makes the control dependency explicit. Due to the fact that there is also data-dependency (the value of *Permitted* is relevant), *Permitted* is added as an object flow node. Finally, the more formal part of the specification must not be forgotten. By using OCL constraints, the relevant pre- and post-condition predicates can be included.

Rule 9 *Pre- and Post-conditions of operation schemata are mapped to pre and post OCL comments to the system class; the predicates of the state schema are mapped to the class as OCL invariants. For Z operations expressive function names are to be chosen, their semantics is to be explained in a legend box.*

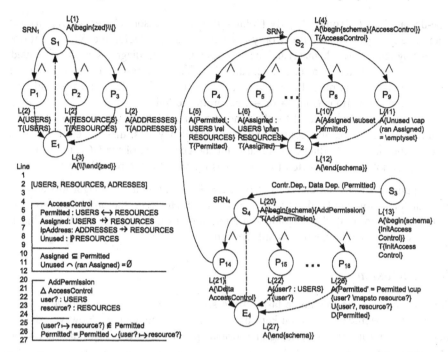

Fig. 4. Parts of the ASRN net representation and source of the AccessControl specification. Primes are mapped to vertices and annotations are used for the transformation process.

Fig. 3(b) demonstrates the result of the transformation to a set of OCL comments. The constructor (initialization schema) gets a postcondition constraint, the three operation schemata get a pre- and post-condition each. The post-condition of *ListUsers*, e.g., tells us that the application does not change the set of resources ($r == r \bullet pre$, the after-state is the same as the before state). The system class is associated with the class invariant. Typically as is, predicate logic, Z functions, and operations are difficult to express in OCL. Here it is suggested to choose mnemonic names instead.

4.3 Automatic Generation

Specification primes are the basic, semantics-bearing elements of a specification. In [4, 11] it is described that state-based specifications can be mapped to a graph representation called ASRN (*Augmented Specification Relationship Net*), and that this graph can be used to detect dependencies by just breaking down the task to reachability conditions. This net is now used to simplify the transformation to UML. A small part of the AccessControl ASRN net can be found in Fig. 4.

The basic idea behind the net is that higher level primes are made up of a set of start and end vertices – which contain prime elements. Every vertex gets annotated (line numbers, text, and definition and use information of literals), and references and dependencies to other primes are expressed by (classified) edges between these primes.

The mapping process to UML is then straight-forward. Rules 1, 2, and 6 are based on the identification of state and operation schemata. Relevant start vertices have to contain type-declarations (T{some_id}). By looking at their successor vertices, operations and state schemata get separated (as only operations contain Delta and Xi annotations referencing other state schemata) and the corresponding UML diagrams can be generated. When all state schemata are identified, rules 3, 4, and 5 are resolved. Associations are resolved by looking at related prime vertices that contain type-declarations and relevant specification annotations (like ↔ or ↠, according to Tab. 1).

The same approach is used for the generation of activity diagrams (rules 7 and 8). As the ASRN also contains control and data-dependency arcs, they are easily mapped to transitions in activity diagrams. Finally, for the generation of the OCL text (rule 9), again the annotations connected to the primes (A(source)) are parsed and printed.

Mapping the rules (on the basis of the ASRN) to a program is straight forward and the transformation can be done in reasonable time. However, the problem is still the neat visualization of all the diagrams - and for an optimal positioning of all the objects on the screen some user action is still needed.

5   Conclusion

Comprehension is an inevitable task during software maintenance and development phases, and specifications, when kept up-to-date, are valid sources. However, due to their complexity it is not surprising that formal specifications languages are said to be write-only languages.

This paper discusses ways in transforming formal Z specifications to UML in order to open the documents to a wider range of stakeholders. Existing approaches only cover static information, but state-based specifications also deal with state changes – and thus dynamics. In contrary to existing approaches (which the pure focus on class diagrams) this paper suggests to make also use of activity diagrams. It explains how to identify control dependencies, which are then the basis for the latter reconstruction of dynamic behavior within declarative specifications.

There are still some limitations that should not be concealed. As with other approaches the issue of scalability is not solved, and in addition to that it is still hard to decide whether a class candidate is a pertinent class or not. To test the applicability of the approach a framework for dealing with large Z specifications (combining slicing, chunking, and UML transformation) is under further development.

The approach does, by far, not lead to a perfect UML representation of the specification. But it provides a good picture of *what* is *in* the specification. In fact it can at least be used to speed up the re-construction of concepts behind. And as dynamics is at least as important as statics, this approach should be a step further into the direction of a more useable framework and increase the use of formal specification.

References

1. Laleau, R., Mammar, A.: An overview of a method and its support tool for generating B specifications from uml notations. In: Fiftheenth IEEE Conference on Automated Software Engineering. (2000)

2. Truong, N.T., Souquieres, J.: An approach for the verification of UML models using B. In: Proceedings of the 11th IEEE Conference and Workshop on the Engineering of Computer-Based Systems (ECBS'04). (2004)

3. Idani, A., Ledru, Y.: Object oriented concepts identification from formal B specifications. In: Formal Methods in Industrial Critical Applications, FMICS'04. (2004)

4. Mittermeir, R.T., Bollin, A.: Demand-driven specification partitioning. In: Proceedings of the 5th Joint Modular Languages Conference, JMLC'03. (2003)

5. Bollin, A.: Maintaining formal specifications. In: Proceedings of the 21st IEEE International Conference on Software Maintenance (ICSM 2005), Budapest, Hungary. (2005) 442–453

6. Spivey, J.: The Z Notation. C.A.R. Hoare Series. Prentice Hall (1989)

7. Glass, R.L.: Facts and Fallacies of Software Engineering. Addison-Wesley (2003)

8. Basili, R.V.: Viewing maintenance as reuse-oriented software development. IEEE Software 7(1) (1990) 19–25

9. Pirker, H.: Specification based Software Maintenance (a Motivation for Service Channels). PhD thesis, University of Klagenfurt (2001)

10. Banker, R.D., Davis, G.B., Slaughter, S.A.: Software development practices, software complexity, and software maintenance performance: A field study. In: Management Science. Volume 44., Inst. for Operations Research and the Management Sciences (1998) 433–450

11. Bollin, A.: Specification Comprehension – Reducing the Complexity of Specifications. PhD thesis, University of Klagenfurt (2004)

12. Dick, J., Loubersac, J.: A visual approach to VDM: Entity-structure diagrams. Technical Report DE/DRPA/91001, Bull, 68, Route de Versailles, 78430 Louveciennes (France) (1991)

13. He, X.: PZ Nets - a formal method integrating Petri Nets with Z. Information and Software Technology 43(1) (2001) 1–18

14. Dupuy, S., Ledru, Y., Chabre-Peccoud, M.: An overview of RoZ: A tool for integrating UML and Z specifications. In: Proceedings of CAiSE'00. (2000) 417–430

15. Idani, A., Ledru, Y., Bert, D.: Derivation of UML class diagrams as static views of formal B developments. In: 7th International Conference on Formal Engineering Methods, ICFEM 2005. (2005) 37–51

16. Kim, S.K., Carrington, D.: A formal mapping between UML models and Object-Z specifications. Lecture Notes in Computer Science **1878** (2000) 2–21

17. Roe, D., Broda, K., Russo, A.: Mapping UML models incorporating OCL constraints into Object-Z. Technical Report ISBN/ISSN: 1469-4174, Imperial College of Science, Technology and Medicine, Department of Computing (2003)

18. Kim, S.K., Carrington, D.: Visualization of formal specifications. In: In Proceedings Sixth Asia Pacific Software Engineering Conference (ASPEC'99), IEEE Computer. Society Press, Los Alamitos, CA, USA (1999) 102–109

19. Kent, S.: Constraint diagrams: Visualising invariants in object-oriented models. In: In Proceedings of OOPSLA'97, ACM Press (1997)

20. Fekih, H., Jemni, L., Merz, S.: Transformation des spècifications B en des diagrammes UML. In: Approches Formelles dans l'Assistance au Développement de Logiciels, AFADL'04. (2004) 131–148

Appendix A - Access Control Specification

$[USERS, RESOURCES, ADDRESSES]$

```
┌─ AccessControl ──────────────────────────────────────────────┐
│ Permitted : USERS ↔ RESOURCES                                 │
│ Assigned : USERS ⇸ RESOURCES                                  │
│ IpAddress : ADDRESSES ⇸ RESOURCES                             │
│ Unused : ℙ RESOURCES                                          │
├───────────────────────────────────────────────────────────── │
│ Assigned ⊆ Permitted                                          │
│ Unused ∩ (ran Assigned) = ∅                                   │
└───────────────────────────────────────────────────────────────┘
```

```
┌─ InitAccessControl ──────────────────────────────────────────┐
│ AccessControl                                                 │
├───────────────────────────────────────────────────────────── │
│ Permitted = ∅                                                 │
│ Assigned = ∅                                                  │
│ IpAddress = ∅                                                 │
└───────────────────────────────────────────────────────────────┘
```

```
┌─ AddPermission ──────────────────────────────────────────────┐
│ ΔAccessControl                                                │
│ user? : USERS                                                 │
│ resource? : RESOURCES                                         │
├───────────────────────────────────────────────────────────── │
│ (user? ↦ resource?) ∉ Permitted                              │
│ Permitted' = Permitted ∪ {user? ↦ resource?}                 │
└───────────────────────────────────────────────────────────────┘
```

```
┌─ ListUsers ──────────────────────────────────────────────────┐
│ ΞAccessControl                                                │
│ resource? : RESOURCE                                          │
│ st! : ℙ USERS                                                 │
├───────────────────────────────────────────────────────────── │
│ st! = dom(Permitted ▷ {resource?})                           │
└───────────────────────────────────────────────────────────────┘
```

```
┌─ AssignResource ─────────────────────────────────────────────┐
│ ΔAccessControl                                                │
│ user? : USERS                                                 │
│ resource? : RESOURCES                                         │
├───────────────────────────────────────────────────────────── │
│ (user? ↦ resource?) ∈ Permitted                              │
│ user? ∉ dom Assigned                                          │
│ Assigned' = Assigned ∪ {user? ↦ resource?}                   │
└───────────────────────────────────────────────────────────────┘
```

$ActiveAccessControl == InitAccessControl \, \mathbin{\raise.2ex\hbox{$\circ$}\kern-.1em\lower.4ex\hbox{$\circ$}} $
$$(AddPermission \lor ListUsers \lor AssignResource)$$

Modeling of Component-Based Self-Adapting Context-Aware Applications for Mobile Devices

Kurt Geihs[1], Mohammad U. Khan[1], Roland Reichle[1]
Arnor Solberg[2], Svein Hallsteinsen[2]

[1] University of Kassel, Wilhelmshoeher Allee 73, FB16,
34121 Kassel, Germany
{geihs, khan, reichle}@vs.uni-kassel.de
http://www.vs.uni-kassel.de/
[2] SINTEF ICT, Strindveien 4,
NO-7465 Trondheim, Norway
{Arnor.Solberg, Svein.Hallsteinsen}@sintef.no

Abstract. A challenge in distributed system design is to cope with the dynamic nature of the execution environment. In this paper, we present a model-driven development approach for adaptive component-based applications running on mobile devices. Context dependencies and adaptation capabilities of applications are modeled in UML. We present our new modeling approach and UML profile. A short description of the required middleware infrastructure is given and the transformation technique of the UML models to platform specific code is briefly introduced. An application example illustrates the modeling and development approach. The presented research results have been obtained as part of the European IST project MADAM.

1 Introduction

Many people carry a mobile device of some sort wherever they go, and an increasingly diverse set of mobile devices (PDAs, smart phones, laptops etc.) are becoming widely available. As a matter of fact, people become more and more accustomed to using mobile services ubiquitously in both work and leisure situations. Clearly, the performance and quality of mobile applications crucially depend on the dynamically changing properties of the execution context, e.g. communication bandwidth fluctuates, error rate changes, battery capacity decreases, and a noisy environment may obliterate the effect of sound output. Therefore, applications on mobile devices need to adapt themselves to their current operational context automatically according to goals and policies specified by the user and/or the developer.

The development of self-adapting applications opens up a great challenge: The range of devices, types of infrastructure, types of context dependencies, ways in which context can change, situations in which users can find themselves and the functions they want, introduce great complexity and demand a systematic, general methodology to design and implement self-adapting applications.

Please use the following format when citing this chapter:

Geihs, K., Khan, M.U., Reichle, R., Solberg, A., Hallsteinsen, S., 2006, in IFIP International Federation for Information Processing, Volume 227, Software Engineering Techniques: Design for Quality, ed. K. Sacha, (Boston: Springer), pp. 85–96.

Our goal is to develop such a methodology for future self-adapting applications. We want to provide users with applications that are robust and retain their usability and good performance even in the case of context changes. At the same time we want to free system developers and system managers from much of the low-level details of configuration, operations and maintenance activities.

In this paper we present the modeling of adaptive applications with UML as part of an MDA-based development approach. Self-adapting applications are built as component frameworks with integrated variability, i.e. the application developer specifies variation points when designing an application. During application runtime, if the context changes, adaptation is performed by selecting a suitable application variant, i.e. component configuration, that fits to the current context conditions. All of this is supported by a powerful middleware platform. The choice of using the UML as the modeling language stems from the intention of achieving the benefits of the MDA approach in the application development and complying with popular UML tool environments. Our UML adaptation model is platform independent and it can be automatically transformed to programming language code.

Section 2 of this paper contains an overview of the basic concepts for adaptation and the system architecture and presents the underlying development approach. In Section 3 we present our modeling approach. A new UML profile facilitates the specification of adaptive applications together with its context dependencies. An example is given to illustrate the approach. Section 4 very briefly introduces the model to code transformation technique. Related work is discussed in Section 5. Finally, in Section 6 we comment on experiences with the approach, and we point to future work.

2 Adaptation Approach

The goal of adaptation is to provide the best possible service to the user based on the current context and user preferences. In order to facilitate the development of applications that are able to adapt to context changes, the developer must specify how alternative variants can be derived. These variants provide the same basic functionality but differ in their extra-functional characteristics and resource requirements. In order to facilitate reasoning and decision making about adaptation, the developer must specify the context dependencies and a utility function that is evaluated to estimate the suitability of a variant in a given context. In the following we present a conceptual model for designing applications with built-in variability and, their relation to the context. The underlying middleware that provides the platform to run the applications is briefly introduced.

2.1 Application Variability Model

In our approach applications are component based and the variability is achieved by applying similar concepts as used by the product family community [1]. The variation points are realized by using the concepts of ComponentType and Plan.

Conceptual Component Model. According to Szyperski [2], a Component is a unit of composition with contractually specified interfaces and explicit dependencies where dependencies are specified by stating the required interfaces and the acceptable execution platform(s). Naturally, components may be composed of other software components and may use other components or resources. Our component model is consistent with the concepts of existing component models like CCM, EJB and .NET with the exception that in our current implementation, we use a single class for realizing the atomic component. But this concept is easily extendable.

The conceptual component model of our approach is shown in Figure 1. A Component has exactly one type. A Component Type can have different realizations. It provides and requires services through ports. The characteristics of the component type are defined through its set of Port Types. The Port Type is specified through its set of extra functional characteristics represented by its required and provided QoS_Properties. The functional characteristics of a Port Type are represented by its provided and required interfaces.

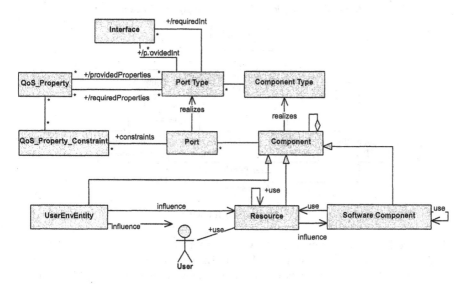

Fig. 1. Conceptual component model

The specification of provided and required services can be seen as defining contracts between components. The Port Types define component contracts through their associated provided and required QoS_Properties. Property constraints associate concrete values with the properties of a component, which may be expressed as constants or as expressions.

A Component can be a SoftwareComponent, a Resource or a UserEnvEntity. A SoftwareComponent can be composed of other components and may collaborate with other software components and use resources through its ports. A Resource represents a run time source of supply and has a limited capacity, which is expressed by its properties. During runtime, consumption and availability of the resource may vary and need to be monitored by middleware services.

The User in the model of Figure 1 represents the actual user of the applications. UserEnvEntity represents entities of interest in the user environment, such as light and noise. The user environment entities may impact resources and other user environment entities.

In our work we have identified three types of context, i.e., user context that relates to the user of a service, system context that encompasses the properties of the execution environment of an application and application context that encompasses the properties of an application providing a service. Context elements are realized through components and context characteristics are expressed as QoS properties of the component.

Dynamic Creation of Application Variants. In our conceptual model an application is represented by a Component Type. The recursive closure of all realizations corresponds to what is often referred to as a component framework [2].

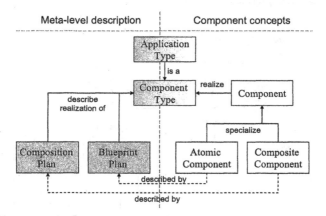

Fig. 2. Component framework

In Figure 2, an application is a software component and an Application Type is considered to be a Component Type. The realization of a Component Type is described using Plans. Components can be atomic as well as composite; accordingly there are two types of Plans: Blueprint Plan and Composition Plan. A Blueprint Plan describes an atomic component and it basically contains a reference to the class that realizes the Component. The Composition Plan recursively describes a composite component by specifying the involved Component Types and the connections between them. A plan represents one possible realization of the associated component type. Variation is obtained by describing a set of possible realizations of a Component Type using Plans.

The representation of applications as Components, Component Types and Plans enables the automatic creation of application variants by recursively resolving the variation points. This reduces the modeling effort significantly. The application developer has to provide only the overall component structure of an application, but there is no need to specify all the possible application variants explicitly. The modeling of one Composition Plan can result in several application variants. In a Composition Plan only the cooperating Component Types are specified, which in turn can have several different realizations described by their corresponding Plans. Besides, if another component is developed that realizes an already existing Component Type further application variants can be derived without much additional modeling efforts. Only the Blueprint Plan and the extra-functional properties of the component have to be specified.

2.2 Middleware Support for Adaptation

The structure of the middleware platform for running the applications is shown in Figure 3. The Context Manager monitors and processes the context information by means of context sensors. The Adaptation Manager receives context information and decides about the adaptation activities. If adaptation is needed, the Adaptation Manager dictates the Configurator to start up the appropriate configuration.

Fig. 3. Middleware building blocks supporting self-adapting applications

The middleware core is responsible for the automatic creation of the application variants as described in the previous section and provides fundamental services for the management of applications, components and component instances. The core relies on the basic mechanisms for instantiation, deployment and communication provided by an underlying distributed computing infrastructure.

The Adaptation Manager reasons on the impact of context changes and is responsible for selecting the application variant (or set of application variants if multiple applications are running) that best fits the current context. In order to evaluate the appropriateness of a particular variant of an application, the utility of the variant is computed. Utility functions along with QoS properties are assigned to each Component Type. For a composite component, the utility value and property constraints can be derived from these.

The Configurator is responsible for the instantiation and configuration of the components that form the selected variants of the running applications.

3 Model Development

We follow the Model Driven Architecture (MDA) approach [3]. An abstract, platform-independent model is needed to capture the adaptation capabilities of complex applications and an automatic transformation to code eases the implementation substantially because it reduces the probability of making mistakes such as omitting possible application configurations in the implementation.

For the platform-independent modeling, we use standard UML 2.0 specification [4]. In addition to this, we extend the standard UML 2.0 specification by introducing a new UML profile, in order to allow generating abstract descriptions of the application's variability and adaptation capabilities. This abstract specification is transformed to appropriate Java code that is responsible for creating the data structures for the Component Types and Plans and for publishing them to the middleware. Our UML-based model builds on experiences with an earlier XML-based model [5].

3.1 UML Profile

We use the UML 2.0 Composite Structure as a baseline in order to model the application architecture. All entities that represent the application context, the resources and the software components (see the conceptual component model in Figure 1) that comprise the applications can be modeled and linked by appropriate associations. For modeling architectural design we have extended the sub-packages InternalStructures and Ports described in the UML 2.0 superstructure specification. The complete description of the profile is beyond the scope of the paper and in the following we present the most relevant part of the profile used for modeling the adaptibilty of applications.

The UML profile defines the component types of the conceptual model by extending the EncapsulatedClassifier of Composite Structures, as shown in Figure 4. Thus, a component type of the conceptual model of Figure 1 is defined as an Encapsulated-Classifier. UserenvEntities, resources and software components are realizations of a Component Type. A Plan describes the realization of a ComponentType.

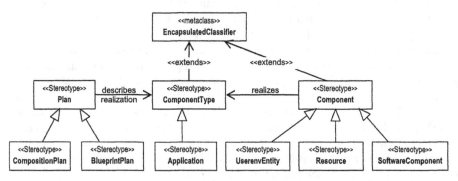

Fig. 4. Plan, Component Type and Component are considered as classes with internal structures

Figure 5 presents the stereotypes for QoS_Property and PortType. The QoS_Property extends the UML metaclass Property in order to express the extra-functional properties of different variants of applications. QoS_Properties are provided or required through ports. Ports realize Port Types. Port Type is an extension of the UML Port metaclass and it is characterized through its provided and required QoS properties.

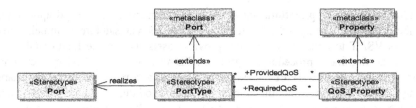

Fig. 5. QoS_Property extends UML Property and PortType is an extension to UML Port meta-classes

For property constraint and utility function we have the following stereotypes: QoS_Property_Constraint, Required_QoS, Provided_QoS and UtilityFunction as shown in Figure 6.

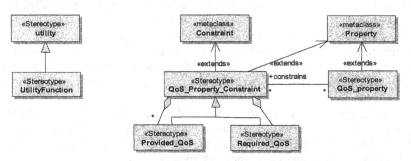

Fig. 6. Property and PropertyConstraint

A QoS_Property_Constraint defines constraints on a Property for a particular component. The Property is provided or required through the port types of the component type. The stereotypes Provided_QoS and Required_QoS include a set of property constraints and indicate if the Property is required or provided respectively. Utility-Function is a generalization of the UML 2.0 standard stereotype <<utility>>, which designates classes having no instances; but denoting non-member attributes and operations. This provides a basic support that satisfies our requirement of expressing the utility of application variants as functions.

3.2 Modeling Example

The modeling technique has been applied to develop two comprehensive distributed applications. Here we use one of them, namely the SatMotion application in order to illustrate the modeling.

The actual modeling of the application starts with the modeling of requirements along with the context and its resources. Here we present a simplified model to focus mainly on the modeling of self-adaptation. Our emphasis is on the variability model of the application which is used to automatically derive the application variants (architecture). During the adaptation process, the suitability of these variants is evaluated and the best fitting variant is chosen to run.

Description of the Application. SatMotion is a commercial distributed application that facilitates the setting up of Internet connections via satellite terminals (also known as VSAT terminals). It basically provides assistance to the field installer on the antenna alignment procedure. It runs on PDAs (e.g. IPAQ) and conventional laptops. The client software of SatMotion consists of a control module, a command editing module, a graphics module, a math processor module, a recording module and an offline analysis module. The server software consists of a communication control module, a storage module and an instrumentation control module.

The SatMotion application offers two main operating modes: Two-Way and One-Way. For both modes, two sub-modes, BasicClient and Recorder, are available which are active depending on the concrete task to be performed by the user. The Two-Way mode implements a two way communication tool able to command the remote instrument, which receives signal traces information from the server and can also send commands to the server side. SatMotion One-Way is a simplified version of the Two-Way mode, enabling just one-way communication for the reception of information from the server. While the Two-Way mode requires a low-latency and highly reliable connection to perform bidirectional operations, the One-Way mode can work with a lower network quality to offer the same real-time signal visualization to the user. Both operating modes, Two-Way and One-Way are complemented by an offline client mode. This variant needs no network connection and is able to play, perform measurements, generate reports etc. on recorded spectrum activity, received previously in an online mode (either One-Way or Two-Way) and stored on the handheld. As indicated by the three different modes, the self-adaptive capabilities of the application address mainly changes in the network context.

The selection of different variants of the application also depends on the internal and external context and resource conditions of the application. Examples for the resources and context elements are: device resources (power drain, power level, memory, processor), user environment (light source, noise), system infrastructure (I/O extension, screen dimensions, screen colours, brightness), network (type, latency, capacity, throughput), application (status, operating mode), etc.

Variability Model of the Application

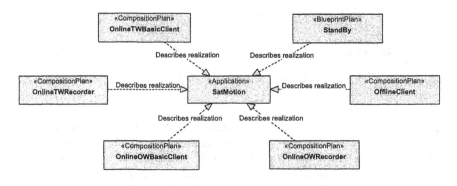

Fig. 7. Plans for the SatMotion application

In the variability model, the SatMotion application is represented as a Component Type that can be realized by any of six Plans, e.g. OfflineClient, OnlineTWRecorder, StandBy etc. as shown in Figure 7. Thus variability is introduced through the possibility of choosing among different plans for the application.

A BluePrintPlan represents the end of the recursion and describes the details of an atomic component. As shown in Figure 7, the SatMotion application can be realized according to one BluePrintPlan and five CompositionPlans. A composition plan is further specified recursively through other composition plans and blueprint plans.

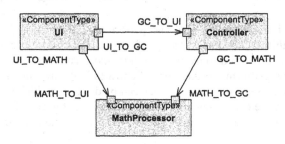

Fig. 8. Component types and their associations in the *OnlineTWBasicClient* Plan

Let us look at the OnlineTWBasicClient plan of Figure 7. Its component composition is shown in Figure 8. The component types *UI, Controller* and *MathProcessor* will be decomposed further until all possible variation points have been resolved and the recursion stops at a BluePrintPlan. Please note that all of these possible variations are evaluated in the Adaptation Manager at run-time in terms of their specified utility.

An example of a BluePrintPlan describing one possible realization of the *Controller* Component Type and providing a *OneWayController* is shown in Figure 9. It contains a definition of a Utility Function, the Component itself and the Property Constraints of the various ports of the component regarding device resources and network.

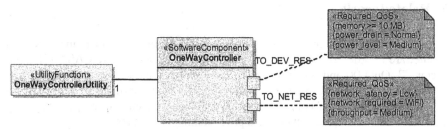

Figure 9: BlueprintPlan for a *OneWayController*

In Figure 9, simple expressions are shown as QoS_Property_Constraints. However, in most cases property constraints can be represented as larger arithmetic expressions involving a number of different QoS_Properties.

It is to note here that there are architectural constraints that can limit the creation of meaningful application variants. For example, a OneWayController can only use a one way mode of the UI, thus its combination with a TwoWayUI will be futile. Moreover, there can be components realized by the same class but with slight changes in their property requirements that can be adjusted by simple configuration parameters. Having separate Blueprint Plans for each of them would cause a big modeling effort. We are currently working on these issues and modeling support will be provided accordingly in the near future.

4 Transformation of the Model to Programming Language Code

Development of the abstract model and performing automatic code generation provides high flexibility. If another target-platform should be addressed, the abstract high level model can be reused, only the transformation has to be adjusted to meet the needs of the new platform. Furthermore, if changes in the overall structure of the applications are necessary, the modifications can be done at the higher abstraction level of the model and the corresponding code is generated automatically. Abstract system specifications are also useful to manage the set of application variants and to ensure completeness.

In our work, we use the Eclipse Modeling Framework, in which UML modeling tools like Omondo and Borland Architect Together can be integrated. The UML model of the application can be exported as XMI according to the metamodel defined by the EclipseUML2, which is a lighter version of the OMG UML 2.0 specification. The UML2 model exported as XMI is taken as input to generate programming language code using MOFScript, which comes as an Eclipse plug-in. The generated code is then published to the middleware.

The transformation technique is introduced for the completeness of the MDA approach; however, this paper focuses mainly on the modeling aspect and the details of the transformation technique are beyond its scope.

5 Related work

There are several research projects dealing with the development of frameworks and middleware in order to support adaptive applications. Examples are CASA [6], Conductor [7], QuO [8] and Rainbow [9]. In these projects, adaptation modeling mainly focuses on the rules and strategies for adaptation. Coming from a different perspective, TRAP/J [10] supports application adaptation for existing Java applications by means of reflection and aspect oriented programming techniques.

Our work is based on the model-driven development paradigm and aims at platform independent but middleware-specific specifications of the variability and adaptation capabilities of applications. In order to allow the selection of the best fitting application variants based on the utility concept, we have to provide modeling support for the extra-functional properties and property constraints of applications. Therefore parts of our UML profile naturally provide similar modeling constructs as OMG's UML Profile for Quality of Service and Fault Tolerance Aspects [11] which includes modeling support for QoS constraints.

Examples for other research projects exploiting the benefits of the model-driven development paradigm and extending UML for providing the platform independent modeling support are MODA-TEL [12], aiming at the MDA-based development of telecommunication systems, and COMBINE [13], dealing with the component based development of enterprise systems. However, these projects focus on the model-driven development of static applications, whereas we aim at modeling the dynamic variability and self-adaptation capabilities of applications.

Another project developing a framework for adaptive mobile applications and services is FAMOUS [14]. However, the project does not emphasize the model-driven development approach and therefore does not aim at automatic code generation from platform-independent models. In [15] an adaptive middleware framework for context-aware applications is presented. However, it lacks the discussion of the development support for adaptive applications.

6 Conclusions

In this paper we have presented a modeling technique for self-adapting, context-aware applications with UML 2.0 in line with the Model Driven Architecture approach of software development. Our focus has been on the specification of application adaptability. The abstract platform-independent adaptation model is transformed to platform-specific code by a transformation.

The specified modeling and transformation techniques have been applied and tested with the development of two real-life commercial distributed applications. Our experiences are promising and support our initial hypothesis: An abstract, platform-independent model facilitates considerably the engineering of adaptation capabilities of complex distributed applications. The model supports dynamic configuration evaluation and selection of suitable application variants at run-time. The automatic transformation to code eases the implementation to a large extent and it reduces the probability of omitting possible application configurations in the implementation.

While working with the trial applications, we have found out that when adaptation occurs often application configurations are evaluated that are practically infeasible. In order to reduce the computational complexity we need to avoid these configuration plans up-front. As future work, we will extend our modeling support for the concepts like architectural constraints and parameterized components in order to solve the above mentioned problems. The transformation support will be improved as well. We will also generalize our notion of context and adaptation towards service contexts and distributed adaptation scenarios where more than one computing device is involved in the adaptation process.

Acknowledgement

The work presented in this paper is done as part of the MADAM [16] project funded by the European Commission under the 6th framework programme. We would like to express our thankful gratitude towards the MADAM consortium and the commission for their valuable support.

References

1. Gomaa, H. and M. Hussein (2003), "Dynamic Software Reconfiguration in Software Product Families", 5th Int. Workshop on Product Family Engineering (PFE), Lecture Notes in Computer Science, Springer-Verlag.
2. Szyperski, C., "Component Software: Beyond Object-Oriented Programming", Addison Wesley, 1997 (2nd ed. 2002, ISBN 0-201-74572-0).
3. OMG MDA Homepage: http://www.omg.org/mda/
4. UML 2.0 Specification: http://www.omg.org/cgi-bin/apps/doc?formal/05-07-04.pdf
5. Kurt Geihs, Mohammad Ullah Khan, Roland Reichle, Arnor Solberg, Svein Hallsteinsen, Simon Merral, "Modeling of Component-based Adaptive Distributed Applications" DADS Track, The 21st Annual ACM Symposium on Applied Computing, Dijon, France, April 23 -27, 2006
6. Arun Mukhija and Martin Glinz, "The CASA Approach to Autonomic Applications", Proceedings of the 5th IEEE Workshop on Applications and Services in Wireless Networks (ASWN 2005), Paris, France, June-July 2005.
7. Mark Yarvis, Peter Reiher, Gerald J. Popek, "Conductor: A Framework for Distributed Adaptation", Proceedings of the Seventh Workshop on Hot Topics in Operating Systems, 1999.
8. Joseph Loyall, Emerging Trends in Adaptive Middleware and its Application to Distributed Real-time Embedded Systems. Third International Conference on Embedded Software (EMSOFT 2003), Philadelphia, Pennsylvania, October 13-15, 2003.
9. Shang-Wen Cheng, An-Cheng Huang, David Garlan, Bradley Schmerl, and Peter Steenkiste, "Rainbow: Architecture-Based Self Adaptation with Reusable Infrastructure", IEEE Computer Vol. 37 Num. 10, October 2004.
10. S. Masoud Sadjadi, Philip K. McKinley, Betty H.C. Cheng, and R.E. Kurt Stirewalt, "TRAP/J: Transparent generation of adaptable Java programs", In Proceedings of the International Symposium on Distributed Objects and Applications (DOA'04), Agia Napa, Cyprus, October 2004.
11. http://www.omg.org/cgi-bin/apps/doc?ptc/04-09-01.pdf
12. A. Gavras, M. Belaunde, L. Ferreira Pires, J.P.A. Almeida. "Towards an MDA-based development methodology for distributed applications." In: Proceedings of the 1st European Workshop on Model-Driven Architecture with Emphasis on Industrial Applications (MDA-IA 2004), CTIT Technical Report TR-CTIT-04-12, University of Twente, ISSN 1381-3625, Enschede, the Netherlands, March 2004, pp. 71-81.
13. http://www.opengroup.org/combine
14. Hallsteinsen, S., Stav, E. and Floch, J., Self-Adaptation for Everyday Systems, ACM SIGSOFT Workshop on Self-Managed Systems (WOSS '04), Newport Beach, CA, USA, 2004.
15. M. C. Hübscher, J. A. McCann, An adaptive middleware framework for context-aware applications, Personal and Ubiquitous Computing, Vol. 10, No.1, pp. 12–20 (2006).
16. MADAM Project Homepage: http://www.ist-madam.org

A Performance Analysis Infrastructure for Component-Based System Hosted by Middleware

Yong Zhang, Tao Huang, Jun Wei, Ningjiang Chen

Institute of Software, Chinese Academy of Sciences, Beijing 100080, China
{yzhang, tao, wj, river}@otcaix.iscas.ac.cn

Abstract. An infrastructure is proposed for automatically modeling the impact of middleware to component-based system at architectural level performance evaluation. The basic ideas behind infrastructure are separation of performance modeling concerns between application and middleware, and declarative performance modeling manner. Taking container style middleware for example, the details of proposed infrastructure are illustrated in this paper, which are well-founded on other existing and proven approaches, such as UML Profile for Schedulability, Performance and Time (UML SPT profile) and Layered Queueing Network performance model generation techniques. To validate proposed infrastructure, a case study is conducted.

1 Introduction

Software middleware helps to alleviate complexity associated with developing distributed software, enables separation of concerns between application logic and system services, such as distributed communication, transaction, message, security, concurrency control, component life cycle management, etc. At the same time, middleware will obviously impact the architecture and performance of component application, which must be taken into account for evaluating the performance of component application from early design specification [1,2,3,4].

At times, middleware as supporting platform is not included as a part of application design description, performance information of which is missing. In order to accurately predict the performance of middleware-based system, some works have been undertaken [5-10], but these approaches require analyst familiar with middleware internal structure and performance modeling technique itself. The steep learning curve behind these methods is one of the major impediments to their adoption.

Our viewpoint is that the modeling process for middleware-based system should be usable in everyday practice by software developer with the help of supporting tool. It should be necessary to automatically construct platform dependent model directly from given application model description and deployment platform. Such tools should be able to read respective model, process it, and produce the composite result suitable for further analysis.

In this paper we propose an infrastructure to support the process, based on separation of concerns and a kind of declarative performance modeling method. Middleware performance concerns are given by platform provider in a manner suitable for

Please use the following format when citing this chapter:

Zhang, Y., Huang, T., Wei, J., Chen, N., 2006, in IFIP International Federation for Information Processing, Volume 227, Software Engineering Techniques: Design for Quality, ed. K. Sacha, (Boston: Springer), pp. 97–108.

declarative modeling. In this paper Extensible Markup Language (XML) Schema is adopted for the purpose. According to predefined Schema, application specific middleware usage and performance information are declared by analyst. Based on proposed infrastructure, the information is automatically weaved into design description of component application. The composite models which include middleware impact and be suitable for derivation of performance analysis model can be got. Thus, different performance modeling concerns of application and middleware are dealt with by different roles in analysis process.

The rest of this paper is organized as follows: a brief survey of related work is given in Section 2; the general description of proposed infrastructure is shown in Section 3; taking a container style middleware for instance, the details of infrastructure are described in Section 4, and a case study based on container middleware is demonstrated in Section 5. Section 6 gives the conclusions of the work.

2   Related Work

Some works have been conducted to investigate the impact of middleware to performance modeling. In [5,6,7], authors model the performance for CORBA-based distributed object system using QN (Queueing Network) / LQN (Layered Queueing Network) formalism. In [8], authors describe a framework for constructing LQN performance model based on the modular structure of Application Server and application components. One of the major drawbacks of these methods is that one must manually construct the performance model by studying underlying middleware, which requires analyst to master middleware details and performance modeling method itself.

In [9,10] authors propose a solution based on empirical testing and mathematical modeling: models describe generic behaviors of application components running on COTS middleware; parameter values in model are discovered through empirical testing. In this solution, incorporating application-specific behavior into the equation is difficult, and the results from empirical testing cannot be generalized across different platforms, which is economically impractical.

In [3,11,12], authors propose applying Model Driven Architecture (MDA) paradigm to analyze the impact of middleware. In [3], authors describe the supporting middleware as a kind of completion information to application design, and suggest the use of MDA idea to supplement it. In [11], authors propose using the Model Driven performance analysis to a distributed middleware based enterprise application developed using EJB. But, neither of [3] and [11] give the concrete transformation details. In [12], authors propose automatic inclusion of middleware performance attributes into architectural UML software models, and the process is illustrated taking a CORBA-based system for an example. But the transformation process of [12] lacks necessary tool supporting. Moreover, only the impacts of distribution communication are discussed.

3 Overview of Infrastructure

The structure of proposed infrastructure is shown in Figure 1, which includes three layers. The top layer is application performance concerns description, and the bottom layer is middleware specific performance concerns, which can be a description library including different kind of middleware. The middle layer will be responsible for finishing the assembling process of application and middleware concerns.

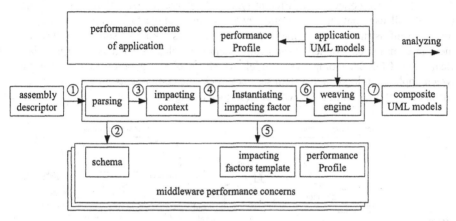

Fig. 1. Structure of proposed infrastructure

In our work we use Unified Modeling Language (UML) as application design specification, and UML SPT performance profile as performance annotation, which has been adopted by Object Manage Group. SPT performance profile extends UML by proving stereotypes and tagged values to represent performance requirements, the resources used by the system and some behavior parameters, to be applied to certain UML behavior model [13,14]. To model performance concerns of middleware, performance profile is also necessary. Here we use UML SPT profile as performance annotation for both application layer and middleware layer.

Performance concerns of different middleware are different, which can be described respectively by platform provider. But a kind of uniform form should be adopted. We present a kind of description in structured XML file in this paper, and illustrate how to use it by container style middleware, by which the information about impacting factors is organized. According to given XML Schema format of a concrete platform, application specific middleware usage information can be provided in a XML file, called assembly descriptor file in our work.

The input of middle layer includes application UML models and application specific assembly descriptor file. According to corresponding XML Schema in middleware model library, an XML parser in infrastructure will parse the assembly descriptor. Then, a middleware impacting context is created, which includes concrete middleware usage and relative performance information. With impacting context, the predefined impacting factors templates of middleware are instantiated. After that, weaving engine will analyze application UML models and insert these impacting factor instances into proper position. The output of infrastructure is composite UML model including middleware impact, from which performance analysis model can be derived. In this paper, we use LQN as target formalism, just one of several possible modeling formalisms [15,2].

4 Modeling for Container Style Middleware

The performance concerns of different type middleware can be different. In this section we will use container style middleware as an example to illustrate the cores of proposed infrastructure. Container style middleware is a kind of supporting environment in common use for server-side component technologies, such as Enterprise Java Beans and CORBA Component Model, which enables separation of concerns between application logic and system services [16]. The components interacting process based on container middleware can be described as Figure 2.

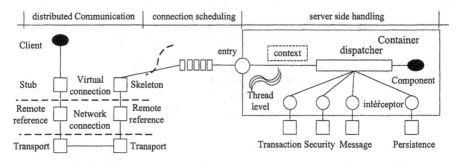

Fig. 2. Component interacting process based on Container middleware

4.1 Modeling Performance Concerns

As illustration, here only three major impacting factors of container middleware are considered: distributed communication, server side connection contention and request processing inside container. We try to build some templates for impacting factors, which can be instantiated according to specific function requirement. The modeling follows the UML SPT profile concepts. We will use scenario-based analysis method [2,13], and scenarios are described by using UML activity diagram with stereotypes and tagged values annotation defined in SPT profile.

The granularity of a scenario step depends on the level of abstraction chosen by the modeler. If finer granularity is required, a step at one level of abstraction can be resolved into a corresponding scenario comprising finer-grained scenario steps. More detailed model which reflects the exact software architecture of middleware, from which more accurate performance estimate can be derived, on the other hand, the system model will be more complex. The tradeoff need be considered.

Distributed communication generally bases on client-proxy-server pattern [17]. Client side and server side components (like stub, remote reference, and skeleton shown in Figure 2) will perform some additional operations on request and response, such as marshaling and un-marshaling. These operations will incur overhead, the impacts of which are modeled in Figure 3. (Here only synchronous call is illustrated).

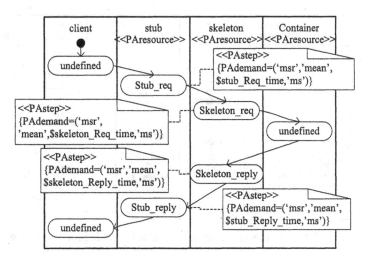

Fig. 3. Modeling overhead of distribution

Relative middleware components are stereotyped as <<PAresource>>, and key actions impacting performance are stereotyped as <<PAstep>>, which demand can be tagged with PAdemand. UML SPT profile provides a useful facility supporting symbolic variables, expressed as *$name*, as well as values for parameters. Here, the demand of each step is described using variable, which will be determined according to application specific model assembly descriptor.

Generally, middleware can process multiple connections concurrently. Here we suppose container middleware using thread pool model. Calls from different client connection will execute in different threads. When the number of client connections exceeds the number of available threads, connections will wait in queue for obtaining thread. The connections can be scheduled based on specific scheduling policy. The size of thread pool and scheduling policy will impact application performance.

Middleware services to be used during invocation usually are declared in application deployment descriptor. To add these services to component system dynamically, architectural pattern similar to chains of interceptor (responsibility) is generally employed in Container middleware [17]. Middleware services serve the request concurrently under the control of different processes/threads. Triggered services will cause overheads.

For convenience, the impact of connection contention and cost of middleware services are modeled in a single UML activity (as shown in Figure 4). The attribute multiplicity, representing the size of thread pool, is described by SPT profile tagged value PAcapacity, and scheduling discipline is described by PAschdPolicy. Each kind of middleware services is abstracted as a service component described by variable *$serviceName_i*. These variables are placeholders for middleware services that will be used in specific application. Here we model each service as a whole, instead of modeling its internals, service demand of which is represented by variable *$ser-viceiTime*.

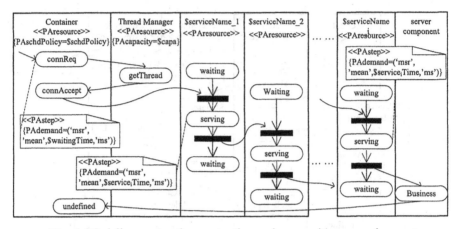

Fig. 4. Modeling connection contention and server side processing cost

4.2 Organizing Concerns Information in XML

The performance concerns discussed in last section should be provided in a manner suitable for declarative modeling. In this paper, we use XML file to organize the information, which complies with the habit of application developer using middleware. At the same time, XML-based description is easily extensible, which provides convenience for further abstracting other impacting factors and refining current factors. The Schema of which is shown in Figure 5.

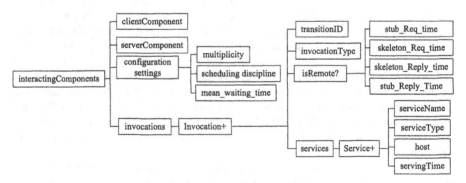

Fig. 5. Schema of model assembly descriptor

The elements in Figure 5 are declared according to each pair of interacting components that use middleware. Element <configuration settings> provides information about modeling connection contention, a sub-element of which <mean_waiting_time> declares the mean waiting time to get a thread for accepting connection. For each invocation between application components, there is a <invocation> declaration: <transitionID> represents the transition (described in application UML activity diagram) referring to this call; element <invocationType> shows that the invocation is synchronous or asynchronous; element <isRemote> specifies service demands of distribution communication phases; Element <services> represents which middleware services will be used by this invocation, in which the service details are specified.

According to the given Schema, application specific model assembly descriptor can be constructed, which is one of inputs to infrastructure. The assembly descriptor provides metadata for assembling component application UML model and middleware impacting factors.

4.3 Weaving Engine

From the assembly descriptor file, middleware impacting context that includes application specific middleware usage and performance information will be created. Using the information, the middleware impacting factors templates are instantiated. Based on impacting context, weaving engine will locate the affected invocations in application UML models, in particular UML activity diagram in this paper, and insert instantiated impacting factors into it. During the process, the original call in activity diagram can need to redirect. The processing steps are illustrated in Figure 6.

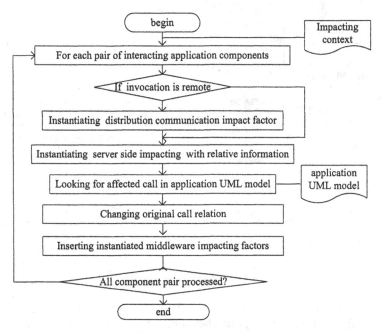

Fig. 6. The weaving process

In addition, the UML deployment diagram of component application need also be changed to reflect the allocation of middleware components to hardware devices.

5 Case Study

To illustrate proposed infrastructure, a case study is conducted, modeling the performance of an online store application based on EJB container middleware. The scenario can be described as Figure 7: *customer* component makes a remote synchronous invocation to *businessBean* component to find required customer information, which need middleware security service; then updates email address of customer to database, during the process middleware transaction service is needed. We will predict the response time of updating customer email information at varying number of clients.

Customer and *businessBean* are implemented as EJB components. The deployment platform we employed is a J2EE Application Server, called *OnceAS* [18]. Client machine generates a number of users who repeatedly generate random requests. There is a think-time distribution that each user uses to determine how long to wait between requests. We let the number of clients vary between 10 and 200 with the increment of 10 clients. The workload is described with PApopulation tagged value. Database is modeled indirectly by specifying as external resource with UML SPT tagged value PAextOp, attached to steps that access database, *getCustomer* and *setEmail*. The detail modeling of database is outside the scope of this paper.

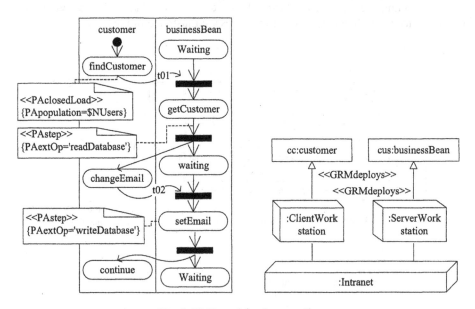

Fig. 7. UML models of case study

With the help of a profiling toolkit *OptimizeIt* [19], service demands of middleware are obtained from a prototype implementation of the case. According to the Schema shown in Figure 5, the model assembly descriptor file of case study is given below. The file, together with the UML diagrams in Figure 7 (in XML format according to XMI standard transformation), will be the inputs to infrastructure.

```
<interactingComponents clientComponent=customer serverComponent=businessBean>
  <configuration settings multiplicity=10 scheduling discipline=FIFO mean_waiting_time=2.8ms/>
    <invocations>
      <invocation transitionID=t01 invocationType=synchronous>
      <isRemote stub_req_time=1.5ms skeleton_req_time=1.9ms
            skeleton_reply_time=3.4ms stub_reply_time=3.2ms getConn=2.8ms/>
      <services>
        <service serviceName=SecService serviceType=Security
              Host =serverWorkstation servingTime=5.3ms/>
      </services>
      </invocation>
      <invocation transitionID=t2 invocationType=synchronous>
      <isRemote stub_req_time=2.1ms skeleton_req_time=2.5ms
            skeleton_reply_time=3.3ms stub_reply_time=2.8ms/>
      <services>
        <service serviceName=TxService serviceType=Transaction
              Host =serverWorkstation servingTime=19.5ms/>
      </services>
      </invocation>
    </invocations>
</interactingComponents>
```

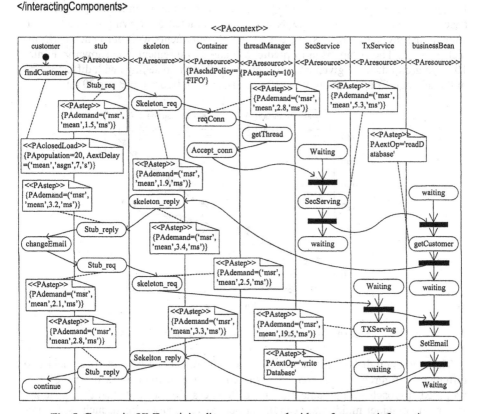

Fig. 8. Composite UML activity diagram annotated with performance information

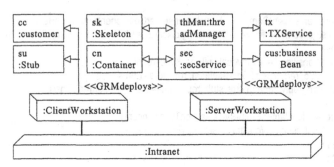

Fig. 9. Composite deployment diagram

By weaving engine, the composite UML models are obtained, as shown in Figure 8 and Figure 9, including activity diagram and deployment diagram. For the sake of clarity, the performance information of application components is not shown in figures.

Using the method proposed in [20], the LQN performance model is obtained from Figures 8 and 9, which can be solved with the model solving tools provided in [21]. For space limitation, the resulting LQN performance model is omitted here. Performance estimates of the resulting LQN model are extracted for varying parameters. To validate the prediction results, we conducted measurements with our benchmark implementation. The comparison of predictions and measurements are shown in Figure 10. Two group data are given under different configuration settings with different size of thread pool: Configuration A has 10 threads, and configuration B has 30 threads.

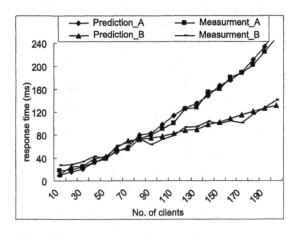

Fig. 10. Comparison of predictions and measurements

The prediction differences shown in Figure 10 are about 12% and 10% under two different configurations respectively. This comparison demonstrates the validity of proposed approach. At the same time, the differences also illustrate that the impacting factors of container middleware can be further extended and refined, such as, the impact of component instantiating, database connection contention, etc. Their aggregate impact may explain the differences.

6 Conclusion

In this paper we propose an infrastructure supporting automatically modeling the middleware performance impact to component-based system. Taking container style middleware as an example, the cores of proposed infrastructure are illustrated. The ideas behind this are separation of performance modeling concerns between application and middleware, and declarative performance modeling manner. We suggest the performance concerns of middleware be provided in a manner of suitable for declarative modeling by platform provider. In this paper, major performance impact factors of container middleware are abstracted, and modeled following the UML SPT concepts. Through a model assembly descriptor file, the model weaving engine is responsible for assembling the performance impacting factors into component application UML model. The prototype of proposed infrastructure has been realized. Using a case study, we validate proposed method.

In the future, several aspects of studying will be conducted. Firstly, we plan to continue to refine and abstract other performance impacting factors of container middleware that are not considered currently, such as more precise thread pool mechanism, instance pool mechanism, database connection contention, and component persistence mechanism, etc. Next, we will improve the abstraction level of middleware impacting factors description. We will try to build UML profile for middleware impacting factors which can be applied to application UML models directly, by using the standard extension mechanism provided by UML [22]. In addition, we will extend middleware concerns library using other type middleware platform, based on the analysis to an open source CORBA middleware project.

References

1. Wolfgang Emmerich: Software engineering and middleware: a roadmap. In: Proceedings of the 22nd International Conference on Software Engineering, on the Future of Software Engineering. ACM, New York, NY(2000) 117-129
2. Simonetta Balsamo, Antinisca Di Marco, Paola Inverardi, Marta Simeoni: Model-Based Performance Prediction in Software Development: A Survey. IEEE Transactions on Software Engineering. Vol.30, No.5, May (2004) 295 – 310
3. M. Woodside, Petriu, D., Khalid Siddiqui: Performance-related Completions for Software Specifications. In: Proceedings of the 24th International Conference on Software Engineering. ACM, New York, NY (2002)22-32
4. Pooley, R., Software engineering and performance: A road-map, In: Proceedings of the 22nd International Conference on Software Engineering, on the Future of Software Engineering. ACM, New York, NY (2000) 189-200
5. Kahkipuro,P.: Performance Modeling Framework for CORBA Based Distributed Systems, PhD thesis, Department of Computer Science, University of Helsinki (2000)
6. Petriu, D., Amer, H., Majumdar, S., Abdull-Fatah, I.: Using analytic models for predicting middleware performance. In: Proceedings of the Second International Workshop on Software and Performance WOSP2000.ACM, New York, NY (2000) 189-194.
7. Williams, L.G., Smith, C.U.: Performance Engineering Models of CORBA-Based Distributed-Object Systems. In: Proceedings of International CMG Conference, Computer Measurement Group (1998) 886-898

8. Jing Xu, A. Oufimtsev, M. Woodside, L. Murphy: Performance Modeling and Prediction of Enterprise JavaBeans with Layered Queuing Network Templates. In: Proceedings of Workshop on Specification and Verification of Component-Based Systems, ACM, New York, NY (2005)
9. Liu, Y., Fekete, A., and Gorton, I.: Design-Level Performance Prediction of Component-Based Applications. IEEE Transactions on Software Engineering, Vol.31, No.11, November (2005) 928-941
10. S. Chen, Y. Liu, I. Gorton, and A. Liu: Performance Prediction of Component-Based Applications. J. Systems and Software. Vol. 74, No. 1, January (2005) 35-43
11. James Skene and Wolfgang Emmerich, Model Driven Performance Analysis of Enterprise Information System, Electronic Notes in Theoretical Computer Science 82 No.6, 2003.URL: http://www.elsevier.nl/locate/entcs/volume82.html
12. Tom Verdickt, Bart Dhoedt, Frank Gielen,and Piet Demeester, Automatic Inclusion of Middleware Performance Attributes into Architectural UML Software Models. IEEE Transactions on Software Engineering. Vol. 31, No.8, August (2005) 695-711.
13. Object Management Group, UML Profile for Schedulability, Performance, and Time, v1.1, 2005.
14. C.M.Woodside and D.C. Petriu, Capabilities of the UML Profile for Schedulability Performance and Time, In Workshop SIVOES-SPT held in conjunction with the 10th IEEE RTAS'2004.
15. M. Woodside, Tutorial Introduction to Layered Modeling of Software Performance, Edition 3.0, http://www.sce.carleton.ca/rads/lqn/lqn-documentation/tutorialg.pdf, Carleton University,2002
16. Ward-Dutton, N: Containers: A Sign Components are Growing Up. Application Development Trends. January (2000) 41-46
17. Douglas Schmidt, Michael Stal, Hans Rohnert, Frank Buschmann, Pattern-Oriented Software Architecture, Volume 2, Patterns for Concurrent and Networked Objects. John Wiley & Sons, New York, NY (2000).
18. http://www.once.com.cn
19. http://www.borland.com/us/products/optimizeit/
20. D.C. Petriu and H. Shen: Applying the UML Performance Profile: Graph Grammar-Based Derivation of LQN Models from UML Specifications. In: Proceedings of 12th International Conference Computer Performance Evaluation, Modeling Techniques and Tools, LNCS 2324, Springer-Verlag, Berlin (2002)159-177.
21. Franks,G.,Hubbard,A.,Majumdar,S.,Petriu,D.C.,Rolia,J.,Woodside,C.M: A toolset for Performance Engineering and Software Design of Client-Server Systems. Performance Evaluation, Vol.24, No.1-2, February (1995)117-135
22. Object Management Group, Unified Modeling Language Specification, Version 1.4.2, http://www.omg.org/docs/formal/04-07-02.pdf

Estimation of mean response time of multi–agent systems

Tomasz Babczyński and Jan Magott

Institute of Computer Engineering, Control and Robotics
Wrocław University of Technology
Tomasz.Babczynski@pwr.wroc.pl

Abstract. The following analytical approaches: queuing network models, stochastic automata networks, stochastic timed Petri nets, stochastic process algebra, Markov chains can be used in performance evaluation of multi–agent systems. In this paper, new approach which is based on PERT networks is presented. This approach is applied in performance evaluation of layered multi–agent system. Time-out mechanisms are used in communication between agents. Our method is based on approximation using Erlang distribution. Accuracy of our approximation method is verified using simulation experiments.

1 Introduction

In this paper, an analytical approach, which is based on stochastic PERT networks, is developed. The approach is applied in performance evaluation of layered multi–agent system. These layers are associated with the following types of agents: manager, bidder, and searcher ones. Our method is based on approximation using Erlang distribution. Erlang distribution is one of probability distributions that are used in evaluation of completion times in stochastic PERT networks. In the paper [4], an approximation method which is based on Erlang distribution has been applied for the above layered multi–agent system. In this paper, there was no bounds for time of waiting for messages from the agents. In present paper, time-out mechanisms are used in communication between the agents. Accuracy of our approximation method is verified using simulator. This simulator has been previously used in simulation experiments with the following multi–agent systems: personalized information system [1], industrial system [2], system with static agents and system with mobile agent [3]. These systems have been expressed in standard FIPA [5] which the JADE technology [6] is complied with.

In section 2, the multi–agent system is described. Then our approximation method is presented. In section 4, accuracy of our approximation method is verified by comparison with simulation results. Finally, there are conclusions.

2 Layered multi–agent system

We consider layered multi–agent information retrieval (*MAS*) system given at Fig. 1.

The *MAS* includes: one manager type agent (*MTA*) as Fat Agent, two bidder type agents(*BTAs*) as Thin Agents, Searcher type agents (*STAs*) as Thin Agents. One *BTA* co-operates with a number of *STAs*.

Please use the following format when citing this chapter:

Babczyński, T., Magott, J., 2006, in IFIP International Federation for Information Processing, Volume 227, Software Engineering Techniques: Design for Quality, ed. K. Sacha, (Boston: Springer), pp. 109–113.

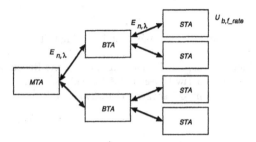

Fig. 1. Layered multi–agent information retrieval system

After receiving a request from an user, the *MTA* sends messages to the *BTAs* in order to inform them about the user request. Then the timer of the *MTA* is started, and the *MTA* is waiting for two responses from the *BTAs*. The waiting time is limited by the termination time *tm*. Having two responses from the *BTAs*, the *MTA* prepares the response for the user. If the maximal waiting time *tm* has elapsed then the *MTA* prepares the response for the user having information received from the *BTAs* until the *tm* has elapsed.

After receiving a request from the *MTA*, the *BTA* sends messages to all *STAs* co-operating with this *BTA*. Then the timer of the *BTA* is started, and the *BTA* is waiting for responses from all its *STAs* but no longer than the termination time *tb*. Having responses from the *STAs*, the *BTA* prepares the response for the *MTA*. If the maximal waiting time tb has been elapsed then the *BTA* prepares the response for the *MTA* having information received from the *STAs* until the *tb* has elapsed.

The *STA* prepares the response by searching in Data Base (*DB*). Each *STA* is associated with one *DB*. The probability of finding the response in the *DB* is denoted by *f_rate*. Time unit is second, and it will be omitted. Searching time is expressed by uniform distribution over the time interval $[0, b)$. Hence, the expected searching time, provided there is the required information in the *DB*, is equal to $b/2$. Searching time is equal to b with the probability $1 - f\_rate$.

Message transmition times between the *MTA* and the *BTA*, and between the *BTA* and the *STA* are given by n stage Erlang distributions with parameter λ for each stage.

3   Erlang distribution based approximation method

We will explain how the expected value of time of receiving of a response by the user is approximated. Because of the lack of space some derivations will be omitted. Probability distributions of times are approximated by Erlang ones [7].

Random variable (*RV*) with this distribution will be denoted by $E_{n,\lambda}$. This *RV* can be interpreted as a sum of n *RVs* with exponential distribution and each with parameter λ. Expected value and variance for this *RV* are equal to $E(E_{n,\lambda}) = n/\lambda$ and $Var(E_{n,\lambda}) = n/\lambda^2$, respectively. For the *RV* T, the squared coefficient of variation (*SCV*) of the T is defined by the formula:

$SCV(T) = Var(T)/E(T)^2$ where: $E(T)$ is the expected value of T, $Var(T)$ is the variance of T. The *SCV* for the $E_{n,\lambda}$ is equal to $SCV(E_{n,\lambda}) = 1/n$.

The *RV* of the *STA* searching time in the *DB* will be denoted by U_{b,f_rate}. This *RV* has the probability density function:

$$f_{U_{b,f\_rate}}(t) = \begin{cases} f\_rate \cdot 1/b & \text{for } t \in [0,b) \\ (1 - f\_rate) \cdot \delta(t-b) & \text{for } t = b \\ 0 & \text{otherwise} \end{cases}$$

Expected value, variance, and *SCV* for this *RV* can be found in [4].

Let us consider the approximation of the probability distribution of the *RV X* of the length of the time interval between the time instant when the *BTA* sends the request to given *STA* and the time instant when the *BTA* receives the response from this STA. This *RV* is given by the expression: $X = E_{n,\lambda} + U_{b,f\_rate} + E_{n,\lambda}$. We suppose that *RVs* of transmission times between agents and *RVs* of searching processes in the *DBs* are independent. The formulae for expected value, variance, and *SCV* of *RV X* can be found in [4].

For multi–agent system described in section 2, the *RVs* of transmission times between agents are two stage Erlang distributions with parameter $\lambda = 1$ for each stage, and will be denoted by $E_{2,1}$.

The *RV X* is approximated by the *RV* $E_{n,\lambda}$, and with the $SCV = 1/n$ such that $|SCV(X) - 1/n|$ is minimal. The expected values of the *RVs X* and $E_{n,\lambda}$ are equal. Hence, the parameter λ is selected according to the equality $\lambda = n/E(X)$.

Let *m* be the number of *STAs* associated with one *BTA*. Let $E_{n,\lambda}(i)$ be such a *RV* $E_{n,\lambda}$ that approximates the length of the time interval between the time instant when the *BTA* sends the request to i^{th} *STA* and the time instant when the *BTA* receives the response from this *STA*. In this case, the *RV Y* of the *BTA* waiting time for all responses from *STAs* is $Y = \max_{i \in \{1,...,m\}} E_{n,\lambda}(i)$. The cumulated distribution function of the *RV Y* is given by the expression: $F_Y(t) = \left(F_{E_{n,\lambda}}(t)\right)^m$. The kth moment (noncentral) of the *RV Y* is obtained by numeric integration of the following formula:

$$\mu^{(k)}(Y) = k \int_0^\infty t^{k-1} \left(1 - F_Y(t)\right) dt$$

Then the *RV Y* is approximated by *RV* E_{n_Y,λ_Y} in the same way as the *RV X* has been approximated by the *RV* $E_{n,\lambda}$.

Now, let us suppose that the *BTA* waits for the responses from the *m STAs* not longer than for the termination time *tb*. Therefore, we analyse the *RV* E_{n_Y,λ_Y} truncated in the *tb*. This *RV* will be denoted by *W*. The *CDF* and the *k*-th moment of the *RV W* are given by the expressions:

$$F_W(t) = \begin{cases} 0 & \text{for } t \leq 0 \\ F'_W(t) & \text{for } 0 \leq t \leq tb \\ 1 & \text{otherwise} \end{cases}$$

$$\text{where} \quad F'_W(t) = \frac{\gamma(n_Y + 1, \lambda_Y t) + \lambda_Y^{n_Y} t^{n_Y} e^{-\lambda_Y t}}{n_Y!} \tag{1}$$

$$\mu_W^{(k)} = \frac{\gamma(n_Y + k, \lambda_Y \cdot tb)}{(n_Y - 1)! \lambda_Y^k} + \frac{tb^k \, \Gamma(n_Y, \lambda_Y \cdot tb)}{(n_Y - 1)!}$$

$$E(W) = \mu_W^{(1)}; \quad Var(W) = \mu_W^{(2)} - (\mu_W^{(1)})^2$$

The *RV W* is not approximated. The *RV* of the length of the time interval between the time instant when the *MTA* sends the request to given *BTA* and the time instant when the *MTA* receives the response from this *BTA* is approximated by the *RV*: $Z = E_{2,1} + W + E_{2,1}$.

The expected value of time of receiving of a response by the *MTA* (or user), i.e. response time, is approximated in the similar way as the expected value of the *RV Y* has been approximated.

4   Accuracy of the approximation method

In order to evaluate the accuracy of the approximation method, the simulation for: the *MAS* containing *m STAs* for each *BTA*, where $m = 3$, 10, have been performed. For each *MAS*, the following values of $f\_rate = 0.1$, 0.3, 0.6, and 0.9 have been considered. The transmission time between agents is given by *RV* $E_{2,1}$. Hence, the mean transmission time between the agents is equal to $E(E_{2,1}) = 2$. In table 1, the percentage errors of

Tab. 1. Percentage errors of mean response time

b	tb	tm	f_rate / m	0.1	0.3	0.6	0.9
16	20	27	3	0.7%	−0.4%	−2.5%	−2.6%
			10	1.4%	1.3%	0.7%	−0.1%
32	38	45	3	0.5%	−0.7%	−3.1%	−2.5%
			10	0.9%	0.7%	0.6%	1.0%
32	380	450	3	17.2%	11.9%	9.8%	7.6%
			10	28.2%	22.3%	24.6%	21.0%

mean response time for choosen values of b, tb and tm are given. In the case when the maximal searching time $b = 16$ and the termination times $tb = 20$, $tm = 27$, we have $b/E(E_{2,1}) = 8$. The approximation results are very good, errors are below 3%. When the maximal searching time $b = 32$ and the termination times $tb = 38$, $tm = 45$, then $b/E(E_{2,1}) = 16$. Even in this case, when the uniform distribution of *RV* of searching time is strongly dominating the Erlang distribution of *RV* of transmission times, the Erlang distribution based approximation is very good. In the third group of results the maximal searching time $b = 32$, the termination times $tb = 380$, $tm = 450$. In this case, $b/E(E_{2,1}) = 16$. Now, the approximation errors are much greater than previously. However, it is not realistic choice of parameters, because the termination time tb is more than 10 times greater than the mean time of the *RV* $X = E_{2,1} + U_{32,f\_rate} + E_{2,1}$.

5   Conclusions

In the approximation method, the *RV* with n stage Erlang distribution is used. It has been obtained from the simulation, that the sum of the *RV* of the Erlang distribution (representing the transmission time) and the *RV* of searching time with uniform distribution can be approximated by the other *RV* of Erlang distribution with suitable number of stages.

Many multi–agent systems have layered structure with the following agents: client assistant, brokers, execution agents. The presented performance approximation method can be used for finding the mean time of response on client request for this class of systems. In the future, we will try to get a better approximation using the general phase type distribution instead of the Erlang one.

References

1. T. Babczyński, Z. Kruczkiewicz, J. Magott, Performance evaluation of multiagent personalized information system, in: Proc. 7th Int. Conf. Artificial Intelligence and Soft Computing - ICAISC, Zakopane, 2004, Lecture Notes in Computer Science / Lecture Notes in Artificial Intelligence (LNCS/LNAI), Springer-Verlag, Vol. 3070, 810-815.
2. T. Babczyński, Z. Kruczkiewicz, J. Magott, Performance analysis of multiagent industrial system, in: Proc. 8th Int. Workshop Cooperative Information Agents - CIA, Erfurth, 2004, LNCS/LNAI, Springer-Verlag, Vol. 3191, 242-256.
3. T. Babczyński, Z. Kruczkiewicz, J. Magott, Performance comparison of multiagent systems, in: Proc. Central and Eastern European Conference on Multiagent Systems – CEEMAS, 2005, LNCS/LNAI, Springer-Verlag, Vol. 3690, 612-615.
4. T. Babczyński, J. Magott, PERT based approach to performance analysis of multi–agent systems, in: Proc. International Conference of Artificial Inteligence and Soft Computing – ICAISC, 2006, LNAI, Springer-Verlag, Vol. 4029,1040-1049
5. Foundation for Intelligent Physical Agents, http://www.fipa.org/specs/
6. JADE, http://jade.tilab.com/
7. MathWorld, Wolfram Research, Inc.,
   http://mathworld.wolfram.com/ErlangDistribution.html,
   http://mathworld.wolfram.com/topics/GammaFunctions.html.

Integrated Approach to Modelling and Analysis using RTCP-nets*

Marcin Szpyrka[1] and Tomasz Szmuc[1]

Institute of Automatics,
AGH University of Science and Technology,
Al. Mickiewicza 30, 30-059 Kraków, Poland
mszpyrka@agh.edu.pl, tsz@agh.edu.pl

Abstract. RTCP-nets are a subclass of coloured Petri nets formed in order to support specification, design, validation, and verification of embedded systems. The advantages of the nets are directly visible in rapid modelling of the so-called rule-based control systems that are widely applied. A method of embedded systems' modelling based on RTCP-nets has been presented in the paper. The formalism is supported by software tool called *Adder*. This tool provides an integrated environment supporting formal specification and design of embedded systems.

1 Introduction

Correctness of a *real time system* is a difficult task due to a high concurrency level and additional time requirements [1]. These features cause, that applications of formal modelling and verification of such systems could be reasonable, especially when the use of these methods is supported by the corresponding software tools. A wide class of real time systems perform on the basis of a set of rules, which are used to compute outputs in response to current state of inputs that are monitored in such system environment. This set of rules specified in the analysis phase as functional requirements may be formally described, and then incorporated into the system model.

A large number of formalisms has been proposed for real-time systems ([1], [2]), e.g. process algebras, Petri nets, temporal\real-time logics, timed automata. Petri nets are one of the most widespread formal methods used in software engineering. The presented approach is based on a subclass of coloured Petri nets (CP-nets [3]), the so-called RTCP-nets. RTCP-nets ([6]) are an adaptation of CP-nets in order to make modelling and verification of real-time systems' easier and more efficient. The main features of RTCP-nets in comparison to timed CP-nets are presented below.

- A priority value is attached to each transition.
- A set of arcs is defined as a relation (multiple arcs are not allowed). Two expressions are attached to each arc: a weight expression and a time expression. For any arc, each evaluation of the arc weight expression must yield a single token belonging to the corresponding type (colour); and each evaluation of the arc time expression must yield a non-negative rational value.

* Research supported from a KBN Research Project No.: 4 T11C 035 24

Please use the following format when citing this chapter:

Szpyrka, M., Szmuc, T., 2006, in IFIP International Federation for Information Processing, Volume 227, Software Engineering Techniques: Design for Quality, ed. K. Sacha, (Boston: Springer), pp. 115–120.

- Time stamps are attached to places instead of tokens. Any positive value of a time stamp describes how long a token in the corresponding place will be inaccessible for any transition. It is possible to specify how old a token should be so that a transition may consume it.

Hierarchical RTCP-nets are based on the construct used for hierarchical CP-nets. Substitution transitions and fusion places ([3]) are used to combine pages but they are a mere designing convenience. A special *canonical form* of hierarchical RTCP-nets has been defined to speed up and facilitate drawing of the models ([6]). RTCP-nets in canonical form are composed of four types of subnets with precisely defined structures: *Primary place pages* are used to represent active objects (i.e. objects performing actions) and their activities. *Primary transition pages* are oriented towards activities' presentation and are second level pages. *Linking pages* belong to the functional level of a model. They are used (if necessary) to represent an algorithm that describes an activity in detail. Moreover, a linking page is used as an interface for gluing the corresponding D-net into a model. *D-nets* are used to represent rule-based systems in the Petri net form.

CASE tools for RTCP-nets called *Adder Tools* are being developed at AGH University of Science and Technology in Kraków. The tools are a free software covered by the GNU Library General Public License. It has been implemented in the GNU/Linux environment by the use of the Qt Open Source Edition. The software can be compiled and run in Mac OS X or Windows systems. *Adder Tools* contain: *Designer* – for design and verification of rule-based systems, *Editor* – for design of RTCP-nets, and *Simulator* – for simulation of RTCP-nets. *Adder Tools home page*, hosting information about current status of the project, is located at *http://adder.ia.agh.edu.pl*.

2   System design process

This paper presents a development process, based on RTCP-nets, that can be used for modelling of real-time embedded systems. A general scheme of RTCP-nets design process is illustrated in Fig. 1. The approach is consistent with general rules of object system development but some elements of structural modelling have been additionally included. The main stages of RTCP-nets design process are given bellow.

1. The first stage consists of system requirements' definition and verification. For the considered control systems, requirements are usually described by the use of decision tables (see [7]).
2. System decomposition is the first step of a model development. It starts with distinguishing objects that constitute the system and with defining attributes that describe their features. Objects are divided into active and passive ones. Construction of primary place pages for active objects ends this development stage.
3. The next stage deals with description of model dynamic that is especially important for reactive systems. Primary transition pages are constructed at this stage. After completion of this stage, RTCP-net represents all elements (objects) that constitute the modelled system and all its activities.
4. The last stage is related to development of functional aspects of the system. Linking pages and D-nets (if necessary) are used for this purpose.

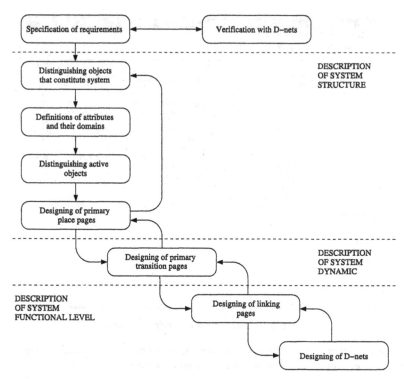

Fig. 1. The RTCP-net development process model

3 Case study

Let consider an office heating/air conditioning control system. A driver turns a heater and an air conditioner on/off to keep the office temperature between $T - 2°C$ and $T + 2°C$, where T is the required temperature. T is set depending on the particular day (D), month (M), and hour (H). All relationships between these attributes are represented in the form of a rule-based system presented in Fig. 2 (the table is based on the example presented in [4]). D, M, and H are conditional, while T is a decision attribute. Each row of the table represents a generalized decision rule ([7]). For example, the first rule means: *If it is any day of the week, the month is: December or January or February, and the time is before 9 or after 17, then the required temperature is equal to* $14°C$.

Any rule-based system is useful when it satisfies certain formal requirements. For intuition, a decision table is considered to be *complete* if for any possible input situation at least one rule can produce a decision. A decision table is *deterministic* if no two different rules can produce different results for the same input situation. The last property means that any dependent (non-necessary) rules were removed. *Adder Designer* enables users to verify a decision table properties automatically.

Design of an RTCP-net starts with distinguishing objects that constitute the modelled system. Any object is represented by a place. For each object, a list of its attributes and their types are defined. The Cartesian product of the defined types specifies the corresponding place type. The following active objects can be distinguished in the

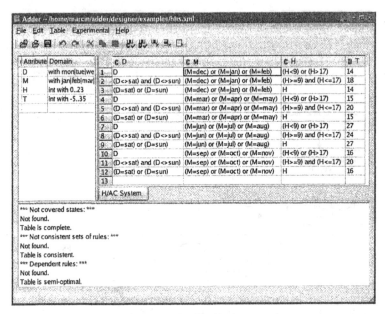

Fig. 2. Example of *Adder Designer* session

considered system: *Driver, AirCond, Heater, Sensor, Office.* The last object represents
the system environment. Examples of definitions of some colours (types) are as follows:

color Temperature = int with -5..35;

color Temperature2 = with normal — heat — cold;

color State2 = with ok — failure;

color DriverState = product Temperature2 * State2;

Primary place pages are used to represent active objects. Any such page is composed
of one place representing the object and one transition for each object activity. Such
a page for the *Driver* is presented in Fig. 3 a). Other primary place pages are designed
in a similar way. Transitions placed on primary place pages are usually substitution
ones. For each of them a *primary transition page* is drawn. Such a page contains all the
places, the values of which are necessary to execute the activity. A primary transition
page for the *Measurement* activity is shown in Fig. 3 b). The place *Timer1* is used to
guarantee, that the temperature will be measured every 15 seconds. If expressions of
arcs surrounding such a transition are not enough to describe the activity, a linking
page (and D-net if necessary) must be constructed. D-net form of the decision table
presented in Fig. 2 is shown in Fig. 3 c). To include such a D-net into the model
a linking page should be constructed. Such a page is used to gather all necessary
information for the D-net and to distribute the results of the D-net activity. Connections
among all pages are represented by the use of a page hierarchy graph (see Fig. 4).

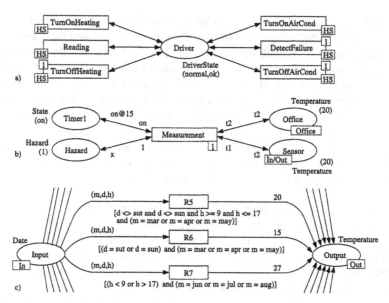

Fig. 3. a) *Driver* primary place page, b) *Measurement* primary transition page, c) Part of D-net

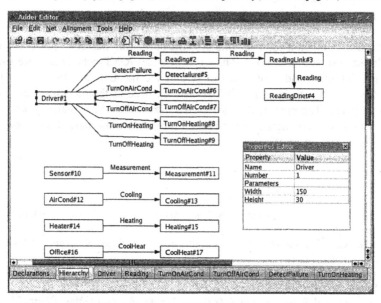

Fig. 4. Example of *Adder Editor* session

4 Model verification

Verification of RTCP-nets may be carried out in two ways. First of all, simulation is used to check how a model works. Adder Simulator supports both interactive and automatic simulation of an RTCP-net. The tool generates a textual report.

Formal verification of RTCP-nets is based on coverability graphs. Two states are considered to *cover* each other, if both have the same markings and the same *level* of tokens accessibility, i.e. in both states, for each place the tokens are already accessible or we have to wait the same number of time units to remove them. A coverability relation is defined on the set of all states and the coverability graph contains only one node for each equivalence class of the relation. If the set of reachable markings of an RTCP-net is finite and each type is finite, then it is possible to construct a finite coverability graph representing the set of all reachable states regardless of the fact the set is finite or infinite ([5]). The coverability graph for an RTCP-net provides similar capabilities of analysis of the net properties as the full reachability graph. For example, the following conclusions are resulted from the graph analysis:

- The heater and air conditioner never work at the same time.
- The heater never works if the temperature is *heat*.
- The air conditioner never works if the temperature is *cold*.
- If the temperature changes from *heat* to *normal*, the air conditioner is immediately turned off.
- The air conditioner (heater) works at least $30s$ and can work incessantly.

5 Summary

A proposal of a method for real-time systems modelling has been presented in the paper. It uses two subclasses of CP-nets – D-nets and RTCP-nets. D-nets are used for the formal definition and verification of system specification, and then are built into system model in the design phase. RTCP-nets are used as the modelling language in the design phase. The presented approach is supported by the so-called *Adder Tools*. The two kinds of Petri nets and the related tools constitute basis for the proposed method for development of real-time systems.

References

1. Cheng A. M. K. *Real-time Systems. Scheduling, Analysis, and Verification.* Wiley Interscience, New Jersey, 2002.
2. Heitmeyer, C., Mandrioli, D. (Eds.) *Formal Methods for Real-Time Computing.* Jonh Wiley & Sons, Chichester, 1996.
3. Jensen K. *Coloured Petri Nets. Basic Concepts, Analysis Methods and Practical Use*, volume 1-3. Springer-Verlag, 1992-1997.
4. Ligęza A. *Logical Foundations of Rule-Based Systems.* Springer-Verlag, Berlin, 2006.
5. Szpyrka M. Analysis of RTCP-nets with reachability graphs. *Fundamenta Informaticae*, 2006 (to appear).
6. Szpyrka M. Fast and flexible modelling of real-time systems with RTCP-nets. *Computer Science*, 6:81–94, 2004.
7. Szpyrka M., Szmuc T. D-nets – Petri net form of rule-based systems. *Foundations of Computing and Decision Sciences*, 31(2):157-167, 2006.

Hybrid modeling and verification of Java based software

Konrad Kułakowski[†]

Institute of Automatics,
AGH University of Science and Technology
Al. Mickiewicza 30, 30-059 Cracow, Poland

Abstract. From the very beginning, notions such as bisimulation and formal methods like temporal logic HML or mu-Calculs were closely connected with process algebra CCS. Another formal method that is widely used for similar purposes is Petri nets formalism. The presented paper shows how the model given in the form of a Petri net could be transformed into an equivalent algebraic model. Some practical application of this method to the analysis of Java based software will be discussed.

1 Introduction

A typical software life-cycle proceeds from the phase of gathering requirements and forming specification to building and delivering a ready-to-use product. Usually it consists of several subsequent steps or phases in which a more and more detailed model of the system is built [1]. In this approach, it is useful to have a method of comparing the initial specification of the system with another (maybe more detailed) specification. One of the formal methods which can be used for this purpose is bisimulation [2].

The hybrid approach to software modeling and verification proposed in this paper is based on labelled Petri nets (LPN) and process algebra CCS. It shifts consideration about the model correctness from labelled Petri nets to the process algebra CCS. This allows for verification of the correctness of Petri nets by means of native algebraic mechanisms and notions. The shift is done by defining simple mapping between both formalisms. This approach does not need a compositional net semantics [3].
Correctness is understood as a relation of satisfying the specification by the given model [4]. Specification could be given in the form of Petri net, and in this case, we would say that the model satisfies the specification if both the LPN representing model and LPN representing specification are bisimilar. Bisimlarity checking is done in CCS. In order to do so, both Petri nets will be transformed into corresponding agent expressions. Specification could also be defined in the form of temporal logic formulas [5, 6]. The presented hybrid approach might also be useful for analysing Java software. In this paper, a sample program based on CyclicBarrier will be analysed in the context of the hybrid approach based on Petri nets and process algebra CCS.

[†] Author was partially supported by MNiSW under grant 4 T11C 035 24

Please use the following format when citing this chapter:

Kułakowski, K., 2006, in IFIP International Federation for Information Processing, Volume 227, Software Engineering Techniques: Design for Quality, ed. K. Sacha, (Boston: Springer), pp. 121–126.

2   Preliminary notions

Definicja 1. *Labelled Petri Net (Labelled Place-Transition net) is a tuple*
$N = (P, T, F, K, W, L, M_0)$ *satisfying the following conditions:*

- *P is a finite, nonempty set of places.*
- *T is a finite, nonempty set of transitions.*
- *$F \subseteq (P \times T) \cup (T \times P)$ is a set of directed arcs of the net known as a flow relation.*
- *$K:P \longrightarrow \mathbb{N} \cup \{\infty\}$ is a function assigning a positive integer to every place. The value $K(p)$, where $p \in P$, indicates the maximum number of tokens that can be held by p. If $p = \infty$, this means that the maximum number of tokens is unlimited.*
- *$W:F \longrightarrow \mathbb{N} \cup \{0\}$ is a function denoting the weight of each arc.*
- *$M_0:P \longrightarrow \mathbb{N} \cup \{0\}$ is a function denoting an initial marking of the net.*
- *$L:T \longrightarrow Act_{LPT}$ is a labelling function which maps transitions to elements of a finite set of Act_{LPT} with a distinguished element τ.*

In the LPT net, an occurrence of transition $t_i \in T$, and in consequence, marking the change from M to M', will be denoted $M \xrightarrow{\ t_i\ } M'$, or $M[t_i\rangle M'$. For every $a \in Act_{LPT}$, $M \xrightarrow{\ a\ } M'$ means that $M \xrightarrow{\ t_i\ } M'$, such as $L(t_i) = a$. The net is called finite if $\forall p \in P\ K(p) \neq \infty$.

Definicja 2. *A reachability graph of the Petri net $N = (P, T, F, K, W, L, M_0)$ is a pair $G = (V, A)$ over T, where:*

- *$V = [M_0\rangle$ is a set of vertices,*
- *T – is a set of transitions ,*
- *$A = \{(M, t, M') : M, M' \in [M_0\rangle \wedge M[t\rangle M'\}$ is a set of arcs labelled by the names of transitions such that $(M, t, M') \in A$ if execution of t cause a change of marking from M to M'.*

The notion of bisimulation was originally defined for process algebra CCS [7], and it also could be easily defined for Petri nets [8]. In both formalisms, bisimulation is defined over the space of states of a system. In CCS there is a set of all possible derivatives of the given agent, whilst in the Petri net, this is a set of all possible markings of the net. Thus, whenever we say that two nets are bisimilar, we mean that their initial markings are bisimilar.

Definicja 3. *Let LPT_1 and LPT_2 be labelled Petri Nets. A strong bisimulation is the relation B between the markings of LPT_1 and LPT_2, such that for all $(M_1, M_2) \in B$ and for all $a \in Act_{LPT}$:*

- *if $M_1 \xrightarrow{\ a\ } M_1'$ then $M_2 \xrightarrow{\ a\ } M_2'$ for some M_2' such that $(M_1', M_2') \in B$ and*
- *if $M_2 \xrightarrow{\ a\ } M_2'$ then $M_1 \xrightarrow{\ a\ } M_1'$ for some M_1' such that $(M_1', M_2') \in B$*

The simlar definition could be given for a weak bisimulation. We would say that M_1 is strongly bisimilar to M_2 and donote it $M_1 \sim M_2$, and M_1 is weakly bisimilar (observable equivalent) to M_2 and denote it $M_1 \approx M_2$. Two Petri nets are in strong (weak) bisimulation if their initial markings are in strong (weak) bisimulation.

Notions like strong and weak bisimulation were originally defined in the context of process algebra CCS. Appropriate definitions, as well as a detailed description of the formalism, might be found in various positions [9, 10].

3 Transformation of Labelled Petri Nets to CCS

Let N be a finite labelled Petri net and $G_N = (V, A)$ be its reachability graph. Because N is finite, G_N is also finite; i.e. both sets V and A are finite. Let us enumerate the set of vertices as follows: $V = (M_0, \dots, M_r)$. Let $O(M)$ be a set of all vertices from V that can be directly reached from M; i.e.:

$$O(M) = \{M_i \in V : M[t\rangle M_i \in A\}$$

For every vertex $M \in V$ let $\Phi(M)$ be the agent in the form:

$$\Phi(M) = \Sigma_{M_i \in O(M)} L(t_i).\Phi(M_i)$$

where t_i is a transition such that $M[t_i\rangle M_i \in A$.

We would say that the symbol Φ denotes transformation of the given Petri net N, with the initial marking M_0, to the corresponding CCS agent $\Phi(M_0)$ according to the scheme presented above.

Let us consider the net N_1 (Fig.1).

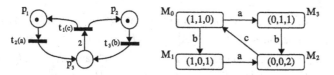

Fig. 1. Petri net N_1 and its reachability graph

Transitions t_1, t_2, t_3, of N_1 are labelled correspondingly: $L(t_1) = c$, $L(t_2) = a$, $L(t_3) = b$. The reachability graph of N_1 contains four vertices that denote four possible markings: $M_0, \dots, M_3$ (Fig.1). According to the assumed transformation algorithm, the algebraic equivalent of N_1 is the CCS agent $\Phi(M_0) \overset{df}{=} \Phi(N_1)$ defined as follows:

$\Phi(M_0) \overset{df}{=} a.\Phi(M_3) + b.\Phi(M_1)$, $\Phi(M_1) \overset{df}{=} a.\Phi(M_2)$, $\Phi(M_3) \overset{df}{=} b.\Phi(M_2)$, $\Phi(M_2) \overset{df}{=} c.\Phi(M_0)$.

Transformation Φ is consistent with the relations of strong and weak bisimulations, which means that if two Petri nets are bisimilar, their algebraic equivalents are also bisimilar.

Theorem 1. *For two finite labelled Petri nets LPN_1, LPN_2 if $LPN_1 \sim LPN_2$, thus also $\Phi(M_0^{(1)}) \sim \Phi(M_0^{(2)})$ where $M_0^{(1)}$ and $M_0^{(2)}$ are initial markings of LPN_1 and LPN_2.*

Proof. Let us assume $LPN_1 \sim LPN_2$. Satisfying the equivalence $\Phi(M_0^{(1)}) \sim \Phi(M_0^{(2)})$ requires:

- $\forall a : \Phi(M_0^{(1)}) \overset{a}{\longrightarrow} A_1^{(1)}$ exists $A_1^{(2)}$, such that $\Phi(M_0^{(2)}) \overset{a}{\longrightarrow} A_1^{(2)}$
  and $A_1^{(1)} \sim A_1^{(2)}$
- $\forall b : \Phi(M_0^{(2)}) \overset{b}{\longrightarrow} B_1^{(2)}$ exists $B_1^{(1)}$, such that $\Phi(M_0^{(1)}) \overset{b}{\longrightarrow} B_1^{(1)}$
  and $B_1^{(1)} \sim B_1^{(2)}$

If for some a exists transition $\Phi(M_0^{(1)}) \xrightarrow{\ a\ } A_1^{(1)}$, it means that by knowing the construction of the agent $\Phi(M_0^{(1)})$, we also know that $M_0^{(1)}[t_i)M_1^{(1)}$, where $L(t_i) = a$ and $\Phi(M_1^{(1)}) = A_1^{(1)}$. In other words, $M_0^{(1)} \xrightarrow{\ a\ } M_1^{(1)}$. Because $LPN_1 \sim LPN_2$ there is $M_0^{(1)} \sim M_0^{(2)}$. Thus, on the basis of these two facts, there is $M_2^{(2)}$ such that $M_0^{(2)} \xrightarrow{\ a\ } M_1^{(2)}$. Let us denote $A_1^{(2)} = \Phi(M_1^{(2)})$. Considering the construction of $\Phi(M_0^{(2)})$, we know that there is transition $\Phi(M_0^{(2)}) \xrightarrow{\ a\ } \Phi(M_1^{(2)})$.

The question arise whether $A_1^{(1)} \sim A_1^{(2)}$, i.e. if $\Phi(M_1^{(1)}) \sim \Phi(M_1^{(2)})$ (and similarly, if $B_1^{(2)} \sim B_1^{(1)}$). Let us note that $M_1^{(1)} \sim M_1^{(2)}$ (as a consequence of $LPN_1 \sim LPN_2$). In other words, using the same reasoning as presented above, but this time applied to the nets $LPN_1(M_1^{(1)})$ i $LPN_2(M_1^{(2)})$ – i.e. to net LPN_1 with marking $M_1^{(1)}$ and net LPN_2 with marking $M_1^{(2)}$, we may show that $\Phi(M_1^{(1)}) \sim \Phi(M_1^{(2)})$, which is of course true if and only if $A_2^{(1)} \sim A_2^{(2)}$ and $B_2^{(2)} \sim B_2^{(2)}$,... and so on. By repeating this operation, we prove equivalences: $A_3^{(1)} \sim A_3^{(2)}, A_4^{(1)} \sim A_4^{(2)}$,... and correspondingly $B_3^{(2)} \sim B_3^{(1)}, B_4^{(2)} \sim B_4^{(1)}$,... etc.

After the r-th iteration, we have to prove that $\Phi(M_r^{(1)}) \sim \Phi(M_r^{(2)})$. These two agents satisfy the relation $\sim$ if $A_{r+1}^{(1)} \sim A_{r+1}^{(2)}$ and $B_{r+1}^{(1)} \sim B_{r+1}^{(2)}$. If in steps l_1, l_2, such that $0 < l_1 < r$, $0 < l_2 < r$, the equivalences $A_{l_1}^{(1)} \sim A_{l_1}^{(2)}$ and $B_{l_2}^{(1)} \sim B_{l_2}^{(2)}$ have been proven, where $A_{r+1}^{(1)} = A_{l_1}^{(1)}$, $A_{r+1}^{(2)} = A_{l_1}^{(2)}$, $B_{r+1}^{(1)} = B_{l_2}^{(1)}$ and $B_{r+1}^{(2)} = B_{l_2}^{(2)}$, we may stop our reasoning at this point. If not, this situation must happen at the latest for $r = pq$, where p is the number of vertices in the reachability graph G_{LPN_1} and q - is the number of vertices in the reachability graph G_{LPN_2}. This is because, if we reach r-th step of out reasoning ($r = pq$), this means that for every pair of agents $\Phi(M_i^{(1)})$, $\Phi(M_j^{(2)})$, where $M_i^{(1)}$, $M_j^{(2)} \in V_{LPN_1}, V_{LPN_2}$, it is true that $\Phi(M_i^{(1)}) \sim \Phi(M_j^{(2)})$.

According to the presented reasoning scheme, the following theorems can also be proved.

Theorem 2. *For two finite, labelled Petri nets LPN_1 and LPN_2, if $LPN_1 \approx LPN_2$, thus also $\Phi(M_0^{(1)}) \approx \Phi(M_0^{(2)})$, where $M_0^{(1)}$ and $M_0^{(2)}$ are initial markings of LPN_1 and LPN_2.*

Theorem 3. *For every two finite labelled Petri nets LPN_1, LPN_2 if $\Phi(M_0^{(1)})$ op $\Phi(M_0^{(2)})$, then LPN_1 op LPN_2, where op $\in \{\sim, \approx\}$, and $M_0^{(1)}, M_0^{(2)}$ are initial markings of LPN_1 and LPN_2.*

4   Hybrid modeling – case study

Petri Nets are very often used in the modeling of reactive systems behaviour. The Petri Net could act both as a specification or as a design. When specification is considered, usually a small Petri Net is used. It defines activities which determine basic system functionality.

The ideas of strong and weak bisimulation could be implemented into the Petri Net formalism. Thanks to the presented transformation, analysis of bisimilarities on the basis of the net's algebraic representation is possible. It also allows us to: model comparisons in terms of bisimulation property and project validation against specification which might be written in the form of a set of temporal formulas.

Different model comparisons

Let us consider a model of a system that consists of several different processes responsible for data processing and one process responsible for printing the result. In our example, data processing consists of two separate activities denoted correspondingly by a and b. Data processing is complete if both activities are done. A result printing is represented by activity c. The order of activities, a and b is not important. Both sequences a, b and b, a are allowed. The only requirement is that a and b must take place before c. In our mini-system, these activities will be modeled by actions; i.e. the activity is complete if an action occurs.

Assuming that actions a and b occur independently (e.g. in a separate processes), a situation like the one described above is modeled by the net N_1 shown in the figure 1. In general, N_1 depicts the system in which two different processes do action a and b, and next they wait until c is done.

This very popular synchronisation model was reflected in modern Java in the form of a *CyclicBarrier* class [11]. It provides a convenient synchronisation aid that allows one thread to wait until other threads complete their tasks. Of course the requirement that before c both actions a and b must occur might be fulfilled differently. Let us consider a *NaivyApp* simple sequential application which may perform two possible scenarios: a, b, c and b, a, c. In deed, these application also meets the requirements that both actions a and b must occur before c.

The behaviour of *NaivyApp* is modeled by the net N_2 shown in the figure 2. This net corresponds to a simple sequential program that performs the actions a, b, c or b, a, c repeatedly in turn.

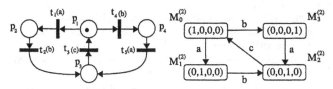

Fig. 2. Net N_2 and its reachability graph

Because both nets N_1 and N_2 represent the programs that satisfy our informal specification, the question comes up whether their behaviours are the same. In order to answer this question, the reachability graph of N_2 is built (figure 2). It enable us to construct agent $\Phi(N_2)$, which is the algebraic representation of N_2.

$$\Phi(M_0^{(2)}) \stackrel{df}{=} a.\Phi(M_1^{(2)}) + b.\Phi(M_3^{(2)}), \ \Phi(M_1^{(2)}) \stackrel{df}{=} b.\Phi(M_2^{(2)}), \ \Phi(M_2^{(2)}) \stackrel{df}{=} c.\Phi(M_0^{(2)}), \ \Phi(M_3^{(2)}) \stackrel{df}{=} a.\Phi(M_2^{(2)})$$

According to the theorem 3, the nets N_1 and N_2 are bisimilar if agents $\Phi(M_0)$ and $\Phi(M_0^{(2)})$ are bisimilar. A quick automatic check proves that $\Phi(M_0) \sim \Phi(M_0^{(2)})$ [12], and thereby it will be shown that $N_1 \sim N_2$.

5 Summary

For several years, a significant increase of demand for reliable multi-threaded software can be be observed. As a result, libraries supporting the building of concurrent applications for many programming languages are available [13, 11] (e.g. a recent version of Java incorporates the new *java.util.concurrent* package). This trend also make stronger a need for the creation of convenient and versatile formal methods that support specification and design of concurrent software.

The hybrid modeling technique presented above helps to achieve this goal. It facilitates using bisimulation in the context of models given in the form of Petri nets. Because of transforming a net to an appropriate CCS agent, it is possible to proceed with further analysis in well defined algebraic formalism, including suitable tools such as CWB [12].

Defining algorithms and methods that shorten the distance between formal methods such as Petri nets or CCS algebra and the Java language will pose a challenge to author in the near future.

References

1. McConnell, S.: Code Complete. Microsoft Press, Redmond, WA. (1993)
2. Bruns, G.: Distributed Systems Analysis. Prentice Hall (1997)
3. Goltz, U.: CCS and Petri Nets. In: Semantics of Systems of Concurrent Processes, Berlin - Heidelberg - New York, Springer (1990) 334–357
4. Kułakowski, K.: Konstrukcja i Analiza Oprogramowania Sterowników Wspomagana Metodami Formalnymi. PhD thesis, Akademia Górniczo-Hutnicza (2003)
5. Groote, J., Voorhoeve, M.: Operational semantics for petri net components (2003)
6. Fencott, C.: Formal Methods for Concurrency. International Thomson Computer Press, Boston, MA, USA (1995)
7. Milner, R.: Communication and Concurrency. Prentice-Hall (1989)
8. Jancar, P., Esparza, J.: Deciding finiteness of Petri Nets up to Bisimulation. Lecture Notes in Computer Science **1099** (1996)
9. Milner, R.: A Calculus of Communicating Systems. Volume 92 of LNCS. Springer-Verlag (1980)
10. Fidge, C.: A comparative introduction to CSP, CCS and LOTOS. Technical report (1994)
11. Lea, D.: Concurrent Programming in Java. The Java Series. Addison-Wesley, Reading, MA (1997)
12. Moller, F., Stevens, P.: Edinburgh Concurrency Workbench user manual (version 7.1). (Available from http://homepages.inf.ed.ac.uk/perdita/cwb/)
13. Niño, J., Hosch, F.A.: An Introduction to Programming and Object Oriented Design Using Java 1.5. Second edn. Wiley, Hoboken, NJ (2005) With CD-ROM.

An evolutionary approach
to project management process improvement
for software-intensive projects

Paweł Pierzchałka

Q-Labs GmbH, Germany
Ingersheimer Str. 20, 70499 Stuttgart
pawel.pierzchalka@q-labs.de, ppierzchalka@yahoo.de

Abstract. Project management plays an important role in software engineering discipline. Project management is about delivering projects "on time", "in budget" and "in quality". Introducing, applying and improving project management process requires systematical and coordinated approach, which helps to overcome organizational barriers, reduce implementation cost, provide knowledge sharing and secure achieved results. Many companies within the software-intensive automotive industry have decided to start the organization-wide process improvement programs. In this context, project management is one of the first key issues on the way to the better processes. This article presents an evolutionary approach to introducing and improving project management organizational methodology. It defines steps needed for incremental implementation of project management in software-intensive organization and its component-projects. It discusses the key success factors, prerequisites, methods and tools used on the way to the better, systematical, universal and practicable project management process.

1 Introduction

Nowadays project management is an increasingly growing discipline. Many international and local organizations (such as *Project Management Institute* in U.S., *Gesellschaft für Projekt Management* in Germany, or *Polskie Towarzystwo Informatyczne, Sekcja Zarzadzania Projektami* in Poland) are supporting the growth and improvement of project management. These organizations promote the usage of the modern project management principles across all disciplines, with a special focus on software industry. They also support practitioners in mastering their project work.

The modern process and quality reference models underline the role of project management in the development work. Such models as CMMI, ISO15504, or PMBOK provide an extensive guidance on project management [1-5].

Project management is now recognized as one of the basic methods in the modern software engineering. It is one of the essential elements enabling the success of the software and system development initiatives [6-8].

The automotive industry has also recognized the importance of project management in the electronic and software-intensive development projects. In the next dec-

Please use the following format when citing this chapter:

Pierzchałka, P., 2006, in IFIP International Federation for Information Processing, Volume 227, Software Engineering Techniques: Design for Quality, ed. K. Sacha, (Boston: Springer), pp. 127–138.

ade electronic and software will account for approximately 90% of all future automotive innovation. Electronic and software are becoming critically important and will share approximately 40% of the cost of car production. At the same time the complexity of the software-intensive systems in modern vehicles is rapidly growing. Nowadays a high number of electronic control units are present in the car. They communicate through internal buses and influence each other. Almost every part of the car is now controlled by electronic and software - starting with engine/gear control, chassis, traction control systems, windows, light control and ending with the modern car navigation and entertainment systems.

The increasing role of software in modern vehicles requires better management of the car development projects. In order to deal with the size and complexity of the vehicle systems, automotive companies have decided to start the company-wide process improvement programs. By introducing process improvement they want to deal better with the increasing complexity, improve product quality, to improve productivity and efficiency of the development departments. Within those process-oriented approaches, project management process plays an important role, already at the beginning of a process improvement initiative.

The experience gained during the implementation of project management in the context of software-intensive automotive systems lead to this work. This article presents an evolutionary approach to introducing and implementing the project management methodology within software-intensive automotive systems. It presents the key factors, methods and selected tools, which lead to the successful and sustaining implementation of the project management within the organization. The special focus is put on the component-projects – projects that aim to develop the single software-intensive component (e.g.: electronic gear control, control panel, roof control panel) resulting from the cooperation between the OEM and suppliers.

2 An Evolutionary Approach to Project Management Process Improvement

The article presents an evolutionary approach to introducing and improving the project management within the context of the organizational process improvement program. It is based on the author's experience collected during the implementation of the project management principles within multiple automotive companies. It presents the suggestion of the Project Management Process Improvement Model (PM-PIM). The article introduces the maturity levels needed for introducing, carefully implementing and then mastering project management within the software-intensive organization. The proposed levels build on each other, e.g.: establishing the project management framework (Level 1) is a prerequisite for starting with piloting and roll-out of project management practices in the component development projects (Level 2). Implemented project management practices (Level 2) are the basis for more advanced project management, including definition of the tailoring guidelines for project management process, quantitative project management and further continuous improvement (Level 3).

The content of the suggested Project Management Process Improvement Model (PM-PIM) is presented on the Figure 1.

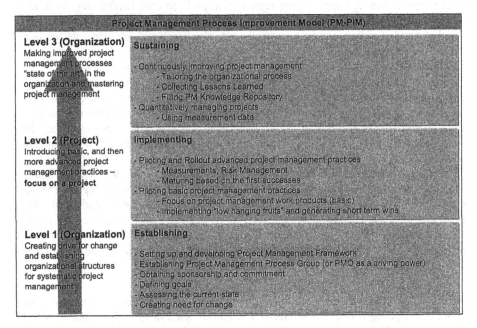

Fig 1. Project Management Process Improvement Model (PM-PIM)

The focus of the model is software-intensive organization and its component-projects. The discussion of the model elements is presented in the article below, taking into account successful and sustaining implementation of project management process improvement.

2.1 Level 1 - Establishing

The Establishing level refers to creating the organizational environment for the successful improvement of project management practices. It is about creating drive for change in project management, assessing the current state of project management practices, defining goals based on the organizational business goals and assessment results, obtaining sponsorship and creating a guiding coalition for the project management initiative, collecting the right people on board and working out the first Project Management Framework. It is the responsibility of the organization to achieve all the points discussed in the Establishing level. Before starting the operational project management process improvement work with the projects, the issues discussed in the Establishing level should already be in place.

Creating need for change. Introducing a systematic project management process is usually linked with the change to the current "lived" processes. Before starting the improvement work the company must understand the reasons for doing the work. There are different sources, which drive the need for change in project management. These sources can be internal (poor results from past projects, firefighting, recall actions, improvement initiatives, business goals, management requirements) or external (market trends, studies, customer expectations, regulatory and governments requirements) to the organization.

There must be a real sense of urgency in the organization to provide a right set-up for project management improvement initiative. The organization must really want to move, to change the current way of working. Usually the best way to achieve this is to learn by its own experience of the problems in the past. Some examples are the firefighting situation at the end of the project, using too many resources on fixing the problems, huge cost overruns or even putting in danger the vehicle development project end milestone – called Start of Production (SOP).

"Feeling the pain" is the best driving factor for starting with the deep-grounded project management process improvement. On the other side, if the company has not experienced any problems itself, it is rather hard for the employees to understand that there is a need for change. It is then the role of management to convince the teams and also themselves that the change and improvement are needed. Creating the need for change - it is about being proactive – thinking about potential problems before they occur.

Assessing the current state. Assessing the current state of project management is about determining where you are now. The current state of the project management processes should be assessed in order to determine, what is already in place and what needs to be done to close the gaps in the current „lived" project management processes.

While assessing the status of the project management practices some process reference models can be helpful. One of the reference models - Capability Maturity Model Integration (CMMI) - provides a description of the "best practices" for project management [2-3]. The project management in CMMI is divided in some Process Areas, both on the fundamental as well as on the progressive level. The fundamental Project Management Process Areas includes Project Planning (PP), Project Monitoring and Control (PMC), and Supplier Agreement Management (SAM). The progressive project management Process Areas includes Integrated Project Management (IPM), Risk Management (RSKM), Integrated Teaming (IT) and Quantitative Project Management (QPM). These CMMI project management Process Areas cover activities related to project planning, monitoring and control. They provide a lot of guidance on what is important for the systematic project management. The CMMI model enables to assess the current project management practices, identify gaps against the CMMI project management practices and define actions, which need to be implemented in order to improve project management practices.

Another alternative to assess project management is using another model - ISO15504 / SPICE [4]. In this model project management plays also a central role. The process group Project Management (MAN3) deals with project management. Some other process groups provide additional details on project management, i.e.: Risk Management (MAN5) or Measurement (MAN6). The usage and importance of the process reference models in the software-intensive automotive industry is well visible at the example of the SPICE model. In the year 2005 the new version of the SPICE model was created with the focus on the automotive industry. The result is Automotive SPICE [5]. This model adds on the additional automotive focus to the standard SPICE model. Project management plays here an important role. Most of German automotive OEMs assess project management implementation of its suppliers, using SPICE as a reference model.

Performing an assessment against the reference model results in a list of the organization's strengths and weaknesses in the project management process. At the end of the assessment the clear picture of the project management current state is available and project management process improvement roadmap is established.

Defining Goals. Goals specify where you want to go. Having the picture of the current state, you can define where are the gaps in the project management process and then you can define where you want to go. The important input for definition of the improvement goals is the result from the assessment of the current project management process. In addition, the goals for project management processes should be derived from the organizational business goals and process improvement objectives. Defining goals for project management visualizes, how the project management fits within the overall process improvement initiative, and also within the business organizational context.

Obtaining sponsorship and commitment. For every improvement initiative there is a need for a strong sponsorship from the senior management. Senior management plays a sponsor role and is responsible for linking the project management process improvement activities to the organization's vision and mission.

It is important that a sponsor has a management role at a high enough level in the organization structure. The sponsor has an authority to direct activities, states the objectives and commits the allocation of resources (people, materials, funding) for project management process improvement initiative.

Senior management sponsor should be involved and committed to the project management improvement activities. This involvement and commitment is demonstrated for example by defining organizational policies, presenting the project management improvement effort goals at the employee forum. The sponsor must "walk the talk". It means, even in the technical problem situation the organization will stick to the project management policies. For example, if the policy states that every project is asked to perform risk management workshop, the senior management will force to do so, even if a project manager will try to avoid it by showing that there is no time for risk management. Another sign of the sponsor commitment to project management improvement initiative is showing interest in the work progress, encouraging and participating in the reviews of project management improvement activities.

It is also the job of a sponsor to remove barriers and obstacles that block the project management process improvement effort. The value of a sponsor cannot be underestimated. Strong, committed and proactive sponsorship is the key factor to the success of project management process improvement activities.

Establishing Project Management Process Group (or PMO as a driving power).
The Project Management Process Group (PMPG) is a group of people interested in
project management. It is a driving power for successful implementation of the
change in project management. This group manages the project management process
definition activities. It is typically staffed by the professionals whose primary
responsibility is coordinating project management organizational process
improvement.

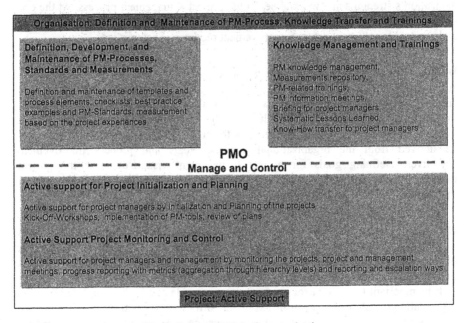

Fig. 2. Role of PMO in the organization

This Project Management Process Group is usually concentrated around Project
Management Office (PMO). The practical experiences show that installing the PMO
in the organization will facilitate and speed up the project management process improvement. PMO is an organizational unit, which is used to centralize the project
management expertise and manage the projects. While introducing a systematic project management, PMO will play an important role, serving the projects with the project management competence, and also supporting by the introduction of the PM
methods and tools. The role of the PMO is presented in Figure 2.

PMO provides support by implementing and improving project management in the
component-project. Some additional PMO features to be underlined while improving
project management processes are:

- Assessing current "lived" PM processes, identifying gaps and defining actions
- Identifying, applying and improving of project management processes
- Using industry-proven PM methods and techniques
- Training-by-doing / coaching / "hands-on" support
- Involving all relevant parties (projects, suppliers, departments and teams)

Setting up and developing Project Management Framework. There is a need to develop and set up the Project Management Framework. It is about preparing the first definition of the project management process. The findings from assessments are used. PMO members contribute with their various project management experience. Best project management practices and guidelines, taken from the reference models are also beneficial. The project management process description is mapped to the organization structure. The objective is not to provide a perfect, 100% ready process description. It is more about the first draft of the project management process, which is good enough to start with the first implementation.

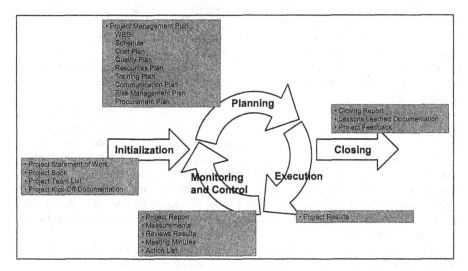

Fig 3. Overview of the project management process with work products

Project Management Framework describes the project management process and includes also the basic set of pre-defined templates describing project management work products (see Figure 3).

In addition, the visualization of the link between project management process and the organization (existing organizational processes, organization departments and teams) is also provided.

2.2 Level 2 – Implementing

The Implementing level is about piloting and rollout of the improved project management practices across the projects within the organization. It is done in two phases. At the beginning basic project management practices are introduced, starting with some selected pilot projects. In the next phase more advanced project management practices are implemented. The objective is to reach all projects in the organization. It is the responsibility of the projects, especially project leaders, to implement the improved project management practices. While implementing the practices the project leaders receive active support from Project Management Office.

Piloting basic project management practices. The first phase of the Implementation level is about implementing the basic project management practices. In some selected pilot projects first elements of project management process are introduced. This first step is to pilot and gain acceptance of the improved project management practices across projects.

At the beginning, it is important to select small improvements with quite a lot of impact on the projects. In order to identify these elements the results of the project management assessment are used. The assessment results make visible, where are the gaps in the project management process and improving which of them can be most beneficial for the projects. It is about picking up the "low hanging fruits - issues with low effort and high positive impact for the projects. They can be quickly implemented in the projects and they bring visible positive improvements in the projects. In consequence, they will generate acceptance for the project management initiative among project leaders. These first "short-term wins" are crucial for the further success of the whole project management improvement initiative. Short-term means here days or weeks, not months.

Project leaders in software-intensive automotive projects are more technical experts than project managers, with a strong orientation on delivering results and less experience in process management. In order to facilitate the project management process improvement, the work should concentrate on working out the project management work products. The work products are the tangible results of the project management process. Concentrating on the work products brings more focus, results in the tangible deliverables and drives the project management work into the right direction. And while working with the work products the people learn how the project management process works.

Some of the project management work products, which are worked out at the beginning of the project management improvement initiative include:

- Statement of Work
- Project Book
- Work Breakdown Structure (WBS)
- Project Management Plan (first draft)
- Project Report (simplified)
- Action List

Introducing these elements brings the first project management benefits into the project life. The role of the Project Book and Project Report are discussed with more details below.

Project Book. The experiences show that introducing the Project Book brings the project management structure in the early phase of the project life. Project Book is the central document for project agreements and starting point for all relevant project information.

The Project Book consists of the following elements:

- Project content (objectives, scope, assumptions & constraints, milestones)
- Project organization (project chart, infrastructure, meetings, tools)
- Roles and responsibilities
- Processes (selection of the processes relevant for the project)

The project leader creates or manages the development of a Project Book. The elements documented it the Project Book create the baseline for further work on the project. The component project is usually placed within the organizational structures, including system projects, product lines, competence centers, organization departments and multiple suppliers. Creating and clarifying elements of the Project Book helps to deal with all these relevant parties. One important issue is to describe the project roles and responsibilities. It helps the project leader to reach commitment on the project from project participants.

Project Report. When the project runs, then the Project Report is a valuable project management tool. Project reporting determines where is the project in terms of schedule, budget, functionality and quality. It is about looking at the decisions needed to be taken, problems or foreseen risks. The project leader creates the Project Report. The status of the project is a result of his professional judgment, with consultation with component-project supplier and other project team members. The Project Report is used to report all relevant aspects of the project to the relevant project stakeholders. It can also be used to escalate the issues, which cannot be solved within the project. Project reporting helps to take decision on the future of the project. It is important to integrate the Project Report in the project lifecycle. The Project Report should be prepared in regular time intervals, for example as a part of the project meeting.

Typical content of Project Report includes:

- Overall project status (e.g.: traffic light with reasoning)
- TOP Topics: Highlights, Decisions, Milestones, Defects, Risks, Non-technical Problems, Next Steps
- Project progress measurements (in more advanced status reporting)

The Project Book and Project Report are discussed here in detail, due to the fact, that they have proven the high usability during the work within the component projects. Other project management work products are also inevitable. Implementing the proper project management you should not forget a careful preparation of the project work breakdown structure and project management plan. You cannot control your project without having a proper plan.

Piloting and Rollout advanced project management practices. In the second phase of the Implementation level more advanced project management practices are introduced. It is about further refining a basic project management practices. Measurements are introduced and risk management process is implemented.

Measurements. Measurements provide an added value for monitoring and control of the project progress. They are collected and analyzed as a part of the project status reporting. They are visually presented in the cockpit chart. The project metrics are derived from the project objectives. The experience shows that usually the following set of measurements will fulfill the project management progress monitoring requirements:

- Milestone Trend Analysis
- Effort / Rework
- Activities / Work Packages
- Functionality / Work Products

- Defects / Problems
- Risks

The measurement process is also introduced. It describes how to define, describe, collect, analyze and report the measurement data. The measurement process provides guidance on how measurement activities should be performed in the project. It provides methods and tools for defining measurement goals, creating operational measurement definitions, and presenting and analyzing the measurement data.

Risk Management. Risk management process describes how to perform project risk management in the structured, organized way. It is about introducing the systematic approach in managing component project risks. It also refers to extending the viewpoint of the technical oriented project leaders. Usually component project leaders understand risk management as the technical analysis of the potential problems in the product. But risk management involves also project or process aspects. Project risks are for example schedule, people resources, budget, interfaces, project stakeholders or politics. Process risks are for example development processes, management processes, standards, policies, quality or communication. Risk management introduces a change in the way of thinking of the project leaders - from the technical product centered to the project, product and process centered. It also introduces another shift in the projects – from the problem solving modus to proactive way of working. Risk Management enables to identify some potential problems before they occur. It is about thinking what can go wrong, and acting against it. Risk management address issues that can endanger the achievement of project objectives (time, scope, budget, quality). Risk management enriches and complements very well with the project management process.

The goal of the rollout phase of the Implementation level is to reach with the improved project management practices all projects within the organization. While implementing the PM-practices, the first experience has been collected. The results and experience achieved by the projects in the Implementing level should be stored and prepared for the further use. It is the role of the organization to make sure that the improved project management will stay and continually improve. This is a topic of Level 3 – Sustaining the project management process improvement.

2.3 Level 3 – Sustaining

The Sustaining level is to ensure that the project management is anchored in the organization. It is about improving the project management practice in the organization. It also means managing the organization's projects based on facts - using the measurement data.

Quantitatively managing projects. The measurements are collected in the projects and used to control the projects at the organizational level. The data are aggregated according to prior defined reporting structures. For example, the measurement data can be aggregated within the department or product line, according to the measurement customer needs and objectives. The measurements are used to take decisions not only at the component project level, but also at the organizational level. The organization is then managing by facts.

Having the measurement data collected, more advanced analyses of the data are performed. They are performed for the identified, selected important project issues. To perform data analyses more advanced quality management tools are used: e.g.: cause-and-effect diagram, Pareto chart, scatter diagram or control charts.

Continuously improving project management. Continuously improving project management means to collect experiences from the implementation of project management process elements in the projects. It is about providing the organizational structures that support and encourage project management process improvement. At this point the role of Project Management Office is important. The PMO drives the project management knowledge management. As a central organizational structure, PMO facilitates further definition, development and maintenance of project management processes and standards. For more information on the PMO role in Sustaining the project management see also Figure 2.

Project management improvement proposals are continuously collected, analyzed and implemented. At the end of projects Lessons Learned workshops are performed with key project participants. All the relevant project management related information is stored in the project management knowledge repository. This information is analyzed, categorized and prepared for the future use. All future projects can use the experience from the past similar projects.

The organization provides the mature, standardized, organization-wide description of the project management process. All projects can use this universal description. The process description must be tuned to the special needs of different departments, or different project arts. The organization provides Project Management Tailoring Guidelines. The Tailoring Guidelines describe, how the project management will be used in the different organizational settings. It describes, what is required in the project management process implementation, and what can be skipped or modified depending on the environment of the project.

3 Summary

Improving project management is about Establishing, Implementing and Sustaining the project management practice in the organization, as summarized in Figure 4.

The article presents an evolutionary approach to project management process improvement, based on the experience with introducing the project management within the software-intensive automotive systems. It systematizes the experience and defines the Project Management Process Improvement Model (PM-PIM). Implementing improvement in project management involves the continuous cooperation between the organization and component projects. The organization creates the required environment, provides support and facilitates the continuous improvement of project management process. The role of the projects is to implement and verify in practice the project management process improvements.

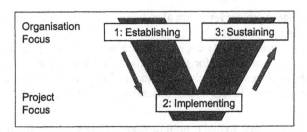

Fig 4. Project Management Process Improvement Model summary

And at the end, it is about successful organizations, happy people and projects being "on time", "in budget" and "in quality".

References

1. A Guide to the Project Management Body of Knowledge, Third Edition, (PMBOK Guide), Project Management Institute, Newton Square, Pennsylvania, USA, 2004
2. Capability Maturity Model® Integration (CMMI^SM), Version 1.1, CMMI Product Team, March 2002 (http://www.sei.cmu.edu/cmmi)
3. CMMI - Guidelines for Process Integration and Product Improvement, Mary Beth Chrissis, Mike Konrad, Sandy Shrum, Addison-Wesley, 2003
4. ISO/IEC 15504 (SPICE) Standard, 2006
5. Automotive SPICE, Process Assessment and Reference Model, Automotive SIG, 2005
6. Project Management, Harold Kerzner, John Wiley & Sons, 2003
7. The Fast Forward MBA in Project Management, Eric Verzuh, John Wiley & Sons, 1999
8. Basiswissen, Software-Projektmanagement, Hindel, Hörmann, Müller, Schmied, dpunkt.verlag, 2004

Improved Bayesian Networks
for Software Project Risk Assessment
Using Dynamic Discretisation

Norman Fenton[1], Łukasz Radliński[2], Martin Neil[3]

[1,3] Queen Mary, University of London, UK
norman@dcs.qmul.ac.uk
[2] Queen Mary, University of London, UK
and Institute of Information Technology in Management, University of Szczecin, Poland
lukrad@dcs.qmul.ac.uk

Abstract. It is possible to build useful models for software project risk assessment based on Bayesian networks. A number of such models have been published and used and they provide valuable predictions for decision-makers. However, the accuracy of the published models is limited due to the fact that they are based on crudely discretised numeric nodes. In traditional Bayesian network tools such discretisation was inevitable; modelers had to decide in advance how to split a numeric range into appropriate intervals taking account of the trade-off between model efficiency and accuracy. However, recent a recent breakthrough algorithm now makes dynamic discretisation practical. We apply this algorithm to existing software project risk models. We compare the accuracy of predictions and calculation time for models with and without dynamic discretisation nodes.

1 Introduction

Between 2001 and 2004 the collaborative EC Project MODIST developed a software defect prediction model [4] using Bayesian Networks (BNs). A BN is a causal model normally displayed as a graph. The nodes of the graph represent uncertain variables and the arcs represent the causal/relevance relationships between the variables. There is a probability table for each node, specifying how the probability of each state of the variable depends on the states of its parents. The MODIST model (used by organisations such as Philips, QinetiQ and Israel Aircraft Industries) provided accurate predictions for the class of projects within the scope of the study. However, the extendibility of the model was constrained by a fundamental limitation of BN modelling technology, namely that every continuous variable had to be approximated by a set of discretised intervals (defined in advance). Since the MODIST project has been completed we have addressed the problem of modelling continuous nodes in BNs. A recent breakthrough algorithm (implemented in the AgenaRisk software toolset) now enables us to define continuous nodes without any restrictions on discretisation. The necessary discretisation is hidden from the user and calculated dynamically with great accuracy. In this paper we describe our work to rebuild the defect prediction model

Please use the following format when citing this chapter:

Fenton, N., Radliński, Ł., Neil, M., 2006, in IFIP International Federation for Information Processing, Volume 227, Software Engineering Techniques: Design for Quality, ed. K. Sacha, (Boston: Springer), pp. 139–148.

using this approach to dynamic discretisation. In Section 2 we provide an overview of the MODIST model and explain the limitations due to static discretisation. In Section 3 we provide an overview of the dynamic discretisation approach and then apply it to construct a revised MODIST model in Section 4. We present a comparison of the results in Section 5.

2 Existing models for software project risk assessment

The defect prediction model developed in MODIST is shown in schematic form in Figure 1.

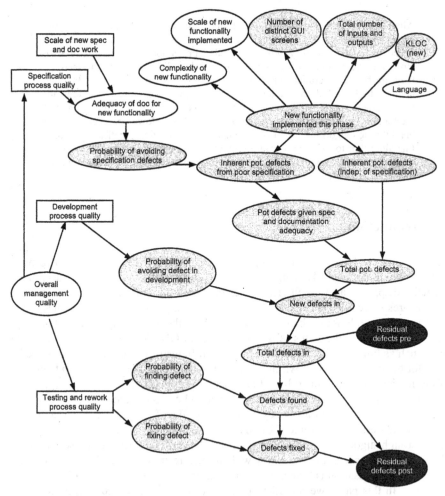

Fig. 1. Schematic view of defect prediction model; adopted from [2, 4]

Its main objective is prediction of various types of defects inserted or removed during various software development activities. All ellipses on this figure indicate a node of a Bayesian Net. Rectangles indicate subnets containing several additional nodes, which do not need to be shown here (since they are not important in this context and would cause unnecessary complexity).

This model can be used to predict defects in either of the following software development scenarios:

1. Adding new functionality to existing code and/or documentation
2. Creating new software from scratch (when no previous code and/or documentation exists).

The model in Figure 1 represents a single phase of software development that is made up of one or more of the following activities:

- specification/documentation,
- development (coding),
- testing and rework.

Such single phase models can be linked together to form a chain of phases which indicate major increments (milestone) in the whole project. This is the reason why in MODIST this model is called "phase-based defect prediction model". In this way we can model any software development lifecycle. More on modelling various lifecycles can be found in [3].

In common with many BN models this model contains a mixture of nodes that are qualitative (and are measured on a ranked scale) such as "Overall management quality" and nodes that are numeric, such as defects found and KLOC. Because generally BNs require numeric nodes to be discretised even if they represent continuous variables there is an inevitable problem of inaccuracy because a set of fixed intervals has to be defined in advance. To improve accuracy in predictions we have to split the whole range of possible values for a particular node into a larger number of intervals. The more intervals we have, the longer the calculation time – (since this includes generating the node probability table (NPT) from an expression in many cases). It is not simply a question of getting the right 'trade-off' because in many cases we need to assume an infinite scale for which, of course, there can never be a satisfactory discretisation.

One proposed solution to the problem has been to minimize the number of intervals by more heavily discretising in areas of expected higher probability, using wider intervals in other cases. This approach fails in a situation when we do not know in advance which values are more likely to occur. Such a situation is inevitable if we seek to use the models for projects beyond their original scope.

Table 1 illustrates node states in the MODIST model for two nodes describing size of the new software: "New Functionality" and "KLOC". Notice that there are several intervals where the ending value is around 50% or more higher than the starting value. The model cannot differentiate if we enter as an observation a starting, ending value or any other value between them. They are all treated as the same observation – middle of the interval.

There were two main reasons for defining such node states:

1. Availability of empirical data that the model was later validated against
2. Calculation time which was acceptable for the number of states.

The node "KLOC" contains intervals with high differences between starting and ending values. But those high differences are for values below 15 KLOC and over 200 KLOC (it was assumed that the KLOC in a single phase would never outside these boundaries). Hence, we can expect that predictions for software size between 15 and 200 KLOC will be more accurate than outside this range.

Table 1. Node for "New Functionality" and "KLOC"

New Functionality				KLOC (new)			
Start	End	Interval Size	Percentage Difference Between Starting and Ending Values	Start	End	Interval Size	Percentage Difference Between Starting and Ending Values
0	24	25	-	0	0,5	0,5	-
25	49	25	**100,0%**	0,5	1	0,5	**100,0%**
50	74	25	**50,0%**	1	2	1	**100,0%**
75	99	25	33,3%	2	5	3	**150,0%**
100	124	25	25,0%	5	10	5	**100,0%**
125	149	25	20,0%	10	15	5	**50,0%**
150	199	50	33,3%	15	20	5	33,3%
200	298	99	**49,5%**	20	25	5	25,0%
299	399	101	33,8%	25	30	5	20,0%
400	499	100	25,0%	30	40	10	33,3%
500	749	250	**50,0%**	40	50	10	25,0%
750	999	250	33,3%	50	60	10	20,0%
1000	1499	500	**50,0%**	60	80	20	33,3%
1500	1999	500	33,3%	80	100	20	25,0%
2000	2999	1000	**50,0%**	100	125	25	25,0%
3000	4999	2000	**66,7%**	125	150	25	20,0%
5000	7999	3000	**60,0%**	150	175	25	16,7%
8000	12000	4001	**50,0%**	175	200	25	14,3%
12001	15999	3999	33,3%	200	300	100	**50,0%**
16000	19999	4000	25,0%	300	500	200	**66,7%**
20000	30000	10001	**50,0%**	500	10000	9500	**1900,0%**

For the "new functionality" node we cannot find any range of intervals with relatively low differences between lower and upper bound in an interval. This means that we will have relatively inaccurate predictions for most software size expressed in function points.

The defect prediction model contains several variables for predicting different types of defects. Most of them have similar states in terms both the number of states and their ranges. Table 2 illustrates intervals for one of them: "defects found".

Table 2. Node states for "defects found"

Defects found				Defects found (cont.)			
Start	End	Interval Size	Percentage Difference Between Starting and Ending Values	Start	End	Interval Size	Percentage Difference Between Starting and Ending Values
1	4	4	**400,0%**	1500	2000	501	33,4%
5	19	15	**300,0%**	2001	3000	1000	**50,0%**
20	39	20	**100,0%**	3001	4000	1000	33,3%
40	59	20	**50,0%**	4001	5000	1000	25,0%
60	79	20	33,3%	5001	6000	1000	20,0%
80	99	20	25,0%	6001	7000	1000	16,7%
100	124	25	25,0%	7001	8000	1000	14,3%
125	149	25	20,0%	8001	9000	1000	12,5%
150	174	25	16,7%	9001	10000	1000	11,1%
175	199	25	14,3%	10001	11000	1000	10,0%
200	249	50	25,0%	11001	12000	1000	9,1%
250	299	50	20,0%	12001	13000	1000	8,3%
300	349	50	16,7%	13001	14000	1000	7,7%
350	399	50	14,3%	14001	15000	1000	7,1%
400	449	50	12,5%	15001	16000	1000	6,7%
450	499	50	11,1%	16001	17000	1000	6,2%
500	749	250	**50,0%**	17001	18000	1000	5,9%
750	999	250	33,3%	18001	19000	1000	5,6%
1000	1499	500	**50,0%**	19001	20000	1000	5,3%

3 Dynamic discretisation algorithm

The dynamic discretisation algorithm [5, 7] was developed as a way to solve the problems discussed in the previous section. The general outline of it is as follows:

1. Calculate the current marginal probability distribution for a node given its current discretisation.
2. Split that discrete state with the highest entropy error into two equally sized states.
3. Repeat steps 1 and 2 until converged or error level is acceptable.
4. Repeat steps 1, 2 and 3 for all nodes in the BN.

The algorithm has now been implemented in the AgenaRisk toolset [1]. Using this toolset we can simply set a numeric node as a simulation node without having to worry about defining intervals (it is sufficient to define a single interval [x, y] for any variable that is bounded below by x and above by y, while for infinite bounds we only need introduce one extra interval).

In the AgenaRisk tool we can specify the following simulation parameters:

- maximum number of iterations – this value defines how many iterations will be performed at maximum during calculation; it directly influences the number of intervals that will be created by the algorithm and thus calculation time,
- simulation convergence – the difference between the entropy error value between subsequent iterations; the lower convergence we set, the more accurate results we will have at the cost of computation time,
- sample size for ranked nodes – the higher value here reduces probabilities in tails for ranked node distributions at the cost of longer NPT generation process [1].

"Simulation convergence" can be set both as global parameter for all simulation nodes in the model or individually for selected nodes. In the second case the value of the parameter for a selected node overrides the global value for the whole model. If it is not set for individual nodes the global value is taken for calculation.

Currently there is no possibility to set the "maximum number of iterations" for a particular node. All nodes in a model use the global setting. This causes the same number of ranges to be generated by the dynamic discretisation algorithm for all simulation nodes in most of the cases. We cannot expect more intervals generated for selected nodes resulting in more accurate prediction there.

4 Revised software project risk models

Table 3 illustrates differences between node types for numeric nodes in the original and revised models.

We do not present number of states for numeric nodes in the revised model because they are not fixed. They rather depend on simulation parameters which are set by users.

In our model all numeric nodes are bound (do not have negative or positive infinity), so we set a single interval for those nodes.

Table 3. Numeric node types in original and revised models

Node	Original model			Revised model	
	Type of Interval	Simulation	Number of states	Type of Interval	Simulation
Prob avoiding spec defects	Continuous	No	7	Continuous	Yes
KLOC (new)	Continuous	No	21	Continuous	Yes
Total number of inputs and outputs	Integer	No	5	Integer	Yes
Number of distinct GUI screens	Integer	No	5	Integer	Yes
New functionality imple-mented this phase	Integer	No	21	Continuous	Yes
Inherent potential defects from poor spec	Integer	No	25	Integer	Yes
Inherent pot defects (indep. of spec)	Integer	No	25	Integer	Yes
Pot defects given spec and documentation adequacy	Integer	No	26	Integer	Yes
Total pot defects	Integer	No	26	Integer	Yes
New defects in	Integer	No	24	Integer	Yes
Total defects in	Integer	No	38	Integer	Yes
Defects found	Integer	No	38	Integer	Yes
Defects fixed	Integer	No	39	Integer	Yes
Residual defects pre	Integer	No	38	Integer	Yes
Residual defects post	Integer	No	38	Integer	Yes
Prob of avoiding defect in dev	Continuous	No	5	Continuous	Yes
Prob of finding defect	Continuous	No	5	Continuous	Yes
Prob of fixing defect	Continuous	No	5	Continuous	Yes

5 Comparison of results

All calculations have been performed on a computer with Pentium M 1.8 GHz Proc-essor and 1 GB RAM under MS Windows XP Professional using AgenaRisk ver. 4.0.4. We ran calculations for the revised model using two values of parameter "maximum number of iterations": 10 and 25. We compared achieved results with the results achieved with the original model.

We observed very significant changes in predicted values for the revised and origi-nal model. Those differences varied among nodes and scenarios. Most of the pre-dicted means and medians were significantly lower in the revised model than in the original (the range of those differences was from -3% to -80%). This result fixed a consistent bias that we found empirically when we ran the models outside the scope of the MODIST project. Specifically, what was happening was that previously, outside the original scope, we were finding some probability mass in the end intervals. For example, an end interval like [10,000-infinity] might have a small probability mass, which without dynamic discretisation, will bias the central tendency statistics like the mean upwards. Only in a few cases did we observe an increase in predicted values. In all of them the differences were small – the highest was around 40%, but most of them did not reach 10%.

We could also observe a decrease in standard deviation for predicted distributions (from -8% to -80%). Partly this is explained by the model no longer suffering from the 'end interval' problem that also skewed the measures of central tendency However, another reason is that dynamic discretisation fixes the problem whereby nodes that are defined by simple arithmetic functions had unnecessary variability introduced. For example, nodes like 'total potential defects', 'total defect in', 'residual defects post' no longer suffer from inaccuracies due entirely to discretisation errors affecting addition/subtraction.

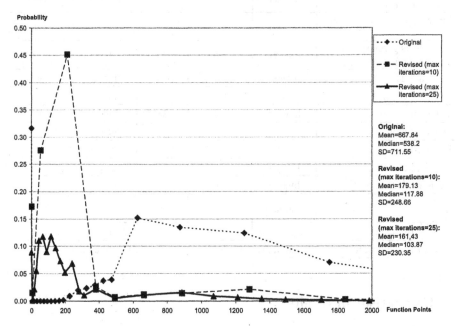

Fig. 2. Comparison of probability distributions for "residual defects post" for original and revised models for selected scenario

The dynamic discretisation algorithm creates node states in such way as to have narrow intervals within the area of highest probabilities and wide intervals where the probabilities are low (Fig. 2). This ensures greater accuracy for predicted values.

The number of intervals created for simulation nodes depends mainly on the parameter "maximum number of iterations". Figure 2 illustrates this. We can observe that in the areas of higher probability more intervals have been created.

Node states are fixed for the nodes not marked as simulation nodes. They do not change according to predicted values for those nodes.

We can observe that predicted values for the node "residual defects post" decreased significantly using the model with simulation nodes compared to the original. This occurred for both tested values of "maximum number of iterations". Predicted values for this node in both cases in the revised model were very similar (Fig. 2). Our results show this was also true in other scenarios and for other nodes.

Table 4. Comparison of calculation times for selected scenarios in original and revised model

Model	Time (in minutes)		Percentage difference in calculation times (compared to original model)	
	Average	Shortest	Average	Shortest
Original	0:13.1	0:11.1	-	-
Revised (Maximum number of iterations = 10)	0:18.7	0:15.7	42.8%	41.4%
Revised (Maximum number of iterations = 25)	2:03.1	1:34.8	839.0%	754.5%

We can observe the great difference between different settings of "maximum number of iterations" in calculation times (Table 4). When we compared calculation times for the revised model setting "maximum number of iterations" to 10 with the original model, we could observe that they increased by just over 40%. Although it was a significant increase in many cases it would make no real difference for end user.

However, calculation times increased very significantly when we set this parameter to 25 – around 8 times longer than in the original model. In this case we get only slightly more accurate predictions, so we must decide if much longer calculations can be compensated by only slightly higher precision.

The latest version of AgenaRisk (which we received just before finishing this research) contains optimizations to the algorithm which result in the times presented in Table 4 being generally halved. However, we cannot present precise information about as we were unable to perform extensive testing of the new algorithm.

6   Summary and future work

Results of our research have led us to the following conclusions:

1. Providing that we set a suitable value for the parameter "maximum number of iterations" the dynamic discretisation algorithm ensures greater accuracy of predicted values for simulation nodes than for nodes with fixed states.
2. Changing numeric node types to simulation nodes caused significant decrease in predicted "number of defects" and standard deviation (in several nodes). This re-

sult fixed a consistent (pessimistic) bias we had found empirically in projects outside the scope of MODIST.

3. Applying the dynamic discretisation algorithm does not force model builders to define node states at the time of creation of the model. This is a very useful feature especially in those cases when we do not know in advance in which ranges we should expect higher probabilities.

4. We can mix simulation and traditional nodes in a single model. We can define fixed node states for some of the nodes while setting others as simulation.

5. The cost of increased accuracy and model building simplicity that comes with dynamic discretisation is increased calculation timebut these increases are insignificant for values which still provide significant increases in accuracy..

Applying dynamic discretisation to the defect prediction model was one of a number of improvements we plan for the MODIST models. The next step will be to build an integrated model from the existing two developed in the MODIST project:

– defect prediction model,
– project level model (that contains, for example, resource information)

We also plan to apply dynamic discretisation to this integrated model and to extend it by incorporating other factors influencing the software development process.

References

1. Agena, AgenaRisk User Manual, 2005
2. Agena, Software Project Risk Models Manual, Ver. 01.00, 2004
3. Fenton N., Neil M., Marsh W., Hearty P., Krause P., Mishra R. Predicting Software Defects in Varying Development Lifecycles using Bayesian Nets, to appear Information and Software Technology, 2006
4. MODIST BN models, http://www.modist.org.uk/docs/modist_bn_models.pdf
5. Neil M., Tailor M., Marquez D., Bayesian statistical inference using dynamic discretisation, RADAR Technical Report, 2005
6. Neil M., Tailor M., Marquez D., Fenton N., Hearty P., Modelling Dependable Systems using Hybrid Bayesian Networks, Proc. of First International Conference on Availability, Reliability and Security (ARES 2006), 20-22 April 2006, Vienna, Austria
7. Neil M., Tailor M., Marquez D., Inference in Hybrid Bayesian Networks using dynamic discretisation, RADAR Technical Report, 2005

Software Risk Management: a Process Model and a Tool

Tereza G. Kirner[1], Lourdes E. Gonçalves[1]

[1]Graduate Program in Computer Science
Methodist University of Piracicaba – SP, Brasil
tgkirner@unimep.br; lgoncalves@unasp.edu.br

Abstract. This paper is concerned with the risks associated with the software development process. A model (*GRisk-Model*) is proposed for the management of such risks and a software tool (*GRisk-Tool*), developed to support the model, is described. Both the method and the tool were created with the participation of senior managers and software engineers of software factories. The model and the tool serve as effective instruments for achieving the continuous improvement of software processes and products.

1 Introduction

Several approaches of software risk management have been proposed and used since Boehm [1], [2] and Charette [4], [5] introduced the topic and its importance in the software engineering context. However, despite of several studies and experiences published about risk management, the software industry, in a general way, does not seem to follow a model to analyze and control the risks through the development of their products.

This article comprises two objectives. The first one is to present a model of risk management process (*GRisk-Model*), that covers all the stages of the software development process. The second is to present a tool (*GRisk-Tool*) that supports this model. The *GRisk-Model* was proposed with basis on the literature and from the experience of managers and senior software engineers of Brazilian software factories. The *GRisk-Tool* implements the proposed risk management model and also was evaluated by professionals, with respect to its functional aspects and obtained benefits.

Section 2 points out the theoretical basis that has supported the proposal of the model and the construction of the tool. Section 3 details the *GRisk-Model* and section 4 presents the *GRisk-Tool*. Section 5 presents the conclusions, stressing the potentialities, limitations and future directions of the work.

2 Related Work

Risk has to do with any variable that can lead to the failure of the project. Generally, risk can include problems related to deadlines, requirements, budget and staff [9].

Please use the following format when citing this chapter:

Kirner, T.G., Conçalves, L.E., 2006, in IFIP International Federation for Information Processing, Volume 227, Software Engineering Techniques: Design for Quality, ed. K. Sacha, (Boston: Springer), pp. 149–154.

According to Pressman [10], there is a considerable debate regarding the accurate definition of software risk, but there is a consensus that risk always involves two characteristics: (a) Uncertainty, which means that an event that characterizes the risk can either happen or not, that is, there is not 100% of probability of the risk to occur. (b) Loss, which means that, if the risk becomes a reality, undesirable consequences will occur involving damages to the product in question.

Risk management comprises a systematic approach of evaluating the risks related to the software development process. A typical risk management model involves the identification and analysis of the potential risks of a project and, moreover, the adoption of monitoring strategies for reducing these risks.

One of the precursors of the area of risk management is Barry Boehm who, in 1988, proposed the Spiral Model that incorporates successive analyses of risks along the software development stages [1]. Later, this same author defined the risk management as a process composed of two phases: (a) Risk evaluation, that includes the identification of the risk, the analysis of the risk, and the prioritization of the risk. (b) Control of the risk, that includes a plan of risk management, the resolution of risks, and the monitoring of the risks [3]. Another well known model of risk management is the RISKIT [11], that incorporates a similar process to that proposed by Boehm [3], including the following stages: (a) definition of a risk management program; (b) review of the objectives of the project; (c) identification of the risks; (d) analysis of the risk; (e) planning of the risk control; (f) control over the risks; (g) monitoring of the risks.

The benefits propitiated by the tools that assist in the software development, as CASE tools, prototyping tools, etc., are unquestionable. Among these tools destined to support the risk management, discussed in the literature, ARMOR [8] and SERIM [7] tools are distinguished.

ARMOR (Analyzer for Reducing Module Operational Risk) aims to detect and evaluate software risks, based, mainly, on statistical models. The execution of the tool includes a series of functions, which make possible to: access the data that are pertinent to the characteristics of software; use and evaluate metrics applied to the software product; evaluate risks of performance; identify, validate, calculate and present the risks related to each software module, including indication of actions for the risk reduction. SERIM (Software Engineering of Risk Management) supports the identification of a reliable process for software development, based on the identification of the potential risks and the stages and activities of the project that need a more accurate attention. After identifying the risks, the tool assists the elaboration of plans for minimizing the latent risks, including since the identification of risks related to the system implementation until the involved costs and the defined deadlines.

3 Risk Management Model

The definition of the *GRisk-Model* counted on the participation of a team of professionals composed of 1 commercial manager, 1 manager of software factory, 3 coordinators of software factories, and 3 senior system analysts. For the stages, phases and activities of the software development, descriptions have been prepared and indicated the classes and the risks associated to those. Periodically, meetings were held in which the group came up with an evaluation of the classes and the risks indicated for each phase and activity. At the end of the work, forms for analysis of the proposed structure were filled up through which the professionals of the work team informed their evaluation and contribution to the model.

Figure 1 illustrates the *G-Risk Model* phases, which occur in parallel to the software life cycle. In the model, the phases are subdivided in activities and both are defined. For each set of phase/activity, the risks, divided in their respective classses, are related.

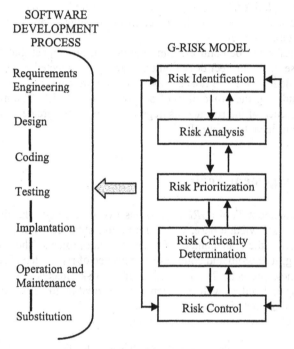

Fig. 1. Overview of the *GRisk-Model*

The classes of risk adopted in the model include:

- Relationship Risks (RR). They are risks that involve the interactions between developers and users, and between different types of users, concerning the definition of system functionality.
- Organizational Risks (OR). They are risks that involve organizational changes that affect the system under development as, for example, organization charts alterations, changes in the user's area, dismissal of professionals responsible for the system, etc.
- Management Risks (MR). They are risks that involve the management of the system development, such as: definition of development methodologies, definition of professionals who will compose the work team; definition of the necessary development environment; definition of resources for the development; etc.

- Financial Risks (FR). They are risks that cause financial expenses beyond the planned one, including high values of proposals, cost of equipments, etc.
- Technical Risks (TR). It is a broad class of risks, which can be caused by the professionals' lack of experience, use of inadequate methodologies and techniques, etc.
- Legal Risks (LR). They are risks related to laws, such as fiscal requirements, licenses for software, changes of tax laws during or after the system development, etc.

As part of the *GRisk-Model*, a list of probable risks, for each phase of the software development was defined [6]. These risks were identified with basis on bibliographical studies and also considering the experience and suggestions of the professional team who participated in the work.

So that the risks can be controlled and monitored, the impact that these risks will be able to cause in the project development and to the expected product must be determined. The degree of risk impact, may it be high, medium or low, will have to be analyzed, considering the probability of occurrence of the risk. The higher the probability of occurrence of the risk and its degree of impact, the greater is the control and monitoring it will have to receive [3].

4 Risk Management Tool

The Risk Management Tool (*GRisk-Tool*) has two objectives. The first objective is the creation of a knowledge base, with information obtained from the *GRisk-Model*, that will be used in the management of risks of future projects. The second objective is the compiling, follow-up and control of occurrence of risks, identified along the development of new projects. The compiling of the risks makes possible to keep the knowledge base updated, as well as to generate information to define metrics concerning to significant impacts for the identified risks.

Figure 2 gives an overview of the tool, which includes the following modules:

- Creation of knowledge base. In this module, the information, already classified in phases and activities of the software development, is loaded in the files.
- Control of risk management. In this module, the information of occurrences of risk identified in the software development process is registered.
- Monitoring and control of risks. This module makes available to the user the register of monitoring carried through a determined risk occurrence.
- Maintenance of knowledge base. In this module, the knowledge base is updated through the registering of risk occurrences.
- Reports and consultations. This module makes available to the user a series of reports and consultations related to the knowledge base contents, risk management, and occurrences about the risk monitoring.

The *GRisk-Tool* was evaluated by six software engineering professionals, including 1 manager of software factory, 3 project managers and 2 senior system analysts. Two of them had participated of the GRisk-Model definition and the other ones did not know the model and the tool. These professionals were invited to participate of the evaluation, in function of their experience on software project management, specifically on risk management.

The tool works on personal computer environment, under Windows operational system (see [6], for a complete description of implementation issues). It was set free for use by the software development team of the software factories that participated of its development. It is being used together with the software development methodology, aiming at the optimization of the software production, in terms of deadlines, costs, and quality.

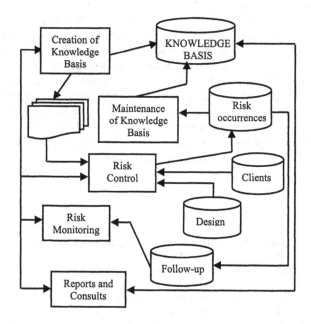

Fig. 2. Overview of the GRisk-Tool

5 Conclusion

This article presented a process model of risk management (*GRisk-Model*) and a tool (*GRisk-Tool*). The *GRisk-Model* was developed with basis on the literature, also getting the experience and effective participation of directors, managers and senior software engineers of Brazilian software factories. The *GRisk-Tool* implements the risk management model and the professional team involved in the definition of this model also evaluated it.

The *GRisk-Model* is characterized by incorporating a knowledge base concerning the software development process. The *GRisk-Tool* supports this model, as well as it offers conditions so that the knowledge base created can be continuously updated and extended with information of new risks related to projects monitored by the tool.

A very important result from the use of the *GRisk-Tool* is to detect potential problems in the software development phases, as well as the impacts and the costs related to such problems. It is possible to get the mapping of these problems from a script of actions to be taken, containing a set of information on different classes of risks related to all stages and activities of the software development, as is shown in the *GRisk-Model*.

As the impact of the risks is determined for each project, it is expected that, with the descriptions included in the tool, metrics can be obtained for determining standards to be applied to the risk impacts. Such metrics and standards have been gradually incorporated in the model and the tool.

It is also expected that the *GRisk-Tool* work as an additional mechanism to assist the software development in the company. The tool offers to the risk management a list of actions to be taken in all stages of software development, thus preventing that the responsible professionals need more accurate knowledge on the subject. With the dynamic updating of the knowledge base, this characteristic becomes an essential factor for the risk management and the success of the project being developed.

Now, some experiments are being conducted, focusing on the use of the model and of tool, in the development of new software projects, in the software factories. It is expected these experiments will provide important information for the improvement and extension of the *GRisk-Model* and the *GRisk-Tool*.

References

1. Boehm, B.W. "A Spiral Model of Software Development and Enhancement", *IEEE Computer*, Volume 21, Number 5, May 1988, pp. 61-72.
2. Boehm, B.W. *Tutorial: Software Risk Management*, IEEE Computer Society Press, New York, 1989.
3. Boehm, B.W. "Software Risk Management: Principles and Practices", *IEEE Software*, Volume 8, Number 1, January 1991, pp. 32-41.
4. Charette, R.N. *Software Engineering Risk Analysis and Management*, McGraw-Hill New York, 1989.
5. Charette, R.N. "Large-Scale Project Management is Risk Management", *IEEE Software*, Volume 13, Number 4, July 1996, pp. 110-117.
6. Gonçalves, E.L. *Risk Management in the Software Development Process*, Master Dissertation, Methodist University of Piracicaba, 2006 (in Portuguese).
7. Karolak, D.W. *Software Engineering Risk Management*, Wiley-IEEE Computer Society Press, Los Alamitos, CA, 2002.
8. Lyu, M.R, Yu, J.S, Keromidas, E., Dalal, S. "ARMOR: Analyser for Reducing Module Operational Risk", *25th Symposium on Fault-Tolerant Computing*, IEEE Computer Society Press, Los Alamitos, CA, 1995, pp. 137-142.
9. Padayachee, K. "An Interpretative Study of Software Risk Management Perspectives", SAICSIT 2002, South Africa, 2002, pp. 118-127.
10. Pressman, R.S. *Software Engineering – A Practitioner's Approach*, 4th edition, McGraw-Hill, New York, 1997.

An Approach to Software Quality Specification and Evaluation (SPoQE)[*]

Iwona Dubielewicz[1], Bogumiła Hnatkowska[1], Zbigniew Huzar[1],
Lech Tuzinkiewicz[1]

[1]Institute of Applied Informatics, Wrocław University of Technology,
Wybrzeże Wyspiańskiego 27, 50-370 Wrocław, Poland
{Iwona.Dubielewicz, Bogumila.Hnatkowska, Zbigniew.Huzar,
Lech.Tuzinkiewicz}@pwr.wroc.pl

Abstract. The paper discusses how to carry evaluation of software product quality within software development process. The evaluation process bases on a quality model being an instance of a quality model. Quality model, elaborated basing on ISO quality standards, may be used both for specification of quality requirements and quality assessment. The evaluation process is presented in terms of activity diagrams. It is generic and may be concretized for two perspectives of software product quality, i.e. external, and internal quality. Simple example illustrates the proposed approach.

1 Introduction

Quality of a software product can be defined as a totality of characteristics that bear on its ability to satisfy stated and implied customer needs [5].

The meaning of the term "software product" is extended to include any artifact, which is the output of any process used to build the final software product. Examples of a product include, but are not limited to, an entire system requirements specification, a software requirements specification for a software component of a system, a design module, code, test documentation, or reports produced as a result of quality analysis tasks [10].

The aim of the paper is to elaborate a generic process of software product evaluation based on current ISO standards, relating to Software Quality Assurance (SQA). The process is independent from specific software development methodology, and shall ensure software product compliance with quality requirements, moreover with required level of this quality.

SQA processes provide assurance that software products and processes in the project life cycle conform to their specified requirements by planning, enacting, and performing a set of activities to provide adequate confidence that quality is being built into the software [10].

[*] The work was supported by polish Ministry of Science and Higher Education under the grant number 3 T11C 06430.

Please use the following format when citing this chapter:

Dubielewicz, I., Hnatkowska, B., Huzar, Z., Tuzinkiewicz, L., 2006, in IFIP International Federation for Information Processing, Volume 227, Software Engineering Techniques: Design for Quality, ed. K. Sacha, (Boston: Springer), pp. 155–166.

ISO standard [3] provides a new supporting process called *Product evaluation*. The process is defined in informal way. The paper formalizes *Product evaluation* process and presents it in the form of activity diagrams. The diagrams, expressed in SPEM notation [9], include roles of stakeholders of software process development, and artifacts related to SQA. Considered activities are based on ISO standard [4], while artifacts are instances of our Software Quality Model of Requirement, Evaluation and Assessment (SQMREA) [6]. The fact that ISO quality models are instances of SQMREA explains why we have called SQMREA in [6] to be a quality meta-model.

The paper is organized as follows. Section 2 gives an overview of software quality generic model. In Section 3 our formalization of evaluation process is given. Section 4, on the base of a simple example, explains how the evaluation process may be instantiated. Finally, Section 5 discusses presented proposals and compares them to current literature.

2 Generic model of software quality requirements evaluation and assessment

Our proposal of software quality generic model for requirement, evaluation, and assessment, called SQMREA, is shown in Figure 1. This is an extended version of the model, presented in [6]. The model is presented as UML class diagram with a set of OCL constraints (omitted in this paper).

The reason of SQMREA introduction is to enable evaluation and assessment of quality levels of intermediate artifacts produced during software development as models, specifications etc., and, finally, the resulting software product.

In general, according to ISO standards, quality assessment can be done from three perspectives: external, internal, and in use perspective. The last perspective relates not only to a software product itself but also to its operation in a specific environment and specific context of use. Therefore, our SQMREA model takes into account only the first two perspectives, which concern only a software product. The external perspective represents a viewpoint of a user, while the internal perspective represents a viewpoint of a software developer.

The choice of quality perspective plays the key role in model instantiation. Each perspective determines a quality model, i.e. the set of selected characteristics and relationships between them. Instances of the generic model embrace not only ISO quality models for a given perspective, but also other models that are different from ISO quality models, for example, dependability models based on IEC 300 series of standards [10]. In the sequel, for the sake of brevity, we confine our consideration to ISO quality models.

To do description of the SQMREA generic model more readable, we have grouped its elements into four packages that are presented in Figure 2.

Two central packages relate to elements of quality model, and software requirements respectively. The right side package relates to subjects of quality assessment, while the left side one defines how to do the assessment.

We start with description of the package *Elements of Quality Requirement Specification*, as comprehensive requirement specification is a starting point both to development process of a software product and to its quality requirement specification and evaluation. This specification is based on user *needs* that are informal by nature. The needs serve as the basis for the formulation of *requirements*. A requirement is defined as *a condition or feature required by user to solve a problem or to reach specific goal* [10]. The requirements should be expressed quantitatively through referring to values of software product *attributes*, i.e. *measurable physical or abstract properties of the product.*

Software Product, Artifact Specification, Need, and *Requirement* classes are abstractions concerning software quality requirements. Their instances are specific for a given software product. An instance of *Software Product* class can be associated with a set of instances of *Artifact Specification* class. In our considerations, we abstract from semantics of instances of *Artifact Specification*, and we concentrate only on associations between this class and other classes. The association to *Artifact Implementation* class reflects obvious relationship between specification and implementation – specification of an artifact may have many implementations. The association to *Requirement* class (a requirement may be decomposed into other requirements) reflects the fact that artifact implementations will be eventually evaluated in context of some requirements. The association to *Attribute* class points the attributes that are involved in artifact specification and should be also present in artifact implementation.

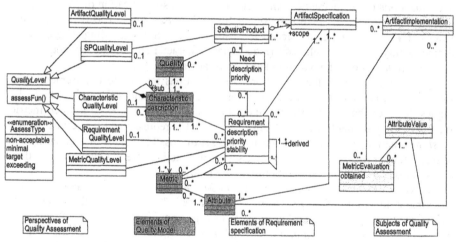

Fig. 1. SQMREA generic model

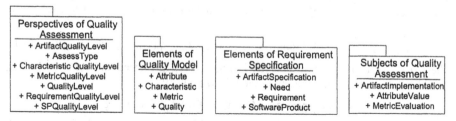

Fig. 2. Elements of main parts of SQMREA model

To do quality requirements measurable the classes of *Elements of Requirement Specification* package are associated with classes of the package *Elements of Quality Model*. The main elements of this package are: *Quality, Characteristic, Metric,* and *Attribute* classes. An instance of *Quality* class is a root of a hierarchy of characteristics and sub-characteristics, and represents a given quality perspective. Standard [1] defines the following characteristics for internal and external quality models: *functionality, reliability, usability, efficiency, maintainability* and *portability*. These characteristics may be subdivided into multiple levels of sub-characteristics. For example, according to this standard, there are the following sub-characteristics for functionality: *suitability, accuracy, interoperability, compliance* and *security*. For an agreed sub-characteristic a set of metrics as functions on attributes is given. Acceptable ranges of the metrics specify recommended values of attributes.

A requirement may be decomposed into other requirements. The leaves of the requirement's tree are associated with metrics by *Metric Quality Level* association class.

The elements of the left side package *Perspective of Quality Assessment* supplement the package *Elements of Requirement Specification* by delivering functions that assess quality levels for: (1) a requirement (*Requirement Quality Level*), (2) a characteristic (*Characteristic Quality Level*), (3) an artifact (*Artifact Quality Level*), and (4) a whole software product (*SP Quality Level*). The mentioned classes (in braces) are specializations of an abstract *Quality Level* class. Each specialization of *Quality Level* class should provide its own assessment function (*assessFun*). The functions yield values of *Assess Type*, i.e. non-acceptable, minimal, target or exceeding. These values define quality of a given element (requirement, characteristic, single artifact, and finally a software product, understood as a set of artifacts).

Assessment functions form a hierarchy of functions relating to requirements (the lowest level), sub-characteristics, characteristics, artifacts and software product (the highest level of the hierarchy). The elementary assessment relates to a given metric for a given requirement (*Metric Quality Level*), and is represented by a respective *assessFun* function. The function classifies the set of possible values of a given metric to one category of *Assess Type*. Other assessment functions are not elementary – they are composed of assessment functions that are at lower hierarchy level.

The values of the assessment function for *Metric Quality Level* are arguments for assessment functions of *Requirement Quality Level*. The values of the assessment functions for *Requirement Quality Level* are arguments for others assessment functions, i.e. *Characteristic Quality Level*, and *Artifact Quality Level*. Assessment of the whole software product (*SP Quality Level*) is done with regard to the results from artifact quality level assessments.

For example, assessment functions defined for *i*-level in hierarchy may take a form as below:

$$ass_{level(i)}(x_1, x_2, \ldots, x_n) = \min(ass_{level(i-1)}(x_1), ass_{level(i-1)}(x_2), \ldots, ass_{level(i-1)}(x_n)) \quad (3.1)$$

where $ass_{level(i-1)}(x_k) \in$ {Non-acceptable, Minimal, Target, Exceeding} for $k = 1, \ldots, n$, and the values are ordered linearly in the following way:

$$\text{Non-acceptable} < \text{Minimal} < \text{Target} < \text{Exceeding}$$

The composition may take different forms, for example, a given higher level assessment function may take a form of weighted sum of values that are results of lower level assessment functions.

The package *Subjects of Quality Assessment* contains the classes that represent instances of artifacts (*Artifact Implementation* class), values of their attributes (*Attribute Value* class), and metric evaluations (*Metric Evaluation* class), calculated based on attribute values.

3   Model of evaluation process

This section presents our formalization of product evaluation process, informally defined in ISO standard [4]. The formalization uses activity diagram for expressing artifacts flow among different roles engaged within the process. Artifacts used within the process are instances of our SQMREA model. Roles are selected from those, proposed in [11].

Model of software product evaluation process is presented in Figure 3.

As was mention in Section 2, the main elements of SQMREA model were divided into four packages. The names of packages are used on the activity diagram as the names of artifacts produced by different activities. This means that a given activity yields all elements from the package. To simplify the picture only the outputs for activities are presented. The output of a given activity is also an input for the following one.

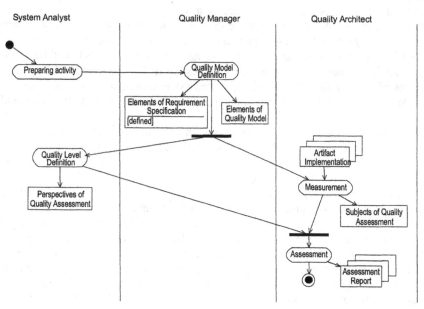

Fig. 3. Model of software product evaluation process

The process starts with *Preparing activity*. This activity can take one of two forms according to the quality perspective. In the case of external quality the activity is substituted by *Software Requirement Specification* activity, and in the case of internal quality – by *Internal Requirement Specification* activity, see Figure 4.

During *Software Requirement Specification* activity system analyst should, first of all, to determine the real purposes of the software. The purposes are expressed as needs, and they are represented by instances of *Need* class in the activity diagram. Needs are written informally, in natural language. Based on them system analyst identifies kinds of output artifacts, elicits quality requirements, and associates artifacts specifications with quality requirements.

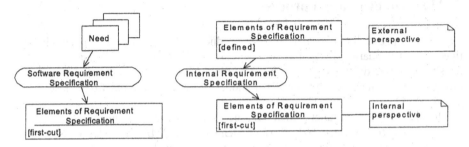

Fig. 4. Details for Preparing activity for external, and internal quality perspective

The requirements at that moment are described informally, what is marked by object-flow state called "first-cut". They take a form of system features. System feature is defined as a general system service that is associated with fulfillment of one or more needs [8]. ISO standard [4] introduces a term *general requirement* for system features description. An example feature for a weapon control system can be defined as: *in the case of attack two independent authorizations are needed* [8].

Based on general requirements system analyst decides what artifacts will be expected to represent a software product from interesting quality perspective (it proposes instances of *Artifact Specification* class). When external perspective is considered the example artifacts may be: executable components, user manual, installation manual, and so on.

Internal Requirement Specification aims with transforming external requirements into internal ones that are associated with internal artifacts. The example internal artifacts may be: software requirement specification, software architecture document, source code, and so on. Needs are omitted at this stage.

The most difficult is *Quality Model Definition* activity as it is responsible for transformation of informally defined, general requirements into formally defined requirements. The main aim of this activity is to elaborate a quality model, expressed in terms of characteristics, metrics, and attributes. These elements must be suitable for interested quality perspective. Their association with not empty set of metrics formally defines the leaves of requirement tree. Some identified attributes may contribute to more than one requirement for a software product. Some of them may be mutually in conflict, which must be resolved.

For each pair: requirement-metric an instance of *Metric Quality Level* class and an instance of *Metric Evaluation* class are created. The assessment function for instances of *Metric Quality Level* will be defined in the next activity, called *Quality Level Definition*. The attribute obtained for instances of *Metric Evaluation* class will be filled in *Measurement* activity.

Quality Level Definition activity yields assessment functions for elements which quality we want to evaluate and assess. This activity is a complex one and can be decomposed, as it is shown in Figure 5. The activity is repeated for each considered quality element we want to evaluate. First of all the assessment function for all pairs: leaf-requirement—metric must be defined. Next, following assessment functions are defined: for each leaf-requirement, for each artifact, and for the whole software product. *Quality Manager* may introduce (or may omit) definitions of assessment functions for selected characteristics from quality model.

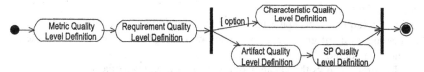

Fig. 5. Details of *Quality Level Definition* activity

The last two activities in Figure 3 are deferred up to artifact implementations are created. *Measurement* activity returns values of attributes used in metrics for any artifact implementation, and deriving from attribute values metric evaluations for each pair: leaf-requirement—metric. These evaluations are represented by *obtained* attribute in *Metric Evaluation* class.

During *Assessment* activity assessment functions, defined in *Quality Level Definition* activity are performed. Results of the functions are gathered in assessment report.

4 Example

Presented example deals with situation when at the beginning of the semester the course timetable for students' courses contains some inconsistencies. The timetable is prepared manually using data from the given external database. So, the *problem* is how to get feasible timetable within a given deadline. A software product, which supports the problem solution, is expected.

The investigation performed by system analyst with administrative staff shows that possible *reasons* of timetable incorrectness come from:

- incomplete or incorrect input data,
- no direct access to database,
- constraints received from teachers,
- temporary overloading of faculty staff at the beginning of the semester.

To resolve problem the following information needs are formulated:

- recording of teacher's constraints up to a given deadline,
- data relating to timetable should be accessible all time they are needed (*),
- preview of current assignments of lecturers and classrooms to courses during the process of timetable preparation (*).

To fulfill these needs requested software product should have the following *features*:

- system is accessible on demand,
- system enables reporting of current resource usage.

In further, we investigate an exemplary quality evaluation process conducted for the needs marked by (*). Additionally, we restrict the example only to external perspective of software product quality.

Activity 1: **Software requirement specification**
Input: User needs
Output: Requirements specification; it contains following requirements:
  R1) Some kinds of analytical reports are expected; the following two of them are further considered:
    Report1 – shows the vacancy of classrooms along weekdays
    Report2 – shows preliminary timetable based on current assignments of lecturers and classrooms to courses
  R2) Report presentation should take a format of pivot tables and pivot charts
  R3) Data for reports are retrieved from the external database
  R4) System is accessible for use in any time when it is needed
  R5) The expected software should be implemented on Microsoft platform.
    Comment: The software functionality is limited to preparation of a set of analytic reports to support current, manually conducted process of timetable preparation.
  Software Product (SP) will consists of two kinds of artifacts:
  - Code: Resource Planning Reports system (RPR system)
  - Documentation: User manual
  The RPR system will operate in conjunction with:
  - DBMS (MS SQL or Access)
  - Excel

Activity 2: **Quality model definition**
Input: Requirement specification, list of artifacts, and ISO quality standards [1], [2].
Output: Elements of quality model – presented in Table 1.

Table 1. Quality model for RPR system

Quality model characteristic/ subcharacteristic	Metric/ Metric_ID	Measurement formula & attributes	Tracing for	Assign to
Functionality/ Suitability	Coverage/ Fsm1	X=1-A/B A–number of function incorrect or missing B–number of function described in requirement specification	R1	Code Doc
Functionality/ Interoperability	Data exchangeability/ Fim1	X=A/B A–number of data formats exchanged successfully with other software B–total number of data formats to be exchanged	R3	Code

Usability/ Usability compliance	Usability compliance/ Ucm1	X=1-A/B A–number of usability compliance. items missing B–total number usability compliance items specified	R2	Code Doc
Reliability/ Recoverability	Availability/ Rrm1	X=A/B A–total available cases of user successfully software use when attempt B–total number of cases of user's attempt to use software during observation time	R4	Code Doc
Functionality/ Interoperability	MS software compliance/ Fim2	X=A/B A–number of Microsoft software products being used B–total number of used software products	R5	Code

Activity 3: **Quality level definition**

Input: Quality model definition for RPR system

Output: During this activity the assessment functions for all elements from assessment perspective package are established. First, the metric quality level assessment functions for any pair: requirement-metric are defined. They are shown in Table 2.

Table 2. Definition of assessment function for metric quality level

Req.	Metric_ID	Assessment function definition
R1	Fsm1	Minimal>0.80; Target=1.0
R2	Ucm1	Minimal>0.5; Target≥0.9
R3	Fim1	Minimal=0.9; Target=1.0
R4	Rrm1	Non-acceptable≤0.5; Minimal<0.9; Target=0.9; Exceeding>0.9
R5	Fim2	Non-acceptable≤0.8; Minimal<1.0; Target=1.0

We have assumed the assessment functions for all quality levels are defined according to the formula (3.1). The only difference is the formula of an assessment function for *SPQualityLevel*, and it is defined as follows:

$$
ass_{SP\text{-}level}(x_{Code}, x_{Doc}) = \begin{cases} \text{Non-acceptable} & \text{if } x_{Code} = \text{Non-acceptable} \\ \text{Minimal} & \text{if } x_{Code} = \text{Minimal} \\ \text{Target} & \text{if } x_{Code} = \text{Target and } x_{Doc} \geq \text{Minimal} \\ \text{Exceeding} & \text{if } x_{Code} = \text{Exceeding and } x_{Doc} \geq \text{Minimal} \end{cases} \quad (4.1)
$$

The assessment functions are accepted or given by user.

Activity 4: **Measurement**

Input: Code and documentation of RPR system.

Output: During this activity the measurement of software artifacts is performed. The resulting metric values are presented in Table 3.

Table 3. Examples of performed measurements for metric level

Metric_ID	Metric	Obtained metric values	
		Code	Documentation
Fsm1	coverage	X = 0.85	X = 0.4

Ucm1	usability compliance	X = 0.9	X = 0.8
Fim1	data exchangeability	X = 1	n/a
Rrm1	availability	X = 0.6	X = 1
Fim2	MS software compliance	X = 1	n/a

*n/a – not applicable

Comment. The measurement of SP is performed in user's environment

Activity 5:   **Assessment**
Input: Results of activities 3 and 4
Output: Quality values for all levels

Using the assessment function (3.1) defined in clause 3, for each level of assessment there were obtained values given in tables 4–7. As each requirement has one associated metric only, the results of quality values for requirement quality level are the same as for metric quality level. The assessments are done independently on each level for every artifact.

Table 4. Obtained quality values for metric and requirement quality level

Req	Metric_ID	Obtained quality values	
		Code	Documentation
R1	Fsm1	Minimal	Non-acceptable
R2	Ucm1	Target	Minimal
R3	Fim1	Target	n/a
R4	Rrm1	Minimal	Target
R5	Fim2	Target	n/a

Table 5. Obtained quality values for sub-characteristic level

Sub-characteristic	Metric_ID	Obtained quality values	
		Code	Documentation
Suitability	Fsm1	Minimal	Non-acceptable
Interoperability	Fim1 Fim2	Target	n/a
Usability compliance	Ucm1	Target	Minimal
Recoverability	Rrm1	Minimal	Exceeding

Table 6. Obtained quality values for characteristic level

Characteristic	Obtained quality value	
	Code	Documentation
Functionality	Minimal	Non-acceptable
Usability	Target	Minimal
Reliability	Minimal	Exceeding

Table 7. Obtained quality values for artifact level

Artifact	Obtained quality value
Code	Minimal
Documentation	Non-acceptable

Final assessment of the RPR system quality is minimal according to (4.1) definition of assessment function for the software product.

5 Conclusions and related works

The paper formalizes and refines ISO standards relating to processes of quality evaluation and assessment [5]. It systematizes notions used for quality specification. The notions are elements of SQMREA model [6]. The developed SQMREA model is general. It enables for instantiations of different kind of quality models, not only those proposed by ISO. For example, it is possible instantiate the quality model for high dependable systems, which concentrates on such characteristics as: safety, security, usability, availability, and reliability [10]. In general, other existing quality models use different notions, but they share the same structural elements (characteristics, subcharacteristics and metrics).

The SQMREA model is our original contribution, while the model of evaluation process is a refined and formalized version of the evaluation process, presented in the series 14598 of ISO/IEC standardization documents. The new elements include definition of roles, specification of artifacts, an assignment of artifacts to roles and activities, performed by roles.

The paper also presents SPoQE methodology for software quality product evaluation and assessment. The methodology is defined in terms of SPEM notation [9], i.e. roles performing some activities on a given set of artifacts. The SPoQE methodology is independent from a software development methodology provided that the methodology distinguishes at least the following two processes, defined in [3]:

- system requirement analysis,
- software construction.

The activities of the proposed software product evaluation process conform to those proposed in [4] with only one difference:

- *measurement* activity in [4] is proceeded with planning activity – we omit this activity as it is part of a management process.

The presented quality evaluation process can be considered as an important part of *Quality Control* process within SQA. It can also be considered within CMM (fourth level) [6] as part of quality management. The SPoQE methodology concentrates on product evaluation only, and does not take into account evaluation of development process. The knowledge about the results of evaluation enables to carry out some corrective actions, and in this way can positively influence the final quality of the software product.

We have not found another approach to software product evaluation based on ISO standard [4].

It is evident that application of proposed method of product evaluation is labour-consuming. The cost-benefits analysis was not the subject of our interests. It can, and should be concern of further investigations as it is obvious that some trade-off between evaluation effort and resulting quality of software product is expected.

In further research we are going to:

- apply and validate SpoQE methodology for industrial projects,
- develop a tool supporting evaluation and assessment of a software product according to SPoQE.

References

1. ISO/IEC 9621-1:2000, Software engineering – Product quality - Part 1: Quality model
2. ISO/IEC TR 9621-2:2002, *Software engineering – Product quality - Part 2: External metrics*
3. ISO/IEC 12247:1995/Amd.1:2002, *Information technology — Software life cycle processes*
4. ISO/IEC 14598-3:2000, *Software engineering – Product evaluation – Part 3: Process for developers*
5. ISO/IEC 25000:2005, Software engineering – Software Product Quality Requirements and Evaluation (SQuaRE) – Guide for SQuaRE
6. Dubielewicz I., Hnatkowska B., Huzar Z., Tuzinkiewicz L., Software Quality Metamodel for Requirement, Evaluation and Assessment, ISIM'06 Conference, Prerov, 2006, Czech Republic, Acta Mosis No. 105, pp. 115–122.
7. Jalote P., CMM in Practice: Process for Executing Software Projects at Infosys, Boston, Addison-Wesley, 2000
8. Leffingwell D., Widrig D., Zarządzanie wymaganiami, (in Polish) WNT, 2003
9. Software Process Engineering Metamodel Specification (SPEM), version 1.0, OMG 2002
10. SWEBOK, Guide to the Software Engineering Body of Knowledge, 2002
11. Unhelkar B., Process Quality Assurance for UML-Based Projects, Addison-Wesley, 2002

Feedback from Users on a Software Product to Improve Its Quality in Engineering Applications

Barbara Begier[1], Jacek Wdowicki[2]

[1] Institute of Control and Information Engineering, Poznan University of Technology,
Pl. M. Sklodowskiej-Curie 5, 60-965 Poznan, Poland
[2] Institute of Structural Engineering, Poznan University of Technology
ul. Piotrowo 5, 60-965 Poznan, Poland

Abstract. Users' involvement in a software process is one of strategies for achieving an improvement of software quality. The described research is referred to the software system applied in civil engineering. The continual feedback from users makes possible to learn the user's point of view and to improve a product just according to her/his notes and expectations. The applied method based on a questionnaire survey has been presented – the layout of questionnaires is the original solution. Four iterations of the collaborative development, including software quality assessment, took place. The level of users' satisfaction from a product is currently better than that at the beginning.

1 Introduction

Users assess the quality of software in practice, after the product is delivered. But software quality is born in the software process which is several times repeated till the withdraw of the considered product. Users' involvement in the process is one of possible strategies which support software quality improvement, like the QAW Method [2], for instance. In general, a cooperation with users is the base of agile methodologies [1]. It is not in contradiction with other trends in software engineering, like the MDA (Model Driven Architecture) recommended by the OMG, for example.

The described research is referred to the class of software products which support calculations in an engineering discipline. General characteristics of the considered products are given in the next section. According to the ISO 9000:2000 the *level of a customer satisfaction* from a product is one of recommended measures of its quality. The level of user's satisfaction from a software product derives from its quality, specified using accepted criteria and particular measures of its assessment.

The presented approach is based on a feedback from users in the product life cycle (see section 3). That feedback must respect accepted methodologies and various constraints [7]. The own experience shows that many users are eager to present their suggestions to improve a product [5, 6]. The presented method has been applied to the software system BW applied in civil engineering – it is briefly described in the section 4. Users of the described class of software are highly qualified experts in their discipline who are able to give valuable feedback to software developers. The assess-

Please use the following format when citing this chapter:

Begier, B., Wdowicki, J., 2006, in IFIP International Federation for Information Processing, Volume 227, Software Engineering Techniques: Design for Quality, ed. K. Sacha, (Boston: Springer), pp. 167–178.

ment of software quality takes place after the next version of the product has been introduced. The questionnaire survey is here the recommended form of a software assessment by its users. The content of a questionnaire must be comprehensive and clear for its respondents. The practice shows that one edition of a questionnaire is far not enough to obtain the successful result.

The described method to provide the valuable questionnaire survey has been developed (see section 5), applied several times in practice and successively improved to learn the user's point of view, including notes given to particular metrics and his/her suggestions to improve the product (see section 6). The obtained results make possible to develop the software product exactly to its users' expectations.

2 The Class of Software Supporting Engineering Calculations

Software products supporting calculations of various constructions in civil engineering represent the class of numerical data processing − the numerical input describe a geometry of a construction, expected loads, coefficients of equations, and parameters which control a running software. Data and results are transformed to graphical forms. Generated technical drawings, charts, and maps of stresses contain technical terms and physical units which must be in accordance with technical terminology and notation. Particular programs of calculations often cooperate with the well known AutoCAD system. Authors of this kind of software focus first of all on a correct software construction [8], starting from mathematical and physical models, then programming numerical calculations providing the required accuracy and visualization of results, including image processing.

The strength of wall constructions is calculated each time in a design process of a building − so the supporting software is applied when such a need arises. The progress in civil engineering (new types of constructions, different environmental conditions including various kinds of loads and applied materials) involves the development of a supporting software. Software products required for engineering purposes are maintained many years and evolve till their withdraw. Applied algorithms are based on stable and repeatedly proven principles of mechanics.

Users of the described class of software products are widely regarded as experts in their domain. High qualified users expect an added value − precise results of computations, according to the requirements and the technical standards. The notions of functionality, reliability and safety constitute the canon of their work. Professionals in civil engineering are able to cooperate with software authors.

The following quality elements, to be considered in a production of that class of software, have been specified [3, 4]:

1. Quality of goals of the software project − the specified level of an automation of designer's work is required in the given area; the specification of the object of calculations and sources of loads should be clearly developed.
2. Quality of requirements − their specification includes the correctness of data describing types of analyzed constructions and all possible loads.
3. Theoretical grounds of accepted technical solutions come from the domain analysis, namely the civil engineering in the presented case.

4. Quality of the software process – specification of the software development cycle is worked out, including the required documentation, and then followed.
5. Quality of software construction providing its modifiability and portability.
6. Quality of interfaces between program modules and the provided proper access to their common data.
7. Specification of software quality criteria and their particular measures to provide a product assessment by its users.
8. Quality of testing – provided test cases assure the correctness of results and make them reliable (although it is not easy to provide the real life data).
9. Quality of the user interface including graphical forms of presentations.
10. Expected verifications of the input data.
11. Required cooperation with the AutoCAD system.
12. Structure, content and language of the documentation, including documents of all changes, test cases, and instructions for users.

All quality elements should be developed, discussed, assessed, and modified by software designers, domain experts and potential users. The domain experts participate obligatory in the software process to provide the quality elements denoted at 1–3 and 8. They also may cooperate with quality engineers and software designers to provide the other quality elements, especially those 4–7 here. In any engineering calculations the correctness of the input data play the more important role than in other fields – any mistake here may result in a construction disaster. At least the elements denoted above from 9 to 12 should be assessed, in the authors' opinion, by all users of the given software product. This statement is developed in the next sections.

3 Software Life Cycle Including a Feedback from Users

Software products applied in civil engineering are developed and improved in their entire life cycle. In the described approach the main source of ideas to improve the product comes from its users, as shown in the Figure 1. The following steps are recommended to provide a regular feedback from users on the given product:

1. Get learn and specify the users' profiles.
2. Specify and plan the forms of users' involvement in the process, mainly in a quality assessment of a product.
3. Specify several dozen of quality criteria and measures.
4. Design the questionnaires with some place left for suggestions of changes.
5. Carry out a survey.
6. Collect results and process them statistically.
7. Record and analyze carefully all suggestions and proposals.
8. Compare current values of given notes with the previous results.
9. Select measures to be improved, choose some suggestions and start the next development cycle to build a new version.

Thus the provided answers and their analysis constitute a basis of software modifications and improvement – one may ***control those features*** which *are specified*, then *implemented, measured, assessed,* and possibly *improved* in the next iteration.

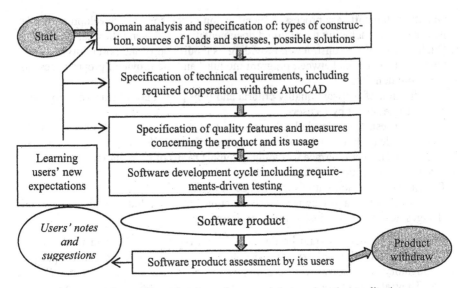

Fig. 1. Software life cycle of a product supporting engineering applications

4 Object of an Assessment − the BW System

The integrated software system BW (its name is an acronym from '*Tall Buildings*' expressed in Polish) has been developed to support the static and dynamic analysis of multi-storey buildings with large three-dimensional coupled shear wall structures. All analyses should be accurate and fast − the calculations are not possible without the computer support. The considered system provides calculations of internal forces, stresses and displacements due to the set of lateral and vertical loads and flexural moments. The static analysis is based on the developed variant of the continuous connection method using differential equations for the usually expected and the extreme stresses, the shear and normal ones [12]. The BW system enables also to analyze the flexural strength of a tall building − its dynamic analysis is performed using the hybrid continuous-discrete approach and the response spectrum technique to estimate the seismic response of a construction [14].

The BW system has evolved for many years. Its maintenance requires to respect principles of software engineering and to pay a special attention to software quality [3, 13]. Several programmers cooperate with the main authors of the technical solution. Its current version follows the Eurocode 8 standard, accepted by CEN (Comité Européen de Normalisation) in 2003. It analyses torsions of the coupled construction due to its displacements resulting from earthquakes or para-seismic effects. The BW system is intended to cooperate with the AutoCAD system to get dimensions of a construction from its technical drawings and also to transfer numerical values in the opposite direction to check visually the correctness of the given data. The BW system generates numerical and graphical results. It has been applied many times in practice to calculate ca 240 constructions, in the home country and abroad.

5 Quality Measures of Software for Civil Engineering Applications

The quality metrics have been specified during four years of work concerning quality of software products developed for civil engineering. Quality criteria and measures result from quality goals of the software project. Quality measures are, at first, the part of software requirements and then they become a subject of a product assessment by its users. The particular metrics have been worked out on a base of quality attributes given in the ISO 9126 [9] and as a result of cooperation with users. The developed decomposition of quality attributes is given in the Figure 2.

The scope of software *functionality* is related to the range of required types of constructions and their loads. The provided cooperation with the AutoCAD system and the data correction also belongs to the product functionality.

The main part of the software product assessment concerns its ***usability***. It refers to the software construction, user interface, ease of learn, and ease of use of the software product. Comprehensive software construction corresponds to subsequent steps of a design process and to designer's decisions made on a base of the obtained values. It is important feature from the user's point of view to provide an easy way to change the former set of input data and to perform calculations starting from the chosen point, not only from the very beginning. An interactive impact on calculations and a possibility to trace them seem to be valuable. User's interface should provide conformity with the terminology and notation used in the given technical discipline.

The usually long period of a program maintenance requires the ***portability*** of the product including an ease of installation on various computer platforms.

All quality measures along with user's subjective impressions constitute the main metric, namely the ***level of user's satisfaction*** from the considered product.

The following measures have been specified and then assessed:

Functionality

M1. Variety of building constructions analyzed by the product.
M2. Sufficient number of various load cases analyzed by the product.
M3. Mode of cooperation with the AutoCAD system, providing an effective way to check the correctness of the input data.
M4. Possibility for presenting subsequent steps of calculations.

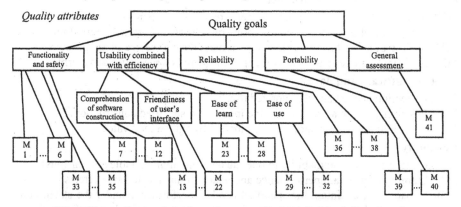

Fig. 2. The quality tree joint for software products applied in civil engineering

M5. Provided on-line correction of data describing the given construction.

M6. Correction of data concerning loads of the construction, including a withdraw of the previously given values.

Comprehension of software construction

M7. Comprehension of all provided software options and their use.

M8. Clarity of software construction and the provided ease of an access to software functions at any moment of use of a product.

M9. Ease of a program navigation using an icon tool bar.

M10. Readable and clear access to software functions by making use of menus.

M11. Provided way to prepare the input data.

M12. Availability of lists of choice for the input data.

Friendliness of screen elements provided by a user interface

M13. Comprehension of the content of lists of choice.

M14. Layout (arrangement) of objects presented on a screen.

M15. Size of character types and other screen elements, including graphics.

M16. Readability and comprehension of legends attached to drawings and charts.

M17. Provided kind and range of physical units.

M18. Conformity of labels, used next to elements of charts and drawings, with the technical notation applied in the given area.

M19. Comprehension of language expressions used in inscriptions and messages; ease of their interpretation (avoiding misinterpretation of them).

M20. Sufficient support with graphical forms.

M21. Proper use of colours applied to screen objects and a background.

M22. Ability to customize views of screen objects to the user's likings.

Ease of learn to use the software product

M23. The time required to learn to use the program.

M24. The initially required help of the program experienced user.

M25. Estimated frequency of mistakes made in one hour of a software use.

M26. Frequency of currently made mistakes compared with that at the beginning.

M27. Usefulness of the provided user's instruction.

M28. Usefulness of the built-in help option.

Ease of use of the software product

M29. Required help of an experienced user after the initial period of learn to use.

M30. Frequency of using the provided forms of help (in a given time period/unit).

M31. Feeling of a comfort of work at any moment during the use of the product.

M32. Sufficient number and clear content of the provided messages and alarms.

Safety of software and data

M33. Protection against an unauthorized user's access.

M34. Possibility to run a program for the incorrectly specified construction.

M35. Possibility to run a program for the incorrectly given load values.

Reliability

M36. Constant standby and ability to operate data (no unpredictable suspensions).

M37. Stability of program performance and a lack of unexpected side effects.

M38. Capability to maintain the specified level of performance under the stated conditions (the same parameters of performance after the multiple use of a product).

Portability

M39. Capability to run on the specified various platforms.

M40. Ease of program installation on any computer platform.

General assessment of the software product

M41. Level of users' satisfaction from the given software product.

6 Software Product Assessment Using a Questionnaire Survey

6.1 Structure and Content of Questionnaires

Each questionnaire includes an initial part which contains questions concerning users' experience with computing tools. Respondents have been asked about software products used at their every day work – a number and a kind of software systems of general purpose, the frequency of using each product, and separately distinguished tools suitably supporting professional applications in civil engineering.

The main part of a questionnaire has been developed to assess, first of all, the usability of the product. In its two first editions this part contained 26 questions, grouped into 3 sections concerning subsequently: user interface, ease of learn, and user's efficiency as a result of the provided ease of use [6]. In two last editions this part has been increased up to 41 questions, containing all measures quoted in the previous section. At the end, users are asked about their general assessment of a given product. An additional point in all four editions was a request for user's suggestions to improve the BW system.

The content of a questionnaire have been improved every year. The aim was to achieve process-able and comparable results. Each group of items has its name corresponding to the quality criterion to keep user's attention on a given subject. Expected forms of an answer should be clearly explained and suggested.

Two first editions showed that some questions were not equally interpreted by all respondents. In a consequence, various forms of answers were given. For example, the question "*A frequency of mistakes made at the very beginning of the software use compared to the current frequency of such mistakes*" was imprecise. The answers were like: a ratio (4:1, for example), number of times, percentage of cases during the use of software, and also in words like "*none*" or "*several*".

Table 1. The fragment of a questionnaire

M	Ease of learn to use the software product	
24	The initially required help of the program experienced user [1 – necessary, 2 – desired, 3 – partial, 4 – occasional, 5 – unnecessary]	
25	Estimated frequency of mistakes made in one hour of software use [1 more than 10, 2 – from 6 up to 10, 3 – from 3 up to 5, 4 – 1 or 2, 5 – zero]	
26	Frequency of currently made mistakes compared with that at the beginning [1 – no difference, 2 – a bit less, 3 – less than a half, 4 – rarely, 5 – by no means]	
27	Usefulness of the provided user's instruction [1 – bad, 2 – insufficient, 3 – sufficient, 4 – good, 5 – very good]	

The need arose to specify precisely the suggested unit of each answer. The set of acceptable values of an answer should be attached to each question. The most comparable are numerals and thus just integers have been suggested as expected forms of answers. In next editions of the questionnaire, the possible forms of each answer along with their meanings were given in square brackets right behind each question as it is illustrated in the Table 1. The last column is reserved for answers.

6.2 Overview of the Obtained Results

The subsequent software quality assessments using a questionnaire survey took place four times – every year, since 2002. The 38 fulfilled copies were obtained in 2002, then 41 in 2003 [6], 36 in 2004, and 30 in 2005. It took 10 up to 15 minutes for each respondent to fulfil a questionnaire. An important question should be answered at the very beginning of the questionnaire survey – if problems in use the considered software product arise from a possible lack of users' experience at computing and software tools, or not. Answers given to the questions in the initial part have confirmed that civil engineers are skilled in computing – all of them use computers every day, all are experienced with popular tools of general purpose like the MS Word and MS Excel. All know and use the AutoCAD system.

All answers given by respondents during each edition of the questionnaire have been entered into the report sheet. Its each row is designed for one question and related answers. The first column points out the number of a question, and the next ones contain provided answers. The following data are calculated and maintained in last five columns: given minimum value, maximum value, sum of provided values, number of answers, and the average of provided answers. The fragment of the report sheet (limited to 15 respondents) obtained in the last edition is given in the Table 2.

In some cases of metrics, for example to assess the '*Feeling of comfort of work at any moment during the use of the product*' or the '*Sufficient number and clear content of the provided messages and alarms*', the average values do not make sense. So despite the comparable numerical results of the assessment the descriptive statistics has been done to present all obtained data on graphs. Two examples of graphs presenting statistical data are shown in the Figure 3 and the Figure 4.

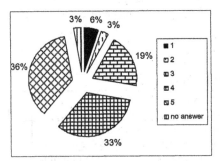   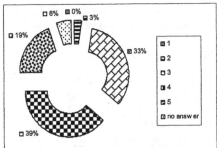

Fig. 3. Results of assessment of the M11   **Fig. 4.** Results of assessment of the M5
    ('*Provided way to prepare the input data*')   ('*Provided on-line correction of data ...*

Table 2. Fragment of the report sheet

User / Question	1	2	3	4	5	6	7	8	9	10	11	12	13	14	15	*min*	*max*	*sum*	*n*	*average*
Functionality																				
M1	5	5	5	5	3	5	5	0	3	5	5	5	3	5	5	3	5	64	14	4.57
M2	5	5	5	3	5	5	5	5	3	5	3	5	5	5	5	3	5	69	15	4.60
M3	3	4	5	5	4	4	3	4	4	3	4	3	5	4	5	3	5	60	15	4.00
M4	4	4	5	4	4	4	5	0	4	4	4	4	4	4	4	4	5	58	14	4.14
M5	3	0	2	4	4	4	4	5	4	3	4	4	3	4	4	2	5	52	14	3.71
M6	3	0	2	4	4	4	4	5	4	3	4	4	4	4	3	2	5	52	14	3.71
Comprehension of software construction																				
M7	5	4	5	4	5	5	5	5	3	4	4	5	4	5	4	3	5	67	15	4.47
M8	4	4	4	5	5	5	5	5	3	5	4	5	4	4	5	3	5	67	15	4.47
M9	4	5	4	5	5	5	5	5	5	5	4	4	4	5	5	4	5	70	15	4.67
M10	4	4	4	5	5	5	5	5	4	4	4	3	4	5	5	3	5	66	15	4.40
M11	4	5	4	5	4	4	4	5	5	4	5	4	4	5	5	4	5	67	15	4.47
M12	4	5	4	5	5	5	5	5	5	4	5	3	4	5	4	3	5	68	15	4.53
Friendliness of screen elements provided by a user interface																				
M13	4	5	4	5	5	4	4	4	5	4	4	4	3	5	3	3	5	63	15	4.20
M14	4	4	5	5	5	5	5	4	4	4	5	5	4	4		4	5	68	15	4.53
M15	3	3	5	5	5	5	5	5	4	4	4	5	5	5	4	3	5	67	15	4.47
M16	4	4	4	3	4	5	5	5	3	4	5	4	4	5	4	3	5	63	15	4.20
M17	5	5	4	5	5	5	5	5	4	4	4	4	5	5	4	4	5	69	15	4.60
M18	5	4	5	4	4	4	4	5	3	4	4	4	4	5	4	3	5	63	15	4.20
M19	4	4	5	5	4	5	4	5	5	5	5	4	5	5	4	4	5	69	15	4.60
M20	5	3	5	5	4	5	5	5	5	4	5	4	5	5	5	3	5	70	15	4.67
M21	5	4	5	5	5	5	4	5	5	4	5	4	5	5	5	4	5	71	15	4.73
M22	4	3	3	3	4	3	4	0	2	3	4	2	4	5	5	2	5	49	14	3.50
Ease of learn to use the software product																				
M23	5	5	5	5	5	5	5	5	5	5	5	5	4	5	5	4	5	74	15	4.93
M24	3	5	4	2	2	3	4	4	2	2	2	4	1	4	4	1	5	46	15	3.07
M25	4	5	4	5	5	4	4	5	5	4	4	5	3	5	5	3	5	67	15	4.47
M26	4	5	4	4	5	4	5	0	1	4	4	5	3	5	5	1	5	58	14	4.14
M27	4	4	4	4	3	3	4	0	2	3	4	4	3	4	3	2	4	49	14	3.50
M28	3	4	3	3	3	3	4	0	3	3	4	4	3	4	3	3	4	47	14	3.36
Ease of use of the software product																				
M29	4	5	5	4	5	5	5	5	0	4	3	5	5	4	5	3	5	64	14	4.57
M30	4	4	3	4	4	4	4	5	3	3	3	4	3	4	5	3	5	57	15	3.80
M31	5	5	5	5	5	5	5	5	5	5	3	5	3	5	5	3	5	71	15	4.73
M32	4	5	4	5	5	5	5	0	3	4	4	5	4	5	3	3	5	61	14	4.36
Safety of software and data																				
M33	4	0	3	2	3	3	4	5	1	2	4	4	1	4	3	1	5	43	14	3.07
M34	3	3	4	4	3	4	4	0	3	4	3	4	3	4	3	3	4	49	14	3.50
M35	3	3	4	4	3	4	4	0	3	3	3	4	3	4	3	3	4	48	14	3.43
Reliability																				
M36	4	5	4	5	5	5	4	5	4	4	5	5	3	4	4	3	5	66	15	4.40
M37	4	5	4	5	4	5	3	5	4	4	5	5	3	4	5	3	5	65	15	4.33
M38	4	5	4	5	4	5	4	5	4	4	5	5	4	4	5	4	5	67	15	4.47
Portability																				
M39	4	0	4	5	5	3	4	0	3	4	4	4	4	5	4	3	5	53	13	4.08
M40	2	5	4	5	5	5	5	5	5	4	5	4	5	5	5	2	5	69	15	4.60
General assessment of the software product																				
M41	4	4	4	5	3	4	5	5	3	4	4	4	0	4	0	3	5	53	13	4.08

The general assessment of the product is relatively high (4.08). And 30 from among 40 particular measures have gained the average notes higher than 4.0. The facilities of data correction are the most difficult to improve them. It seems to be the

general problem concerning any kind of software product − how to provide the satisfying level of verification and correction of data.

The highest average notes gained all measures concerning the comprehension of
software construction and its reliability. The worst notes were given to the measures
of safety of programs and their data − fortunately, these are not the key measures in
the case of software products supporting applications in civil engineering.

In some metrics the maximally different results have been obtained. For example,
in the case of M24 and M26 the range of values is from 1 to 5. There is a correlation
between an experience in using the AutoCAD system and other software for engineering applications − users who assess their experience in using those products as the
average require the help of an experienced user. The other explanation associates a
user with his/her professional environment − respondents who cooperate with experienced users do not complain about the ease of learn to use the product.

7 Software Quality Improvement Resulting from the Users' Involvement in a Product Assessment

All notes and suggestions given by users have been carefully analyzed after each
questionnaire survey. Fortunately, many of the polled users show their willingness to
influence on a software product − each second respondent gave his/her particular
suggestions, although the weight of them was not equal − from a suggestion of using
boldface elements or letters on a specified chart, to identify a danger of loosing some
data in the case of a too fast click in the described circumstances. Users' remarks and
expectations regarding each new version of the BW product concern:

  a) improvement of some specified software features and a system usage,
  b) close cooperation with the AutoCAD system,
  c) an increasing number of types of analyzed building constructions.

The chief of an assessment and the developers' leader (both are the authors of the
presented paper) have worked out three *enumerated lists of suggested changes*, separately for each kind of the listed above problems. Each item on a list has its several
initially specified attributes: number, name, date of registration, weight (assigned
using three different colors), description, justification (goal and related quality measures), addressee. The developed lists are transferred each time to programmers who
then are obliged to fulfill several other attributes and explain what real modifications
of the software product have been made. Thus the history of all changes and their
justification is maintained − it also shows the favorite areas of programmers' work.
The reality shows that programmers are eager to improve first of all the interface with
the AutoCAD system. Thus the new or widely modified pre- and postprocessors co-
operating with the AutoCAD have been subsequently developed. But the note given
to the mode of cooperation with the AutoCAD (M3) remains the same, namely 4.00.

Authors of the BW system have taken into account many critical remarks concerning their product and have eliminated its some weak points pointed out in the questionnaire survey. So the directions of software product improvement follow exactly
the users' notes, given opinions, and submitted suggestions.

Average values of most measures have grown since the previous assessment. For example, the variety of building constructions analyzed by the program BW (M1) has gained the average note 4.57 (previously 3.94). The comprehension of all provided software options and their use (M7) arose from 4.12 up to 4.47, the provided way to prepare the input data (M11) previously achieved an average 3.71 while 4.47 last time, and the availability of lists of choice for the input data (M12) got 3.94 and 4.53, respectively. The estimated frequency of mistakes made in one hour of software use (M25) has been currently assessed much better (4.47) than before (3.47). Also the average note given to the frequency of currently made mistakes compared with that at the beginning (M26) has grown from 3.82 up to 4.14. The feeling of comfort of work at any moment during the use of the product (M31) arose from 3.94 up to 4.73.

Usefulness of user's instruction (M27) and that of the built-in help option (M28) is still problematic and even a bit worse than previously: 3.50 and 3.36 instead of 3.88 and 3.56, respectively. So some help of the program experienced user (M29) is still required at the beginning (it got the average note 4.57 recently, and previously 3.82).

Again and again the data correction is assessed as a weakness of the product – the provided on-line correction of data describing the given construction (M5) and the similar measure related to the loads of the building (M6) are both currently assessed equally as 3.71 and are a bit worse than previously (3.76 and 3.88, respectively).

After four iterations of software development including periodical quality assessment of the product by its users, the average level of users' satisfaction from a product is slightly better (4.08) than that obtained the previous time (4.0).

8 Conclusions

Evaluation of software quality based on data coming from software users is the current problem in software engineering. The experience using a questionnaire survey to gain a continuous feedback from users on a software product has been described. Conclusions are related to: the form and the layout of the questionnaire, the obtained results, and the general idea of the applied approach. Some remarks concerning the content of the questionnaire are given in the section 6.1. After the careful analysis there are still some doubts if names of metrics and expressed possible answers are phrased well. Maybe the Likert scale will be used in the next edition of the questionnaire. In this method each item of the questionnaire is the statement and the respondents are asked to indicate their degree of agreement with the provided statements.

Users' expectations are growing every year. It is a real risk – if a software product remains unchanged then the general note given in its assessment may be each time worse than it was before. Notes are given to the particular measures of the software product in the changing environment – the level of average user's skills is growing. Also a range of users' expectations increases according to the hierarchy of needs described by Maslow [10] – users propose new requirements after their basic needs are satisfied. So the gained results of questionnaires may surprise when strictly compared – the new results may be worse than previous ones, although many improvements have been done in the meantime.

Despite all differences between the software products applied in civil engineering and any other software *the idea to incorporate users to the software process* looks promising. At least the ***periodical assessment of the software product*** by its available (possibly all) users is worth working out and decidedly recommended here. The assessment is based on the questionnaire survey. The content of a questionnaire and all forms of the expected answers should be carefully specified to get valuable results and to avoid misunderstandings. In other words, the questionnaire itself should be periodically improved, too. Users' answers and suggestions are a base of the specification of required changes. The history of all justified changes is maintained.

References

1. Agile Modeling(AM) Home Page, http://www.agilemodeling.com/, 2001–2005
2. Barbacci M. R., Ellison R., Lattanze A. J., Stafford J. A., Weinstock Ch. B., Wood W. G.: Quality Attribute Workshops (QAWs), 3rd edn, CMU/SEI-2003-TR-016, Carnegie Mellon Software Engineering Institute, Pittsburgh (USA), August 2003, http://www.sei.cmu.edu/pub/documents/03.reports/pdf/03tr016.pdf
3. Begier B., Wdowicka E., Wdowicki J.: On the methodics providing software quality in civil engineering applications. In: Tasso C., Adey R. A., Pighin M. (eds.): Software Quality Engineering. Computational Mechanics Publications, Southampton-Boston (1997) 71–80
4. Begier B., Wdowicki J.: Quality criteria of software provided for the calculations of constructions in civil engineering (in Polish). In: Tadeusiewicz R., Ligęza A., Szymkat M. (eds.): The 3rd National Conference on Methods and Computer Systems in Research and Engineering MSK'01, Conference proceedings. Kraków (2001) 233–238
5. Begier B.: Software quality assessment by users. In: Huzar Z., Mazur Z. (eds.): Problems and methods of software engineering. Wydawnictwa Naukowo-Techniczne (2003) 417–431
6. Begier B., Wdowicki J.: Quality assessment of software applied in civil engineering by the users. In: 4th National Conference on Methods and Computer Systems in Research and Engineering MSK'03 (in Polish). Kraków (2003) 547–552
7. Begier B.: The UID Approach – the Balance between Hard and Soft Methodologies. In: Zielinski K., Szmuc T. (eds.): Software Engineering: Evolution and Emerging Technologies. IOS Press, Amsterdam (2005) 15–26
8. Cooke J.: Constructing Correct Software. The Basics. Springer Verlag, London (1998)
9. International Standard ISO/IEC 9126-1:2001, Software engineering – Product quality, Part 1: Quality model. ISO Copyright Office, Geneva (2001)
10. Maslow A.: Motivation and Personality, Harper and Row (1954)
11. Sikorski M.: Usability management in information technology projects (in Polish). Wydawnictwo Politechniki Gdanskiej, Gdansk (2000)
12. Wdowicki J., Wdowicka E.: System of Programs for Analysis of Three-Dimensional Shear Wall Structures. The Structural Design of Tall Buildings, Vol. 2 (1993) 295–305
13. Wdowicki J., Wdowicka E., Tomaszewski A.: Integrated System for Multi-storey Buildings – Use of Software Engineering Rules. In: European Conference on Computational Mechanics ECCM-2001, Cracow, Poland (2001) 1–20
14. Wdowicka E., Wdowicki J., Błaszczynski T.: Seismic analysis of the 'South Gate' tall building according to Eurocode 8. In: The Structural Design of Tall and Special Buildings, Vol. 14, John Wiley & Sons, Ltd, 1 (2005) 59–67

Reaching and Maintaining High Quality of Distributed J2EE Applications – BeesyCluster Case Study***

Paweł Czarnul

Faculty of Electronics, Telecommunications and Informatics
Gdansk University of Technology, Poland
pczarnul@eti.pg.gda.pl

Abstract. The paper presents design recommendations, selected and representative implementation and configuration errors encountered during development of BeesyCluster – a J2EE component-based system for remote WWW/Web Service file management, task queuing, publishing services online for other users with credential management and team work support. Based on a QESA methodology developed previously, we build a quality tree by including the aforementioned but generalized recommendations, errors, and solutions for multi-tiered distributed J2EE applications. This allows to validate other similar applications in the future against errors we have identified and solutions we recommend thus creating a quality checklist for other J2EE developers.

1 Introduction

Although the market offers applications in a variety of fields, there is a growing need for high quality software. This is true especially in view of a large collection of open source code available on the Internet but of variable quality. The latter can be used or embedded into larger projects to solve specific tasks (within the limitations imposed by licences).

It is the quality of the development process, the methodology used, design practices and implementation techniques that contribute to the final quality of the product.

For complex applications, designers and programmers might reuse solutions to similar problems faced by others before which is often expressed as design patterns. Certainly a check-list of typical implementation errors, especially for distributed Internet-based applications, would also be useful to eliminate bugs quickly. Of equal importance are activities and issues that show up during software configuration, deployment and maintenance, usually very time-consuming but nevertheless required.

2 Motivations and Goals

Based on the facts derived above, we can conclude that every effort that classifies recurring design/implementation/deployment/maintenance problems and solutions can help improve new projects.

* partially covered by the Polish National Grant KBN No. 4 T11C 005 25
** calculations carried out at the Academic Computer Center in Gdansk, Poland

---

A research team led by the author of this paper has successfully designed, implemented and deployed a large Web-based portal for accessing HPC (High Performance Computing) clusters, file and task management, queuing, making tasks available to others via WWW with a virtual payment subsystem and a team work environment, described in detail in paragraph 4 and [1–3]. BeesyCluster was deployed at Academic Computer Center, Gdansk, Poland as an access portal to HPC clusters including a 288-processor IA-64 holk, a 64-processor SGI Altix 3700 system and others[1]. 21 designers, programmers and documentation writers have contributed to the project over 3 years. The goal of this paper is to use the experience we have gained during the development of BeesyCluster (ca. 100 KLOC) and turn it into a concise check-list in the form of a quality tree. The paper identifies and suggests solutions to:

1. selected design problems – this will include comments on the usage of existing patterns and possibly identification of new recommendations,
2. selected implementation errors – especially useful since provides a check-list of problems the programmer might face in own applications,
3. system configuration/management/deployment problems – can be non-trivial, time-consuming and require much experience for complex J2EE and distributed systems.

Since J2EE imposes API and the multitiered architecture, this serves as a common denominator for applications considered which in turn makes this approach viable.

The quality tree which includes common J2EE problems and implementation errors is defined to automate the process of checking other applications against errors identified in BeesyCluster and making it easier to eliminate them. Each application can be evaluated in a special QESA tool, codeveloped by the author before.

3   Related Work

Firstly, existing J2EE design patterns are directly related to our work here as provide reference solutions to typical design problems encountered during development of J2EE applications. As [4] suggests the patterns are:

- reusable – can be used for several applications, are also expressed in general terms so can be applied to problems in various areas,
- developed and improved by knowledgeable designers and programmers.

[5] lists various design patterns for J2EE applications important of which are: Intercepting Filter, Front Controller, Session Facade and Web Service Broker for exposing selected services for SOAP calls.

As for avoiding implementation errors, there exist Code Conventions for the Java Programming Language ([6]) to save on software maintenance (80% of the lifetime cost of software according to [6]). Java practices are collected in [7] including issues for servlets/JSPs, coding exceptions, input/output, collections and common practices

---

[1] https://beesycluster2.eti.pg.gda.pl/ek/Main from anywhere, https://karawela.task.gda.pl:8443/ek/Main from Gdansk University of Technology

like defensive copying, using testing frameworks like JUnit etc. Still, J2EE specific errors are not addressed.

Secondly, we try to automate the process of checking the quality of design, implementation, configuration by including the identified practices, errors into a quality tree. This is related to existing general software quality models and defect classification methods.

There are several general quality approaches available. The Goal-Question-Metric (GQM, [8]) method first specifies goals to achieve, formulates questions which help achieve the goal, defines metrics for which data is collected and answers the questions ([8]). COCOMO ([8]) and Function Points ([8]) can be used to measure the required effort and software size. Software Process Improvement and Capability Determination (SPICE, [8], [9], published as ISO/IEC TR 15504) is an international initiative aimed at the standard of software process assessment, used in the context of process improvement or process capability determination either of an organization or a supplier. SPICE defines a framework for performing evaluation, required activities, defines how to conduct software evaluation. [10] presents system-level quality metrics for component-based systems that can help managers decide whether existing components should be reused.

In this work a QESA approach, introduced by us in [11] for improving design of an application for management of ship containers, will be used to build a quality tree including design practices, errors and recommended solutions. Paragraph 6 discusses the QESA methodology and compares it to defect classification methods like IBM's Orthogonal Defect Classification and HP's Company-Wide Software Metrics ([12]).

4 BeesyCluster

BeesyCluster can be seen as an access portal to a network of clusters/supercomputers/PCs with WWW and Web Service interfaces. Figure 1 depicts the architecture of the system with main modules and relationships (described in detail in [1]). The user sets up an account in BeesyCluster through which (single sing-on) can access accounts on many different clusters/supercomputers/PCs. Users can manage files and run sequential or parallel tasks (interactively or queued) on their accounts on clusters/supercomputers/PCs via WWW and Web Services. Furthermore, users can publish their services (applications, sequential or parallel, run interactively or queued on clusters/supercomputers as well files) to other users of BeesyCluster. For the use of services (if not specified as free of charge), users-providers earn points which can be spent on running services published by others. Users can register new clusters or individual PCs in the system just by providing a login/password to any system account and can run tasks, edit files and publish services from there.

BeesyCluster is representative in terms of:

distributed architecture – the user connects to BeesyCluster via WWW or Web Services while the system uses SSH to connect to accounts on remote clusters/PCs and run tasks there – we run several demanding parallel applications using this system (described e.g. in [13]),

access via multiple popular interfaces – WWW and Web Services (its efficiency in BeesyCluster tested in [2]),

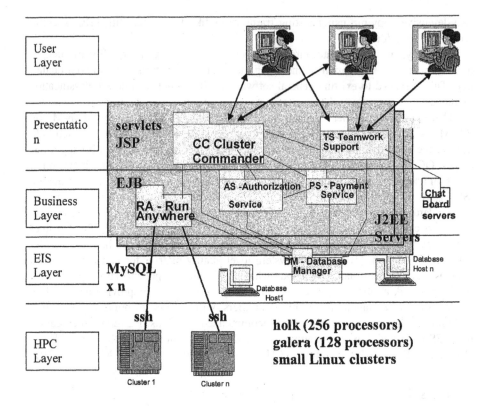

Fig. 1. Architecture of BeesyCluster

grid computing – the user can mark an application to be available as a service via WWW or Web Services from both accounts on clusters as well as even desktop PCs – this implements controlled resource sharing i.e. grid computing,

data replication – uses data replication in several databases for which consistency must be maintained and is handled by a custom-built distributed database replication mechanism on MySQL outside of J2EE,

clustering – uses multiple J2EE servers to increase availability and reliability,

session and security handling using WWW and Web Services (described in paragraph 5.1) – handling security identities and rights to the resources (digital signatures with asymmetric cryptography are used),

modular design – the system is composed of modules which can be implemented independently and share the same top-level compilation scripts,

variety of interactive services via applets – BeesyCluster uses two dedicated Java servers for chat and a board shared by users for interactive collaboration, another applet implements an online remote shell on clusters,

building scientific workflows – services on clusters can be combined into complex scientific workflows ([3]).

5   Classification of Patterns/Solutions to Typical Errors Identified during Development of BeesyCluster

5.1   Selected Design Problems/Solutions in BeesyCluster

In this paragraph, we distinguish selected design problems and their solutions in BeesyCluster (Table 1, [1]). This is done in view of the existing J2EE design patterns, also in a broader context of current and future technologies which are suggested for implementation.

Tab. 1: Selected Design Problems/Solutions in BeesyCluster

Problem	Solution
Portable Authorization and Session Management for Various System Interfaces and Clients	Since complex applications can use various interfaces like WWW, Web Services, listen on sockets using a proprietary protocol, wait for a file system change etc., a portable and compatible way of authorization and session management between calls must be used. BeesyCluster suggests a way in which the user logs in with a username/password and obtains an encrypted token which is passed with following calls (steps analogous to publishing data in UDDI). In the system there is a dedicated business component for authorization based on a database. Then for: 1. WWW requests: authorization can be done within an Intercepting Filter ([5]) which verifies the token by calling the business component per each request before delegating the request to following components, possibly Front Controller. Although J2EE has a way of defining roles that may access Web components and J2EE server users may be mapped to these roles, this way is more flexible since can employ e.g. runtime variables as time of day or IP into granting access. The token which handles session information may be stored in a cookie or in a session object on the server and be identified by a cookie. 2. Web Services or other interfaces: a method for logging in is a first required step which returns a token which is then used as an additional parameter to successive calls ([3] explains the way it is implemented in BeesyCluster). "Business" Web Services (which call EJBs) call a business component to verify access. Similarly, the proprietary protocol for TCP communication might use the same token. This means that the user could possibly start a session using WWW and finish using Web Services from another device.
Separation of Java Code from Web Pages and Instant Review of Page Changes	Although the J2EE standard defines the presentation layer (servlets, JSPs) and business logic layer (EJBs), still servlets and especially JSPs can contain control statements (patterns like Front Controller or Composite View [5]) as well as formatting for Web pages. It can be recommended to use a technology purely for presentation/formatting output. In our case, we used Velocity which displays (using proper templates) output variables (from proper business methods) or arrays set in servlets. Furthermore, changes in templates do not require recompilation which speeds up the development.
continued on next page	

continued on next page

Problem	Solution
Multiple Extensible Interfaces to the System and Business Layer Separation	In today's world, apart from the WWW interface for human-system interaction over the Internet, complex applications need means to communicate among themselves. We used Web Services (based on AXIS), currently an element of J2EE, to provide such possibilities. In fact the Web Service Broker pattern suggests this approach. Still, other interfaces might be needed like more efficient proprietary protocols over TCP etc. J2EE is well prepared for this as business methods may be called by endpoints handling these interfaces e.g. servlets/JSPs for WWW, Web Service for SOAP, a server listening on sockets etc. From this perspective, it seems crucial that business methods are sufficiently isolated (Session Facade [5]).
Minimizing latency to data layer and external systems	This should be done by proper caching of data: 1. when fetching data from external systems or the database, part of it should be reused for following client requests if possible (e.g. reloading the left panel of the file manager does not cause querying of the right panel of another cluster), 2. in the presentation layer: technologies like AJAX allow to exchange XML data with the server without reloading the entire page.
Uniform Logging Facility	Logging can be incorporated into an Intercepting Filter but only for presentation layer components. A dedicated logging component (e.g. bean) is suggested recording the id of the calling module, time, the user who has requested the operation, users whom the operation affects, priority, description. It is recommended to define logging levels to reflect the J2EE layers (presentation, business). Logging in the presentation layer should be turned off when EJBs already log detailed information.
Transparent Parallel and Reliable Access to Data	Usually data would be retrieved from a database by entity beans (BMP or CMP). Still, it is desirable that there is a mechanism, transparent to the programmer, that hides potentially parallel access to several databases for both increasing throughput of e.g. SELECT queries and reliability (if some database nodes fail). This can be configured in both commercial engines and e.g. MySQL where a master node and slave database server nodes can be configured. Within BeesyCluster, an extension to the MySQL solution was implemented which changes a slave to the master if the current master fails. Additionally, synchronization algorithms can be changed to e.g. quorum consensus and others easily ([1]). This in fact suggests a more complex sequence diagram for the standard Data Access Object pattern ([5])
Client-aware Interface	Although fast broadband Internet connections have become mainstream, the client-system data transfer should be client-aware because of mobile devices like palmtops or mobile phones with limited memory and processing capabilities (MIDP 2.0 requires 128KB for the Java runtime heap, 8KB for persistent data, a screen of 96x54 pixels). Crucial Web, Web Service or other resources should take the maximum returned data size parameter. This can be done with the standard request e.g. by: 1. another request parameter for HTTP transfer, 2. another header in a SOAP message for Web Services ([14]). Revert to a basic but functional interface for less capable browsers.
Minimize Response Time by Advance Queries	Periodic calls with output to be used by user queries (e.g. monitoring the state of remote systems or databases to be queried next) should be done by threads in the background (threads or separate servers). The output (possibly somewhat out-of-date) is fetched when the user request is handled. JMS communication with threads is suggested.

5.2 Selected Implementation Errors Identified during Development of BeesyCluster

Table 2 lists selected implementation errors or recommendations identified during the development of the system. These are likely to occur in other complex applications.

Tab. 2. Selected Implementation Errors Identified during Development of BeesyCluster

Layer	Errors or Recommendations to Avoid Errors
Presentation Layer	1. Initial values not filled in web forms. 2. Presentation layer servlets and JSP pages using hardcoded ids (e.g. clusters or users) not from the database thus making it inconsistent with ids used by the business layer components. 3. Specific parameters (text boxes) cause problems (e.g. spaces in the names of directories). 4. Access to specific servlets or JSP pages should not be granted to users with restricted privileges (missing conditional instructions). 5. Test functionality of the interface using 1 client, always use 20+ concurrent client requests from various nodes to test response times, isolation of transactions, potential deadlocks when referring to same resources. 6. Always disable display of exception details for production version, log details to a log, always print information to a log in catch blocks. 7. Avoid a long sequence of page reloads (3+) to complete a task, could be completed within one page (using e.g. AJAX). 8. Use only one way of fetching session information in web components.
Presentation--business Layer Interaction	1. When processing in business method takes 5+ seconds, call it asynchronously, store a handle and allow to retrieve status or make the presentation layer show progress until results are available. 2. Data presentation not handled properly for certain input data to the business layer or error codes from the business layer not interpreted.
Business Layer	1. Errors in EJB components which are likely to be detected only during the real deployment of that module. Example: errors of task submission to a real cluster from the module (via the Jsch Java library). 2. Long response times or hangs when submitting many requests to an external system in a short time frame – configure external systems properly. On cluster holk command must be run via a proxy node - initially via rsh. rshd on holk refused connections in the case of many concurrent requests (ports up to 1023 can only be used). Using ssh solved the problem.

5.3 System Configuration/Deployment Errors and Solutions

Management of configurations especially in the case of multiple installations of a system, possibly on different architectures is challenging. BeesyCluster's official release runs on Solaris while the development version on Linux.

Tab. 3: System Configuration/Deployment Errors and Solutions

Issue	Items
Security	1. HTTP connection available after testing, should leave only HTTPS. 2. Errors with certificates in HTTPS access from certain browsers (error for self-signed certificates where Common Name (CN) of the issuer and CN of the entity the certificate was issued to are identical - Mozilla, Konqueror). 3. Securing physical access to servers (accidental restarts by other users). 4. Hide URLs for services where possible (e.g. by a proper Front Controller pattern passing parameters for selected URLs). 5. Write a client for exposed URLs requesting with random parameters and use it for testing.
Database Configuration	1. Error in scripts filling the database with initial data (SQL statements not accepted by later MySQL versions, worked correctly on the version, BeesyCluster was originally deployed on). 2. Modification of a single node of a cluster of replicated databases. During some tests using one node, only a single database was modified and another backed up as a master.
System Configuration	1. Problems with specific versions of required libraries e.g. xdoclet pre 1.2.2 caused compilation errors while newer versions worked correctly, 2. Problems with migration from Java 1.4 to 1.5, qualified names should be used in the code due to the conflict with classes from Java 1.5, 3. Inconsistent configuration (versions of software) and startup scripts across the cluster of servers, need for a tool updating all nodes or NFS, 4. Some services would not start properly after system was restarted although the core of the system worked correctly (Java chat/whiteboard servers). 5. Uniform configuration and compilation scripts for all modules are recommended. It is possible to define a top-level build.xml file so that a new module can simply be added by copying its directory into the existing sources and no or very few additional changes are required. 6. Failures of operating system servers cause selected servers used by the system to fail. Creation of a simple monitoring tool with restart of services is recommended.
Versioning	1. Components were updated on one of the J2EE servers instead of all the servers which resulted in errors on those servers. Use a distribution tool to distribute changes to all servers. 2. Submission of incorrect versions of components to a server for deployment – already corrected errors/bugs would show up again.

In view of clustering and replication to increase the number of clients the system can handle in parallel/concurrently and inconsistencies of configuration across the cluster, errors of this type in BeesyCluster (Table 3) can be applicable to other systems as well.

6 Quality Modeling and Evaluation in QESA

6.1 QESA Methodology

The QESA methodology ([11]) uses a generic QESA quality tree (Figure 2) to evaluate the quality of a product or phase by general top-level external quality attributes each of which is defined by either four or five quality factors at the second level (several translation functions are available). In the QESA methodology, these two levels are fixed since are thought to be general enough to suit any application, development phase or product. Depending on whether a development phase or a product is evaluated, factors will be further defined by more precise metrics at the lower and measures at the lowest level of a four-level quality tree – both chosen by the user to suit the application. As an example attribute *dependability* defined by factor *error-tolerance* could be defined by metric *presentation layer errors* and this by question *whether access to page tested when no user logged in*. Then answers to questions in measures or their numerical values propagate up the tree and generate final values for quality attributes.

QESA allows e.g. metrics to contribute to a factor by a decreasing function. Usually a more complex and fancy user interface improves visual effects while decreases interaction performance. Measures being in fact internal quality attributes are defined with values in their own domain (e.g. seconds or LOCs) and normalized into the [0,1] range. Quality attributes, factors and metrics are defined within the range [0;1], the higher value meaning better quality at the highest level.

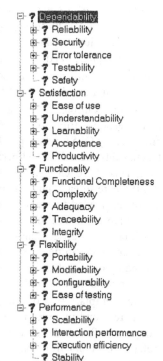

Fig. 2. QESA Quality Tree - Two Top Levels

In fact, as applied during classes on Software Quality courses at Faculty of Electronics, Telecommunications and Informatics, Gdansk University of Technology, the QESA quality tree could be used in many ways, two of which are:

1. During the software development cycle, a new quality tree is created for each phase with metrics and measures specific for the given phase.
2. For the comparison of products e.g. complete applications, a reference quality tree is created with metrics and measures specific for the given type of product and evaluation is performed for each product. Values can be compared in the QESA system. In particular, an aggregate value for higher level factors and attributes can be compared.

6.2 Modeling Quality of BeesyCluster as a Template for New Applications

Modeling quality of BeesyCluster as a quality tree will allow other applications to be verified against the errors, deficiencies and design strategies suggested in paragraph 5.

For the BeesyCluster system, we have created quality models (trees) with metrics and measures specific for distributed and parallel applications which is our area of expertise ([13], [3]). Quality trees refer to:

design – measures are simply questions whether the design principles given in paragraph 5.1 are met (yes/no) or in what degree (numerical value),

implementation – whether the code has been validated against the errors listed in paragraph 5.2 and other basic coding standards,

testing – system tested for some implementation errors from paragraph 5.2 and configuration/deployment from paragraph 5.3.

As an example, the programmer/user of a new system specifies in the testing phase response times or whether form parameters have been tested. The values are processed by QESA which produces a final quality values for dependability, satisfaction, functionality, flexibility and performance. If the quality is satisfactory a new phase may start. This approach is similar to IBM's Orthogonal Defect Classification from 1992 ([12]) where in each phase numbers of defects of eight types are noted depending on the repair needed for the defect. Then the changes of distribution of defects between phases are compared to expected patterns. Process Inferencing Tree is built to track defect changes between phases. Similarly, in tracking quality QESA is similar to HP's Company-Wide Software Metrics from 1987 ([12]) which classifies defects into types depending on the phase and assigns mode e.g. *missing* for missing error checking. If other projects data is available, trends can be observed.

An exemplary part of the QESA quality tree for BeesyCluster's testing is shown in Figure 3 and includes the metrics and measures corresponding to items listed in paragraph 5.3. Resulting quality charts for BeesyCluster without the identified points (related to errors from paragraph 5.3) improved are shown in Figure 4 and after corrections in Figure 5. After the improvements the system can still be corrected e.g. a better interface can be engineered (as also reported by the attendees of a training course) or the response time can be reduced thanks to faster hardware.

For distributed J2EE applications such as BeesyCluster, the highest-level quality attributes given the largest weights (angles in Figures 4 and 5) are:

1. dependability especially error-tolerance i.e. how the system tolerates errors (here we assume that if several issues identified in BeesyCluster are not checked and tested for, the system may give undefined results), reliability (the system must be available and functional at all times) and security since providers must be certain their resources cannot be compromised beyond what they permitted,
2. functionality mainly functional completeness in the case of BeesyCluster being remote task execution, management, making resources available, receiving proper payments for the resources checked out etc.,
3. performance especially interaction performance (the system must respond in less than a few seconds for any request), scalability (must scale well with the number of servers and users).

The presented quality tree is available from the author. The QESA (SOJO in Polish) system can be downloaded from http://fox.eti.pg.gda.pl/~pczarnul/SOJO-1.0.zip. A Web-based version of QESA is available at http://153.19.53.71/qes/page.tytul.php.

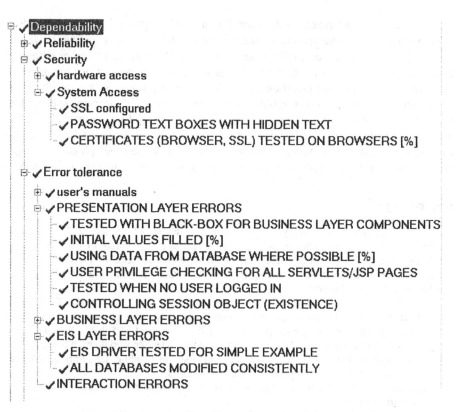

Fig. 3. Part of a QESA Quality Model for BeesyCluster's Testing

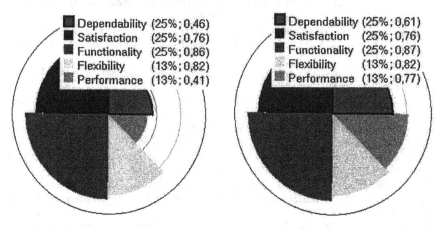

Fig. 4. Quality before Improvement   **Fig. 5.** Quality after Improvement

7 Summary

The model used, especially the quality issues specific for J2EE applications and identified above, can make design, implementation and development of other similar applications easier and faster. Products for design, implementation and testing for other J2EE applications can be validated against items identified in this paper while QESA can produce a quantitative quality value which can be compared to other systems. One of the original goals of the QESA initiative was the creation of distinct models, including translation functions (how the values of lower level nodes are translated to higher levels), coefficients of translation functions, metrics and measures specific for the given application class and the given development phase. This is especially useful in case of distributed applications due to their complex nature. The model proposed in this work is based on real world errors encountered during the development of a large production J2EE-based application and can be either used as provided or improved.

References

1. Czarnul, P., Bajor, M., Banaszczyk, A., Buszkiewicz, P., Fiszer, M., Fraczak, M., Klawikowski, M., Rakiej, J., Ramczykowska, K., Suchcicki, K.: The architecture of beesycluster: a front-end to a collection of clusters accessible via www/web services. In: Proceedings of VI Conference on Computer Engineering (KKIO 2004), Gdansk, Poland (2004) 437–450 in Polish, ISBN 83-204-3051-8.
2. Czarnul, P., Bajor, M., Fraczak, M., Banaszczyk, A., Fiszer, M., Ramczykowska, K.: Remote task submission and publishing in beesycluster : Security and efficiency of web service interface. In Springer-Verlag, ed.: Proc. of PPAM 2005. Volume LNCS 3911., Poland (2005)
3. Czarnul, P.: Integration of compute-intensive tasks into scientific workflows in beesycluster. In: Proceedings of ICCS 2006 Conference,, University of Reading, UK, Springer Verlag (2006) Lecture Notes in Computer Science, LNCS 3993.
4. Sun Microsystems: BluePrints, Patterns (2006) http://java.sun.com/blueprints /patterns/index.html.
5. Alur, D., Crupi, J., Malks, D.: Core J2EE Patterns: Best Practices and Design Strategies. 2nd edn. Prentice Hall / Sun Microsystems Press (2003) http://www. corej2eepatterns.com/index.htm, ISBN:0131422464.
6. Sun Microsystems: Code Conventions for the JavaTM Programming Language (1999)
7. O'Hanley, J.: Collected java practices (2006) Canada, http://www.javapractices. com/Table-OfContents.cjp.
8. Fenton, N.: Ensuring quality and quality metrics. In: Software engineering. MIKOM (2000) ISBN 83-7279-028-0.
9. Emam, K.E., Drouin, J.N., Melo, W.: SPICE The Theory and Practice of Software Process Improvement and Capability Determination. Wiley (1997) ISBN 0-8186-7798-8.
10. Sedigh-Ali, S., Ghafoor, A., Paul, R.A.: Software engineering metrics for cots-based systems. IEEE Computer Society Press, Computer **34**(5) (2001) 44–50 ISSN:0018-9162.
11. Czarnul, P., Krawczyk, H., Mazurkiewicz, A.: Quality driven development methodology for network applications. In: ISThmus'2000 Conference, Poznan, Poland (2000)
12. Fredericks, M., Basili, V.: Using defect tracking and analysis to improve software quality. Technical report, Experimental Software Engineering Group, University of Maryland, College Park, Maryland USA (1998)
13. Czarnul, P., Grzeda, K.: Parallelization of electrophysiological phenomena in myocardium on large 32 & 64-bit linux clusters. In Springer-Verlag, ed.: Proceedings of Euro PVM/MPI 2004, 11th European PVM/MPI Users' Group Meeting. Volume LNCS 3241., Budapest, Hungary (2004) 234–241
14. Nilo Mitra, Ed.: SOAP Version 1.2 Part 0: Primer. W3C Recommendation. (2003) http://www.w3.org/TR/soap12-part0.

Automatic software validation process

Maciej Dorsz[1], Mariusz Wasielewski[2]

[1] Poznan University of Technology,
60-965 Poznań, Poland
Maciej.Dorsz@cs.put.poznan.pl
[2] Projekty Bankowe Polsoft Sp. z o.o,
60-965 Poznań, Poland
Mariusz.Wasielewski@pbpolsoft.com.pl

Abstract. This article presents the Automatic Software Validation tool (ASV), which is deployed in one of the Polish software companies. This system helps to automatically test web applications, create its simulations, which are helpful during end-user training, and then test those simulations. The tool was invented to speed the process of testing one of the company's applications working in more than 12 Polish financial institutions. The clients' system settings and database schemas are different, therefore while introducing a new system functionality it is not enough to test one system version, but repeat tests for all 12 different parameters settings. Manual testing is very time-consuming and expensive. Every night ASV tool, basing on CVS, ANT and HttpUnit, fully automatically prepares the current system version, deploys it twelve times on Tomcat server with different parameters settings, executes tests, creates application simulations, tests those simulations and sends a summary report.

1 Introduction

Rapid and almost aggressive software development, as can be noticed in the recent years, calls for radical testing effort [1]. Inadequate software testing costs the economy of United States about 59 billion dollars every year. It has been estimated that possible improvements in software testing infrastructure could reduce that cost at about 22 billions [12]. Models and standards related to software development such as CMMI, eXtreme Programming, ISO 9001:2000, RUP place great attention to careful validation of the final product [2,3,4,8]. This article presents the way of putting software testing infrastructure improvements into practice.

About two years ago one of the Polish software company applications was deployed in more than 12 financial institutions. In this article it will be named: AMLPortal (Anti Money Laundering Portal). Although application source codes are the same for all customers, unfortunately, all of the customers have got different parameters settings. Those parameters customizes presentation and business tires according to individual customer's requirements. Moreover, there are some differences in database schemas. The team developing this product prepared Ant script to generate a ready for deployment application [1]. AMLPortal is written in Java, therefore

Please use the following format when citing this chapter:

Dorsz, M., Wasielewski, M., 2006, in IFIP International Federation for Information Processing, Volume 227, Software Engineering Techniques: Design for Quality, ed. K. Sacha, (Boston: Springer), pp. 191–197.

Ant script simply generates .war file. Then, CruiseControl was installed to take care of storing in CVS repository only versions which can be compiled [5,6]. With time, the problem of software validation process appeared.

AMLPortal is used to search for amount, suspected and related banking transactions. One of its functionality is manual transaction adding to the AMLPortal database. The transaction form has about 45 different fields, such as: transaction number, date, owner data, beneficiary data, addresses, bank account numbers, remarks etc. Almost each of the customers uses unique form to add a bank transaction manually. The form can have additional fields, which may be used by one or some of the customers. Moreover, the clients uses different data validation. Therefore, not fulfilled *beneficiary address* for some clients is correct, for some it is shown as a warning, and for the others it is marked as an error. The example is presented in Figure 1.

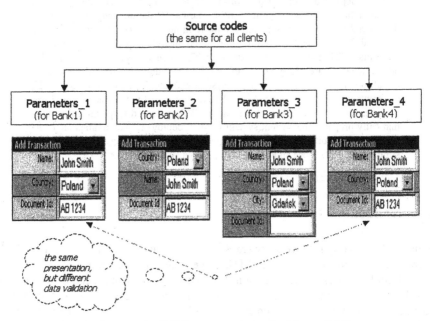

Fig. 1. The example of different presentations and data validations

The difficulty of testing the AMLPortal application will be shown on the example. Let's consider the case that a computer scientist changed a form for manual bank transactions adding. Because the system source codes, JSP pages, libraries, etc. are the same for all customers, this person introduced the change only once. However to carefully test it, one needs to test a new AMLPortal version 12 times, namely, for each set of the client's specific parameters settings. It is very time-consuming, expensive, and monotonous. Therefore, an application for automatic software validation was proposed.

2 Automatic Software Validation

The Automatic Software Validation tool (ASV tool) builds a system version, deploys it on the Tomcat server with client's specific parameters, tests it, deploys the same system version with parameters for next client, test it, etc. and finally send a report. In Figure 2 the diagram outlining the process of automatic software validation is presented.

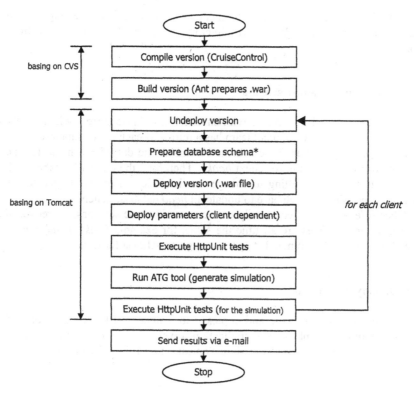

Fig. 2. The diagram outlining the process of automatic software validation

The diagram as well as an asterisk meaning are explained in detail in following sections.

2.1 Version compilation

CruiseControl periodically compiles the *head version* stored in CVS repository. If the compilation process fails, the application development team is obliged to repair the system version or rollback introduced changes. Therefore, in the end of the day, the *head version* can always be compiled.

2.2 Building the version

AML Portal is a web application written in Java. ASV tool uses Ant script to generate the current system version. Ant script, on the basis on the *head version* stored in CVS, prepares .war file.

2.3 Undeploying version

On the Tomcat server, the undeployment process is easy. It is enough, to *stop* the server, delete content of WEB-INF directory as well as the content of WORK directory.

2.4 Preparing database schema

This stage is marked in Figure 1 with an asterisk, because currently is not fully automatic. Application development team has a mirror of each client database schema, for example *bank1_head* database schema resembles the database schema for the *head version* of the application for client *bank1*. Therefore, there are 12 database schemas. A computer scientist willing to change the database schema is obliged to inform a person responsible for database to update all *head* database schemas.

Therefore ASV tool works only with correct database schemas. Moreover, the database schemas names are all time the same, for example *bank1_head, bank2_head* etc. ASV runs SQL commands to prepare a given schema for tests.

2.5 Deploying version

ASV tool unpacks .war file and copies it to Tomcat WEB-INF directory. If ASV worked with more sophisticated application servers, the deployment procedure would be more complex. However, regarding Tomcat server it is really simple.

2.6 Deploying parameters

Every client has individual system parameters. For example *bank1* may have parameter called *is_beneficiary_address_recquired* set to '1' that means it is required. Another one, may have it set to '2' what would mean that it will be marked as *warning.* The others may have it set with value designating 'not required'. For AML portal way of storing parameters is quite sophisticated, for the sake of clarity, it will be assumed that each client has a separate parameter file called: *bank1_AMLPortal.parameters, bank2_AMLPortal.parameters,* etc. In such files are all parameters describing system presentation and business login nuances, but also many other like database connection settings, mailer settings etc.

ASV tool simply copies the right parameters file to Tomcat WEB-INF/etc directory. Then ASV tool *starts* Tomcat server.

2.7 Executing HttpUnit tests

There is only one set of HTTP tests for AMLPortal application [7]. It means that automatic tests do not check client's specific functionality. They are general and focus on system functions which are used by all customers. Therefore, the option prepared and visible only for one client is not tested in this way. However, the main AMLPortal functionality concerns bank transactions management: inserting it into system, searching for amount, suspicious and related transactions, and exporting the founded transaction to an external institution, called: The General Inspector of Financial Information [10].

In order to make HttpUnit tests general the test which adds banking transaction has to add a bank transaction with filled in field *beneficiary address*. Then regardless of the parameter *is_beneficiary_address_recquired* value the bank transaction can be added properly.

2.8 Use ATG tool to generate AMLPortal simulation

AMLPortal was deployed in 12 institutions. It had meant many end-user training. In order to support that process Automatic Training Generation (ATG) tool was invented [4,5]. ATG on the basis on HttpUnit tests saves subsequent .html pages. HttpUnit uses *WebConversation* object to obtain connection with web page. Then it can *set* and *get* html form elements' values, clicks buttons and links. This tool bases on html protocol.

Then it changes their content by adding JavaScript. Finally, Automatic Training Generation tool prepares the simulation of a real application. The simulation is a set of .html pages powered with JavaScript. The end-user may "start" simulation and use it almost as a real system. Because the simulation is a set of static pages, the end-user does not need network connection, running database with an AMLPortal schema and application server.

Automatic Software Validation tool runs Automatic Training Generation tool to prepare AMLPortal simulation.

In case when generation simulations are not needed, processing concerning ATG should be excluded from application testing.

2.9 Executing HttpUnit tests for the simulation

Next, the same tests as were used for testing the real application are used to test generated simulation. Because the simulation visual side resembles the original application, and was created by saving .html files, the fields, links, and button names and their arrangement are the same. In order to test the static simulation pages, they are deployed on application server. Therefore in practice, HttpUnit is testing a web application, which, in fact, is a set of static pages.

2.10 Sending results

After repeating steps from 2.3 to 2.9 twelve times, ASV tool prepares a report and sends it via email. A report structure is shown in Figure 3.

```
-----start: 2006.02.03----
Bank1: passed
Bank2: passed
Bank3: failed
Bank4: passed
Bank5: failed
Bank6: passed
(...)
----------------
Bank3: Executing HTTPUnit tests : AddingTransactionTest
            <exceptions part>


----------------
Bank5: Deploying parameters:
            FileNotFoundException (file: Bank5.parameters)

-----end: 2006.02.03----
```

Fig. 3. The report structure

3 ASV in practice

The Automatic Software Validations tool can be used for the testing of one system version with only one parameters setting. However, it is really profitable for testing a versions with a few sets of parameters.

Table 1. Some of the ASV tool properties

Property name	Value	Comment
server_path	C:\tomcat	# Tomcat installation path
war_path	D:\AMLPortal\war	# generated AMLPortal .war path
properties_path	D:\AMLPortal\properties	# path to clients properties files
simulations_path	D:\AMLPortal\simulations	# path to generated simulations
start_time	02:00	# ASV starts at 2:00 a.m.
clients_list	bank1, bank2...	# list of clients
CVSROOT	:pserver:cod@10.5.5.10: /amlportal	# cvs repository path
(...)		

ASV tool is deployed in one of the Polish companies, whether it will be an Open Source application has not been decided yet. It would be not difficult to adapt ASV to another environments. To use it one needs CVS repository, Ant script to compile and generate versions and HttpUnit tests. It is not necessary to use CruiseControl, also simulation generation with ATG tool may be used on demand. ASV tool properties are placed in *properties* file, some of them are shown in Table 1.

4 Summary

This article presents Automatic Software Validation tool, which allows one to automatically test the application *head version* with many different parameters settings. Basing on CVS repository, Ant and HttpUnit this tool can automatically prepare system version, then for each client deploy it, execute tests, create an application simulations and even tests those simulations. Finally, ASV sends a report.

The next development phase for ASV tool means the development of GUI side as well as integrating it with CruieControl reports. Automatic preparation of database schemas would be really helpful. Moreover, statistics about automatic testing and its results should be gathered.

References

1. Ant, http://ant.apache.org
2. Beck, K., Extreme Programming Explained. Embrace Change. Addison-Wesley, Boston, (2000)
3. CCTA, Managing Successful Projects with PRINCE 2, The Stationary Office, London (2002)
4. CMMI Product Team, Capability Maturity Product Integrations (CMMI), v1.1, Staged Representation, CMU/SEI-2002-TR-004, Software Engineering Institute, Pittsburgh PA, December (2001)1. Jefferies, R., eXtreme Testing: Why aggressive software development calls for radical testing effort, STQE Magazine, March/April (1999)
5. Concurrent Versions System, http://www.nongnu.org/cvs
6. CruiseControl, http://cruisecontrol.sourceforge.net/
7. HttpUnit, http://HttpUnit.sourceforge.net/
8. International Organization for Standardization, Quality Management Systems – Guidelines for performance improvements, ISO 9004:2000, ISO publication, December (2000)
9. Maciej Dorsz, Jerzy Nawrocki, Anna Demuth: ATG 2.0: the platform for automatic generation of training simulations, Software Engineering: Evolutions and Emergining Technologies, IOS Press, Krzysztof Zieliński, Tomasz Szmuc (ed.) (2005)
10. Ministry of Finance, Poland, http://www.mf.gov.pl
11. Rational Software Corporation, Using Rational Robot (2001)
12. RTI, National Institute of Standards and Technology, The Economic Impacts of Inadequate Infrastructure for Software Testing, Final Report, May (2002)

j2eeprof – a tool for testing multitier applications

Paweł Kłaczewski and Jacek Wytrębowicz

Institute of Computer Science of Warsaw University of Technology
P.Klaczewski@elka.pw.edu.pl, J.Wytrebowicz@elka.pw.edu.pl

Abstract. Quality assurance of multitier application is still a challenge. Especially difficult is testing big, distributed applications written by several programmers, with the use of components from different sources. Due to multi threaded and distributed architecture, their ability to be observed and their profiling are extremely difficult. *J2eeprof* is a new tool developed for testing and profiling multitier applications that run in the J2EE environment. The tool is based on the paradigm of aspect insertion. The main goal of *j2eeprof* is to help in fixing of integration errors and efficiency errors. This paper presents the concept of *j2eeprof* and gives some insides of *j2eeprof* development. On the beginning we give some introduction to the methods of software profiling, and a brief characteristic of existing profilers, i.e., *JFluid, Iron Track Sql, OptimizeIt Server Trace* and *JXInsight*. Next we present the architecture of *j2eeprof*, and we describe how it collects data, what protocols it uses, and what kind of analysis it supports. On the end we demonstrate how *j2eeprof* works in practice. In conclusions we list the strong and weak points of this tool, which is still in a beta version. *J2eeprof* is planned to be offered as an open source for the programmer community.

1 Introduction

Software testing and software profiling are time consuming tasks, especially during development of multitier, distributed applications. Sometimes these tasks take more time than coding. They are crucial when the target application is safety or business critical. We mean by testing the process of defect discovery in a developed code. We mean by profiling the process of performance analysis of an application.

Because Java Platform Enterprise Edition (J2EE) is a widely used programming platform for developing and running distributed multitier architecture applications, we have focused our attention on testing and profiling applications that run in the J2EE environment. The result is *j2eeprof* [7] - a new tool to help in fixing of integration errors and efficiency errors. Integration testing and profiling need very similar methods and tools. We shortly describe them.

To make not frequent or exceptional conditions testable we have to extend the tested application to make controllable its execution flow. During an execution flow a programmer collects selected data for subsequent analysis. Selection of the data depends on programmer aim, it could be: remote function checking, bottleneck discovery, time consumption of selected functions and memory consumption. In general, there are two methods of data gathering: sampling and tracing∞. The advantage of sampling is that this method slightly influences the tested application in contradiction to the tracing

Please use the following format when citing this chapter:

Kłaczewski, P., Wytrębowicz, J., 2006, in IFIP International Federation for Information Processing, Volume 227, Software Engineering Techniques: Design for Quality, ed. K. Sacha, (Boston: Springer), pp. 199–210.

method. The advantage of tracing is the possibility to achieve very high accuracy but when accuracy is higher – the execution time is more and more disturbed.

Extensions that make the execution flow controllable are included in the application code by a programmer. Sampling can be performed without any modification of the application code. Tracing can be achieved by altering the code or by modification of its environment, or both. The Java Platform Debugger Architecture (JPDA), which is a collection of APIs to debug Java code, is a good example of a tool for environment modification. A disadvantage of JPDA is the limited set of low-level events that the programmer can observe. The abstraction level of virtual Java machine is not suitable for J2EE application analysis. The programmer gets too much low level data, which are difficult to analyze. Altering of the application code can be done by hand, can be processed by a compiler (e.g., as for *gprof* Unix tool), or after compilation. There are Java libraries, e.g., BCEL[1], ASM [3], which allow altering a Java bytecode during loading. The programmer has to point where and how the automatic code altering should be performed.

The amount of data collected during an application run is usually huge. Sometime some compression or aggregation methods have to be used for their collection. A programmer needs to have some tools for filtering the collected data and for their visualization in an interactive manner. G. Ammons, T. Ball and J. R. Larus [1] have proposed to build a structure called Calling Context Tree (CCT) – as an aggregation method. Every tree node keeps some measurements of an executed function. Any path in the tree represents a possible execution sequence of modules (the module can be a method, a component, a layer, or a node belonging to a distributed system). Figure 1 depicts an exemplary execution path of a function X that executes 6 modules (AB notation means that A module calls B module). A tree representation is more expressive.

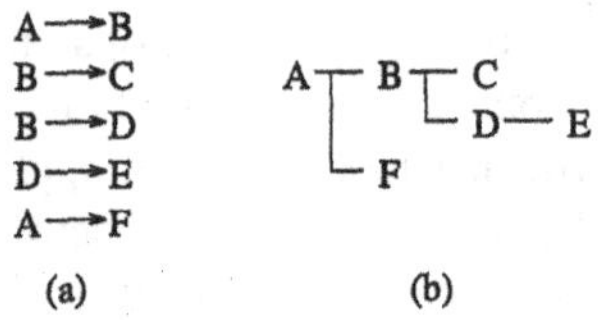

Fig. 1. Execution path visualization a) sequential, b) context tree

It helps to find bottlenecks related to different load of data or user connections. There are more ways of execution path visualization as Fig 2 shows. Nowadays profilers generate a layered representation of full tree of execution calls (Fig 2b). The width of every rectangle may depict execution time of relating module. Complex applications give very big trees. To make them more readable reduced graphs can be generated (Fig. 2c, 2d). Most profilers allow for simple filtering of presented data with predefined set of views. However there are exceptions: a programmer using *ejp*[2] can implement own filters. *XDSE* profiler [2] stores full execution trace in an XML database. Next a programmer can define filtering by XQuery language and select a visualization form.

---

[1] http://jakarta.apache.org/bcel

[2] http://ejp.sourceforge.net

M(A(B()C())D(C())A(B()C())D(C())A(B()B()C()C()))

(a)

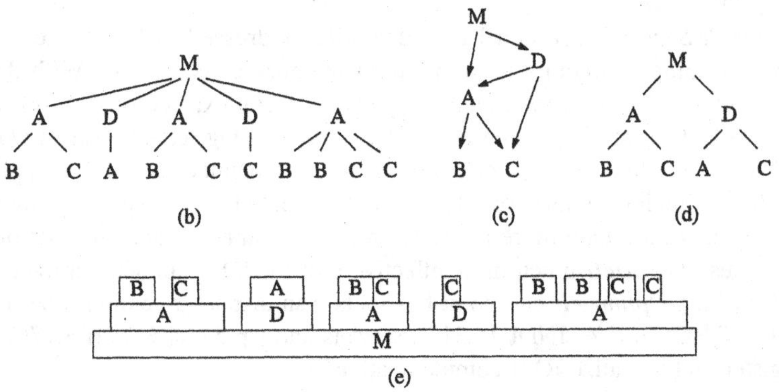

(b)   (c)   (d)

(e)

Fig. 2. Execution path visualization a) layered representation, b) full tree of execution calls, c) reduced call graph, d) context call tree. e) trace graph

Profiling of a distributed system is difficult. Every distinct element has to be observed independently. Next, a profiler has to correlate collected data before filtering and presentation. A correlation method based on independent clocks is not accurate and leads to interpretation errors. Much efficient is to include tracing into a communication mechanism used by separate instances. Authors of [8] describe a tool that traces TCP messages. For better efficiency, a profiler could use some marking of messages that concern the analyzed application/purpose. *Pinpoint* project [6] is based on modification of *Jboss*[3] application server – in this way a distributed application, which works on *Jboss* servers, can be easily and efficiently traced. When a programmer uses CORBA, then we can take advantage of built in interceptor mechanism for message marking. The interceptor is a function written by the programmer and called during communication.

There are several commercial profilers addressed to J2EE environment, but we do not know any such a tool from public domain. Profilers created for Java programmers, not only for those who use J2EE, are more numerous. Let take a look on some of them – the most interesting in our opinion. *JFluid* profiler [5], from Sun Microsystems, works only with the *NetBeans* programmer framework. It provides some means for analysis of: memory consumption, execution time and execution flow. Programmer can point some Java methods for analysis. *JFluid* process the code statically to discover all methods, which could be executed by those selected. Next it alters them to make them traceable. It visualizes only the traces that belong to the execution context of selected methods. The altered code has constant time overhead, that allows subtracting it from measured values, and present more accurate data. Because *JFluid* co-works with extended (tuned for it) virtual java machine it is a fast and efficient tool.

Iron Track Sql[4] is a free tool for performance monitoring of java applications that interact with databases. It builds a log of every database query, its time and duration. It allows for some filtering, e.g., to register only these queries whose duration overcomes

---

[3] http://www.jboss.org

[4] http://www.irongrid.com/catalog/product_info.php?products_id=32

a defined threshold. It is based on a database proxy, which makes all required logs. The programmer has to use the *p6spy* driver (an element of *Iron Track Sql*) in place of standard jdbc driver.

OptimizeIt Server Trace is a Borland profiler addressed to J2EE. It can gather data using probing or tracing. It can monitor memory consumption. With this tool the programmer can visualize execution paths as a context tree or as a full tree of execution calls. OptimizeIt presents j2ee services trace using sets of abstract words. In example word "ejb load" stands for ejb load life cycle method. Tool hides application server internal implementation of ejb load and presents it to user in simplified form. Profiling statistics are then more readable and free of unnecessary information. This feature makes *OptimizeIt* much more effective tool for J2EE application tracing than standard profiler. *OptimizeIt* can point hot spots, can display execution time of every layer, e.g.: JDBC 23,68%, JNDI 15.31%, servlets and jsp 57.84%, EJB 3,17%. It can even register and visualize RMI communication.

JInspired company offers the *JXInsight* profiler. This tool is very similar to *OptimizeIt Server Trace*. The difference is that *JXInsight* has more functions for monitoring of database queries. It can display correlations between distributed events using CORBA interceptors. Both *OptimizeIt* and *JXInsight* are very complex and powerful tools, which allow multitier visualization of execution paths.

There are many other profilers but most of them suit only development of standard Java programs running on a single machine. They are inefficient for development of J2EE applications, which are distributed and use a server code. Usually the programmer does not know the server code (it is a black box for him). And the server code is a significant part of the application. The only corrections and optimizations, the programmer can make, are inside his code. Hence only tools like *OptimizeIt* and *JXInsight* can really help to profile J2EE applications.

2   j2eeprof insides

J2eeprof is profiler designed for applications running in J2EE environment. J2EE provides variety of services. Programs work in a container i.e., servlet container or ejb container. Container provides services, can manage component life cycle and enhance program behavior. The way program uses services can be specified in code or configuration descriptor. When configuration is used it is impossible to inspect program behavior only by reading its code. This makes testing more difficult to the programmer. Another problem arises, when J2EE application is profiled using standard java profiler. There is huge amount of container implementation code execution registered together with program code. The performance impact is large and results contain plenty of superfluous information.

In order to capture accurate view of execution flow, *j2eeprof* uses tracing. *J2eeprof* comes with ability of selective program tracing. It registers J2EE services and program execution at high level of detail. By inspecting trace programmer can find out all the interactions of J2EE services with program. The tool has significant ability to shape profiling scope. *J2eeprof* addresses also distributed nature of ejb components. It is able to track communication between remote ejb components and deliver distributed system trace.

J2eeprof is designed for profiling applications that run in a distributed environment. Thus tool itself is distributed as well. There are three major modules of *j2eeprof*: data collection module, transport module and visualization module. The data collection is installed on distributed system nodes and acts as client in the client-server *j2eeprof* architecture. Visualization module is responsible for trace analysis and visualizations. The data is transported from remote data collections modules to visualization module by transport module.

2.1 Data collection

Data collection module uses tracing method to collect profile data. Its implementation is based on the aspect oriented programming (AOP). Aspect is a program module that implements some common functionality and has no dependencies on other program modules. AOP consists of two elements: aspect weaver and composition language. Aspect weaver is responsible for composition of aspects and other modules into final application. Composition language controls the weaver. *J2eeprof* uses *Aspectwerkz*[5], open source AOP library, as a basis for data collection module. *Aspectwerkz* weaver is capable of dynamic aspect insertion. This feature enables profiler to temporarily modify tested code and change profiling scope on every program execution. *Aspectwerkz* uses *AspectJ*[6] composition language. The point of program code, where aspect can be inserted, is called join point. It can be i.e., a method or a construction invocation. Pointcut is *AspectJ* definition that pick out a set of join points. *AspectJ* gives *j2eeprof* capability to define profiling scope with detail. Important feature in J2EE environment is that a join point can define interface and polymorphic execution. J2EE is specified by a set of interfaces. *J2eeprof* can profile application server standard services by tracing them at the interface level. This method provides the right level of abstraction. Tracing implementation details of application server not only has negative performance impact, but also has no value for the application developer, as he cannot modify server code. Still the application code can be traced with much greater detail – up to every method call.

Data collection module implements a set of aspects. Data collection aspect is responsible for registering information on program execution. AOP composition language allows mixing of aspects in order to register traces on different detail level. Data trace representation (see Fig. 3) in *j2eeprof* consists of 4 elements. *PathNode* is a node of trace path. *PathNode* can contain other *PathNode* in the way it make call tree. *PathNode* is a base class for a concrete node, which may represent method execution or distributed call. Nodes belong to an execution thread, which is represented by *ThreadNode*. *SystemNode* is a node of distributed system. *System* abstracts whole observed system. The representation can describe nodes on different level of abstraction.

There are 2 generic aspects that trace method executions: *MainAspect* that registers only method signatures and ParametersAspect that registers also parameter values. An aspect collects information about several attributes: start and end time, information on

---

[5] http://aspectwerkz.codehaus.org

[6] http://www.eclipse.org/aspectj

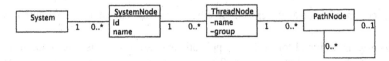

Fig. 3. Trace model

exception, path node name (e.g. method signature) and execution thread. There is also one additional attribute – category that is specified in aspect definition, and it is used later for data analysis.

2.2 Data transport

Gathered data are transmitted by transport module. The module consists of three parts: data sender, transport protocol and data receiver. Data transport module can write data to file or send over TCP/IP. The most important element is the protocol. *J2eeprof* uses binary protocol that is built in a way to keep network traffic low. We have executed several tests to measure *j2eeprof* overhead. The results (Table 1) have shown that the most time consuming is I/O. The more data is sent the more impact on performance is made (see test 3 and 4 in Table 1). During execution of test 3 all gathered data been discarded, during execution of test 4 the same data have been written into a file. I/O slow down factor was about 6. Addition of a simple compression method resulted in better overall performance. *J2eeprof* uses dictionary compression for most frequently sent data – event labels. *MainAspect* sends approximately 30 bytes per start method event and 22 bytes per exit method event. Executions with tracing turned off (test 1) and with *AspectWerkz* (test 2) empty aspect have shown a difference of performance overhead. Encoding overhead (test 3) is 3,232.98 ns but 509.68 ns (test 2) is the effect of using *AspectWerkz* and cannot be avoided. Write to the file (test 4) slows down by 17,421.38 ns. *J2eeprof* performs almost twice better as *Log4J*[7] (test 7). The maximum time was taken from *j2eeprof* statistics. It indicates that writing into a file gives more stable effects compared to sending over TCP/IP, however the second choice is much more convenient for a user.

Tab. 1. Measured performance overhead

no	test	mean time[ns/per call]	max time[ms/per call]
1	no aspects	31.63	
2	NullAspect	509.68	
3	MainAspect (no I/O)	3,232.98	
4	MainAspect (file)	20,654.36	58
5	MainAspect (tcp local)	33,639.00	308
6	MainAspect (tcp)	36,767.00	949
7	Log4J (file)	41,199.31	

2.3 Distributed tracing

J2eeprof can profile distributed J2EE systems. Execution path on each distinct node of analyzed system is recorded. But it is also required to match right local paths and

---

[7] http://logging.apache.org/log4j

reconstruct distributed path. Tagging messages exchanged between nodes can do this. This method has top accuracy over others, and is not affected by time differences of the nodes. EJB protocol – RMI/IIOP supports sending additional information in protocol tier, without changing interface on an application tier (Fig. 4). Corba Interceptor documentation [4] describes this feature. *J2eeprof* tracing mechanism can be enabled in the configuration file of application server, with no need to modify program or server code. The method is protocol dependent; *j2eeprof* comes with implementation for standard EJB protocol RMI/IIOP and *Jboss* RMI. But this solution is well suited for J2EE environment. J2EE specification requires application servers to provide transaction support and user authentication over remote calls. These services are defined in application configuration descriptors. Thus communication protocols must be able do support rpc-level communicates tagging. *J2eeprof* inject into EJB communication apart of transaction id and user information his own data.

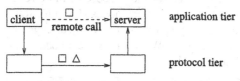

☐ information passed by application
△ extra tracing information passed by protocol tier

Fig. 4. Protocol tracing

Distributed paths require trace model to be improved. Model is extended by addition of two new nodes (*PathNode* subclasses). *RPCCallNode* (RC) represents an rpc call on the client side. *RPCReceiveNode* (RR) represents an rpc call on the server side. Figure 5 depicts reconstruction of a distributed path. On rpc call event – *j2eeprof* tags outgoing message with *rpcId* – auto generated id, unique in jvm scope, and *node id*(specified in configuration file). On rpc receive event – *rpcId* tag and *node id* are added to RR event. *Node id* attribute is saved in RR.sourceNodeId field. Paths merging is performed by matching RC-RR pairs. Match criteria is:

1. RC.rpcId=RR.rpcId
2. RC is registered on system node defined in RR.sourceNodeId

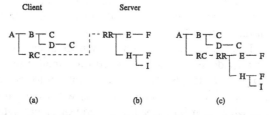

Fig. 5. Reconstruction of a distributed path a) local path on client side b) local path on server side c) completed distributed path

2.4 Visualisations

J2eeprof supports several visualizations. Profiler provides data analysis on summarized trace data as well as on raw trace. Many of these visualizations are found in other tools, but distributed trace view is an original extension of them.

J2eeprof can summarize trace in form of CCT and flat list. Both views display total number of invocations, total, mean, minimum and the maximum execution time. CTT view provides "drill up" and "drill down" functions. "Drill up" displays all contexts in which selected node was called. "Drill down" selects all possible executions rooted in a selected node.

Raw trace can be visualized as a graph or tree. Figure 6a shows graph of a trace. The Graph is similar to tree view but every node has a rectangle form. The length and position represents execution time. For the purpose of more readable view, there is an option for displaying only top-level trace nodes (Fig. 6b). Raw trace data can be queried. The result is indicated in graph view (Fig. 6) by changing color of nodes. Raw trace views are connected each other. When user selects node in the tree list, focus in other view is set to this node.

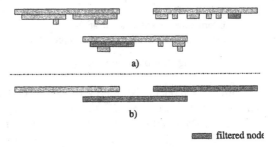

a)

b)

▨ filtered node

Fig. 6. Trace visualization a) detail, b) summary

Ability to collect distributed trace is quite uncommon in profilers. Thus there are not many ready to use solutions. Distributed trace requires special view. *J2eeprof* comes with original solution to this problem.

Figure 7 depicts "rpc view". The view captures distributed path on all nodes it belongs to. Apart of the path itself, the view contains also context of path on each distinct node. The view is horizontally divided in two zones. On the top, there is distributed path. On the bottom, there is context of the fragment of graph view. The view has also several vertical zones, each on every node along the distributed path. Double vertical lines divide system nodes. Doted lines mark time margin zone. In margin zone the top part of view is frozen on the contrary to the context shown in bottom part of the view. Timeline in context view is wider than in distributed path view. Thus in a case when distributed path execution of given system node is very short, still the context view show some information.

The path on Fig. 7 starts on Node 1, paths a and b. Execution of c is an rpc call. That part is shown on left part of the figure. D path is executed on Node 2 - middle part of the graph. Paths a,b,c are marked with grey color as they do not belong to Node 2. Last part of the figure, on the right, displays end of paths back on Node 1.

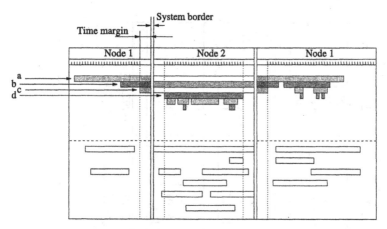

Fig. 7. Distributed trace view

3   j2eeprof in practice

J2eeprof was tested with *Rubis*[8] [9] – J2EE auction site benchmark. *Rubis* was created
to compare performance of several distinct implementations of the same program. Each
implementation uses different framework or technology. *J2eeprof* was tested with two
of them. First is BMP_EntityBean_ID_BMP that is based on Entity Beans and bean
managed persistence (denoted as bmp). The second EJB_CMP2 (denoted as cmp)
uses Entity Beans, Session Facade design pattern and container managed persistence.
Two of *Rubis* functions where choosen for the test. *SearchItemsByCategory* shows
list of auction items. The second *RegisterUser* registers new auction site user. These
functions are very different. First one is data intensive read only function, while the
second is transactional read and write function. Profiling scope included all *Rubis* code
method calls and tracing of JDBC and JTA services on interface level. Table 2 presents
performance overhead of j2eeprof in J2EE enviroment.

Test were performed on the open source application servers: *Jboss* 3.2 and *JOnAS*
4.5.3. *JOnAS* was configured to use iiop protocol, profiling scope included protocol
tracing (using CORBA interceptors). Rubis comes with dedicated load test tool. Load
tests were set to run for 5 minutes with 10 virtual users. Test where performed on
AMD Athlon XP 1600+, 756RAM, Linux Slackware 10 operating system.

Rubis tests contain random factor, thus test count varies between tests. It also depends
on test performance. Jonas bmp test with *j2eeprof* has very large overhead and test
count is much lower than test without profiling. *J2eeprof* performance overhead factor
varies from 1.1 in jboss cmp test to 56.77 in jonas bmp test. On *Jboss* server overhead
is related only to profiling scope. Since number of registered events is reasonably small,
overhead is up to 77%. IIOP protocol tracing adds overhead to *JOnAS* test results.
JOnAS tests performed slower than *Jboss* tests with exception of SearchItemsByCategory
test (jonas cmp). The reason is that *Jboss* optimizes local ejb calls, *JOnAS* not.

Table 3 presents some insights of Rubis implementation derived from trace data.
On *JOnAS*, bmp performed slower than cmp version but jboss cmp is slower than jboss

---

[8] Rice University Bidding System (Rubis), http://rubis.objectweb.org

Tab. 2. Measured Rubis performance overhead

	SearchItemsByCategory				RegisterUser				
	test count	time[ms] avg	time[ms] min	time[ms] max	avg overhead	test count	time[ms] avg	time[ms] min	time[ms] max	avg overhead
no profiling (Rubis performance statistics)										
jboss cmp	89	233	146	519		17	67	29	279	
jboss bmp	109	196	72	769		8	50	17	144	
jonas cmp	86	198	115	406		10	585	121	2333	
jonas bmp	78	1,037	196	3,484		5	342	174	546	
j2eeprof (Rubis performance statistics)										
jboss cmp	89	395	235	1,329	1.77	7	74	52	198	1.10
jboss bmp	52	226	100	520	1.15	5	76	36	201	1.52
jonas cmp	74	599	211	5,554	3.03	15	5,148	197	19,813	8.80
jonas bmp	12	33,051	16,426	67,706	31.87	1	19,415	19,415	19,415	56.77
j2eeprof (j2eeprof performance statistics)										
jboss cmp	87	290	175	684		6	70	45	134	
jboss bmp	50	146	24	399		5	42	30	55	
jonas cmp	72	718	165	4,710		15	5,104	193	19,252	
jonas bmp	9	42,197	15,220	66,204		1	15,864	15,864	15,864	
j2eeprof (no CORBA tracing, Rubis performance statistics)										
jonas cmp	75	557	177	3,167	1.14	5	3,521	176	16,795	
jonas bmp	46	2052	283	5,799	9.08	6	2,295	314	6,847	

Tab. 3. Rubis tests results

	jboss cmp	jonas cmp	jboss bmp	jonas bmp
concurrent threads	7	14	4	18
SearchItemsByCategory				
jdbc (time percent)	51.72	67.84	27.43	3.93
jdbc/ejb.load	1	0.77	1	1
jdbc/ejb.find	1	0.00	1	1
rmi (time percent)	0	2.41	0	18.60
rmi/per client call	0	2	0	42
RegisterUser				
jdbc (time percent)	23.64	42.58	9.05	34.25
jdbc calls/per client request	11	6.33	6	35
rmi (time percent)	0	0.39	0	2.88
rmi/per client call	0	2	0	8

bmp. Bmp *Rubis* implementation calls ejb entity components within web tier that results in large number of remote calls. Such design is described as J2EE anti-pattern. *Jboss* optimizes such calls but on *JOnAS* there is a remarkable average overhead of rmi call – 108.975 ms. Cmp version uses better design – Session Facade that minimizes remote calls, there are only 2 rmi calls in SeachItemsByCategory compared to 42 in bmp test.

The most efficient jdbc use is done by jonas cmp version. Each pair of ejb.find and ejb.load methods result at most one jdbc call. *JOnAS* probably makes use of cache since jdbc calls are performed only in 77% of ejb.find calls in SearchItemsByCategory test. Other *Rubis* versions does not perform jdbc optimization, every ejb.load and ejb.find call results in jdbc.call. Despite of jonas cmp efficiency, the best performer is jboss bmp. *JOnAS* and *Jboss* differ also in number of observed threads. *Jboss* delegates one thread to a server client request so number of concurrent threads is equal to number of concurrent requests. *JOnAS* passes control to different thread in every rmi call. The protocol tracing mechanism is necessary to obtain complete paths in such case, although significantly increases performance overhead.

4   Conclusions

The purpose of *j2eeprof* is to help in testing and profiling of J2EE distributed applications. Using it a programmer can easily analyze interactions between his code and other components or environment. Programmer does not have to modify his code to gather data. *J2eeprof* uses RMI/IIOP to mark and trace communication messages – giving accurate data about interactions between distributed components. The programmer decides on which abstraction level he wish to analyze his code, then he controls the trace information using *aspectwerkz* library. The advantage of the aspect approach is, that the programmer can easily monitor the interactions between his code and a J2EE server code. The strong features of *j2eeprof* are: flexibility in use, ability to fit gathered data to programmer needs, and high accuracy of registered traces from distributed components.

A week feature of *j2eeprof* is remarkable and varied execution time overhead. All profilers that work on tracing basis, in place of sampling basis, have this disadvantage. Because *j2eeprof* gathers full execution trace with programmer-defined data, not just execution statistic, the overhead is higher than other profilers put in. To obtain accurate time characteristics, the programmer has to take other profiler that works on sampling basis. *J2eeprof* is small and simple tool comparing with commercial *OptimizeIt* and *JXInsight* profilers. Although it is free, easy to use and we find it very useful.

References

1. G. Ammons, T. Ball and J. R. Larus: Exploiting hardware counters with flow and context sensitive profiling. In Proceedings of the SIGPLAN '97 Conference on Programming Language Design and Implementation,pages 85-96, Las Vegas, 1997.
2. C. Anslow, S. Marshall, R. Biddle, J. Noble and K. Jackson: Xml database support for program trace visualization. In Australian Symposium on Information Visualization, volume 35, 2004.
3. E. Bruneton, R. Lenglet and T. Coupaye: Asm: a code manipulation tool to implement adaptable systems. In Adaptable end extensible component systems, Grenoble, France, 2002.
4. Interceptors Published Draft with CORBA 2.4+ Core Chapters, Document Number ptc/2001-03-04. http://www.omg.org/cgi-bin/doc?ptc/2001-03-04
5. M. Dmitriev: Design of jfluid: A profiling technology and tool based on dynamic bytecode instrumentation. Technical report, Sun Microsystems, Nov. 2003.
6. E. Kiciman: Pinpoint: Status and future directions. 2003 www.stanford.edu/~emrek/pubs/roc-retreat-2003-pinpoint.pdf
7. Paweł Kłaczewski: Testability Issues of Multitier Applications (in polish). Master thesis, Institute of Computer Science of Warsaw University of Technology, 2005.
8. Marcos K. Aguilerai, Jeffrey C. Mogul, Janet L. Wiener, Patrick Reynolds and Athicha Muthitacharoen: Performance debugging for distributed systems of black boxes. In Proceedings of SOSP, Bolton Landing, NY, Oct. 2003.
9. E. Cecchet and A. Chanda and S. Elnikety and J. Marguerite and W. Zwaenepoel: Performance Comparison of Middleware Architectures for Generating Dynamic Web Content, 4th ACM/IFIP/USENIX International Middleware Conference, Rio de Janeiro, Brazil, June, 2003.

An Analysis of Use Case Based Testing Approaches Based on a Defect Taxonomy

Timea Illes[1], Barbara Paech[1]

[1] University of Heidelberg, Institute of Computer Science
Im Neuenheimer Feld 326
Germany-69120 Heidelberg
{illes, paech}@informatik.uni-heidelberg.de

Abstract: Use cases are a well-established means for requirements elicitation and specification. Recently, several approaches have argued to take use cases also directly as the basis for testing. In this paper we analyze use case based testing approaches on the basis of a defect taxonomy. For this purpose, we propose a taxonomy classifying typical defects which need to be uncovered during system testing. Then, we survey current approaches to derive test cases from use cases and discuss their ability to reveal these defects.

1 Introduction

Since their original introduction in [15], use cases (UC) have gained an increasing popularity. They are a well-established means for requirements elicitation and specification, modeling the behavior of a system from the user's point of view.

Recently, several approaches have been proposed which take UCs as input for test case development. The need to employ documented requirements as a basis for testing has already been recognized in the year 1979 [19]. A more recent survey insists on the necessity of using UCs as a basis for system testing [28]. UC based testing claims to offer a lot of advantages. One of these advantages is that UCs are widely used as inherent part of most object oriented analysis and design methodologies. Furthermore, the use of UCs as a basis for both, for software development as well as for testing, provides a uniform notation and a high reusability of requirements engineering artifacts. Additionally, the integration of testing activities into early development stages is alleviated. Finally, the development of test cases in parallel to UCs enables an early validation of the requirements.

But how well can these approaches support system testing? In order to answer this question, this paper examines which typical defects can be revealed during system testing and discusses the ability of current approaches to reveal the identified defect classes. The contribution of this paper is three-fold. First, we propose a defect classification for system level tests. Then, we evaluate current approaches for UC based testing with respect to their ability to reveal these defect classes. Finally, we add a testing perspective to requirements engineering (RE). The defect classes show how testers think about requirements and systems and what kind of information they need.

Please use the following format when citing this chapter:

Illes, T., Paech, B., 2006, in IFIP International Federation for Information Processing, Volume 227, Software Engineering Techniques: Design for Quality, ed. K. Sacha, (Boston: Springer), pp. 211–222.

Related work. In [12] four approaches addressing the derivation of test cases from requirements are compared. Only two of them are based on UCs. Furthermore, the comparison is very superficially based on criteria such as the use of standards or the availability of a tool supporting the approach. In [2] an overview of the approaches to test case generation during RE is given. In contrast to this paper, the authors do not focus on UC based testing techniques and consequently they do not consider all approaches discussed in this paper. Additionally the comparison of the approaches is ad-hoc without a systematic definition of criteria.

Overview. The remainder of this paper is organized as follows. Section 2 starts with a brief introduction to the basic concepts of UC based testing. Section 3 introduces the defect taxonomy. Section 4 gives an overview of current approaches for UC based test case derivation and discusses how well they address the defect classes proposed in Section 3. Section 5 concludes the paper.

2   UC Based Testing – The Overall Approach

This section introduces some basic concepts. We explain the notions of UCs, of system testing and UC based testing. Additionally, we give an overview on UC based testing approaches considered in this paper.

2.1   Terminology

In the context of this paper we define UCs, based on the definition proposed in [22] as follows: *A UC is a sequence of steps executed cooperatively by the system (system steps) and outside actors (actor steps) in order to yield an observable result to the actor(s), including alternatives and exceptions.* Consequently, UC descriptions typically contain information on *tasks or goals (*Which tasks/goals of the actor(s) should be fulfilled by the UC?), *actors* (Who initiates/participates in the UC?), *preconditions* and *postconditions* (Which conditions have to be fulfilled before respectively after the UC execution?) as well as *actor steps* (actions to be performed by the actors, including input data) and *system steps* (actions to be performed by the system, including output data). Optionally, information on *rules* (describing complex functional or causal interrelations) as well as on *quality requirements* (e.g. usability or performance) can be added to the UC description.

According to the definition proposed in [13], *system testing* is concerned with the process of testing an integrated system in order to verify that it meets the specified requirements. For this purpose a finite set of test cases has to be developed, in order to execute the system under test (SUT) with different inputs. A *test case* contains a set of input values, execution preconditions, expected results and execution post conditions.

UC based testing is an approach to system testing, where test cases are defined and selected on the basis of the requirements specified in terms of UCs. Therein, UCs play different roles:

During testing, actual behaviour is compared with the expected behaviour in order to decide, whether a test was passed or not. The source to determine the expected behaviour of the SUT is called test oracle. Consequently, the UC specification serves as *test oracle* in UC based testing, i.e. the UC specification is the source to define the expected output and post conditions as a result of the input and preconditions defined in a certain test case. If the actual behaviour corresponds to the expected behaviour, the SUT meets the specified UC. Since complete testing is impossible, a finite set of test cases has to be selected according to some coverage criteria indicating which parts of the SUT should be executed. Coverage criteria are determined according to a coverage item. In the case of UC based testing, UCs serve as *coverage items*. A weak coverage criterion is e.g. UC coverage, which requires at least one test case per UC. A stronger coverage criterion is e.g. path coverage which requires at least one test case per UC path.

2.2 Considered Approaches

Table 1 gives an overview on the approaches and the particular models into which UCs are transformed.

Table 1. Overview of the approaches and corresponding models

Approach (ID, Name)		Model Transformation
A	Path Analysis [1]	UC, no transformation
B	Testing with UCs [24]	State charts, Activity Diagrams
C	Extended UCs [4]	Tabular representation
D	Requirements by Contracts [21]	UC transition system (nodes: system states, transitions: instantiated UCs)
E	TOTEM [6]	Activity Diagrams, Sequence Charts, regular expressions
F	SCENT [25]	Annotated state charts, dependency charts
G	Simulation and Test Model [29]	Extended interaction overview charts, state charts
H	Purpose Driven Testing [3]	Goal Graphs (different abstraction level)
I	ASM based Testing [11]	Abstract state machines

For our analysis we selected approaches according to the following criteria:

(a) The approaches are based on UC descriptions or UC diagrams
(b) For each of the following approach classes we selected representative approaches.

Model exploration approaches exploit the information contained in UCs *as is*. Most approaches of this class are white papers. We selected the Path Analysis approach (A in Table 1) because it was the only approach of this class mentioning the GUI.

Model extension/transformation approaches extend the information contained in UCs by test related information. Additionally, an informal or structured UC model is transformed into a semi-formal, mostly graphical model. When appropriate, the resulting model is retransformed into a new model. On the basis of the resulting model, test cases are (semi-) automatically derived. For this purpose the models are traversed according to some coverage criteria, where a path usually corresponds to a test case. The approaches B-H in Table 1 belong to this class. We selected the approaches so that all target models (e.g. state charts or a proprietary model) are represented. Additionally we included the approach B in Table 1 as it addresses inter-software defects.

Model formalization approaches take an informal or structured UC model as input and transform this into a formal model. On the basis of this model, test cases can be automatically generated according to specific coverage criteria defined for that model. As a representative of this class we selected the ASM Based Testing approach (I in Table 1).

3 Defect Taxonomy

We now identify typical defect classes which need to be uncovered during system testing. We based our defect classification on taxonomies proposed in [5, 16]. In contrast to these defect taxonomies, which address defect classes at different phases of the development life cycle, e.g. defects in the requirements specification document, we restricted our taxonomy to defects which can be detected during *system testing*. Additionally, we refined the resulting taxonomy by analyzing further defect classifications like those proposed in [17, 18, 27] with respect to their applicability for system testing. In contrast to our taxonomy, these classifications have a particular focus on e.g. defects in e-commerce applications [27] or taxonomies for security issues [17] and [18]. Finally, we validated our taxonomy by investigating, to what extend defects captured in bug reports for open source software can be classified according to our taxonomy. For this purpose we investigated several bug reports stored in the bug tracking system of the mozilla.org [7] database. The defects recorded in this database refer to software such as the web browser Firefox [10], the Email Client Thunderbird [26] and other mozilla.org projects [20]. Due to the comprehensiveness of the database, we only considered "blocker", "critical" and "major" defects. Additionally we investigated defect lists of two open source CRM (Customer Relationship Management) projects [9, 23]. The result is a list of defect classes for system testing. Each defect class can be refined by subclasses. The defect classes are not orthogonal, i.e. a defect can be categorized into more than one defect class. Additionally, a defect can also be associated to a combination of defect classes. In the following, we present a short definition and corresponding examples of typical subclasses for each defect class.

Completeness defects subsume all defects related to an incomplete implementation of the specified functionality. Typical defects in this class are *missing functionality defects* (the implementation of a specified or desired requirement is missing) and *undesired functionality* (additional, undesired functionality has been implemented). There are two typical defects which can occur in the presence of additional, undesired functionality: *prevention defects* (if additional functionality prevents the execution of the desired functionality) and *overlapping defects* (if additional functionality and desired functionality overlap).

Input/Output defects subsume all defects related to wrong input respectively to wrong output data of the SUT. Typical input/output defects include *boundary defects* (e.g. date < 21.02.2006 instead of date < 13.02.2006), defects concerning *wrong size, shape or format* of the data or *combination defects* (i.e. defects which occur, when certain input values respectively output values are combined).

Calculation defects subsume all defects resulting from wrong formula or algorithms in the SUT (e.g. defect in the search algorithm: The system looks for product descriptions, containing *all* of the key words entered by the customer, instead of finding also products containing *at least one* of the entered keywords).

Data handling defects subsume all defects related to the lifecycle and the order of operations performed on data. Typical data handling defects include *duplicated data* (e.g. system fails when creating duplicated data) or *data flow defects* (defects related to the sequence of accessing a data object (e.g. data update before the data has been created).

Control flow and sequencing defects subsume all defects related to the control flow or the order and extent to *which* processing is done, as distinct from *what* is done [5]. Typical control flow defects concern *wrong sequencing* of the actions performed or *iteration and loop defects,* which subsume all defects related to the control flow of iterations and loops.

Concurrency defects subsume all defects related to the concurrent execution of parts or of multiple instances of the SUT. Typical defects contained in this class include priority defects and race condition defects. *Priority defects* are related to the assignment of a wrong priority (too high, too low, priority selected not allowed), e.g. a phone call on a mobile phone does not pre-empt the execution of an arbitrary function when a phone call has been received). *Race condition defects* are related to the competition of processes for a limited resource, e.g. for time, or for shared data.

GUI defects subsume all defects related to the user interface, which are not usability defects. Typical defects of this class are *display defects* (defects related to the display and highlighting of the information on the screen, e.g. failure to clear or update part of the screen or failure to clear highlighting) and *navigation defects* (e.g. missing or disabled menu entries).

NFR (non-functional requirement) defects subsume all defects related to the quality of the SUT. According to [14], defects concerning *functionality, reliability, usability, efficiency, maintainability and portability* belong to this category.

Inter-Software defects subsume all defects concerning the interface of the SUT to other software systems. Typical defects of this class are *input/output defects* (if there is a syntactic or semantic misunderstanding between the interacting software systems), *concurrency defects* (e.g. if the SUT and a COTS component compete for the same data) or *completeness defects* (e.g. if functionality of the third party software is missing).

Hardware defects subsume all defects concerning the interface of the SUT to the hardware. Typical defects of this class are *input/output defects* (e.g. incorrect interpretation of returned status data).

4 Evaluation of the Approaches

UCs are intuitive, informal and thus easily readable for different stakeholders. Consequently, UCs are well suited in the context of requirements elicitation and specification. However, when UCs are used as a basis for test case derivation the perspective changes. In this case, the stakeholders of the UC specification are testers, who aim to find defects in the SUT. The aim of this paper is not the evaluation of the UC concepts itself, but the efficiency of UC based testing techniques.

Based on the defect taxonomy introduced in Section 3, we now discuss the defect classes with respect to their ability to be revealed by UC derived test cases. Additionally, for each defect class typical solutions are presented. Table 3 summarizes the result of our analysis. A „+" indicates that the corresponding defect class is well addressed by an approach, a "(+)" indicates that the corresponding defect class is partially considered (e.g. parts of the possible defects in the defect class are addressed). A "-" indicates that the approach does not consider the corresponding defect class at all.

In order to assure comparability of the approaches, we assume a correct UC specification and evaluate the efficiency of the techniques with respect to a given correct specification. All techniques assume a correct requirements specification because the test case set derived is as good as the UCs themselves. Some approaches give guidance for the specification and validation of use cases. But this aspect is not part of our evaluation. Furthermore, to assure an efficient evaluation, we focus on defects which can be associated with a single defect class and do not consider defects which result by all possible combinations of different defect classes.

4.2 Completeness Defects

In general missing UC implementation is revealed easily on the basis of a UC specification. Most approaches will uncover a missing UC implementation, since they iterate over all UCs and perform some analysis *per* UC, e.g. determine all paths within a UC or develop a new model e.g. a state chart representation *per* UC. Consequently, there is at least one test case per UC which would detect the missing implementation of a UC. Whether missing parts of an UC can be uncovered, depends on which coverage criteria the corresponding approach defines, e.g. path coverage will easily uncover a missing case within a UC. Coverage criteria will be discussed along with control flow and sequencing defects. As the approaches [21] and [3] focus on the *interaction* between UCs, they are not well suited to uncover missing parts *within* a UC.

4.3 Input / Output Defects, Calculation and Data Handling Defects

The detection of input/output defects, calculation defects as well as data handling defects depends on the accuracy with which the respective details have been documented. Due to the fact that UCs are typically phrased in natural language, they are imprecise. Therefore, test cases derived from UCs will hardly reveal *input/output defects*, *calculation defects* as well as *data handling defects*.

Input/Output Defects. In [4] the concept of extended UCs is introduced. Extended UCs express the relationship between system state (precondition of a UC), a combination of inputs and the expected results in terms of a decision table. For each combination of inputs and system state which results in distinct classes of SUT behaviour a new relation in terms of a new row in the decision table is defined. Then, test cases are derived using combinatorial strategies. Following this approach, input/output defects can easily be uncovered. A light weight approach is the annotation of UCs or the models derived on the basis of UCs with test related data including input values or possible ranges for the input or output data. This is the case in [25] and [3].

Calculation Defects. Calculation defects are not addressed by any particular approach especially. However, the approach proposed in [4] is suited best for this purpose. The tabular representation, relating a combination of inputs and system states to outputs can easily be adapted to the creation of test cases, which test e.g. a formula specified within a UC with different input combinations.

Data Handling Defects. In [6] the life cycle of a „business object" and related defects are addressed by representing the life-cycle of these objects in terms of activity diagrams, which relate UCs to each other. The UCs are grouped into swimlanes, where each swimlane represents the life cycle of a business object from its creation until its deletion. UCs grouped into the same swimlane manipulate (read, write) the corresponding object. Valid sequences of UCs are generated by traversing the activity diagram. A path in the activity diagram represents a test case, and thus a possible life-cycle of a business object. In [21] pre and post conditions of a UC are expressed in terms of contracts on the inputs respectively on outputs of a UC e.g. an item has to be created so that the UC delete item can be executed. Thus, sequences in the life cycle of business objects can be created by concatenating UCs so that the post condition of one UC represents the precondition of the next UC. However, both approaches consider only valid paths. Negative test cases, e.g. which test unwanted behaviour are not created.

4.4   Control Flow and Sequencing Defects

Sequences of interaction between user and system as well as alternatives and exceptions within a UC can easily be expressed. Hence, control flow as well as sequencing defects in the implementation of that particular UC can easily be detected. But since UCs comprise self-contained coherent units of functionality, they are not suited to express the interplay between distinct UCs. Consequently, test cases which verify the correct implementation of the interaction *between* UCs are hard to be derived from UC specifications.

Some approaches [1] and [8] require structural coverage of UCs by test cases, e.g. path coverage. Thus, each path in a UC is executed by at least one test case. Consequently, these approaches will likely reveal control flow defects *within* the implementation of a UC. In [1] all paths of a UC are required to be uncovered by a test case. In [8] test cases are derived which exercise all combinations of executing and non-executing an <<extends>> relationship. Most approaches transform the UC model into another, more formal model e.g. a state chart or a sequence diagram representation and require coverage of the new model. This is the case in [24, 6, 25, 29 and 11]. Usually the models are then traversed according to coverage criteria of the new model. As the transformation into a new model is not automatic, there is a risk not to consider all information defined in a UC, and thus, not to detect all defects which would be detected based on the original UC specification.

Control flow defects in the implementation of the interaction *between* UCs are especially addressed in [3, 6, 21, 24, 25 and 29]. In [3] the interaction between UCs realizing a user goal is addressed. In [6] valid sequences of UCs are expressed in terms of activity diagrams. Test cases are derived by traversing all valid sequences. In [21] contracts on the execution of a UC are defined by expressing pre and post conditions of a UC. On the basis of these contracts, a transition model of valid UC sequences can be defined by concatenating post conditions of a UC with the precondition of another UC. Test cases are generated from the transition model according to given coverage criteria. In [24] state models derived from single UCs are merged by "composition". Test cases are then derived by covering all valid state combinations in the "composed" state model. In [25] the interaction between UCs is expressed in a new diagram type, the so called "dependency chart". Dependency charts can express dependencies between scenarios, e.g. sequential dependencies, alternatives or iterations. The authors use the term "scenario" equivalent to the term "use case". Test cases are derived from dependency charts mainly by trying to break the constraints defined. The authors give advice on how to break these constraints. In [29] sequential dependencies between UCs are identified and represented in terms of an UML interaction overview diagram. This diagram is then transformed into a state chart model which is traversed in order to derive test cases for each path in the state chart. No approach, except the one introduced in [25], considers invalid paths and the systematic derivation of test cases for trying to execute invalid paths.

Table 2 summarizes the evaluation of the approaches according to their efficiency to detect control flow defects *within* the implementation of a UC and respectively in the implementation of the *interaction between* UCs. Approaches which consider both defect subclasses are highlighted in light grey.

Table 2. UC based testing approaches and control flow defects

	Path analysis [1]	Purpose Driven Testing [3]	Extended UCs [4]	TOTEM [6]	Structural Testing with UCs [8]	ASM Based Testing [11]	Requirements by Contracts [21]	Testing with UCs [24]	SCENT [25]	Simulation and Test Models [29]
Control flow defects within the implementation of a UC	+	-	-	+	+	+	-	+	+	+
Control flow defects in the implementation of the interaction between UCs	-	+	-	+	-	-	+	+	+	+

4.5 Concurrency Defects

Expressing constraints on the parallel execution is not supported by UCs. Thus, UC derived test cases will hardly uncover concurrency defects.

Concurrency defects are addressed in [29] by defining dependencies between UCs and documenting these dependencies in terms of UML interaction overview diagrams. The dependencies concerning constraints on the parallel execution cover: *parallel execution* (when two or more UCs can be executed in parallel), *pre-emption/suspension* (when one UC pre-empts the execution of another UC having a higher priority), *exclusion* (when a UC can not be executed during the execution of another UC) and *multi-instantiation* (when multiple instances of a UC may be executed at once). Exclusion and suspension are not part of UML 2.0 interaction overview diagrams. Thus, two additional stereotypes have been added to denote the corresponding relationships. The approach also contains a methodology to transform these diagrams into state machines which are traversed and covered in order to obtain test cases. Concurrency is also addressed in [25]. Dependency charts can express constraints on the parallel execution of scenarios. Thus, enforced, prohibited as well as an accidental parallelism can be expressed in terms of relationships between scenarios. Furthermore, constraints on the starting time (scenarios have to start/end at the same time or scenarios have to start one after the other with a given time interval between them) as well as data/resource dependencies can be included. Test cases for each identified dependency have to be developed. The authors propose to focus on "unwanted" behaviour by defining test cases which try to break dependency constraints. In [24] the necessity of modelling parallelism is stated, but how this should be expressed and how corresponding test cases should be derived is not explained. In [6] it is possible to express that the executions of two UCs are independent of each other. But, there is no advice on how to derive test cases which address parallelism.

4.6 GUI & NFR Defects

UCs specify the functional requirements for a system, i.e. they indicate "*what*" should be realized by the system, in contrast to non-functional requirements, which describe "*how well*" a requirement should be realized. The latter can not be expressed well in terms of UCs. Furthermore, UCs abstract from a specific user interface, they specify e.g. that an actor initiates a particular function, but they do not define whether this action occurs by clicking on a hyperlink of a web interface or by selecting a menu item from a windows-based system. Consequently, UCs are not well suited to derive test cases for this class.

GUI defects are considered solely in [1] and [25]. In these approaches, GUI-related information can be annotated to test cases [1] or to intermediate models derived from UCs [25]. The authors do not illustrate how this information can be systematically used to develop (further) test cases.

Non-functional defects, especially performance defects are addressed in [25] only. According to this, the semi-formal models developed on the basis of scenarios are annotated with non-functional requirements. When test cases are derived by covering the state chart, these requirements have to be considered.

4.7 Inter Software Defects

UCs abstract from the internal realization of the functionality, more precisely they describe the functionality without specifying, whether it will be realized by the SUT or by a third party component. Accordingly, the defects detected by UC derived test cases are mostly independent of the realizing (sub)system. A missing case within the implementation of a UC will e.g. be detected by a test case derived from this UC, independent of the realizing (sub)system. There are, however particular cases, which have to be considered.

The first case concerns *undesired functionality* of a third party system. In the case of COTS-software, which is intended to be used in different contexts, the functionality provided is often much more comprehensive than the functionality needed in the context of the SUT. Consequently, prevention defects (e.g. settings in a web browser prevent the execution of parts of a web based application written in JavaScript) as well as overlapping defects (e.g. when the "back" functionality in a web browser and the "back" functionality in the web application interleave) are very likely to occur. The second particular case concerns *known defects* in third party software. These defects represent a special kind of control flow defects, namely exception handling defects, where the SUT has to deal with exceptions of third party software.

As the architectural decisions, as well as decisions concerning which components will be developed and which will be bought, occur at a later development stage as the development of the UCs, the information on additional functionality is not contained in UCs. Therefore, UC derived test cases will hardly uncover the defects mentioned before.

Inter software defects are addressed in [24] and in [25] in the requirements specification phase, where guidance is given on how to identify the interface of the SUT. According to this, all hardware interfaces as well as software interfaces to the SUT are identified. These interfaces are considered (and covered) during the system test. In [29] concurrency defects mainly in the context of distributed components of a software system are addressed. Nevertheless, none of these approaches deals with overlapping functionality or with known defects in the third party software.

Table 3. UC based testing approaches and addressed defect classes

	Path analysis [1]	Purpose Driven Testing [3]	Extended UCs [4]	TOTEM [6]	Structural Testing with UCs [8]	ASM Based Testing [11]	Requirements by Contracts [21]	Testing with UCs [24]	SCENT [25]	Simulation and Test Models [29]
Completeness	+	(+)	+	+	+	+	(+)	+	+	+
Input / Output	-	(+)	+	-	-	-	-	-	(+)	-
Calculation	-	-	(+)	-	-	-	-	-	-	-
Data Handling	-	-	-	(+)	-	-	(+)	-	-	-
Control flow/ Sequencing	(+)	(+)	-	+	(+)	(+)	(+)	+	+	+
Concurrency	-	-	-	-	-	-	-	-	+	+
GUI	(+)	-	-	-	-	-	-	-	(+)	-
NFR	-	-	-	-	-	-	-	-	(+)	-
Inter Software	-	-	-	-	-	-	-	(+)	(+)	(+)
Hardware	-	-	-	-	-	-	-	(+)	(+)	-

4.8 Hardware Defects

UCs not only abstract from the realization, but also from the underlying hardware and external devices. Indeed, most defects at the interface of the SUT occur in the hardware. But as stated in [16], a *software* defect will also occur, if the software system does not recognise and treat a defect in the hardware. Hence, test cases have to be defined, which address defects in the software concerning the exception handling of hardware defects. Since UCs do not contain information on hardware, UC derived test cases are not well suited to reveal this type of defects.

Similar to software defects, hardware defects are addressed in [24] in the requirements specification phase. Hardware interfaces to the SUT are identified and documented. These interfaces can be considered during system testing. In [25] dependency charts, an annotation can be associated to a causal dependency concerning constraints on hardware, e.g. a printer has to be connected before a particular scenario can be executed (e.g. printing a document).

5 Conclusion and Future Work

In this paper we identified defect classes and discussed their ability to be uncovered by UC based testing approaches. Control flow and completeness defects are addressed by almost all approaches. No approach proposes a methodology to enrich UCs with GUI and NFR related information and to systematically derive test cases for testing the GUI and non-functional requirements. SCENT [25] is the most comprehensive approach, addressing more defect classes than all other approaches which have been analysed. It is a lightweight approach for UC based testing which addresses most of the defect classes by annotating UC derived models with test related information. In order to define a middleweight and more thorough approach for UC based testing, some issues concerning the integration of the GUI and of NFRs must be considered. Our future work will address the definition of an integrated model for RE and test development which allows the detection of NFR and GUI defects. Furthermore, we aim at designing a thorough evaluation of the approaches according to a strong benchmark.

References

1. Ahlowalia, N.: Testing from Use Cases Using Path Analysis Technique, International Conference On Software Testing Analysis & Review, (2002)
2. Allmann, C., Denger, C., Olsson, T.: Analysis of Requirements-based Test Case Creation Techniques, IESE-Report No. 046.05/E, (2005), http://www.iese.fraunhofer.de/pdf_files/iese-046_05.pdf, last visited July 2006
3. Alspaugh, T.A., Richardson, D.J., and Standish, T.A.: Scenarios, State Machines and Purpose Driven Testing, 4th International Workshop on Scenarios and State Machines: Models, Algorithms and Tools (SCESM'05), St. Louis, USA, (2005)
3. Binder, R.: Testing Object-Oriented systems, Addison-Wesley, (2000)

4. Beizer, B.: Bug Taxonomy and Statistics, Appendix, Software Testing Techniques, Second Edition, Van Nostrand Reinhold, New York, (1990)
5. Briand, L., and Labiche, Y.: A UML-based Approach to System Testing, Technical Report, Carleton University, (2002)
6. Bugzilla, https://bugzilla.mozilla.org/, last visited July 2006.
7. Carniello, A., Jino, M., and Lordello, M.: Structural Testing with Use Cases, WER04 - Workshop em Engenharia de Requisitos, Tandil, Argentina, (2004)
8. Compiere, http://www.compiere.org/, last visited July 2006
9. Firefox, http://www.firefox.com/, last visited July 2006
10. Grieskamp, W., Lepper, M., Schulte, W., Tillmann. N.: Testable Use Cases in the Abstract State Machine Language, Second Asia-Pacific Conference on Quality Software (APAQS'01), (2001)
11. Gutierrez, J.J., Escalona, M.J., Mejías, M., Torres, J., Álvarez, J.A.: Comparative Analysis of Methodological Proposes to Systematic Generation of System Test Cases from System Requirements, Proceedings of the 3rd International Workshop on System Testing and Validation, (SV'2004), ISBN: 3-8167-6677, Paris, France, (2004), pp. 151-160
12. International Software Testing Qualifications Board, ISTQB Standard Glossary of Terms used in Software Testing V1.1, (2005)
13. International Standard ISO/IEC 9126, Information technology - Software Product Evaluation - Quality Characteristics and Guidelines for Their Use, International Organization for Standardization, International Electrotechnical Commission, Geneva, (1991)
14. Jacobson, I., Christerson, M., Jonsson, P., and Oevergaard, G.: Object-Oriented Software Engineering: A Use Case Driven Approach, Addison Wesley, (1992)
15. Kaner, C., Falk, J., and Nguyen, H. Q.: Testing Computer Software, 2nd Ed., Wiley, New York, (1999)
16. Krsul, I.: Software Vulnerability Analysis, Department of Computer Sciences, Purdue University, Ph.D. Thesis, COAST TR 98-09; (1998)
17. Lough M.L.: A Taxonomy of Computer Attacks with Applications to Wireless, PhD Thesis, Virginia Polytechnic Institute, (2001)
18. Meyers, G.J., The Art of Software Testing, John Wiley & Sons, New York, (1979)
19. Mozilla.org, http://www.mozilla.org/, last visited July 2006
20. Nebut, C., Fleurey, F., Le Traon, Y., and Jézéquel, J.-M.: Requirements by contracts allow automated system testing, Proc. of the 14th. IEEE International Symposium on Software Reliability Engineering (ISSRE'03), (2003)
21. Object Management Group. UML Superstructure Specification, v.2.0, (2005)
22. opentaps, http://www.opentaps.org/, last visited July 2006
23. Rupp, C., and Queins, S.: Vom Use-Case zum Test-Case, OBJEKTspektrum, vol. 4, (2003)
24. Ryser, J., and Glinz, M.: SCENT: A Method Employing Scenarios to Systematically Derive Test Cases for System Test, Technical Report, University of Zürich, (2000/03)
25. Thunderbird, http://www.mozilla.com/thunderbird/, last visited July 2006
26. Vijayaraghavan, G.: A Taxonomy of E-Commerce Risks and Failures. (Master's Thesis) Department of Computer Sciences, Florida Institute of Technology, Melbourne, FL, May 2002
27. Weidenhaupt, K., Pohl, K., Jarke, M., and Haumer, P.: Scenario Usage in System Development: A Report on Current Practice. IEEE Software, (1998)
28. Whittle, J., Chakraborty, J., and Krueger, I.: Generating Simulation and Test Models from Scenarios, 3rd World Congress for Software Quality, (2005)

Minimizing Test Execution Time During Test Generation

Tilo Mücke and Michaela Huhn

Technical University of Braunschweig, 38106 Braunschweig, Germany
{tmuecke,huhn}@ips.cs.tu-bs.de,
WWW home page: http://www.cs.tu-bs.de/ips

Abstract. In the area of model based testing, major improvements have been made in the generation of conformance tests using a model checker. Unfortunately, the execution of the generated test suites tend to be rather time-consuming. In [1] we presented a method to generate the test suites with the shortest execution time providing the required coverage, but this method can only be applied to small models due to memory-consumption. Here we show how to generate test suites for a number of different test quality criteria like coverage criteria, UIOs, mutant testing. Moreover, we present heuristics to significantly reduce test execution time that are as efficient as a naive testsuite generation. Our optimization combines min-set-cover-algorithms and search strategies, which we use to enlengthen generated test cases by promising additional coverages. We compare several heuristics and present a case study where we could achieve a reduction of the test execution time to less than 10%.

1 Introduction

In the last decade, models have been discovered as an invaluable source for deriving test cases. Many authors proposed model checking [2–4] or other search strategies [5] to automatically generate test sequences from behavioral (semi-)formal models. The success of model based testing has its reasons in the wide acceptance of model based development in practice, in particular in the embedded domain where substantial verification and testing of systems is obligatory.

We present an approach to model based test generation that uniformly handles a number of well-established test quality criteria like test purposes [5], coverage criteria [4], and mutation testing [6] and applies them on behavioural models. Our key technology for test case generation is model checking on state based systems. In a preparatory step, test quality criteria are split into subgoals that can be achieved by a test case and the models are instrumented by adding auxiliary variables and test drivers to direct the search for test cases to the subgoals. Using this procedure systematically, large testsuites for involved test quality criteria can be generated automatically.

However, many generated testsuites expose long test execution times which is a limiting factor in several real-time domains: For instance, in railway interlockings, traffic or process control systems some actions need relevant time for execution. We address this problem by combining heuristic search algorithms with min-set-cover algorithms for minimizing the test *execution* time of the testsuites but preserving the test quality.

A second problem of automated test generation is the fault recognition rate. As recently observed by Heimdahl [7], structural test quality criteria tend to produce

Please use the following format when citing this chapter:

Mücke, T., Huhn, M., 2006, in IFIP International Federation for Information Processing, Volume 227, Software Engineering Techniques: Design for Quality, ed. K. Sacha, (Boston: Springer), pp. 223–235.

testsuites that just satisfy the criteria instead of verifying the correct behavior. We cope with this weakness by using strong quality criteria [8], by enlengthening the test cases with UIOs (see section 2.6), and by extending test cases gathering additional coverage (see section 3). Consequently, our approach has the potential to generate test cases with a higher fault recognition rate.

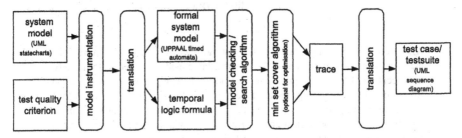

Fig. 1. Automated model based test case generation

Figure 1 summarizes the procedure for test case generation. Initially, the instrumentation of the model has to be adapted according to the selected test quality criterion. The different instrumentations are described in Section 2. The details on the translation from UML statecharts [9] to the input language of the UPPAAL model checker [10] and back can be found in [1]. Section 3 is concerned with the combination of search heuristics for test case generation and min-set-cover algorithms to optimize testsuites with respect to test execution time. The results of a case study are reported in Section 4 and we conclude in Section 5.

2   Test Case Generation

In this section we describe the instrumentation of models for test case generation via model checking for three different test quality criteria:

1. A *test purpose* is given by a test expert. It consists of a desired property or a critical operation sequence. Test cases checking the property or executing the sequence are generated.
2. *Coverage criteria* are definitions of model element type dependent, structural properties which have to take place during test case execution. E.g. state coverage demands each state to be visited at least once.
3. *Mutant testing* demands that every mutated model has to be uncovered as erroneous by the testsuite, unless it behaves equivalent to the original model. The mutants are generated automatically by so called mutation operators. E.g. arithmetic operator replacement (AOR) replaces each occurrence of an arithmetic operator by any other arithmetic operator.

We decompose each test quality criterion into subgoals which are to be achieved and call them *partial coverages*. Partial coverages are encoded as predicates that shall be satisfied on some execution like "*state s has to be reached*". For our purposes, the system model consists of a family of UML statecharts [9] modeling the behavior of the system components. UML statecharts extend final state machines by the concepts of hierarchy, concurrency and communication via events. Transitions can be labeled with events, guards and actions. Additionally, we use a time event after(t) with the obvious meaning. There exist a number of formal semantics for statechart dialects and we will use the approach from [11, 12] to transform statecharts into the input language of the UPPAAL model checker [10] and translate the output traces of the model checker back into sequence diagrams. UPPAAL supports the verication of real-time constraints, a feature we use for the generation of time annotated test cases. The real-time annotations within the models result from measuring and approximating the execution times of actions from previous versions of the components. Test purposes are given in terms of predicates or UML sequence diagrams for scenarios. To illustrate test case generation for the quality criteria, we use a simple running example: The control of a dimmer switch.

2.1   Example: Dimmer Switch

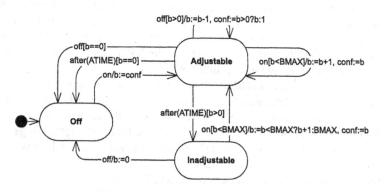

Fig. 2. Statechart of the dimmer switch

The dimmer switch is controlled by two buttons (events): on and off. The brightness b of the connected lamp is the only observable output of the system and can be adjusted within the values 0 (light off) and BMAX. When the on button is pushed, the lamp lights with the brightness b that is memorized (conf) from the previous use. After turning the dimmer on, the brightness can be modified smoothly by pressing the buttons on and off. If for the time ATIME no button is pressed, the brightness will become inadjustable. Pushing the off button turns the lamp off immediately. By pressing the on button, the lamp returns into adjustable mode. The statechart model of the dimmer switch is shown in Fig. 2.

2.2   Test Driver

For test case generation, a test driver has to be added which feeds the system under test with all possible inputs. This test driver has to be implemented non deterministically (see figure 3). Technically, the test driver is put in parallel to the statecharts modeling the system which leads to a product construction at the level of model checking. Fortunately, the test driver consists of only one state.

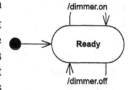

Fig. 3: Test driver

2.3 Test Purpose: Property

First we consider properties that shall be checked by tests. An example property for this model is:

	temporal logic formula	meaning
1	$E <> (b > 0)$	The lamp can be turned on.

In case a property can be directly expressed as a path quantified state predicate the model instrumentation can be omitted. The only thing to do is to add a query at the level of the model checker, i.e., $E <> p$ (on some trace p happens) in UPPAAL syntax. For a property $E <> p$ the model checker returns a trace if it is satisfiable.

2.4 Test Purpose: Interaction Sequence

Often a test purpose can be naturally described as a sequence of operations or interactions. Thus, sequence diagrams are a widely used representation in testing which we use as well. Figure 4 shows a sequence diagram where on is pressed, it is waited ATIME and then off is pressed, demanding that the brightness is set to 0. Afterwards conf is set to 2 and on is pressed, so that b will be 2.

To generate a test case including this sequence, the test driver is modified. It consists now of it's nondeterministic part which is needed to reach a state where the sequence can be executed and a simple representation of the activities in the sequence diagram from the point of view of the test driver, see Figure 4 (right). To generate a test case containing this sequence we ask the model checker for a path reaching the partial coverage: $E <> testdriver.Finished.$

Possible actions of the test driver are (1) sending and (2) receiving events, (3) changing and (4) monitoring global variables, and (5) evaluating time constraints. How these actions are translated from sequence diagrams in test drivers is formally described in [11]. Time constraints are realized during translation to UPPAAL timed automata.

To generate more than one trace per sequence diagram, one can vary the state at which the execution of the sequence starts which will lead to additional partial coverages representing different settings where the scenario is executed.

2.5 Coverage Criteria

A model checker can as well be used to generate test cases for coverage criteria. In [1] it is shown, how models are instrumented and properties are generated to achieve state coverage, transition coverage, modified condition/decision coverage, boundary coverage and dataflow coverage. The instrumentation adds new coverage variables to the system, which are set, whenever a partial coverage is achieved. E.g. to achieve transition coverage each transition is once supplemented with a statement setting the coverage variable to true. Thus with a query $E <> (coverageVar)$ the appropriate partial coverage can be achieved. Other coverage criteria require splitting of transitions (modified condition/decision coverage) or adding auxiliary variables (dataflow coverage). The new coverage criterion boundary coverage is now used as an example to show an instrumented version of Fig. 2.

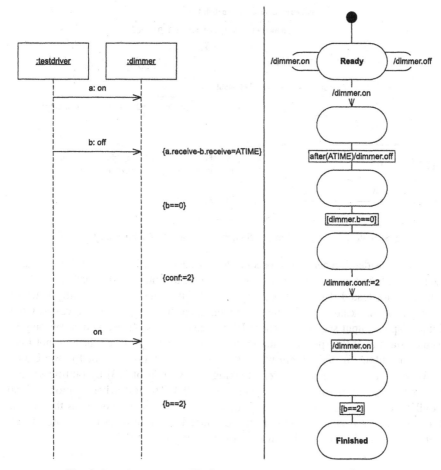

Fig. 4. Statechart of a modified test driver for the sequence diagram

Boundary Coverage demands that for each guard containing a relational operator a test case is generated for which the operands are as close as possible to the boundary. To achieve this criterion, the structure of the statechart is changed by splitting transitions. Each transition with a relational operator in its guard is split in two transitions, one of which fires for the closest operands possible only and is instrumented by a coverage variable and another one which conserves the behavior by firing in all other possibilities. Figure 5 shows, how the Dimmer Switch is instrumented to enable the model checker to generate test cases using the testdriver from Fig. 3 and the queries:
$E <> B1 == true$, $E <> B2 == true$, and $E <> B3 == true$.

2.6 Unique Input Output Sequences

Recent results by Heimdahl [7] indicate that a testsuite generated for structural coverage criteria like state or transition coverage may be weak w.r.t. its fault detection ability. But fault detection is the overall aim of testing.

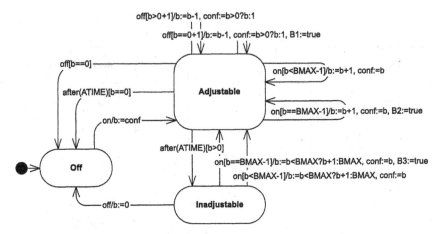

Fig. 5. Statechart of the Dimmer Switch instrumented for boundary coverage

Let us consider a generation procedure for a testsuite satisfying transition coverage. It will generate test cases in which the last step is the execution of the desired transition. Thus, it is not tested if the correct target state of the transition is actually reached. To overcome this kind of problems, we enlengthen the test cases by so called UIOs (Unique Input Output sequence). These UIOs consist of a sequence which can only be executed starting at the specific state. From all other states, provided they are not trace equivalent, outputs of the system will differ from the outputs described in the UIO.

We generate UIOs using model checking in a variant of [13] by putting several systems with partly modified initial states in parallel. The test driver is modified, so that all systems are triggered with the same inputs. A comparator compares the outputs of the systems. As soon as a system has produced different output compared to all other systems, a UIO for the initial state of this system is found.

2.7 Mutant Testing

Mutant testing requires, that each mutation of the original model is either equivalent to the original model or found as erroneous by the test suite. The mutants are generated by mutation operators.

The classical mutation operators [6] can be applied to code only. Thus, in the case of statecharts, they can be applied to guards and actions. Common mutation operators are: (1) LCR, AOR, ROR which replace each occurrence of a logical, arithmetical, or relational operator by any other operator of the same type, (2) UIO which negates, increments and decrements each arithmetic expression, (3) AAR, ACR, ASR, ... replace each occurrence of a variable, constant or array by each compatible variable, constant or array, (4) CRP, DSA slightly change constant values, (5) SDL deletes each statement, and many more.

On the model-layer, these mutation operators have to be supplemented by mutation operators working with the structure of the automata [14]. Some of these operators are already handled by mutating guards and actions. Examples for other operators are: (1) state missing, (2) transition missing, (3) replace origin state of a transition, (4) replace target state of a transition, (5) replace triggering event, (6) replace triggered event, and (7) replace event recipient.

To generate mutant killing test cases, the original model has to be executed versus a mutated program. They both have to be triggered by the same inputs. A mutant is found as erroneous, if the outputs differ. Thus, the same technique we used for UIO generation is applied for generating mutant killing test cases.

Detecting unsatisfiable coverages is done by using the query $A[]c == false$ for a partial coverage c. If the subgoal cannot be achieved, it is is eliminated.

3 Strategies to Generate Time Optimized Testsuites

After instrumenting the model according to a test quality criterion, the statecharts modeling the system are transformed into a semantically equivalent family of timed automata that serves as formal system model for UPPAAL. Details on the construction, e.g. syntactic restrictions on the UML model elements, the translation of timing constructs, the handling of event queues and UML run-to-completion semantics, can be found in [11].

In [1] we investigate a technique to generate the *time optimal* testsuite. We achieved a significant reduction in test execution time, but the technique suffers from high memory consumption, i.e. it is restricted to small models.

Alternatively, we consider heuristics to efficiently generate testsuites with optimized but not necessarily minimal execution time. We generate an optimized testsuite in two steps:

1. We generate a test case for each partial coverage we are interested in, thereby following the work of Hong et.al. [4]. These test cases build a testsuite for a given test quality criterion as each required partial coverage is achieved at least once. Moreover, some partial coverages may be satisfied by more than one test case[1]. To increase the basis for optimization we enlengthen the test cases by adding a path starting from its final state and leading to a state where some additional coverage is satisfied. We consider several search heuristics to generate a testsuite of promising long test cases. The amount of redundancy with respect to the achieved coverages is controlled by a parameter of the search.

2. We use min-set-cover-algorithms [15, 16] to optimize test execution time of a testsuite but retain the required partial coverages. Since the testsuite has been enlarged, a min-set-cover-algorithm works on a broader basis from which it eliminates test cases that are redundant w.r.t. the achieved coverages. Again we consider different heuristics to improve test execution time.

3.1 Building a Redundant Testsuite

For a succinct description of the heuristic search we use pseudo code. The basic function is called *tcGenerate* and generates a *single test case* as follows: The model is instrumented and transformed to the model checker input language, then the model

---
[1] A test case for the coverage c_1 may reach other coverages on the way.

checker is employed for searching a trace and finally the resulting trace is retranslated into a sequence that can be executed on the system model. The concepts needed to realize *tcGenerate* have been described in Section 2:

$$tcGenerate : Models \times (Traces \cup \{\varepsilon\}) \times PC \rightarrow Traces \cup \{\varepsilon\}$$

tcGenerate takes a statechart model $m \in Models$, an initial segment of a test case $t \in Traces \cup \{\varepsilon\}^2$ and a partial coverage pc from the set of interesting partial coverages PC. It returns a test case tc that extends t, i.e. $tc = t \cdot u$ for some suffix u, and satisfies the given partial pc, if possible. Otherwise, it returns ε. With each generated test case tc we store two attributes: $t_{exec}(tc)$, the test case execution time, and $subPC(tc)$, the subset of PC that is achieved when executing tc.

Now we consider three search strategies that use *tcGenerate* to generate *testsuites* for a given model and a set of partial coverages PC:

$$search : Model \times \wp(PartCov) \rightarrow \wp(Traces)$$

The naive search strategy simply generates one test case for each required partial coverage $pc \in PC$ by successively calling *tcGenerate*. Thus the size of the testsuite is $O(|PC|)$.

The depth 2 search aims to enlengthen a test case by a suffix that achieves an additional partial coverage. The initial parts are generated by the naive search strategy and then an extension for each partial coverage is searched:

function depth2Search(model, PC)
    testsuite=naiveSearch(model, PC); extension=∅;
    foreach testcase ∈ testsuite do
       foreach pc ∈ PC do
          extendedTestcase=tcGenerate(model, testcase, pc);
          if (extendedTestcase≠ε) then extension=extension ∪ {extendedTestcase};
       od;
    od;
    return testsuite ∪ extension;
The number of generated test cases is in $O(|PC|^2)$.

Heuristic Search enlengthens only the best test cases for a partial coverage which has been achieved rarely so far. Therefore we need two ranking functions. *getBestTestcase*[3] returns the test case with the maximal value for $|PC(tc)|/(t_{exec}(tc) + t_{reset})$ which has not been enlengthened in all possible ways. The function *getWorstPartialCoverage* gives us the partial coverage which has been achieved least often in the testsuite and in particular not in the chosen test case. The parameter *amount* controls how many test cases are generated. In our experiments we used $10 \cdot |PC|$ which seems to generate a sufficiently large set for the subsequent reduction phase.

---

[2] If t is given as sequence diagram the model is instrumented as described in Sec. 2.4.

[3] A promising test case achieves many partial coverages in short execution time.

```
function HeuristicSearch(model, PC)
   testsuite=naiveSearch(model, PC);
   for i=1 to amount do
       testcase=getBestTestcase(testsuite);
       pc=getWorstPartialCoverage(testsuite);
       extendedTestcase=tcGenerate(model, testcase, pc);
       if (extendedTestcase≠ ε) then testsuite=testsuite ∪ {extendedTestcase};
   od;
   return testsuite;
```

3.2 Optimizing Testsuites by Min-Set-Cover-Algorithms

Originally, a min(imal)-set-cover algorithm constructs a small subset from a set of sets, such that the union of sets in the small subset equals the union of the sets in the original set. Since the minimal set cover problem is NP-complete [17], heuristic algorithms are used. Here we want to adopt min-set-cover algorithms to eliminate test cases, that are redundant w.r.t. the partial coverages they achieve, from the testsuite, thereby reducing test execution time of the testsuite.

$$minsetcover : \wp(Traces) \times \mathbb{R} \to \wp(Traces)$$

minsetcover takes a testsuite and the reset time t_{reset} of the system that has to be added after each test case to sum up the execution time of the testsuite.

A simple Greedy algorithm can be applied on a minimal set cover problem by complementing the usual approach [15], i.e., we start with the full testsuite and try to eliminate test cases but keep the same coverage. To select the next candidate for elimination the function *entry* is used. In the simplest variant of a greedy algorithm we set $entry(testsuite, \dots, i, \dots) = testsuite_i$.

```
function greedyMinSetCover(testsuite, t_reset)
   reducedTestsuite=testsuite;
   for i=1 to |testsuite| do
       testcase=entry(testsuite, reducedTestsuite, i, t_reset);
       if (|testsuite.subPC|==|(reducedTestsuite\{testcase}).subPC|)
           then reducedTestsuite=reducedTestsuite\{testcase};
   od;
```

The bidirectional Greedy Algorithm (see [15]) uses the same *entry* function but is applied to the testsuite twice running from both directions through the testsuite.

A sorted Greedy algorithm improves testsuite optimization even further by using a better *entry* function that sorts the test cases according to their quality, weakest test case are returned first. For this purpose, the function *getBestTestcase* from the heuristic search is recycled.

A force directed algorithm is derived from force directed scheduling algorithms [16]. In difference to the previous greedy algorithms, the order in which the test cases are selected as candidates for elimination is not fixed a priori, but depends on the test cases that are still in the testsuite. We introduce a new function

$$timesCovered : PC \times Testsuites \rightarrow \mathbb{N}$$

to calculate how many test cases of a testsuite satisfy a partial coverage.

The *entry* function selects the test case with the lowest quality according to

$$quality(tc) = \frac{\sum_{pc \in PC} \begin{cases} \frac{1}{timesCovered(pc, reducedTestsuite) - 1} & : \quad pc \in subPC(tc) \\ 0 & : \quad else \end{cases}}{t_{exec}(tc) + t_{reset}}$$

The meaning of the formula is as follows: The numerator contains a metric for the assets achieved by the test case tc. The asset is the smaller the more frequent a partial coverage is achieved by other test cases in the testsuite. If tc is the last test case achieving a partial coverage, the asset is set to infinity, which maximizes its quality and prevents tc from elimination. In the denominator we have the test execution time of tc and the reset time. Thus faster test cases are favored.

Finally, we combine a search for test case generation and an optimization by a min-set-cover algorithm: $MinSetCover(search(model, PC), t_{reset})$.

4   Case Study: Robot Control

Tab. 1. Optimised testsuites generated for the robot control software by *EGRET*

component	RobotHardware	SensorModule	Planner (6 variants)	ControlThread	CycleThreadCheck	CycleThread	skPrControl	skPrInterface	RoboProgClient	GUI	RoboProgServer
number of configurations	27	10^4	216	10^7	256	10^{10}	10^7	10^8	10^{10}	10^5	10^7
number of partial coverages	1	7	3	14	5	38	12	7	32	16	19
testcase reduction (greedy) [%]	0	50	67	86	60	81	83	86	81	88	53
testcase reduction (heuristic) [%]	0	50	67	86	80	97	92	86	97	88	93
time reduction (greedy) [%]	0	50	69	86	60	81	82	83	79	76	54
time reduction (heuristic) [%]	0	50	69	86	80	92	88	83	93	76	92

The presented techniques have been implemented in our *Extendable Generator for Efficient Testsuites* (*EGRET*). *EGRET* imports UML models with some syntactic restrictions from Rhapsody for Java (from i-logix) in the XMI1.2 format. A model diagram as well as a statechart for each class is required. AND-states, method-calls which are not used for sending events, all other data types but bounded integers and booleans, and events with parameters are forbidden. However, we are working on a version supporting top-level concurrency, OR-states within the statecharts, the call of non-recursive functions and events with parameters. The exported system definition is instrumented and translated to timed automata. Coverage criteria, search strategies and min-cover-set-algorithms are plug-ins. Thus the tool can easily be extended. We are using UPPAAL as a model checker for test case generation. Some search strategies already use the possibility of a distributed execution of the model checker to lower test generation time even more. The traces which are output of the model checker and specify the test cases are translated into an XML-format which can be executed by a testdriver via a middleware on the components under test.

In the Collaborative Research Centre 562 "Robotic Systems for Handling and Assembly", a robot control software for parallel and hybrid kinematic machines has been developed. All components of the system have been modelled during the development process using sequence diagrams and later on statecharts [18]. The system consists of 16 components, with 27 up to $\sim 2 * 10^{10}$ configurations each, resulting in a state space of about $5 * 10^{93}$ states. The test generator is capable of generating conformance testsuites for all components and interoperability testsuites for pairs of communicating processes.

We applied *EGRET* to the statechart description of the robot control software, using different optimisation techniques. Table 1 shows, how the testsuite size can be reduced by a simple search combined with a bidirectional greedy algorithm and a heuristic search combined with a force directed greedy algorithm. The second approach reduces the test execution time up to 7% of the execution time of the unoptimised testsuite. The best results have been achieved in optimising the testsuites of large components, like the RoboProgClient, the RoboProgServer and the CycleThread. However, in case of smaller components, the results for the heuristic search and the simple search both combined with min-cover-set-algorithms are the same.

5 Conclusion

We presented an approach for automated model based testsuite generation. We considered a catalogue of test quality criteria, namely the test of system properties or interaction sequences, various coverage criteria, and mutant testing. We showed how to uniformly instrument state based models by adding variables or specific test drivers such that a model checker searching for a subgoal encoded as partial coverage will generate a trace that can serve as a test case for that subgoal. Thus, not only formal test quality criteria like coverages but also expert knowledge and existing tests in terms of sequence diagrams are integrated in an automated, formally founded test case generation smoothly.

Next we compared several heuristics for optimizing the test execution time without decreasing the test quality. We combined search algorithms, adding redundancy on the required coverages to a testsuite, with different min-set-cover algorithms that preserve the set of coverages but minimize the execution time.

Our experimental results on the case study are promising under three aspects: First, the test execution time could be significantly reduced. Second, the heuristics for optimization are efficient w.r.t. time and memory consumption such that our approach is applicable on medium sized real world case studies at least which is an significant improvement compared to other approaches. Third, our approach favors the generation of long test cases on which several subgoals (partial coverages) are tested. Thus, we avoid weaknesses w.r.t. the fault detection rate that were observed on other approaches to automated testsuite generation.

In future, we will investigate the interdependence between different strategies for automated model based testsuite generation and the ability to detect faults running the testsuite. First insights have been given in [7, 8], but a more systematic investigation can lead to valuable hints for what kind of systems which strategy can be recommended. Additionally, we plan to extend our work on mutant testing for state based models and investigate alternative heuristic optimization algorithms for testsuite generation like e.g. genetic algorithms.

References

1. Mücke, T., Huhn, M.: Generation of optimized testsuites for UML statecharts with time. In Groz, R., Hierons, R.M., eds.: TestCom. Volume 2978 of LNCS., Springer (2004) 128–143
2. Engels, A., Feijs, L., Mauw, S.: Test generation for intelligent networks using model checking. In Brinksma, E., ed.: Tools and Algorithms for the Construction and Analysis of Systems. (1997)
3. Rayadurgan, S., Heimdahl, M.: Coverage based test-case generation using model checkers. In: Intl. Conf. and Workshop on the Engineering of Computer Based Systems. (2001) 83–93
4. Hong, H., Lee, I., Sokolsky, O., Cha, S.: Automatic test generation from statecharts using model checking. In Brinksma, E., Tretmans, J., eds.: Workshop on Formal Approaches to Testing of Software (FATES). (2001) 15–30
5. Pretschner, A.: Classical search strategies for test case generation with constraint logic programming. In Brinksma, E., Tretmans, J., eds.: Workshop on Formal Approaches to Testing of Software (FATES). (2001) 47–60
6. King, K.N., Offutt, A.J.: A Fortran language system for mutation-based software testing. Software–Practice & Experience **21**(7) (1991) 685–718
7. Heimdahl, M.P., Devaraj, G., Weber, R.J.: Specification test coverage adequacy criteria = specification test generation inadequacy criteria? In: Proceedings of the 8th IEEE International Symposium on High Assurance Systems Engineering (HASE), Tampa, Florida (2004)
8. Heimdahl, M.P., Devaraj, G.: Test-suite reduction for model based tests: Effects on test quality and implications for testing. In Wiels, V., Stirewalt, K., eds.: Proc. of the 19th IEEE Intern. Conference on Automated Software Engineering (ASE), Linz, Austria (2004)
9. OMG: Unified modeling language specification (2003) Version 1.5.
10. Larsen, K.G., Pettersson, P., Yi, W.: UPPAAL in a nutshell. International Journal on Software Tools for Technology Transfer **1**(1-2) (1997) 134–152
11. Diethers, K., Goltz, U., Huhn, M.: Model checking UML statecharts with time. In Jézéquel, J.M., Hußmann, H., Cook, S., eds.: UML 2002, Workshop on Critical Systems Development with UML. (2002)
12. Diethers, K., Huhn, M.: Vooduu: Verification of object-oriented designs using uppaal. In Jensen, K., Podelski, A., eds.: TACAS. Volume 2988 of Lecture Notes in Computer Science., Springer (2004) 139–143
13. Robinson-Mallett, C., Liggesmeyer, P., Mücke, T., Goltz, U.: Generating optimal distinguishing sequences with a model checker. In: A-MOST '05: Proceedings of the 1st International Workshop on Advances in Model-based Testing, New York, NY, USA, ACM Press (2005) 1–7
14. Sugeta, T., Maldonado, J.C., Wong, W.E.: Mutation testing applied to validate SDL specifications. In Groz, R., Hierons, R.M., eds.: TestCom. Volume 2978 of LNCS., Springer (2004) 193–208

15. Offutt, J., Pan, J., Voas, J.: Procedures for reducing the size of coverage-based test sets. In: Proceedings of the Twelfth International Conference on Testing Computer Software. (1995) 111–123
16. Paulin, P., Knight, J.: Force-directed scheduling for the behavioural synthesis of asics. IEEE Trans. on Computer-Aided Design **8**(6) (1989) 661–679
17. Garey, M., Johnson, D.: Computers and Intractability: A Guide to the Theory of NP-Completeness. Freeman and Company (1979)
18. Steiner, J., Diethers, K., Mücke, T., Goltz, U., Huhn, M.: Rigorous tool-supported software development of a robot control system. In: Robot Systems for Handling and Assembly, 2nd Colloquium of the Collaborative Research Center 562. (2005) 137–152

An Integrated Regression Testing Framework to Multi-Threaded Java Programs

Bixin Li[1,2], Yancheng Wang[1], and LiLi Yang[1]

[1]School of Computer Science and Engineering, Southeast University
No.2 Sipailou Road, Nanjing 210096, Jiangsu Province, P.R.China
[2]State Key Lab. for Novel Software Technology, Nanjing University
No.22 Hankou Road, Nanjing 210093, Jiangsu Province, P.R.China
bx.li@seu.edu.cn; http://cse.seu.edu.cn/people/bx.li

Abstract. Regression testing is a process to retest modified programs to examine whether or not new bugs were introduced by a modification. Currently, most of the selective regression testing methods have been presented to test non-concurrent programs, but few of them discussed the regression testing of concurrent programs. In this article, a selective regression testing framework based on reachability testing is proposed to solve the retesting problems in testing multi-threaded Java programs, where both the identification of related components and the selection of test cases are mainly concerned. The integration of selective regression testing techniques and the idea of concurrent programs reachability testing makes the framework be efficient. The adaptation of *ESYN-sequence* based test data coverage adequacy criterion improves the ability to find bugs.

Key words: Regression testing; Multi-threaded program; Reachability testing

1 Introduction

Regression testing is a process to retest modified programs to examine whether or not new bugs were introduced by a modification. In other word, one goal of regression testing is to ensure that new functionality will not affect adversely the correct functionality inherited from the original program. Selective regression testing attempts to identify and retest only those parts of the program that are related to a modification. There are two important problems need to be solved in selective regression testing[3][4]: how to identify those existing tests that must be rerun since they may exhibit different behavior in the changed program? and how to identify those program components that must be retested to satisfy some coverage criterion? But it is very pity that even though many regression testing methods have been proposed to test sequential programs, few discussed the regression testing of multi-threaded Java programs. On the other hand, Java is one of current main stream languages that is widely used to develop software in different application areas, where Java supports concurrent programming with threads. A thread is in fact a single sequential flow of control within a program, and each thread has a *beginning*, an *execution sequence*, and an *end*. However, a thread itself is not a program, it can not run on its own, it must runs within a program. Programs that has multiple synchronous threads are called *multi-threaded programs*. Fig. 1 shows a simple concurrent Java program that implements the *Producer-Consumer* problem.

Please use the following format when citing this chapter:

Li, B., Wang, Y., Yang, L., 2006, in IFIP International Federation for Information Processing, Volume 227, Software Engineering Techniques: Design for Quality, ed. K. Sacha, (Boston: Springer), pp. 237–248.

ce1. public class Prod_Coms {	te24. public void run(){
me2. public static void main(String[] args) {	s25. while(true){
s3. Buffer q = new Buffer();	s26. inname=q.Read();
s4. new Thread(new Producer(q)).start();	s27. use();
s5. new Thread(new Comsumer(q)).start();	}
}	}
}	s28. public use()
ce6. class Producer implements Runnable {	{
ce7. Buffer q;	...
ce8. String name;	s29. System.out.println(" Used name is:"+inname);
e9. public Producer(Buffer q)	...
{	}
s10. this.q=q;	}
}	ce30. class Buffer {
te11. public void run(){	ce31. String name="unknown";
s12. int i=0;	ce32. boolean bFull=false;
s13. while(true)	me33. public synchronized void Write(String value){
{	s34. if (bFull)
s14. if(i==0){	s35. try {wait();} catch (Exception e) {}
s15. name="EvenNumber";	s36. name= value;
}	s37. try {Thread.sleep(1);} catch (Exception e) {}
else {	s38. bFull=true;
s16. name="OddNumber";	s39. notify();
}	}
s17. i=(i+1)%2;	me40. public synchronized String Read(){
s18. q.Write(name);	s41. if(!bFull)
}	s42. try {wait();} catch (Exception e) {}
}	s43. bFull=false;
}	s44. notify();
ce19. class Comsumer implements Runnable{	s45. return name;
ce20. Buffer q;	}
ce21. String inname;	}
e22. public Comsumer(Buffer q){	
s23. this.q=q;	
}	

Fig. 1. A Java program describing the *Producer-Consumer* problem

The program creates two threads *Producer* and *Consumer*. The *Producer* generates an even or an odd alternatively, and stores it in a Buffer object. The *Consumer* consumes all integers from the Buffer as quickly as they become available. Threads *Producer* and *Consumer* in this example share data through a common Buffer object.

To execute the program correctly, two conditions must be satisfied: the *Producer* can not put any new integer into the Buffer unless the previously putted integer has been picked up by the *Consumer*; the *Consumer* must wait for the *Producer* to put a new integer into the Buffer if it is empty. In order to satisfy the these two conditions, the behaviors of the *Producer* and *Consumer* must be synchronized in two ways: ① the two threads must not simultaneously access the Buffer. A Java thread can handle this through the use of *monitor* to lock an object. When a thread holds the monitor for a data item, other threads are locked out and cannot inspect or modify the data. ② the two threads must do some simple cooperation. That is, the *Producer* must have some way to inform the *Consumer* that the value is ready and the *Consumer* must have some way to inform the *Producer* that the value has been picked-up. This can be done in Java by using a collection of methods of **Object** class, where method wait() is for helping threads wait for a condition, and notify() or notifyAll() is for notifying other threads when that condition changed.

In this article, we suggest an integrated regression testing framework to test the multi-threaded Java programs. The rest of this article is organized as follows: section 2 introduces several basic concepts and terminologies; section 3 introduces the integrated framework; section 4 discusses the selective regression testing which will be adopted in our framework; section 5 introduces the reachability testing based on extended synchronization sequence; section 6 gives the case study; section 7 concludes the article and discusses the works in the future.

2 Several concepts

In this section, we will clarify the meanings of some key concepts used in this article so that we have a common concept foundation.

A *synchronization object* refers to an accessed shared variable. A *synchronization operation* refers the operation on a synchronization object, it can be divided into *synchronization reading operation* and *synchronization writing operation* on shared variables.

A *synchronization event* is the process of synchronization operations on synchronization objects. A *synchronization sequence* (or *SYN-sequence*) means a sequence of synchronization events arranged in time order, which is the executive order of the synchronization events in concurrent programs. A Feasible *SYN-sequence* means the synchronization sequence that can be really executed in the source code, while a valid *SYN-sequence* refers to the ones that are specified to be able to be executed by a software specification. In general, the feasible *SYN-sequences* and the valid ones of a program should be consistent, otherwise, there is an error in the implementation of the program under test[5]. An *event code block* (or *ECB*) is defined as the code fragments that are related to an event happened, it can be divided into *synchronization event code block* (or *SECode*) and *non-synchronization event code block* (or *NECode*). *SECodes* means the code fragments relating to a synchronization event, *NECode* means the code fragments relating to a non-synchronization event.

3 Basic Idea of the Framework

3.1 Test-data Adequacy Criterion

A test-data adequacy criterion is a minimum standard that a test suite for a program must satisfy[1]. An adequacy criterion is specified by defining a set of program components and what it means for a component to be exercised. An example is the *all-statements* criterion, which requires that all statements in a program must be executed by at least one test case in the test suite. Here statements are the program components and a statement is exercised by a test if it is executed when the program is run on that test. Satisfying an adequacy criterion provides some confidence that the test suite does a reasonable job for testing the program. In this article, the test-data adequacy criterion is a criterion based on Java multi-threaded Flow Diagram (or JMFD), we call it **all-feasible-ESYN-sequences** criterion:

– The *all-feasible-ESYN-sequences* criterion is satisfied by a test suite T if for each *ESYN-sequence* S there is some test case X in T that exercises S. An *ESYN-sequence* is exercised by test case X if it is executed when the program is run with input X.

3.2   Basic Testing Steps

In this framework, the regression testing method to test multi-threaded Java programs is suggested based on traditional selective regression testing and improved reachability testing. The regression testing steps are listed here, but the detailed discussion will be presented in section 4 and section 5:

1. Identify all *ECBs* to be tested.
2. Based on the criterion of covering all feasible *ESYN-sequences*, we select an appropriate test case subset T' from T, satisfying $T' \subseteq T$.
3. Compute the feasible *ESYN-sequence* and test it deterministically for each test case in T' based on the idea of reachability testing.
4. Judge whether or not it is necessary to design new test cases to meet the coverage criterion. If the answer is positive, we should create new test cases T''.
5. Compute the feasible *ESYN-sequence* and test it deterministically for each test case in T'' based on the idea of reachability testing.
6. Create the new available test case set for the modified program based on T, T' ,T'' and record the related running information that is useful to the regression testing performed next time.

Being similar to traditional regression testing methods, step 1 and 2 are the basic tasks to select the test case set. The big difference is that this method chooses to cover all feasible *ESYN-sequences* as the criterion, but traditional methods choose to cover all feasible *SYN-sequences*, paths or branches. In this framework, the *ESYN-sequence* is composed of one or more *ECBs*, whereas each *ECB* consists of one or more $SECodes$ and $NECodes$.

4   Identifying All *ECBs* To Be Tested

To identify the *ECBs* is to find all *ECBs* that are related to a modification, different kinds of modifications will have different affections on a *ECB*, so it is necessary to clarify which types of modification will be included in this article.

4.1   Types of the Modification

The types of program modification included in this article should be *corrective modification* and *progressive modification*, thereinto:

1. Corrective modification only changes the internal behavior of a *ECB*, but doesnt change the dependence relationships between two *ECBs*.
2. Progressive modification not only changes the internal behavior of a *ECB*, but also change the dependence relationships between two *ECBs*.

Each of them can still be divided into following three sub-types of modifications: ① *statement modification* means doing some modifications to a statement or a control predicate. ② *statement insertion* means inserting a statement or a control predicate to a program. ③ *statement deletion* means deleting a statement or a control predicate from a program.

We have different ways to identity the related *ECBs* when we do different modifications to the multi-threaded programs. In this article, we will borrow concurrent program slicing techniques to identify and capture those interested *ECBs* .

4.2 Slicing Multi-Threaded Java Programs

As to concurrent programs, there are several kinds of techniques are adopted to slice them, thereinto, the technique based on *MDG* (multi-threaded dependence graph), which was proposed by Zhao[9], is the representative one of them. For easy to understand, we iterate it here in brief. The *MDG* of a concurrent Java program is composed of a collection of thread dependence graphs each representing a single thread in the program, and some special kinds of dependence arcs to represent thread interactions between different threads. Then, the two-pass slicing algorithm based on *MDG* can be described as follows: in the first pass, the algorithm traverses backward along all arcs except *parameter-out* arcs, and set marks to those vertices reached in the *MDG*; In the second pass, the algorithm traverses backward from all vertices having marks during the first step along all arcs except *call* and *parameter-in* arcs, and sets marks to reached vertices in the *MDG*. The slice is the union of the vertices of the *MDG* has marks during the first and second steps. Similarly, we can also apply the forward slices of concurrent Java programs. In addition to computing static slices, the *MDG* is also useful for computing dynamic slices of a concurrent Java program.

4.3 Identifying the *ECBs*

In multi-threaded Java programs, the *ECBs* to be identified is the same level as method, there are two strategies to identify the related *ECBs* using program slicing: according to the first strategy, we first compute the statement-level static slice with respect to the slicing criterion ¡s, v¿, where s is the modified point and v is the modified variable; if a *ECB* includes a statement or control predicate in the static slice, then mark the *ECB*. By this way, we can identify all related *ECBs*. Obviously, we can do this easily by using the method proposed by Zhao[9]. According to the second strategy, we can use hierarchical slicing model[8] to identify all related *ECBs*.

In this article, we will discuss how to use the first strategy to identify *ECBs* to be related to the modification, the steps that we propose in this article to identify *ECBs* are as follows:

1. Create Java multi-threaded program dependence graph (*MDG*).
2. Compute statement-level static slice using the modified statement and variable as the slicing criterion, basing on the graph-reachability algorithm.
3. Mark the *ECBs* that include the statements or control predicates in the static slice.

Forward slicing can be used to identify the *ECBs* affected directly or indirectly by the modified value of the variables. while, the backward slicing algorithm can be used to identify the *ECBs* which directly or indirectly affect the values of variables to be modified.

There are different identification methods of *ECBs* for different types of program modification. In this article, as examples, we only discuss the types of modifications and identification methods listed in Tab. 1. In general, for each symbol + in Tab. 1, we should compute a slice.

Tab. 1. The identification methods and the types of modifications

Types of modification / Identifying methods	Corrective modification			Progressive modification		
	Statement correction	Statement deletion	Statement insertion	Statement correction	Statement deletion	Statement insertion
Backward slicing	-	-	+	+	-	+
Forward slicing	-	+	+	+	+	+

Corrective Modification For corrective modification, the dependence representation in the dependence graph of program P is completely same as that of program P', because such modification does not change the dependence relationships between *ECBs*, Therefore, for program P', it is enough to build the internal dependence relationships only for the *ECBs* related to the modification. Based on the modified statement and the variables used in it, we can compute the corresponding slice for three types of modifications so as to identify the *ECBs* related to these modifications. The computing steps are as follows:

1. *Statement modification*: compute the forward or backward slice for such modified statement in program P'. The *ECBs* that include a statement or control predicate in the slice will be regarded as the related *ECBs*.
2. *Statement insertion*: compute the forward or backward slice for such inserted statement in program P'. The *ECBs* that include a statement or control predicate in the slice will be regarded as the related *ECBs*.
3. *Statement deletion*: compute the backward slice for such inserted statement in program P. The *ECBs* that include a statement or control predicate in the slice will be regarded as the related *ECBs*.

Progressive Modification For progressive modification, we need to build complete *MDGs* for program P and P' respectively, because the dependence relationships between *ECBs* have been changed after the modification, we should treat them differently. As we know, there are three kinds of dependence relationships between *ECBs*, i.e., *synchronization dependence*, *data dependence* and *control dependence*. Synchronization dependence is produced by calling methods wait and notify to activate event synchronizing. Data dependence is produced by the definition of a variable in one *ECB*, whereas the use of the variable in another *ECB*. Control dependence is produced by the happening of one event will be dependent on the condition in another event of the same thread. For progressive modification, we can deal with it regarding to following two cases: (1) The dependence relationships between *ECBs* have been changed but the structure of organizing *ECBs* remains unchanged. Under this condition, the modification to *ECBs* will cause the change of data dependence and control dependence, but won't cause synchronization dependence to change. For that, we can identify those *ECBs* related to computing the corresponding slice over the *MDG* of the modified program P'

based on above three types of modification: *statement modification, statement insertion and statement deletion.* (2) Both the dependence relationships between *ECBs* and the structure of organizing *ECBs* have been changed after the modification. The reason that causes the structure of organizing *ECBs* to change is the *insertion* and *deletion* of the synchronization *ECBs*. Therefore, we can identify those related *ECBs* as following steps:

1. The deletion of the synchronization *ECBs*: In the *ECBs* deleted from program *P*, find the statement and variables which have dependence relationships with other *ECBs* in program *P* and use these statements and variables as slicing criteria to compute the backward slices. The *ECBs* related to these slices will be regarded as the related *ECBs*.
2. The insertion of the synchronization *ECBs*: In program *P'*, find those inserted *ECBs* and determine the statements and variables which are dependent on other *ECBs* in program *P'*, we use these statements and variables as slicing criteria to compute the forward slices and backward slices. The *ECBs* related to these slices will be regarded as the related *ECBs*.
3. The movement of the synchronization *ECBs* can be used replace the insertion and deletion of the synchronization *ECBs*. If the result of moving synchronization *ECBs* causes the dependence relationships to change, we use the changed statements and variables as the slicing criteria to compute slices so as to determine those related *ECBs*. Otherwise, we needn't do anything.

4.4 Identification Algorithm: Identifying All Related *ECBs* By Using Both Backward and Forward Slicing

Program modification includes corrective modification and progressive modification. Progressive modification consists of two kinds of types: the first type has not affected the structure no matter what change you have done, the second type has changed the structure when you do some modification. The second type is a kind of complex one that can be regarded as the composition of many single-statement modifications, so it can be divided into single statement modifications. To deal with such modification, it is needed not only rebuild the program dependence graph of *P'*, but also repartition the set of *ECBs* of *P'* . We compute the *ECBs* to be related for each modification to simple statement, the resulting set of these *ECBs* will be the set of *ECBs* related to the second modification.

Once the related *ECBs* are identified, we can perform the regression testing to Java multi-threaded programs as following steps : (1) choose appropriate test cases based on the relationships between old test cases and the identified *ECBs*; (2) compute the feasible *ESYN-sequences*; (3) do the deterministic testing based on selected test cases and the feasible *ESYN-sequences*.

How to build the relationships between old test cases and the identified *ECBs* and how to choose properly test case are two important and complex questions, we won't discuss them in details in this article. For simplicity, here we will focus on the identification of related *ECBs* after the introduction of the regression testing method and the construction of *ESYN-sequence*. As a case study, we use simple selection criterion: *for a given test case, if some related ECB is included in one of its ESYN-sequence, the test case is also regarded as a selected test case.* Even through the precise is not very high, this technique can insure that the set of selected test cases is safe.

5   Reachability Testing

In this section, we explain how to generate effective test sequences to satisfy the *all-feasible-ESYN-sequences* criterion.

5.1   *JMFD*: A Java Concurrent Model

To describe exactly the concurrent mechanism of a multi-threaded Java program so as to generate *ESYN-sequence*, we borrow the model from Li's method and extend its functionality by adding some new elements[7]. We call this model Java multi-threaded flow diagram (*JMFD*), where the node denotes *event*, the edge denotes *flow*. The steps for constructing *JMFD* are as follows:

1. Use square with round corner notation to denote the start node and end node of the program, marked with start or end.
2. Use square notation, with the formula S_r or S_w being filled in it, to denote synchronization read or write event respectively; use ellipse notation with a name to denote a non-synchronization event; the *creation* and *run* event of a thread is denoted as a non-synchronization event with *Tname.start* being filled in it.
3. Use solid line directed edge to denote the control flow in a program; use uniform dashed line directed edge to denote the concurrent flow in multithreaded programs.
4. Use nonuniform dashed line directed edge to denote the synchronization control flow among the synchronization events of different threads.
5. Starting from the main thread, construct the *JMFD* hierarchically till the *JMFD* for the whole program has been constructed.

In this article, we mainly concerns the behavior feature of a multi-threaded Java program for a given test case. Therefore, firstly, we should build the *JMFD* of a multi-threaded Java program for the special test case. Fig 2 shows the *JMFD* of the program in Fig. 1.

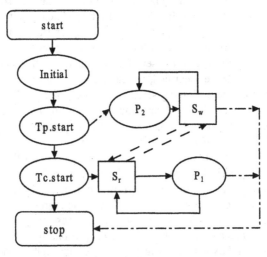

Fig. 2. The *JMFD* of *Producer-Consumer* program

5.2 Computation of the *ESYN-sequences*

For the feasible *SYN-sequence* S of concurrent program P, the prefixes of other feasible *SYN-sequence* of P are called the *race variants*[5], and accordingly, for the feasible *ESYN-sequence* S' of concurrent program P', the prefixes of other feasible *ESYN-sequence* of P' are also called the race variants.

We can compute the race variants of synchronization sequence by building a race variant diagram that is a tree, where the node denotes a general prefix of a given feasible synchronization sequence S or denotes one of its race variants. The creation process of the tree nodes in the race variant diagram is completed by considering the all possible orderings of synchronization read or synchronization write event. The building process of race variant diagram is in fact the process to compute the variants of synchronization sequences, when the whole race variant diagram is constructed, the computation process of race variants of a synchronization sequence ends. To compute other feasible synchronization sequence, we must use a given test case and corresponding race variant of S to execute the replay operation of a concurrent program based on the prefix[2]. From the definition of *ESYN-sequence*, we have following proposition:

Proposition 1 If the time-order remains unchanged, a *SYN-subsequence* of a feasible *ESYN-sequence* is a feasible *SYN-sequence*.

So, we can compute *EYSN-sequence* by extending the computing algorithm of *SYN-sequence* so that it can deal with non-synchronization event[5][6]. For instance, *SYN-sequence*$[1] = (S_w^1, S_r^1, S_w^2, S_r^2, ...)$ is a feasible synchronization sequence in the *Producer-Consumer* program in Fig 1, the *Consumer* thread exercises the event sequence $S[2] = (S_r^1, P_1, S_r^2, P_1, ...)$, meanwhile, the *Producer* thread exercises the event sequence $S[3] = (P_2, S_w^1, P_2, S_w^2, ...)$. The event sequence $S[3]$ shows that the synchronization event S_w^1 must happen after the non-synchronization event P_2, and that the non-synchronization event P_2 must happen before the synchronization event S_w^2. Similarly, the non-synchronization event P_1 must happen between the synchronization events S_r^1 and S_r^2. So, if we insert the non-synchronization event P_1, P_2 into *SYN-sequence*$[1]$ according to the *event sequence constraint conditions* during the thread execution[5], we can obtain the *ESYN-sequence*. Tab. 2 shows a set of *ESYN-sequences*, which is computed over the *SYN-sequence*$[1]$.

Tab. 2. The feasible *ESYN-sequences* computed from the *SYN-sequence*$[1]$

No.	*ESYN-sequence*
1	$(P_2, S_w^1, P_2, S_r^1, P_1, S_w^2, S_r^2, ...)$
2	$(P_2, S_w^1, P_2, S_r^1, S_w^2, P_1, S_r^2, ...)$
3	$(P_2, S_w^1, S_r^1, P_2, P_1, S_w^2, S_r^2, ...)$
4	$(P_2, S_w^1, S_r^1, P_2, S_w^2, P_1, S_r^2, ...)$

The *event sequence constraint condition* during the thread execution are as follows:

- All events in the thread, including synchronization event and non-synchronization event, must be in time-order, i.e., the event sequence belonging to the same thread in a *ESYN-sequence* must be consistent with the thread executon event sequence

- The running of events in a thread must happen after the thread is created. As a example, in Fig.2, the event in *Consumer* thread must happen after the Initial event in the main thread.

The algorithm for constructing *ESYN-sequence* is as follows:

1. For a given test case X and a given *SYN-sequence* S, compute the race variants of *SYN-sequence* S, by changing its race condition.
2. Basing on the event sequences constraint conditions during the thread execution, add all the non-synchronization events related to race variants of the *SYN-sequence* to the race variant so as to construct the race variant of the *ESYN-sequence*.
3. Using test case X and the race variant of each the *ESYN-sequence* of S to perform the multithreaded program replay operation based on prefixes so as to compute the other feasible *SYN-sequences* and feasible *ESYN-sequence* produced.
4. For each new *SYN-sequence*, repeat steps 1,2 and 3 till no new *ESYN-sequence* produced.

6 Case Study

6.1 Corrective Modification

Fig. 1 is a typical Java multithreaded program of the *Producer-Consumer* problem. The program code can be divided into five non-synchronization *ECBs* including Initial, Tp.start, Tc.start, P_2 and P_1, and two synchronization *ECBs* including S_w and S_r. Fig 2 is a *JMFD* of the program in Fig.1 where statement 3 forms the non-synchronization event Initial representing the initialization operation, statement 4 and 5 forms non-synchronization events for the creation of threads Tp.start and Tc.start, respectively.p is the name of *Producer* thread, c is the name of *Consumer* thread. The statements from 10 to 17 form the non-synchronization event P_2 in the *Producer* thread, representing the event of producing data; statement 18 calls synchronization method Write, which forms the synchronization event, marked as S_w. Similarly, statement 26 calls synchronization method Read, which forms the synchronization event, marked as S_r.

The method called by statement 27 forms the non-synchronization event representing the consuming operation. Now, suppose that we do some changes to the program, for example, we change statement s38:bFull=true to bFull=false, then the process is as follows using our regression testing method: firstly, we should create the multi-threaded program dependence diagram, and know from the *MDG* where such modification has not caused the change of dependence relationships, so we can operate along the *case-modification* branch in the identification algorithm for identifying *ECBs* for the corrective modification. In program P', we use ¡s38,bFull¿ as slicing criterion to compute forward slice and backward slice: the backward slice is −s41,s42″ and the forward slice is −me2, s4, te11,s13,s18,me33,s38″. The *ECBs* are related to these resulting slices are: non-synchronization event code blocks Tp.start and P_2, and synchronization event code blocks S_w and S_r. All these *ECBs* are the *ECBs* related to the statement modification. Finally, we should select appropriate test case to finish the reachability testing, and ensure each related *ECB* will be covered by a test case at least. In other words, the coverage criterion is to cover all feasible

ESYN-sequences which includes the related *ECBs*. The testing result shows that there are some faults with the corrective modification to statement 38, it makes infeasible *ESYN-sequence*=(P_2, S_w^1, P_1, S_w^2) become feasible *ESYN-sequence*

6.2 Progressive Modification

Suppose that we delete the statement s39 in the program in Fig.1, the consequence is that the dependence edge from statements s39 to s42 will be deleted. Such modification causes the dependence relationships between *ECBs* to change, it belongs to the type of progressive modification. After the construction of *MDG* and *JMFD* of program P, we can obtain the set of *ECBs* of program P by identifying the *ECBs* along the type of statement deletion of progressive modification. The concrete steps are: (1) compute the backward static slice w.r.t. slicing criterion ¡s39,monitor¿ in program P based on the identification algorithm of related *ECBs*, the result is –s39,s42″. The related *ECBs* that we have are synchronization event code blocks S_w and S_r; (2)select enough test case related to cover those related *ECBs* so as to do reachability testing and ensure each related *ECB* will be covered by at least a test case; (3)perform the reachability testing process. The result shows that there are some faults with the deletion of statements s39,it will cause the deadlock of the program and make the feasible *ESYN-sequences* covering S_w and S_r become infeasible *ESYN-sequences*.

7 Conclusion

In this article, we suggest a regression testing framework to test Java multi-threaded programs based on the integration of both the improved reachability testing and traditional selective regression testing of sequential programs. The adoption of selective regression testing technique makes the efficient be high, the use of reachability testing solves the problems that caused by the non-deterministic behavior of the multi-threaded programs. Meanwhile, program slicing techniques are borrowed to identify the related *ECBs* so as to increase the safety and decrease the total cost of the regression testing.

Acknowledgments. This work is partially supported by the National Science Foundation of China (No. 60473065) and partially supported by the open foundation of State Key Lab. for Novel Software Technology, Nanjing University(No.A2005 08). The authors also thank those anonymous reviewers for their valuable suggestions on the draft.

References

1. D. Binkley. *The application of program slicing to regression testing.* Information and Software Technology (I&ST) special issue on program slicing, 40 (11-12): 583-594, 1998.
2. R.Carver and K. Tai. *Replay and testing for concurrent programs.* IEEE Software, 3(1991):66-74
3. T. L. Graves, M. J. Harrold, J. Kim, A. Porters, G. Rothermel. *An empirical study of regression test selection techniques.* ACM Transactions on Software Engineering and Methodology. 10(2), 2001.

4. R. Gupta, M. J. Harrold, and M. L. Soffa *An approach to regression testing using slicing*. In: Proceedings of the Conference on Software Maintenance, November 1992.
5. G. H. Hwang, K. C. Tai, and T. L. Huang. *Reachability testing: an approach to testing concurrent software*. In: Proceedings of First Asia-Pacific conference on software Engineering, 246-255, 1994.
6. J. Lei, R. Carver. *Reachability testing of concurrent programs*. Technical Report GMU-CS-TR-2005-1, George Mason University.
7. S. Li, H. Chen, and Y. Sun. *A framework of reachability testing for Java multi-threaded programs* IEEE International Conference on System, Man and Cybernetics, 3(2004):2730-2734
8. B. Li, X. Fan, J. Pang, J. Zhao. *A model for slicing Java programs hierarchically*. J. Comput. Sci. & Technol, 19(6):848-858, 2004.
9. J. Zhao. *Slicing concurrent Java programs*. In: Proceedings of Seventh International Workshop on Program Comprehension, 126 -133, 1999

DynAlloy as a Formal Method for the Analysis of Java Programs

Juan P. Galeotti and Marcelo F. Frias

Department of Computer Science
School of Exact and Natural Sciences
University of Buenos Aires
Argentina
e-mail: {jgaleotti, mfrias}@dc.uba.ar

Abstract. DynAlloy is an extension of the Alloy specification language that allows one to specify and analyze dynamic properties of models. The analysis is supported by the DynAlloy Analyzer tool. In this paper we present a method for translating sequential Java programs to DynAlloy. This allows one to use DynAlloy as a new formal method for the analysis of Java programs. As an application showing the utility of this formal method toward this task, we present JAT, a tool for automated generation of test data for sequential Java programs, implemented on top of the DynAlloy Analyzer.

1 Introduction

Alloy [9] is a relational modeling language. Its simplicity, object-oriented flavor, and automated analysis support, have made this formal language appealing to a growing audience. The Alloy Analyzer [10] transforms Alloy specifications (models) in which domains' sizes are bounded to a fix scope, into propositions that are later fed to SAT-solvers such as Berkmin [6] or MChaff [15]. Then, given an assertion to be verified in the model, the Alloy Analyzer attempts to produce a model of the specification that violates the assertion. If no such model is found within the provided scopes, we can gain more confidence that the analyzed property holds in the model. Of course, a counterexample suffices to show that the model is flawed. We will include a description of Alloy's syntax and semantics in Section 2. It is nevertheless worth mentioning at this point that Alloy models are static. That is, while Alloy functions seem to model an input–output behavior by relating input and output variables, the classical first-order semantics prevents actual state change or evolution.

The DynAlloy specification language was first introduced in [4] as an extension of the Alloy language allowing us to cope with the lack of dynamics of Alloy. DynAlloy's semantics is based on dynamic logic [8], making then possible to specify atomic actions (and complex actions from these) that actually modify the state. It also allows one to assert properties about these actions by means of partial correctness assertions [2]. In [3] we presented the DynAlloy Analyzer, which allowed us to effectively analyze DynAlloy specifications.

Please use the following format when citing this chapter:

Galeotti, J.P., Frias, M.F., 2006, in IFIP International Federation for Information Processing, Volume 227, Software Engineering Techniques: Design for Quality, ed. K. Sacha, (Boston: Springer), pp. 249–260.

Contributions of the Paper

- From the foundational point of view, this paper introduces a translation of sequential Java programs to DynAlloy. This translation provides us with a new formal method for the analysis of Java programs using the DynAlloy Analyzer.
- In the applications side, we introduce JAT (Java Automated Testing), an application of DynAlloy to the automated generation of test data for sequential Java programs. JAT allows a user to generate test data according to various structural testing criteria such as statement coverage, branch coverage or path coverage. JAT also provides the user with information about non reachable code, and profits from the existence of invariants and pre conditions written in JML [14], and previous partial test suites, if these are available.

The paper is structured as follows. In Sections 2 and 3 we give brief introductions to Alloy and DynAlloy, respectively. In Section 4 we show how to translate sequential Java programs to DynAlloy. In Section 5 we present JAT, compare it with related work, and evaluate its performance through examples. Finally, in Section 6 we present our conclusions.

2   The Alloy Specification Language

In this section, we introduce the reader to the Alloy specification language by means of an example. This example intends to illustrate the standard features of the language and their associated semantics, and will be used in further sections.

Suppose we want to specify systems handling lists. We might recognize that, in order to specify lists, a data type for the data stored in the lists is necessary. We can then start by indicating the existence of a set (of atoms) for data, which in Alloy is specified using a *signature*:

$$\text{sig } \textit{Data } \{\ \}$$

In this signature we do not assume any properties about the structure of data.

With data already defined, we can now specify what constitutes a list. A possible way of defining lists is by saying that a list consists of a datum, and an attribute *next* relating the current node to the remaining part of the list:

$$\text{sig } \textit{List } \{\text{ val : lone } \textit{Data},$$
$$\text{next: lone } \textit{List } \}$$

The modifier "lone" in the above definition indicates that attributes "val" and "next" may relate a list with at most one element. These are *partial* functions from *List* to *Data* and *List* to *List*, respectively.

Alloy allows for the definition of signatures as subsets of the set denoted by another "parent" signature. This is done via *signature extension*. For example, one could define other (perhaps more complex) kinds of lists as extensions of the *List* signature:

$$\text{sig } \textit{Empty } \text{extends } \textit{List } \{\}$$
$$\text{sig } \textit{TwoList } \text{extends } \textit{List } \{ \text{ val2: Data } \}$$

```
problem ::= decl*form            expr ::=
decl ::= var : typexpr            expr + expr (union)
typexpr ::=                       | expr & expr (intersection)
type                              | expr − expr (difference)
| type → type                     |~ expr (transpose)
| type ⇒ typexpr                  | expr.expr (navigation)
                                  | *expr (refl. trans. closure)
form ::=                          | ^expr (transitive closure)
expr in expr (subset)             | {v : t/form} (set former)
|!form (neg)                      | Var
| form and form (conj)
| form or form (disj)             Var ::=
| all v : type/form (univ)        var (variable)
| some v : type/form (exist)      | Var[var] (application)
```

Fig. 1. Grammar of Alloy

As specified in these definitions, *Empty* and *TwoList* are special kinds of lists. In *TwoList*, a new attribute val2 is added to each list. As the previous definitions show, signatures are used to define data domains and their structure. The attributes of a signature denote *relations*. For instance, the "val" attribute in signature *List* represents a binary relation, from list atoms to atoms from *Data*. Given a set L (not necessarily a singleton) of *List* atoms, L.next denotes the relational image of L under the relation denoted by next. Signature extension, as we mentioned before, is interpreted as inclusion of the set of atoms of the extending signature into the set of atoms of the extended signature.

In Fig. 1, we present the grammar and the (informal) semantics of Alloy's relational logic, the core logic on top of which all of Alloy's syntax and semantics are defined. Adding a bit more of notation, given singleton unary relations $A = \{a\}$ and $B = \{b\}$, we define $A \to B = \{\langle a, b \rangle\}$. Given a binary relation R, we define the update of R by the pair $A \to B$ by

$$R \mathbin{++} (A \to B) = \{\langle x, y \rangle \in R : x \neq a\} \cup \{\langle a, b \rangle\} \ .$$

So far, we have just shown how the structure of data domains can be specified in Alloy. These models can be enriched with the addition of *operations*, *properties* and *assertions*. Following the style of Z specifications, operations in Alloy can be defined as expressions, relating states from the state spaces described by the signature definitions. Primed variables are used to denote the resulting values, although this is just a convention not reflected in the semantics. In order to illustrate the definition of operations in Alloy, consider, for instance, an operation that specifies the appending of a datum to the front of a list (usually called Cons):

$$\text{pred Cons}(d : Data, l, l' : List)\{ \\ l'.\text{val} = d \text{ and } l'.\text{next} = l\} \tag{1}$$

As the reader might expect, a model can be enhanced by adding properties (axioms) to it. These properties are written as logical formulas called *facts* in Alloy. We reproduce some here. It might be necessary to say that lists are acyclic

```
fact AcyclicLists{ all l : List  |  l !in l.(^next) }
fact OneEmpty{ one Empty }.
```

The keyword "one" states that the set (unary relation) Empty is a singleton. More complex facts can be expressed by using the quite considerable expressive power of the relational logic. Assertions are the *intended* properties of a given model. Consider, for instance, the following simple Alloy assertion, regarding the presented example:

assert ToEmpty{ all l: *List* | l != Empty implies Empty in l.^next }

This assertion states that non empty lists (eventually) reach the empty list. Assertions are used to check specifications. Using the Alloy analyzer it is possible to validate assertions by searching for possible (finite) counterexamples for them under the constraints imposed in the specification.

3   The DynAlloy Specification Language

DynAlloy is an extension of the Alloy modeling language. It allows us to define atomic actions that modify the state, and build more complex actions from the atomic ones. Atomic actions are defined by means of pre and post conditions given as Alloy formulas. For instance, atomic actions that retrieve the first element in a list, or remove the front element from a list are specified by

act Head(l : List, d : Data)   act Tail(l : List)
  pre = { l != Empty }   pre = { l != Empty }
  post = { d' = l.val }   post = { l' = l.next }

The primed variables d' and l' in the specification of actions Head and Tail denote the value of variables d and l in those states reached *after* the execution of the actions. While actions may modify the value of all variables, we assume that those variables whose primed versions do not occur in the post condition retain their corresponding input values. Thus, Head modifies the value of d, but l keeps its initial value. This allows us to use simpler formulas in pre-post conditions.

Equally important, DynAlloy allows us to assert properties about complex actions by means of partial correctness assertions. For instance,

{ l != Empty }
Head(l, d);
Tail(l)
{ Cons(d',l',l) }

The syntax of DynAlloy's formulas extends the one presented in Fig. 1 with the addition of the following clause for building partial correctness statements:

formula   ::=   ... | {*formula*} *program* {*formula*} "partial correctness"

Figure 2 shows how complex actions are built from atomic ones. Figure 3 describes the semantics of DynAlloy.

One of the important features of Alloy is the automatic analysis possibilities it provides. Similarly, in [3] we show how to translate DynAlloy specifications to Alloy specifications in order to achieve analyzability. We reproduce the fundamental aspects

$$
\begin{aligned}
act \quad ::= \quad & p\{pre(\overline{x})\}\{post(\overline{x})\} && \text{``atomic action''} \\
| \quad & formula? && \text{``test''} \\
| \quad & act + act && \text{``non-deterministic choice''} \\
| \quad & act\,;act && \text{``sequential composition''} \\
| \quad & act^* && \text{``iteration''}
\end{aligned}
$$

Fig. 2. Grammar for DynAlloy's Actions

$$
M[\{\alpha\}p\{\beta\}]e = M[\alpha]e \implies \forall e'\,(\langle e, e'\rangle \in P[p] \implies M[\beta]e')
$$

$$
\begin{aligned}
P &: program \to \mathcal{P}\,(env \times env) \\
P[\langle pre, post\rangle] &= \{\,\langle e, e'\rangle : M[pre]e \wedge M[post]e'\,\} \\
P[\alpha?] &= \{\,\langle e, e'\rangle : M[\alpha]e \wedge e = e'\,\} \\
P[p_1 + p_2] &= P[p_1] \cup P[p_2] \\
P[p_1\,;p_2] &= P[p_1]\,;P[p_2] \\
P[p^*] &= P[p]^*
\end{aligned}
$$

Fig. 3. Semantics of DynAlloy.

of this translation below, and refer the reader to [3] for optimizations. We define below a function $wlp : program \times formula \to formula$ that computes the weakest liberal precondition [2] of a formula according to a program (composite action). We will in general use names $x_1, x_2 \ldots$ for program variables, and will use names $x'_1, x'_2, \ldots$ for the value of program variables *after* action execution. We will denote by $\alpha|^v_x$ the substitution of all free occurrences of variable x by the fresh variable v in formula α.

When an atomic action a specified as $a\{pre(\overline{x})\}\{post(\overline{x}, \overline{x'})\}$ is used in a composite action, formal parameters are substituted by actual parameters. Since we assume all variables are input/output variables, actual parameters are variables, let us say, $\overline{y}$. In this situation, function wlp is defined as follows:

$$
wlp[a(\overline{y}), f] = pre|^{\overline{y'}}_{\overline{x}} \implies all\ \overline{n}\left(post|^{\overline{n}}_{\overline{x'}}|^{\overline{y'}}_{\overline{x}} \implies f|^{\overline{n}}_{\overline{y'}}\right). \tag{2}
$$

A few points need to be explained about (2). First, we assume that free variables in f are amongst $\overline{y'}, \overline{x_0}$. Variables in $\overline{x_0}$ are generated by the translation function $pcat$ given in (3). Second, $\overline{n}$ is an array of new variables, one for each variable modified by the action. Last, notice that the resulting formula has again its free variables amongst $\overline{y'}, \overline{x_0}$. This is also preserved in the remaining cases in the definition of function wlp.

For the remaining action constructs, the definition of function wlp is the following:

$$
\begin{aligned}
wlp[g?, f] &= g \implies f \\
wlp[p_1 + p_2, f] &= wlp[p_1, f] \wedge wlp[p_2, f] \\
wlp[p_1\,;p_2, f] &= wlp[p_1, wlp[p_2, f]] \\
wlp[p^*, f] &= \bigwedge_{i=0}^{\infty} wlp[p^i, f].
\end{aligned}
$$

Notice that wlp yields Alloy formulas in all these cases, except for the iteration construct, where the resulting formula may be infinitary. In order to obtain an Alloy formula, we can impose a bound on the depth of iterations. This is equivalent to fixing a maximum length for traces. A function $Bwlp$ (bounded weakest liberal precondition) is then defined exactly as wlp, except for iteration, where it is defined by $Bwlp[p^*, f] = \bigwedge_{i=0}^{n} Bwlp[p^i, f]$, and n is the scope set for the depth of iterations.

We now define a function $pcat$ that translates partial correctness assertions to Alloy formulas. For a partial correctness assertion $\{\alpha(\overline{y})\} \ P(\overline{y}) \ \{\beta(\overline{y}, \overline{y'})\}$

$$pcat\left(\{\alpha\} \ P \ \{\beta\}\right) = \forall \overline{y}\left(\alpha \implies \left(Bwlp\left[p, \beta|\frac{\overline{x_0}}{\overline{y}}\right]\right)|\frac{\overline{y}}{\overline{y'}}|\frac{\overline{y}}{\overline{x_0}}\right) . \qquad (3)$$

Of course this analysis method where iteration is restricted to a fixed depth is not complete, but clearly it is not meant to be; from the very beginning we placed restrictions on the size of domains involved in the specification to be able to turn first-order formulas into propositional formulas. This is just another step in the same direction.

4   Translating Java Programs to DynAlloy

It will be made clear in this section that once DynAlloy is available, translating Java becomes immediate. It is also clear that other programming languages, or description languages, can be easily translated to DynAlloy without requiring complicated ad-hoc translations. In Fig. 4 we present the grammar for the subset of Java we will translate in this article. We have also dealt with dynamic dispatch, but is not treated in this paper due to space limitations.

```
program  ::= classdecl* procdecl*
classdecl ::= class class {class field;}
procdecl ::= class static proc (class var,){stmt}
stmt     ::= var = new class()
           | var = expr
           | expr.field = expr
           | while pred { stmt }
           | if ( pred ) stmt else stmt
           | stmt ; stmt
expr     ::= null | var | expr.field
           | expr.proc(expr,. . .,expr)
pred     ::= expr (boolean)
           | expr == expr | !expr | expr && expr
```

Fig. 4. The syntax of a subset of Java

In order to handle aliased objects appropriately, we adopt the object model of JAlloy [11]. The JAlloy model of the List signature requires just a basic signature for lists without fields

$$\text{sig List } \{ \ \} \ ,$$

and fields are considered as binary relations

$$\text{val : List} \rightarrow \text{lone Val,}$$
$$\text{next : List} \rightarrow \text{lone List .}$$

These binary relations can be modified by the DynAlloy actions. We will in general distinguish between simple data that will be handled as values, and structured objects. Action SetNext is now specified as follows:

$$\text{act SetNext(l1, l2 : List, next : List} \rightarrow \text{lone List)}$$
$$\text{pre = \{ l1 != Empty \}}$$
$$\text{post = \{ next' = next ++ (l1 } \rightarrow \text{l2) \}}$$

We introduce now in DynAlloy atomic actions that create objects, and atomic actions that modify an object's field. We denote by Objects_C the unary relation (set) that contains the set of objects from class C alive at a given point in time. This set can be modified by the effect of an action. In order to handle creation of an object of class C in DynAlloy, we introduce an atomic action called NewC, specified as follows:

$$\text{act NewC(o : C)}$$
$$\text{pre = \{ true \}}$$
$$\text{post = \{ } o' \text{ !in Objects}_C \text{ and } o' \text{ in Objects}_C' \}$$

Notice that Objects_C should have been passed as a parameter. In order to maintain notation simple, we keep this kind of variables global. An atomic action that sets the value of field f of object o, is described in DynAlloy as follows:

$$\text{act Setf(o : C, v : C', f : C } \rightarrow \text{C')}$$
$$\text{pre = \{ o in Objects}_C \text{ \}}$$
$$\text{post = \{ f' = f ++ (o } \rightarrow \text{v) \}}$$

From the class extension hierarchy in Java, a signature extension hierarchy is defined in DynAlloy. A class declaration

$$\text{class C \{}$$
$$C_1 \text{ field}_1;$$
$$\vdots$$
$$C_k \text{ field}_k;\}$$

produces a DynAlloy model that includes definitions for a signature C and the necessary actions for creating objects and modifying their fields:

$$\text{sig C \{ \}}$$

$$\text{NewC(o : C)}$$

$$\text{Setfield}_1(o : C, v : C_1, \text{field}_1 : C \rightarrow C_1)$$
$$\vdots$$
$$\text{Setfield}_k(o : C, v : C_k, \text{field}_k : C \rightarrow C_k)$$

We proceed now to the translation of simple statements.

$$\text{v = new C } \mapsto \text{ NewC(v) .}$$

In order to translate assignment of an expression to a variable, we introduce action VarAssign as follows:

$$\text{act VarAssign}(v1, v2 : C)$$
$$\text{pre} = \{\ \text{true}\ \}$$
$$\text{post} = \{\ v1' = v2\ \}$$

The translation then becomes:

$$v = e\ \ \mapsto\ \ \text{VarAssign}(v,e)\ .$$

In order to translate the assignment of an expression e to the f-field of an object o, we use action Set$f$. The translation of the statement then becomes:

$$o.f = e\ \ \mapsto\ \ \text{Set}f(o,e,f)\ .$$

For more complex program constructs, the translation is defined as follows,

while pred {stmt}	$\mapsto$	$(\text{pred}?;\textbf{stmt})^{*};(!\text{pred})?,$
if (pred) stmt1 else stmt2	$\mapsto$	$(\text{pred}?;\textbf{stmt1}) + ((!\text{pred})?;\textbf{stmt2}),$
stmt1 ; stmt2	$\mapsto$	$\textbf{stmt1};\textbf{stmt2},$

where the boldface **stmt**, **stmt1** and **stmt2** stand for the recursive application of the translation to the statements stmt, stmt1 and stmt2, respectively.

5   Test-Data Generation with JAT

JAT is a tool that generates test input data for Java methods according to different white-box testing criteria. The current prototype of JAT does statement coverage, branch coverage and path coverage. In order to obtain a finite Alloy formula, we finitize the code. This is done by performing up to a predetermined (user defined) number of loop unrolling or recursive call unfolding. Also, for those methods called from the analyzed method that are provided with a JML contract, the user can choose whether she/he prefers to use the contract in the test generation process, or rather to inline the code in the caller method.

In Section 5.1 we describe the architecture of JAT. In Section 5.2 we present a case study. Finally, in Section 5.3 we analyze related work.

5.1   The Architecture of JAT

Figure 5 provides the architecture of JAT. Boxed entries in the figure correspond to processes, while non boxed entries correspond to data. Arrows show the flow of data between processes. JAT takes, as a mandatory input, compilable source Java code, together with an indication of the method to be tested. Optional inputs to the tool are a partial JUnit [12] test suite, and JML [14] annotations for data invariants and pre conditions of methods.

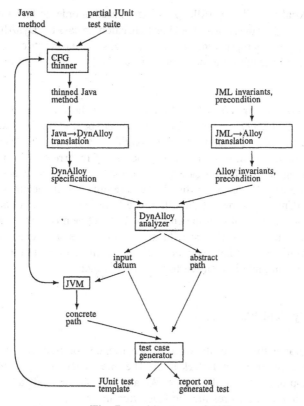

Fig. 5. Architecture of JAT

The Control Flow Graph Thinner The thinner starts by constructing the method's control flow graph (CFG). Given the source code for the method under analysis, and the partial test suite (if any tests are available), the CFG thinner analyzes the coverage produced by the provided test suite. It runs first the method under analysis in all input data available in the provided test suite, and marks the traversed statements and conditions in the CFG. In this way we have a partial coverage of the CFG. Notice that a good starting test suite will greatly improve the test input data generation process.

The CFG thinner then produces appropriate subgraphs of the CFG to be translated to DynAlloy in order to look for new test input data. From the supplied subgraph of the CFG, JAT produces one input datum. The source method is then executed on this input, and the coverage marking in the original CFG is updated by adding the marking of the newly covered statements and conditions. The thinning process then starts again from the newly marked CFG.

Notice that retrieving proper subgraphs of the CFG allows us to get better analysis times by reducing the size of the problem to be solved.

The JML→Alloy Translator JML [14] preconditions and data invariants allow us to generate better test input data, i.e., generation of data that does not satisfy invariants or is not expected as input from the method is prevented.

The DynAlloy Analyzer The DynAlloy Analyzer is used in order to find a model of the specification produced by the Java→DynAlloy translation. In case the DynAlloy Analyzer succeeds in finding an appropriate model, from this model we can retrieve a path on the DynAlloy code (and therefore on the original Java code), as well as an input datum i.

The Test Case Generator We will call the path in the Java code inferred from the DynAlloy Analyzer *abstract*, as opposed to the *concrete* path in the Java code obtained by executing the Java source code with input i on the Java virtual machine. Although it seems like both paths ought to be the same, the use of incorrect JML specifications may produce wrong paths. The test case generator then generates the concrete path and compares the abstract and concrete paths. If they are different, it generates a report for the user, and a JUnit test showing the difference between the value obtained by the concrete execution and the value at the end of the abstract path is generated. This helps the user in finding bugs in the JML specifications. In case the abstract and the concrete path agree, a JUnit test template is generated containing a description of the found input datum. This template is then fed to the CFG thinner.

5.2 Case Study: Red-Black Trees

In order to evaluate the usability of JAT, we looked for branch coverage in an implementation of sets using red-black trees. The implementation was obtained from the class TreeMap in the java.util package. We analyzed the method "add" that inserts an element in a tree and restores the red-black tree invariant.

In order to handle trees whose height is less than or equal to 6, we performed up to 6 loop unrolls in method treeInsert. The total number of lines of code checked, considering the inlined methods and the loop unrolls, is of approximately 230 lines. There are 16 branches to be covered. Following the technique we described in Section 5.1, the CFG thinner produced 9 subgraphs of the CFG. Looking for test inputs from these 9 CFGs allowed us to cover 15 out of the 16 branches, within a scope of 4. Actually, the remaining branch corresponds to an if statement where the if branch is always taken.

In Table 1 we present the analysis times of JAT using DynAlloy. SAT-solvers are usually very sensitive to increases in scope. Fortunately, test input data generation most of the times requires small structures to achieve a high coverage, and therefore SAT-solving becomes a viable technique. This hypothesis on the factibility of using small scopes is known as the *small scope hypothesis*. Different columns show the analysis time for different scopes. Running times were computed in a computer with a 64-bit AMD Athlon 3200 with 2 GB of RAM running on a dual channel architecture. Time is expressed in seconds.

Scope	3	4	5	6	7	8	9	10	11
	52	56	63	80	101	101	102	120	150

Tab. 1. Running times for the generation of test data.

5.3 Related Work

A vast amount of research on test input data generation has been done in the last few years. Some research, as is the case in the SLAM project [1] or in the case of the DART tool [5], assumes absence of aliasing. On the other hand, we aim at the analysis of programs that make extensive use of complex structures. Other research points toward specification testing. For instance, TestEra [13] uses the Alloy Analyzer for specification based testing. Tools such as CUTE [16], Symtra [18], or the work of Visser et al. [17] using Java Pathfinder, base their research on symbolic execution. We solely depend on SAT-solving for analysis purposes. An approach close to ours is the one followed in the INKA tool [7]. The tool handles complex data structures in C, but cannot handle dynamic allocation.

6 Conclusions

We have presented a novel formal method for the analysis of Java programs based on a translation of Java programs to DynAlloy, and the use of SAT-solvers. The experiments we have conducted show that JAT can be effectively used in the analysis of non trivial Java methods that create objects and handle complex data.

References

1. Ball. T, *A Theory of Predicate–Complete Test Coverage and Generation*. Technical Report MSR-TR-2004-28, Microsoft Research, Redmond, WA, April 20004.
2. Dijkstra E. W. and Scholten C. S., *Predicate calculus and program semantics*, Springer-Verlag, 1990.
3. Frias, M. F., Galeotti, J. P., Lopez Pombo, C. G., and Aguirre, N. M. *DynAlloy: Upgrading Alloy with actions*. In *Proceedings of the 27th. International Conference on Software Engineering*, G-C. Roman, Ed. Association for the Computer Machinery and IEEE Computer Society, ACM Press, St. Louis, Missouri, USA, 2005, 442–450.
4. Frias M.F., Lopez Pombo C.G., Baum G.A., Aguirre N.M. and Maibaum T.S.E., *Reasoning About Static and Dynamic Properties in Alloy: A Purely Relational Approach*, in ACM-Transactions on Software Engineering and Methodology (TOSEM), 14(4), 478 – 526, 2005.
5. Godefroid P., Klarlund N. and Sen K., *DART: Directed Automated Random Testing*, in Proceedings of the ACM SIGPLAN 2005 Conference on Programming Languages Design and Implementation (PLDI), 2005.
6. Goldberg, E. and Novikov, Y. *BerkMin: A fast and robust sat-solver*. In *Proceedings of the conference on Design, automation and test in Europe*, C. D. Kloos and J. da Franca, Eds. IEEE Computer Society, Paris, France, 142–149, 2000.
7. Gotlieb A., Denmat T. and Botella B., *Constraint-Based Test Data Generation in the Presence of Stack-Directed Pointers*, in Proceedings of ASE'05, Long Beach, CA, USA, ACM Press.
8. Harel D., Kozen D. and Tiuryn J., *Dynamic Logic*, MIT Press, October 2000.
9. Jackson, D. *Alloy: a lightweight object modeling notation*. ACM Transactions on Software Engineering and Methodology 11, 2, 2002, 256–290.
10. Jackson D., Schechter I. and Shlyakhter I., *Alcoa: the Alloy Constraint Analyzer*, Proceedings of the International Conference on Software Engineering, Limerick, Ireland, June 2000.

11. Jackson D. and Vaziri, M., *Finding Bugs with a Constraint Solver*, in Proceedings of the International Symposium on Software Testing and Analysis (ISSTA), August 21-24, 2000, Portland, OR, USA. ACM, 2000, pp. 14–25.

12. JUnit: http://www.junit.org.

13. Khurshid S. and Marinov D., *TestEra: Specification-Based Testing of Java Programs Using SAT.*, Automated Software Engineering 11(4): 403–434 (2004)

14. Gary T. Leavens, Albert L. Baker, and Clyde Ruby, *Preliminary Design of JML: A Behavioral Interface Specification Language for Java*. TR 98-06-rev27, Iowa State University, Department of Computer Science, April 2005.

15. Moskewicz, M. W., Madigan, C. F., Zhao, Y., Zhang, L., and Malik, S. *Chaff: engineering an efficient SAT solver*. In *Proceedings of the 38th conference on Design automation*, J. Rabaey, Ed. ACM Press, Las Vegas, Nevada, United States, 2001, 530–535.

16. Sen K., Marinov D. and Agha G., *CUTE: A Concolic Unit Testing Engine for C*, in Proceedings of the ACM SIGSOFT Conference on Foundations of Software Engineering, Lisbon, Portugal, 2005.

17. Visser W., Pasareanu C., Khurshid S., *Test Input Generation with Java PathFinder*, in Proceedings of the ACM/SIGSOFT International Symposium on Software Testing and Analysis, ISSTA 2004, Boston, Massachusetts, USA, July 11-14, 2004. ACM 2004, pp. 97–107.

18. Xie T., Marinov D., Schulte D. and Notkin D., *Symtra: A Framework for Generating Object-Oriented Unit Tests Using Symbolic Execution*, in Proceedings of TACAS 2005.

Verification of UML State Diagrams Using Concurrent State Machines

Jerzy Mieścicki

Institute of Computer Science, Warsaw University of Technology
00 665 Warszawa, ul. Nowowiejska 15/19
email: J.Miescicki@ii.pw.edu.pl

Abstract. Numerous research projects are done in academia as well as in industry aimed to support the design process based on UML and Model Driven Architecture with new methods and tools that would help to verify both static and dynamic aspects of UML model, to generate the code from it etc. Much attention is paid to the verification of system's behavior by model checking. In a research project done in the Institute of Computer Science, Warsaw University of Technology, an own model checking environment COSMA is used for these purposes. The approach is based on Concurrent State Machines (CSM), a finite state model well-suited to the representation of systems of concurrent, communicating components. In the paper, the representation of UML state diagrams in terms of CSM is explained and illustrated with an example.

1   Introduction

The progress in the area of new ideas and standards related to Unified Modeling Language (UML, e.g. [1], [2]) is accompanied with an extensive research aimed to support the designer with methods and tools for the verification of static as well as dynamic aspects of a designed system, for generation of code immediately from the UML specification etc. Among other topics, much attention is paid to the behavioral verification of UML models using *model checking* techniques.

The general idea of model checking ([3], [4]) is to construct a *finite-state* formal structure S, representing the behavior of a system to be verified (e.g. a Labeled Transition System, a reachability graph etc.). Then, the property we want to verify (π, say) has to be formally specified: e.g. as a formula of some temporal logic, or a Büchi automaton [4]. Then, we have to check if $S \models \pi$, that is, if π holds for S. The evaluation of $S \models \pi$ involves the exhaustive inspection of S.

Notice that as S is finite, the evaluation of any (properly specified) property is decidable and can be algorithmized, at least if we postpone problems related to the size of S and to the complexity of algorithm. This way, the system designer can be equipped with a set of ready-to-use algorithms and techniques for the analysis of system's properties. Moreover, if the checked property does not hold, he/she can obtain a *counterexample*, i.e. the path of events leading to the just-identified failure. This provides the feedback information enabling the designer to identify and correct the component which is responsible for a negative outcome of the checking. Unfortunately, finite state methods suffer also some drawbacks. Their very nature prohibits the use of infinite buffers,

Please use the following format when citing this chapter:

Mieścicki, J., 2006, in IFIP International Federation for Information Processing, Volume 227, Software Engineering Techniques: Design for Quality, ed. K. Sacha, (Boston: Springer), pp. 261–271.

dynamic creation/destruction of processes makes a problem, etc., and the main challenge the model checking is confronted with is the exponential explosion of the model.

Practical implementation of the above general idea of model checking involves multiple decisions. Usually, systems consist of multiple components which share the common resources and communicate among themselves. How their behavior is to be specified and how these individual behaviors are to be composed into one, finite state behavioral model S ? How this model has to be stored, remembering that its size may be of order of $10^{20} - 10^{50}$ states or even more? What should be a form of specification of properties? How to perform effectively an exhaustive inspection of such an large model S? All these questions can be solved in many ways, so that there is a range of different software tools (or model checkers) designed for these purposes. Among the most frequently referenced ones are SPIN [5], SMV [6], FormalCheck [7] and - for checking systems with real-time constraints - Uppaal [8] and Kronos [9]. A few dozen of other tools of this type have been implemented for academic and research purposes.

In the context of the verification of UML models[1] the primary form of behavioral specification of objects are - quite naturally - UML state, collaboration and sequence diagrams, supported by practically all CASE tools. Since the first attempt by Lilius and Paltor (vUML tool, [11]), a most typical approach is the conversion of UML state diagrams (serialized into XMI format) into the input language of some renowned model checker (usually SPIN's Promela language). Later on, the verification itself is entrusted to the model checker. A good example can be project Hugo [14] [12] [13], where UML diagrams are converted into inputs of two separate model checkers (SPIN and Uppaal, the latter one for the verifiation of timed models) and - aditionally - to the third module which has to generate the Java code.

In contrast to this, in the research project COSMA (Institute of Computer Science, WUT, [15]) an original model checking software environment is used, implemented within the project. The conceptual framework of COSMA are Concurrent State Machines (CSM; [16]). CSM support the communication among system components as well as two aspects of concurrency: possible simultaneous occurrence of communication events (formally - symbols instantaneously broadcasted to all system components) and simultaneous execution of actions of components . No special mechanism for interleaving actions or sequencing the input is assumed. However, single symbols, communication delays, nondeterministic loss of symbols, (finite) buffers as well as specific sender - receiver pairs (instead of broadcast-mode communication) can be also modeled, but as a deliberate decision rather than as an implicit general assumption.

Below, in Section 3 we introduce the idea of a system of CSM and the way the behavior of individual machines is composed into one graph of all-system behavior. To support reader's intuition, the presentation of the CSM model is preceeded by a known example of ATM-Bank system (Section 2). Subsection 3.3 will be devoted to the process of verification, specifically - to the technique of stepwise model reduction [17] which at least helps to overcome the exponential explosion of the model. In Section 4 the main problems with the conversion of UML state diagrams into CSM are summarized.

---

[1] see e.g. [10] for concise identification of problems and the basic literature.

2 The ATM-Bank example

As an illustration, let us consider a system (frequently used also elsewhere in the literature), consisting of single automatic teller machine (ATM) and a bank computer. Simple UML state diagrams of system components are shown in Fig. 1 and 2. The ATM provides the interface to the User (not shown). ATM communicates to the User by displaying the following texts:

InsertCard, EnterPIN, EnterAmount, TakeCard, TakeMoney, CardInvalid

while the User is expected to respond appropriately with events like *Card* (inserting the card into ATM slot), *PIN* (entering PIN), *Amount* (entering the amount), *CardRemoved* (removing the card) or - finally - *Money* (signifying that the User gets the money from the machine).

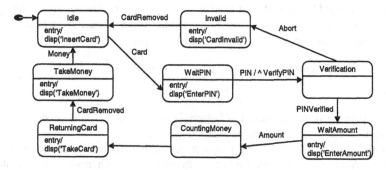

Fig. 1. State machine diagram for ATM

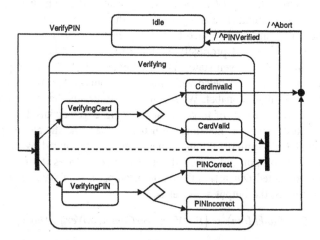

Fig. 2. State machine diagram for Bank

Just for an illustration, assume that we want to model-check the following properties:

- π_1: It is always so that whenever card is inserted then eventually that card is removed before the card can be inserted anew,
- π_2: It is always so that whenever card is inserted then eventually money is paid.

We expect, of course, that for the correct system the first requirement should be evaluated to *True*, while the latter one should be *False*.

3 Concurrent State Machines (CSM)

3.1 Definition of CSM

Let *AP* stand for an universal set of atomic propositions. From these atomic propositions, constants $0, 1$, operators $!, +, *$ (Boolean negation, sum, product, respectively), and parentheses, we build Boolean formulas, obeying the well-known, conventional syntax and semantics. Let $\mathcal{BF}$ be an universal set of all Boolean formulas. The alphabet of formula f (denoted $\alpha(f)$) is the set of atomic propositions referred to in it[2]. Notice that $\alpha(1) = \alpha(0) = \emptyset$, as actually neither 0 nor 1 refer to any atomic proposition.

Formally, a Concurrent State Machine m is a tuple

$$m = < N, edges, form, out, n_0 >$$

where:

- N - finite set of nodes (states of behavior), $n_0 \in N$ is the initial node,
- $edges \subseteq N \times N$ - set of directed arcs,
- $form : edges \rightarrow \mathcal{BF}$ - labeling function, attributing Boolean formulas to edges,
- $out : N \rightarrow 2^{AP}$ - output function, attributing to each node a set of atomic propositions $p \in AP$ that are *True* for this node,

It is convenient to think of CSM models as of labeled graphs (Fig. 3). Rounded boxes represent states, initial state is highlighted with a thicker borderline. In upper part of the box the state name is identified (e.g. *Idle, CardOK, Verifying, InvCard*) and below a set of propositions that are *True* for this state is enumerated (so-called *output set* of a given state). Directed edges of the CSM graph define the next-state relation. Edges are labeled with Boolean formulas rather than with individual symbols from some input alphabet. We require that a machine has to be *complete*, i.e. for any state, the Bolean sum of formulas at outgoing edges equals 1.

In the context of behavior modeling we usually understand the atomic propositions as the communication symbols (signals, messages etc.) produced by the machine in a given state as its output and received (or "watched for") as its input. Machine's *output alphabet* (denoted $Out(m)$) is the union of output sets of states. For instance, for machine from Fig. 3, the output alphabet is:

$$Out(BankMain) = \{PINVerif, verCompl, doVerif, Abort\} \tag{1}$$

---

[2] We require the formulas $f \in \mathcal{BF}$ be 'minimal', in a sense that their alphabets are minimal. So, for instance, 1 is used instead of $(a+!a)$, a instead of $(a*b + a*!b)$ etc.

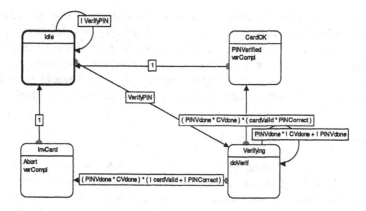

Fig. 3. Example Concurrent State Machine (BankMain)

In the CSM framework it is assumed that the truth value of *all* propositions from the output alphabet of the machine are fully determined by the output function of the (present) state. In other words, we assume that as long as the machine is in state $n \in N$, all propositions $p \in out(n)$ are *True* while all the other ones from machine's output alphabet (i.e. $q \in Out(m) - out(n)$) are *False*. This can be represented by the *state output formula* (denoted $\varphi(n)$) which is *True* for state n. For instance, for state *InvCard* (Fig. 3) - the state output formula is:

$$\varphi(InvCard) = !PINVerif * verCompl*!doVerif * Abort \qquad (2)$$

as $out(InvCard) = \{Abort, verCompl\}$, etc. We say that in state *InvCard* the machine 'produces' two output symbols: *Abort* and *verCompl*, in *Verifying* - one symbol (*doVerif*), while in *Idle* no output symbol is produced.

Similarly, the *input alphabet* of machine m (denoted $Inp(m)$) is the union of alphabets of all edge formulas. Any proposition $p \in Inp(m)$, when *True*, signifies that the symbol p (signal, message, ...) is present in machine's input. For instance, for machine from Fig. 3:

$$Inp(BankMain) = \{VerifyPIN, PINVdone, CVdone, cardValid, PINCorrect\} \qquad (3)$$

Notice that it is not required that input and output alphabets have to be disjoint.

The next-state semantics of machine's behavior is as follows. At any instant of time the machine is in exactly one of its states; initially - in the initial state. In any (present) state n, machine produces its output symbols (making some atomic propositions *True* and the other ones *False*) and simultaneously evaluates the formulas on the edges outgoing from n. If a formula is *True*, then its edge is *enabled*[3]. If only one edge is enabled (deterministic case) - it becomes *active*. If more than one edge is enabled then one of them is selected as active. The choice is nondeterministic and fair[4]. If the

---

[3] Due to completeness, there is always at least one enabled edge.

[4] Of course, the next-state semantics refers to a single execution of the machine. However, in the context of model checking, all the edges that are enabled in a given state point out to *reachable* states. Thus, the reachability graph of the machine (as well as of the whole system, se below) contains all the edges which are labeled with non-zero formulas.

selected active edge (n, n') points out to a state $n' \neq n$ (different than the present one) then the machine executes the transition to n'. Transition is instantaneous (zero time). Otherwise, i.e. if $n' = n$ - machine remains in n. Notice that formula **1** is always *True*, so the edges (n, n') (where $n' \neq n$) labeled with it represent spontaneous transitions, executable regardless of machine's input. Similarly, formula **0** would mean that the edge is never enabled: such an edge can be simply removed from the graph.

3.2   System of CSM and its product

Now, consider a finite (nonempty) set M of Concurrent State Machines. For any two machines $m_i, m_j \in M$, if $Out(m_i) \cap Inp(m_j) \neq \emptyset$ then there is a communication from m_i to m_j (m_i and m_j are 'communication partners'). If $Inp(m_i) \cap Inp(m_j) \neq \emptyset$ then the two machines share the same input. A set M of CSM is a *system* of CSM, iff either $| M |= 1$ (one-component system) or any $m \in M$ has at least one communication partner or shares the input with at least one other machine.

The overall output alphabet of system M (denoted $OUT(M)$) is the union of output alphabets of all $m \in M$. Similarly, the input alphabet of M ($INP(M)$) is the union of input alphabets of all $m \in M$. The set difference $E(M) = INP(M) - OUT(M)$ is the set of atomic propositions which are inputs of machines $m \in M$ but are not produced inside the system. We assume that these symbols $p \in E(M)$ come from an unknown environment of system M and at any instant of time they can be either *True* or *False*[5].

The global behavior of a system of CSM is represented by system's reachability graph RG. The algorithm of obtaining RG has been developed and implemented as one of modules of COSMA environment [16]. Its idea is as follows. The state of the system is a vector of states of system components. Algorithm starts from system initial state which is the vector of initial states of components. In a given system state, system produces the *set union* of outputs of components. As the system output alphabet $OUT(M)$ is known, for any system state $\bar{n}$ the state output formula $\varphi(\bar{n})$ is determined, analogously as in Eq. 2. From state $\bar{n}$, a set of states is *hypothetically* immediately reachable. The hypothetical edge that would lead from $\bar{n}$ to some $\bar{n}'$ should be labeled with the Boolean product of $\varphi(\bar{n})$ and the product of appropriate edge formulas of individual system components. If this product equals **0**, then the state (although it was *hypothetically* reachable) proves not to be *actually* reachable and is not included into the emerging graph. Otherwise, the state is included and the edge with an appropriate labeling formula is created[6]. The process continues until no new reachable states emerge.

The resulting graph is again a single CSM called a *product* of machines. The product is commutative and associative, which supports the compositionality of the model.

The overall organization of the example system from Section 2 is shown in Fig. 4. It consits of two subsystems (ATM and Bank), where ATM is a single CSM (Fig. 5) and Bank itself is composed from three components: Bank-Main (Fig. 3)

---

[5] Notice that by the above definition the alphabet of propositions coming from the environment and produced inside M are disjoint.

[6] It should be emphasized that the propositions $p \in OUT(M)$ are eliminated from these formulas. Indeed, for any system state $\bar{n}$ the truth value of all output propositions is known so that we can substitute **0** for propositions that are *False* in this particular state and **1** otherwise.

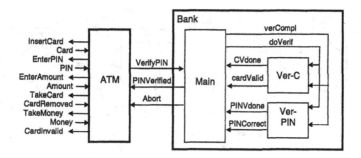

Fig. 4. Structural block diagram of the example system

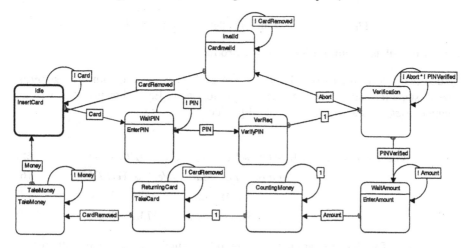

Fig. 5. CSM model of ATM

and two orthogonal machines, one for the verification of the card, the other for the verification of PIN (Fig. 6). Directed arrows in the block diagram from Fig. 4 indicate the communication between machines: for instance, *VerifyPIN* is the output symbol from ATM and input proposition for BankMain, etc. These communication relationships can be easily specified in terms of intersections of input/output alphabets.

Additionally, we prepare the CSM model of expected behavior of the User (not shown for the sake of the economy of space). It has 10 states and 16 edges and generally is analogous to the ATM (Fig. 5) to/from which it communicates. The CSM product of the whole system is a new machine:

$$System = User \otimes ATM \otimes BankMain \otimes VerC \otimes VerPIN \qquad (4)$$

It has as few as 28 (reachable) states (out of $10 \times 9 \times 4 \times 4 \times 4 = 5760$ elements of Cartesian product of sets of components' states) and 46 labeled edges.

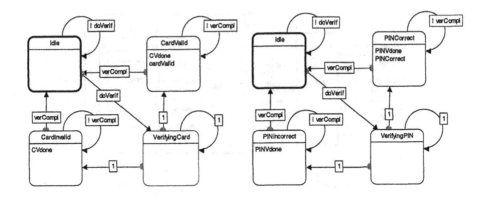

Fig. 6. CSM models of Ver-C (left) and Ver-PIN (right)

3.3 Multi-phase computation of CSM product

Notice that due to the associativity of CSM product, we can obtain the *System* in several steps instead of the one ('flat') operation, as in Eq. 4. For instance, we can compute *System* as a sequence of partial products:

$$System = User \otimes (ATM \otimes (BankMain \otimes VerC \otimes VerPIN)), or \qquad (5)$$

$$Bank = BankMain \otimes VerC \otimes VerPIN \qquad (6)$$

$$ATMandBank = ATM \otimes Bank \qquad (7)$$

$$System = User \otimes ATMandBank \qquad (8)$$

However, if we know what properties are to be verified, we can significantly reduce the partial products before they are used in the next step of product computation. In our example we want to verify the properties π_1, π_2, specified at the end of Section 2. They refer only to propositions *Card*, *CardRemoved* and *Money* (in the interface between User and ATM).

Now, suppose that we have just computed the partial product *Bank* (as in Eq. 6. Actually, it has 15 states and 32 edges. However, from the viewpoint of the next step (Eq. 7) the only relevant states are the ones which either produce or receive symbols to/from ATM, i.e. *Verify*, *PINVerified*, *Abort* (easily identifiable in the block diagram from Fig. 4). Remaining (irrelevant) states and edges can be merged in order to obtain compressed, much smaller version of the partial product. The algorithm for partial product compression (given a set of relevant symbols) has been implemented as a part of COSMA environment. The result of its application to *Bank* (or *NewBank*) is shown in Fig. 7[7]. Notice that *NewBank* has only 4 states and 7 edges (compared with 15/32 of the 'original' *Bank*).

The same procedure can be continued with successive subproducts. We substitute *NewBank* instead of *Bank* in Eq. 7, compute *ATMandBank*, compress again the resulting product into *NewATMandBank* (leaving as relevant symbols only these from ATM-User

---

[7] The algorithm attributes new, technical identifiers to merged states

interface). Finally, we compute and compress (*NewSystem = User ⊗ NewATMandBank*). This time, compression involves hiding all propositions except *Card*, *CardRemoved* and *Money*, (necessary and sufficient) for the evaluation of π_1 and π_2. The result, shown in Fig. 8, is so elementary that one can analyze it just by naked eye. Indeed, the graph shows that *NewSystem1* $\models \pi_1$ (it is true that whenever *Card* is inserted then eventually *CardRemoved*) while *NewSystem1* $\not\models \pi_2$ (it is not true that whenever *Card* is inserted then eventually *Money* is paid).

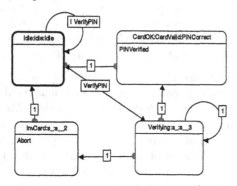

Fig. 7. *NewBank* or compressed product ⊗{*BankMain, VerC, VerPIN*}

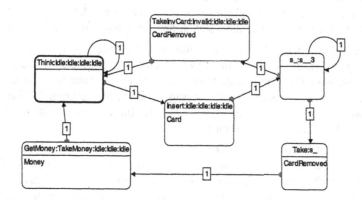

Fig. 8. *NewSystem* or compressed product for the evaluation of π_1 and π_2

It should be mentioned that in the case of larger (also: uncompressed) graphs the verified properties are expressed as formulas in QsCTL (a version of CTL) and evaluated using one of modules of COSMA environment ([18]), with possible edition of counterexamples etc.

4 Conversion of UML state diagrams into CSM

The example discussed above shows that the CSM model and COSMA tool is a noteworthy conceptual framework for behavioral verification of systems. Multi-phase product computation and compression of partial products seem to be an important advantage, as a powerful technique that can overcome (or relax, at least) the exponential model explosion and provide readable evaluation results. However, if such COSMA-style model checking has to support MDA approach - we should have algorithms and tools for converting UML state diagrams into Concurrent State Machines. The software module for converting UML state diagrams (from their XMI specification) into CSM is now under implementation within the COSMA project. Below, we briefly comment on main problems encountered during the implementation. Unfortunately, the results of algorithmic conversion are hardly readable in practice, so that the CSM models of ATM and Bank discused in preceding sections have been prepared manually, just to provide illustrative examples highlighting the nature of CSM model.

First of all, CSM are best tailored to modeling of *control-dominated* systems. Simple types of data (not only boolean, but also short integers, like counters etc.) are acceptable, but may significantly increase the size of product. Also, infinite buffers are excluded and finite ones have to be modeled as separate machines, which may lead to a substantial complication of the model. Dynamic object creation/destruction also contradicts the finite-state nature of the CSM model. On the other hand, the same limitation face practically all finite state methods and model checkers. Moreover, it should be mentioned that the COSMA environment supports also Extended CSM (ECSM, [19]), which allow for the definition of all types of variables and attributing the pieces of C/C++ code to states and transitions of CSM. Of course, systems of ECSM are no longer model-checkable: they can be either simulated or excuted, but we can verify their control- and communication flow 'skeletons' before the code is added.

Conversion of "flat" UML diagrams, like the ATM from Fig. 1, is rather a simple task (compare Fig. 5). However, in CSM the outputs are attributed to states (like in Moore automata) rather than to transitions (like in Mealy automata and state diagrams), therefore in order to produce *Verify* message to Bank the additional CSM state is introduced (*VerReq*). The "self-loops" at CSM states (making the conditions of staying in states explicit) are merely a technical trick.

Composite states (like the AND-state *Verifying* in Fig. 2) cause more problems. First, not only the diagram itself (here: BankMain), but also each of nested subdiagrams (Ver-C and Ver-PIN) must be separate CSM. If so, Ver-C and Ver-PIN have to remain in *some* CSM state even though a higher-level diagram (BankMain) had just returned to *Idle*. Generally, if the composite state can be entered through H or H* pseudostates, then upon exit from this (UML) state all the nested machines have to remain "frozen" in their present (CSM) states. If for the subdiagram the default initial state is specified - then the same trigger which pulls off the higher-level diagram from (UML) composite state forces all the nested sub-machines to get back to their initial (CSM) states. This calls for additional (appropriately labeled) edges in CSMs, from each state back to the initial one. Moreover, in order to keep the sub-machines frozen while the higher-level machine is not in "their" composite state, to each composite state a default technical output symbol is attributed (not provided by the designer at UML level) which multiplies (in a sense of Boolean product) all the formulas at the transitions in its sub-machines. This way these transitions are temporarily disabled. It is the above conventions why algorithmically generated CSM models are hardly readable.

Fortunately, the mentioned technical symbols can be easily hidden during compression and do not influence the readability of final evaluation results.

Among other problems is the conversion of other pseudostates, like Fork - Join bars as well as junction and branch pseudostates. They involve a specific exchange of synchronization symbols among sub-machines, but still can be rather naturally modeled in terms of CSM (see Fig. 3 and 6). Notice that for a subsystem of CSM, aimed to represent a nested composite state we can compute a local CSM product, as we did e.g. for Bank (Eq. 6). This operation "flattens" the behavioral specification and helps to understand the details of cooperation among machines.

The most challenging problem for the COSMA project is now the introduction of real-time constraints to CSM. In this paper we have used just a basic version of the CSM model, where the the only representation of the flow of time are states, in which a machine can nondeterministically remain for an unspecified but finite time (e.g. *CountingMoney* in Fig. 5 or *VerifyingCard, VerifyingPIN* in Fig. 6). The research on the theory and implementation of Timed CSM is in progress.

References

1. *Unified Modeling Language*: www.omg.org/technology/documents/formal/uml.htm,
2. B. P. Douglass: *Advances in the UML for Real-Time Systems*, The Addison-Wesley object technology series, 2004.
3. B. Berard (ed.) et al.: *Systems and Software Verification: Model-Checking Techniques and Tools*, Springer Verlag, 2001,
4. E. M. Clarke, O. Grumberg, D. A. Peled: *Model Checking*, MIT Press, 2000.
5. SPIN: http://spinroot.com/spin/
6. SMV: http://www-2.cs.cmu.edu/ modelcheck/smv.html
7. FormalCheck: www.cadence.com/datasheets/formalcheck.html
8. Uppaal: http://www.uppaal.com/
9. Kronos: http://www-verimag.imag.fr/TEMPORISE/kronos/
10. M. Gallardo, P. Merino, E. Pimentelis: Debugging UML Designs with Model Checking, *Journal of Object Technology*, vol. 1, no. 2, July-August 2002, pp. 101-117.
11. J. Lilius and I. Paltor. vUML: A tool for verifying UML models. In *Proceedings of 14th IEEE International Conference on Automated Software Engineering*, IEEE Press, 1999.
12. T. Schafer, A. Knapp, S. Merz. Model checking UML state machines and collaborations. *Electronic Notes in Theoretical Computer Science*, 55(3), 2001.
13. A. Knapp, S. Merz, Ch. Rauh, Model Checking Timed UML State Machines and Collaborations, W. Damm and E.-R. Olderog (Eds.): *FTRTFT 2002*, LNCS 2469, pp. 395-414, Springer-Verlag, 2002.
14. Project Hugo: http://www.pst.informatik.uni-muenchen.de/projekte/hugo/
15. *COSMA*: www.ii.pw.edu.pl/cosma/
16. J. Mieścicki: Concurrent State Machines, the formal framework for model-checkable systems, *ICS Research Report*, 5/2003,
17. J. Mieścicki, B. Czejdo, W. B. Daszczuk: Multi-phase model checking in the COSMA environment as a support for the design of pipelined processing. *Proc. European Congress on Computational Methods in Applied Sciences and Engineering ECCOMAS 2004*, Jyväskylä, Finland, 24-28 July 2004.
18. W. B. Daszczuk: Temporal model checking in the COSMA environment (the operation of TempoRG program). *ICS Research Report*, 7/2003, Warszawa, 2003.
19. A. Krystosik: ECSM - Extended Concurrent State Machines. *ICS Research Report* 2/2003,

Aspect-oriented Response Injection: an Alternative to Classical Mutation Testing

Bartosz Bogacki, Bartosz Walter

Institute of Computing Science, Poznań University of Technology, Poland
{Bartosz Bogacki, Bartosz.Walter}@cs.put.poznan.pl

Abstract. Due to increasing importance of test cases in software development, there is a need to verify and assure their quality. Mutation testing is an effective technique of checking if tests react properly to changes by introducing alterations to the original source code. A mutant which survives all test cases indicates insufficient or inappropriate testing assertions. The most onerous disadvantage of this technique is considerable time required to generate, compile mutants and then execute test cases against each of them. In the paper we propose an aspect-oriented approach to generation and execution of mutants, called response injection, which excludes the need for separate compilation of every mutant.

1 Introduction

Along with growing popularity of agile methodologies and open source movement, unit testing has become one of the core practices in modern software engineering. It is particularly important in eXtreme Programming [2], which explicitly diminishes the importance of other artifacts than source code and tests cases. In XP unit test cases not only verify if software meets functional requirements, but also enable refactoring, alleviate comprehension and provide guidance on how the production code should be used. Therefore, they contribute to many other important practices of XP.

Test-first coding [3] is an example of a practice which employs the test cases in an infrequently used way. It reverses the traditional order of activities at software development: the test cases get written prior to the production code and play the role of formally expressed requirements. System to be implemented is then treated as mere fulfillment of contracts imposed by tests. Poor quality tests effectively prevent such system from being successfully completed. Quality is here interpreted as the ability to discover possible flaws in the production code, which in turn requires the tests to cover every single piece of the code. The resulting measure, test coverage, is one of most important indicators assessing test quality. It reflects the percentage of source code covered by test cases. Low coverage indicates that tests are unlikely to discover changes or bugs introduced to the production code.

Mutation testing [4] is another technique introduced to verify the quality of the test suite. Unlike the coverage metrics, which only determine the constructs that are executed by tests, it figures out how test cases actually react to a faulty response from the source code. It is based on the assumption that high quality test cases discover any al-

Please use the following format when citing this chapter:

Bogacki, B., Walter, B., 2006, in IFIP International Federation for Information Processing, Volume 227, Software Engineering Techniques: Design for Quality, ed. K. Sacha, (Boston: Springer), pp. 273–282.

teration within the source code which makes the code to behave even slightly differently. The erroneous response is most often generated through simple source code modification. Hence, we use the term *mutation* and the faulty programs are called *mutants* of the original. Mutant is killed by test cases when it causes them to fail.

Mutation testing is considered an effective method of detecting code uncovered by test cases. Unfortunately, it has not been widely adopted by the software industry, mainly due to its high computational complexity and resulting low performance. Typically, every testing cycle includes multiple phases. First, the code needs to be analyzed and mutants get created, so that each mutant contains a single modification. Then every mutant is compiled and presented to all existing test cases, which themselves are not mutated. The time spent on processing a single mutant is a sum of all these factors, and then is multiplied by the number of mutants, which in total is quite complex. Therefore, mutation testing is still practically inapplicable for medium or large scale systems that comprise large number of tests.

In the paper we present *response injection* [15] – a novel approach to mutation testing, which employs aspect-oriented programming (AOP) [1, 8] to produce and execute mutants. It addresses mainly the complexity, which is the most onerous disadvantage of traditional mutation testing. Use of aspects removes the need for multiple compilations, which significantly reduces time required for testing.

In the section 2 of the paper we briefly summarize the status of research on mutation testing and present two existing frameworks: Jester and MuJava. Section 3 describes the concept of aspect-oriented mutations, presents its architecture and an example of use. Results of early evaluation are given in section 4. Finally, in section 5 we provide conclusions and directions for further research.

2   Overview of mutation techniques

Mutation testing, introduced in 1977 by Hamlet [4], has been developing for years as an academic research topic rather than an industry method of testing the tests. There are two main directions of works: one related to the scope and nature of changes, specifically the mutation operators and their variations, and the other one focused on performance improvement. The former one has been driven by the shift in the dominant paradigm of programming from structural to object-oriented. The efforts related to performance adhered to three basic rules: *do faster*, *do smarter* and *do fewer*. The first one targets at faster generating and executing mutants, the second one applies techniques of reusing the already acquired information in processing subsequent mutants, and the latter attempts to limit the number of mutants without loosing information. In order to preserve mutant's properties, Offutt [13] identified three conditions that it must satisfy:

1. The **reachability condition** is that the mutated statement must be reached by a call fro the test case;
2. The **necessity condition** is that once the mutated statement is executed, the test case must cause the mutant program to behave erroneously; the fault that is being modeled must result in a failure in the program's behavior;

3. The **sufficiency condition** states that the incorrect state must propagate to the calling test case and result in a failure.

A high quality mutant is expected to satisfy all these conditions. However, traditional mutation testing techniques often fail in achieving this goal.

2.1 Jester

Jester [6] is an open source, free mutation testing framework for Java developed and maintained by Ivan Moore. It became widely known in 2001, after the paper on Jester was presented on XP'2001 conference [12]. A testing cycle in Jester comprises thre phases: introducing a change to a source file, recompiling that file and running all tests. The mutation operators available in Jester are defined by user, but their capabilities are limited to plain text replacement. Examples include modifying literals, changing "true" to "false" and vice-versa, altering conditionals by replacing "if (" with "if (true ||" or "if(false &&", etc. The important disadvantage of Jester is that it performs no code analysis, which means it may easily produce equivalent or even invalid mutants. It results in lots of errors which require manual analysis and recovery. The critical issue concerning Jester is its poor performance, mainly due to necessity of compiling the source code after each mutation is created.

Although Jester may be a an acceptable opportunity for small programs, its applicability to larger projects is limited.

2.2 MuJava

MuJava is another mutation testing framework for Java. It has been developed by Ma, Offutt and Kwon [11] in response to Jester's basic deficiency: performance. MuJava utilizes two different methods to mutate programs: MSG for altering code behavior and bytecode instrumentation for changing program structure. It also employs a wide range of mutation operators, which allows for performing diverse mutations at different levels of code composition.

MSG method [14] is based on metamutants, derived from the program under test. They abstract the pieces of prospective code to be mutated, so that it can be instantiated with concrete values during execution. Every instance of metamutant is an ordinary mutant, which introduces a single fault. Because metamutants are compiled only once, they significantly improve the testing performance.

Bytecode manipulation is performed in MuJava with a BCEL, a specialized Java library which facilitates creation and instrumentation of the bytecode inside Java VM. It is employed to modify the structure of the tested bytecode, e.g. to add a field or a method to a class, to implement an interface in a class or to change inheritance hierarchy.

Both mutating techniques operate at low level, which removes the need for altering source code. The gain in performance of mutant generation and execution comes primarily from removal of the recurring compilation phase. Experiments determined the speedup of entire testing process to 5.1, while only in mutant generation phase it is even 9.3 times faster than with Jester [11]. However, we found no experiments comparing directly MuJava and Jester's performance.

3 Mutants generator

3.1 Concept of response injection

In traditional model of mutation testing, mutants are generated by small source code modifications, which preserve program's syntactic correctness. Modifications are introduced separately to ensure their effects do not compensate. A mutation can be recognized if it affects the method behavior verified by test cases. The behavior can be tested either directly, by examination of return value or exception thrown, or indirectly, if it changes the internal state of object. This leads to the conclusion that mutants are discovered in one of two ways: either by direct verification of method call result, or by examination of object attributes. To depict the above, let us consider the exemplary source code presented in Figure 1 and its test case in Figure 2.

```java
public class Foo {
  public int bar(int a)
      throws IllegalArgumentException {
    if ((a > 5) || (a < 1)) {
      throw new IllegalArgumentException();
    }
    int c = a;
    for (int i = 0; i < a; i++) {
      c *= 10;
    }
    return c;
  }
}
```

Fig. 1. Exemplary source code under test

```java
public void testBar () {
  assertEquals (3000, new Foo().bar(3));
  try {
    new Foo().bar(6);
    fail ("Exception not thrown for value: 6");
  } catch (IllegalArgumentException e) {}
  try {
    new Foo ().bar(0);
    fail ("Exception not thrown for value: 0");
  } catch (IllegalArgumentException e) {}
}
```

Fig. 2. Exemplary JUnit test method for method *bar()* in class *Foo*

For the above source code (Figure 1) the test (Figure 2) will fail (kill mutant) if the return value of the call to the method `Foo.bar()` with parameter a equal to 3 will be different than 3000 or an unexpected exception will occur, or if parameter *a* equal to 0 or 6 will not make the method to throw an expected exception. However, no mutation will be found if it does not affect the method outcome, for example if the condition   `if((a>5)||(a<1))`   would   be   replaced   with `if((a>5)||(a<1)||(a<10))`.

To create mutants sufficiently fast we need a method to non-invasively modify behavior of selected methods (one at a time), so that it poses a mutated effect on its callers without need for re-compilation at every change. This led us to selection of aspect-oriented programming (AOP) [8, 10].

AOP was originally invented as a response to an inability of object-orientated paradigm in providing encapsulation of features crosscutting unrelated parts of the developed system. Aspects allow for grouping such features and applying them to selected *joinpoints* – well defined points in program execution. Joinpoints with specifically defined criteria, called *pointcuts*, once captured, execute associated pieces of code (called *advices*) or change the program structure.

In the example (see Figure 2) all calls to `Foo.bar()` could be captured on the fly and their actual results (return value and/or exceptions) were mutated as if the modification had been introduced directly in the source code. We called this idea *response injection*, because the mock method response is injected instead of the actual object. Exemplary AspectJ implementation is shown in Figure 3.

```
public aspect FooMutant {
    int around():
        // capture a call to method bar()
        // defined outside this aspect
        call(public int bar(int))
            && !within (*..*Mutant) {
            // and return a mutated value instead
            return Integer.MAX_VALUE;
        }
}
```

Fig. 3. Exemplary aspect mutating behavior of method *bar()*

3.2 Architecture

The proposed system is composed of two collaborating aspects: *MutantGenerator* and *MutantExecutor*.

The first one captures the original flow of the code executed by a test case and is responsible for mutating the results of the tests method. It takes over the control at every method call and has a choice of replacing its execution with own code or proceeding with the existing one. In order to better mimic the normal program flow, the aspect executes each test case twice. During the first pass it captures the information from the original program flow and generates mutants. During the second pass, it runs the test once per each mutant and looks if the mutant is killed. Figure 4 depicts the original program flow with sequence diagram.

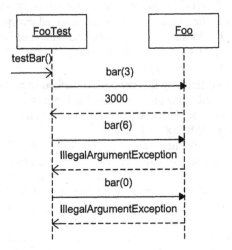

Fig. 4. Sequence diagram for original program flow

As a comparison to the original flow, Figure 5 presents the program flow with MutantGenerator aspect.

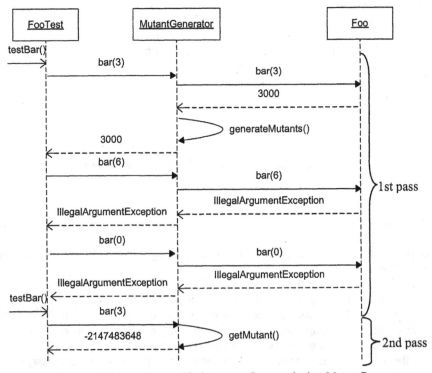

Fig. 5. Sequence diagram for modified program flow employing *MutantGenerator*

Each test case must be executed a number of times, once for each mutant. This leads to introduction of another aspect, `MutantExecutor`, that wraps the test code execution. Its responsibility is to handle each call to the testing method in test case and wrap it with subsequent executions of mutants generated by `MutantGenerator`. MutantExecutor plays the role of meta-mutant, which includes all mutants for a given method, but requires only a single compiling. It also intercepts any exceptions, assures that they do not propagate to the JUnit TestRunner and instead presents results of the test case execution. Figure 5 presents the sequence diagram for the testing routine with both `MutantGenerator` and `MutantExecutor`.

For the prototype implementation we used AspectJ [1, 8, 10] compiler to build code and tests, and JUnit [7] as a testing library.

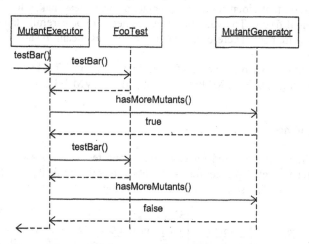

Fig. 6. Sequence diagram for modified program flow employing both *MutantGenerator and MutantExecutor*

3.3 Mutation example

Currently the prototype uses only simple mutation operators, dealing with changing primitive types and String objects, yet they seem sufficient to present the idea. For example for `int` variable of value `result` the mutations include: `-result`, `result+n`, `result-n`, `Integer.MIN_VALUE`, `Integer.MAX_VALUE`, and `0`, where n is a random integer. The only mutation we currently apply to objects is `null` value. In future, we plan to introduce more sophisticated mutants for objects (which could benefit from an on-fly object creation with dynamic proxy).

Considering our exemplary code, for `Foo.bar(3)` call, we end up with the following mutants: -3, $3 + n$, $3 - n$, -2147483647, 2147483647, 0. All such mutants get killed by the test case.

4   Early evaluation results

In order to evaluate the proposed solution, we conducted an experiment with the prototype tool. As an object of experiment we selected Commons Lang v2.1 [5] from the Apache Jakarta Project. Commons Lang features a very good code coverage: it includes over 1250 tests, with 90.9% of conditionals coverage and 91% of statements coverage. The size of the code measured in NCLOCs (non-commented lines of code) exceeded 13K.

To setup a context for our evaluation we decided to compare the results with Jester's. We selected Jester due to its popularity in eXtreme Programming community. However, Jester deficiencies prevented it from objective and unbiased evaluation. A mutation that violates the code syntactic correctness makes Jester hang, which requires manual fixing. To avoid that the code needs to be carefully tagged, which affects the measurement. Therefore, the experiment was meant to show a tendency, not exact results.

Experiment was performed on a PC with Intel Pentium 1.7GHz Centrino with 1GB of RAM, running Windows XP Professional and Java VM 1.4.2_08.

4.1   Performance

Execution time was measured for Commons Lang test cases. As we were unable to execute Jester for entire project due to the abovementioned facts, we decided to limit the experiment to a few selected test suites only. Figure 7 presents the results.

TestSuite	Jester	Response Injection	LOC	NCLOC	Tests #	Speedup
MathTestSuite	1532 sec.	50 sec.	4908	1988	163	30.6
BuilderTestSuite	782 sec.	49 sec.	6836	2310	247	16
EnumTestSuite (enum)	82 sec.	41 sec.	921	222	63	2
EnumTestSuite (enums)	85 sec.	45 sec.	916	225	64	1.9
ExceptionTestSuite	278 sec.	39 sec.	1912	765	62	7.1
MutableTestSuite	58 sec.	38 sec.	1376	378	49	1.5
TimeTestSuite	2250 sec.	69 sec.	3456	1652	40	32.6
AllLangTestSuite	*no data*	76 sec.	39175	13838	1245	approx.1776

Fig. 7. Summary of generation, compilation and execution times for selected test suites of Apache Jakarta Commons Lang project

Reducing the scope of the experiment does not significantly affect compilation time for our prototype, because it still requires compiling entire project with AspectJ. This introduces a constant timing factor, which is independent from size of the tested package, while Jester requires a repeated compilation of every mutant.

The results obtained from Jester and the aspect tool cannot be directly compared.; however, the results allow for drawing some conclusions. Despite of inaccuracies in measurement, the aspect-oriented response injection tool appeared considerably faster for all packages that could be compared with Jester. The gain appears higher for larger testing suites, which could suggest that it could be exploited in production environment.

4.2 Quality

Effective mutation testing benefits not only from performance gain. The other factor is mutants quality, interpreted as their ability to discover bugs with minimal effort.

Adherence to Offutt's conditions is one of quality measures. Noticeably, the response injection approach fulfills all of them. Reachability is ensured by the mutants generation process: mutated statement is always reachable for a test case, because it was injected in response to a call to the statement in test code. Similarly, the necessity condition is preserved as well: the mutated code actually behaves incorrectly, because its response is altered. Sufficiency condition, which requires that a fault is propagated up to the test case, is satisfied by mutating directly the actual method called by the test case.

To assess the quality of generated mutants we analyzed classes from *org.apache.jakarta.commons.math* package. Jester produced 1136 mutants for that package, and 189 of them survived the testing phase. We reviewed them manually in order to assess their applicability in test code improvement. In most cases they have not been killed because they did not meet some of the Offutt's conditions (reachability, necessity or sufficiency).

For the same code base the aspect-oriented tool generated 1978 mutated responses. Test cases indicated that only 3 injected responses did not make any test case to fail. All of them required more strict assertions to be introduced to the test cases, but did not violate any of the conditions.

5 Conclusions

The results of initial evaluation of the presented tool show that use of aspects in mutation testing appears a promising opportunity. The prototype we built generates the mutants much faster than popular Jester, while preserving three required properties: reachability, necessity and sufficiency. The main functional difference is that it traverses the existing test cases to learn the code usage, and then evaluates if the tests are exhaustive enough. Jester, on the other hand, mutates the code independently from test cases, which allows it for assessing the code coverage. That is the reason why the quality of mutants generated by the prototype cannot be directly compared to the Jester's. However, it appears to produce mutants of higher quality by avoiding the redundant equivalent mutants. It also, unlike Jester, performs mutation in strict accordance with the test coverage.

Use of aspects preserves the production source code intact and also allows for various mutation operators, changing both behavior and structure of the code under test.

Further directions of research and development include support for objects, implementation of other mutation operators and a larger scale evaluation.

282   *Bartosz Bogacki, Bartosz Walter*

Acknowledgements

The work has been supported by the Rector of Poznań University of Technology as a research grant BW/91-429.

References

1. AspectJ Project HomePage, http://www.eclipse.org/aspectj/ (visited in January 2006)
2. Beck K.: Extreme Programming Explained. Embrace change. Addison-Wesley, 2000.
3. Beck K.: Test-Driven Develoment. By Example. Addison-Wesley, 2003.
4. Hamlet R.G.: Testing programs with the aid of compiler. IEEE Transactions on Software Engineering, Vol. 3(4), July 1978, pp.279-290
5. Jakarta Commons Lang Project, http://jakarta.apache.org/commons/lang/
6. Jester HomePage, http://jester.sourceforge.net/ (visited in January 2006)
7. JUnit HomePage, http://www.junit.org (visited in January 2006)
8. Kiczales G., Lamping J. et al.: Aspect Oriented Programming. In: Proceedings of ECOOP 1997, Lecture Notes in Computer Science 1241, Springer Verlag, pp. 220-242.
9. Kim S., Clark J., McDermid J.: Assessing test set adequacy for object oriented programs using class mutation. In: Proceedings of Symposium on Software Technology (SoST'99), pages 72-83, Sept. 1999.
10. Laddad R.: AspectJ in Action. Manning Publications, 2003
11. Ma Y., Offutt J., Kwon Y. R.: MuJava. An automated Class Mutation System. In: Software Testing, Verification and Reliability. June 2005. Vol. 15(2), pp. 97-133.
12. Moore, I.: Jester a Junit test tester. In: Proceedings of the 2nd International Conference on Extreme Programming and Flexible Processes in Software Engineering, XP2001. Springer 2001.
13. Offutt A. J.: A Practical System for Mutation Testing: Help for the Common Programmer. Test Conference, 1994. Proceedings., International.
14. Untch R., Offutt A. J., Harrold M. J.: Mutation analysis using program schemata. In: Proceedings of the 1993 International Symposium on Software Testing, and Analysis, pages 139-148, Cambridge MA, June 1993
15. Bogacki B., Walter B.: Evaluation of test code quality with aspect-oriented mutations. In: Abrahamsson P., Marchesi M., Succi G.: Proceedings of 7th International Conference in Extreme Programming and Agile Processes in Software Engineering, Oulu (Finland), June 2006, Lecture Notes in Computer Science 4044, Springer Verlag, pp.202-204.

Advanced mutation operators applicable in C# programs

Anna Derezińska

Institute of Computer Science, Warsaw University of Technology, Nowowiejska 15/19
00-665 Warsaw, Poland
A.Derezinska@ii.pw.edu.pl

Abstract. This paper is devoted to advanced mutation operators for C# source code. They deal with object-oriented (OO mutations) and other complex features of the code. They require structural information about a code, unlike the standard mutations. Applicability of OO operators in C# is compared with those for other OO languages. Operators for specific features of C# language are also proposed. The detailed specification of operators can be provided in terms of pre- and post-conditions of a program transformation. Based on the operators' specification, the generation of mutated C# programs can be automated.

1 Introduction

Mutation testing is a fault-based testing technique used for evaluating tests and for measuring the effectiveness of test cases [11]. Mutations are simple changes inserted into a source code. They are defined in terms of mutation operators in order to make the automated testing process. Standard (traditional) mutation operators can be easily specified for many languages, e.g. an operator replacing an arithmetic operator "+" with "-". Testing of new features in object-oriented languages require more complex operators. The changes, introduced by these operators, should be consistent, for instance, with the inheritance hierarchy of classes. These operators take into account information that is non-local to the placement of the change in the source code.

This paper is devoted to advanced mutation operators specialized for C# code. They can be more dependent on the programming language than the standard mutation operators. The known (from Java [3,7,10] and C++ [4]) object-oriented operators were revised and adopted for C#. Some of the operators have altered definition or different scope of application due to different constructs used in the C#. New operators for specific, not only object-oriented, features of C# were also proposed.

Mutation operators were usually defined informally and illustrated by code examples [3,7,10]. It is not sufficient for the precise definition of advanced mutation operators. To make a definition unambiguous an operator can be specified as a program transformation with pre- and post-conditions. This approach is presented in the paper. Precise specification of operators allows effectively generating mutated programs (so-called *mutants*) that could be successively compiled. The specification and the quality of selected operators were verified in experiments on functional and unit tests [5,6].

Please use the following format when citing this chapter:

Derezińska, A., 2006, in IFIP International Federation for Information Processing, Volume 227, Software Engineering Techniques: Design for Quality, ed. K. Sacha, (Boston: Springer), pp. 283–288.

2 Object-oriented mutation testing

In object-oriented programs standard mutation can be used for intra-method level testing. Object oriented languages provide also new constructions that are not tackled directly by standard mutation operators. The research on the OO mutation was done mostly on Java programs [1,3,7-10]. Mutation of object-oriented features of a UML class specification and C++ code was studied in [4]. To my best knowledge the only research on OO mutation in C# was performed by Baudry et al. [2]. They referred to standard mutation operators, invocation of an exception and only two OO operators. The OO operators were not studied in detail but announced in their Mutator tool. Other C# mutation tools (Nester) support so far only the standard mutation operators.

An important issue is determining the quality of mutation operators in order to choose the best ones to be applied [8]. A good operator should satisfy the following conditions: (1) reflect typical errors of program developers, (2) generate proper and non-equivalent mutants, (3) be effective in qualification of tests. An *equivalent mutant* gives for any input exactly the same output as the non-mutated program. The judgment about the equivalence is very effort-consuming. Some mutation operators can generate mutants that are killed very easily by any test. Such operators are not useful in qualification of tests, although they can mimic typical errors of developers. Although OO operators generate fewer mutants than standard operators [9], we would like to limit the number of mutants and choose the most appropriate operators for C#.

3 Advanced mutation operators for C#

The comprehensive set of mutation operators for C# language is presented in tab. 1. The relations for previously defined operators for Java [3,7,10] and/or for C++ [4] are indicated in the column "Ref". The differences between the applicability of the corresponding operators in different languages were examined [5]. Also eight new operators concerning the specific features of C# were defined. Different groups of operators are discussed below. For the brevity reasons, a description and a specification is given only for two exemplary operators, OPD and IOK.

An informal description of advanced operators is not sufficient for their precise specification. Therefore, any operator could be specified using pre- and post-conditions of the transformation of program P to a mutant P_{Oi}' (i-th mutant after applying operator O on P). The pre- and post-conditions are specified using logical predicates with quantifiers (exists $\exists$, for all $\forall$) and operators (and, not, or, xor, $\Leftrightarrow$, $\Rightarrow$). In post-conditions, the elements marked with the apostrophe (eg. x') relate to elements changed in the mutant P_{Oi}'. Different features of the elements are defined by Boolean values using the dot notation. For example:

x.class   True if x is a class
z.override   True if z has the modifier *override*
x.z.method   True if z is a method declared in x (or inherited by x)

The following expression denotes that s is a syntactically and semantically correct part of instruction p (is used in p): $s \otimes p$, or equivalently "s" $\otimes$ p for complex s. The full notation of the specification and specifications of operators are given in [5].

Table 1. Advanced mutation operators for C#

	Operators	Inv	Spec	Appl	Ref
AMC	Access modifier change	-			[10,7,4]
IHD	Hiding variable deletion		-		[10,7]
IHI	Hiding variable insertion		-		[10,7]
IOD	Overriding method deletion		-		[10,7]
IOP	Overridden method calling position change		-		[10,7]
IOR	Overridden method rename	-	-	-	[10]
ISK	*Base* keyword deletion				[10]
IPC	Explicit call of a parent's constructor deletion		-		[10]
PNC	*New* method call with child class type		-		[10,7]
PMD	Member variable declaration with parent class type				[10,7]
PPD	Parameter variable declaration with child class type				[10,7]
PRV	Reference assignment with other compatible type				[10,4]
OMR	Overloading method contents change				[10]
OMD	Overloading method deletion			-	[10,7]
OAO	Argument order change			-	[10,7]
OAN	Argument number change			-	[10,7]
JTD	*This* keyword deletion				[10]
JSC	*Static* modifier change			-	[10,7]
JID	Member variable initialization deletion				[10]
JDC	C#-supported default constructor create				[10]
EOA	Reference assignment and content assignment replacement			-	[10,3]
EOC	Reference comparison and content comparison replacement			-	[10,3]
EAM	Accessor method change			-	[10,3,4]
EMM	Modifier method change			-	[10,3,4]
MNC	Method name change				[3,4]
MBC	Member changed				[4]
MCO	Member call from another object				[4]
MCI	Member call from another inherited class, MCR in [2]				[4,2]
RFI	Referencing fault insertion				[2]
EHR	Exception handler removal				[7]
EHC	Exception handling change	-			[7]
DMC	Delegated method change				
DMO	Delegated method order change				
DEH	Method delegated for event handling change				
PRM	Property replacement with member field				
IOK	*Override* keyword substitution				
OPD	Overriding property deletion				
OID	Overriding indexer deletion				
NDC	Namespace declaration change				

Inv - invalid operators (listed for compatibility reasons),
Spec - differences in specification to Java or C++,
Appl - differences in meaning or application scope to Java or C++

Several object-oriented inter-class mutation operators can be applied in the similar way in different languages. These operators refer mainly to usage of classes related by inheritance, e. g. PMD, PPD, PRV. Also the operators dealing with incorrect calling of methods are language-independent, e. g. MCO, MNC, MBC, MCI.

Some mutation operators are not appropriate for C# programs. This was stated by a code analysis and experiments [5,6]. These operators (AMC, IOR, EHC) are listed for compatibility reasons and indicated in the column "Inv" of the Table 1.

Other operators for C# have to be specified in a different way than the corresponding operators for C++ or Java (the column "Spec" of the table 1). The specification has to take into account new features of C#. For example, extended usage of keywords (*new* - in operators IHD, IHI), keywords newly introduced in C# (*override* - in operators IOD, IOP).

Regardless of an operator specification its application can be different in the considered languages (the column "Appl" in table 1). They can have a different meaning, or the scope of the application can be broader or narrower than that from Java or C++.

The JSC operator for C# deletes the *static* modifier for any member of a class. The reverse operation (adding *static* modifier as in the JSC operator for Java) could be omitted, because it provides non-compiled code in most cases.

The EOA operator replaces assignment of an object reference pointing to an object with the clone (duplicate) of this object. It intends to check a possible mismatch of objects and object references. In C# the overloaded *Clone()* method creates an object duplicate and is defined for many types. The EOA operator can be applied for a class which has its *Clone()* method.

The EOC operator replaces one kind of comparison with another one (== with *Equals()* or v.v.). In C# the default *Object.Equals* method calls *Object.ReferenceEquals* which results in a reference comparison instead of a value comparison. For many types *Equals* method is overloaded to implement value comparison. The user can overload *Equals* method and the operator == for own declared types.

Operators EAM and EMM dealing with accessor and modifier methods (*get* and *set*) have a minor significance in C# because a new element - *property* can be used.

New mutation operators for the specific features of C# were also defined. They are dealing with delegates, properties, indexers, override modifier and namespaces. *Properties* are values that can be stored or retrieved of a class using an accessor (*get*) and a modifier (*set*). Properties can be overriding in the similar way as methods do. The OPD operator deletes a whole definition of a property from the derived class, e. g.:

```
OPD: Original code                    Mutated code
public class Figure                   public class Figure
{       public virtual double  Area   {       public virtual double  Area
        {       get                           {       get
                {       return 0;}                    {       return 0;}
        }                                     }
}                                     }
public class Square : Figure          public class Square : Figure
{       public override double Area   {       _____        }
        {       get
                { return Math.Ar(base. 2); }
        }
}
```

The operator forces the usage of the appropriate property from the base class. It can be applicable only if the class does not inherit from an abstract type, otherwise a compilation error would be detected because the class does not implement inherited abstract member. A specification of the OPD operator is given below:

OPD Pre: $\exists_x$ x.class and $\exists_y$ y.class and   y.x.public_inherited and
and not x.abstract and $\exists_z$ (y.z.property and z.override)

OPD Post: not y'.z'.property

Indexers are used to index a class in the same way as an array. The OID operator deletes a whole definition of an indexer from the derived class. This operator can be defined in the similar way as the OPD operator.

In properties the *set* modifier uses an implicit parameter called *value*, whose type is of the property. By convention names of properties begin with capital letter, while names of fields with a small one. By mistake a property can be called instead of a field or vice versa. The PRM operator replaces those two names.

Omission of the keyword *override* in a method declaration is a common mistake of C# program developers, who have habits from C++ or Java. In C#, special keywords (*override, new*) denote override or hide of a method from the base class. The IOK operator substitutes an *override* occurrence with the *new* keyword, or vice versa (*new* with *override*). This substitution cannot be revealed by a compiler.

IOK: Original code   **Mutated code**

```
public class  Figure                        public class  Figure
{       public virtual void Draw()          {    public virtual void Draw()
        { ..... }                                  { ..... }
}                                           }
public class Square : Figure                public class Square :  Figure
{       public override void Draw()         {       public new void Draw()
        { .....          }                          { ..... }
}                                           }
```

This mutation will be detected if polymorphism is used. In the above example an object of *Square* can be referenced as a *Figure*. After mutation a method *Draw* called for this object will invoke a method from class Figure instead of class *Square*.

IOK Pre: $\exists_x$ x.class and $\exists_y$ y.class and y.x.public_inherited and
$\exists_z$ (x.z.method and (z.override or z.new))

IOK Post: (z.override $\Rightarrow$ z'.new) and (z.new $\Rightarrow$ z'.override)

In C# *delegates* are the object-oriented equivalents of function pointers. However, unlike function pointers, delegates are type-safe and secure. Delegates can be used in callback and event-handling scenarios. The DMC operator changes a delegated method into another method visible in this context and taking the same types of parameters. The operator simulates a fault, when a developer used by mistake a different method as a callback. The DMO operator changes the order of assignment of delegated methods. The DEH operator changes a method delegated for the event handling. Simulated fault can be for example caused by misleading of elements during construction of a GUI. The operators on delegates are extensively studied in [6].

The *namespace* statement is used in C# to define a new namespace, which encapsulates the classes. The NDC operator changes a namespace declaration. It is used only if exists an appropriate declaration of the class in both namespaces.

4 Final Remarks

The object-oriented mutation operators adopted for C# programs and other advanced operators dealing with new programming features were studied. Defining a mutation operator as a program transformation with pre- and post-conditions allows to give a precise specification of the operator. It is especially important for complex operators dealing with structural features of a program. Based on provided specifications of operators a tool for mutation of C# programs is currently under development.

The application of selected mutation operators for C# was evaluated in experiments. They allowed verifying the specifications, comparing usefulness of operators and suitability for the test selection. The sets of functional tests and unit tests were used [5,6]. The preliminary results showed that object-oriented operators IHD, IHI, IOD, IOP, IOK, OPD and OMD generated proper, non-equivalent mutants and were selective in assessment of the quality of functional tests. Mutants generated by the PRM operator were non-equivalent but killed by all functional tests. Among the operators dealing with exception handling and delegates two operators EHR and DMC were the most promising ones. The evaluation of mutation operators for C# and comparison with other testing criteria needs still further experiments.

Acknowledgment This work was supported by the Polish State Committee for Scientific Research under the project 4 T 11 C 04925.

References

1. Alexander, R. T., Bieman, J. M., Ghosh, J. M., Bixia, J.: Mutation of Java objects, Proc of 13th Int. Symp. on Software Reliability Eng., (2002) 341-351
2. Baudry, B., Fleurey, F., Jezequel, J-M., Traon, Y. Le.: From genetic to bacteriological algorithms for mutation-based testing, Sof. Testing Verif. and Reliab., vol 15, no 2, (2005)
3. Chevalley, P.: Applying mutation analysis for object-oriented programs using a reflective approach, Proc of 8-th Asia-Pacific Softw. Engin. Conf., ASPEC (2001) 267-270
4. Derezińska, A.: Object-oriented mutation to assess the quality of tests, Proc. of 29th Euromicro Conf., Belek, Turkey, 1-6 Sept. 2003, IEEE Comp. Soc. (2003) 417-420
5. Derezińska, A.: Specification of mutation operators specialized for C# code, ICS Res. Raport 2/05 WUT (2005)
6. Derezińska, A.: Quality assessment of mutation operators dedicated for C# programs, accepted for Inter. Conf. on Quality Software, QSIC06, Beijing, China, Oct. (2006)
7. Kim, S., Clark, J., McDermid J. A.: Class Mutation: mutation testing for object-oriented programs, Proc of Conf. on Object-Oriented Soft. Systems, Erfurt, Germany, Oct. (2000)
8. Kim, S., Clark, J., McDermid J. A.: Investigating the effectiveness of OO testing strategies with the mutation method, J. of Soft. Testing, Verif, and Rel., 11(4) (2001) 207-225
9. Ma, Y-S., Offutt, J., Kwon, Y-R.: MuJava: an automated class mutation system, Softw. Testing, Verif. and Reliab., vol 15, no 2, June (2005)
10. Ma, Y-S., Kwon, Y-R., Offutt, J.: Inter-class mutation operators for Java, Proc. of Inter. Symp. on Software Reliability Engin., ISSRE'02, IEEE Computer Soc., (2002)
11. Voas, J.M., McGraw, G.: Software fault injection, Inoculating programs against errors, John Wiley & sons Inc. (1998)

An Open Platform of Data Quality Monitoring for ERP Information Systems

Paweł Sieniawski[1] and Bogdan Trawiński[2]

Wroclaw University of Technology, Institute of Applied Informatics
Wybrzeze S. Wyspianskiego 27, 50-370 Wroclaw, Poland
[1]p.sieniawski@columb-technologies.com, [2]trawinski@pwr.wroc.pl

Abstract. In the paper an Open Platform of Data Quality Monitoring developed to audit data maintained in any enterprise resource planning (ERP) system is presented. Data quality of a database is verified according to a control schema defined in XML. Elementary tests can be developed using external test library written in .NET code embedded in XML and therefore can be easily incorporated into the Platform. Openness of the Platform makes it possible to use complex control techniques without the necessity to introduce any specific meta language. In order to evaluate the Platform tests for six different ERP systems were carried out using several data quality metrics. Results of the investigation proved the usefulness and flexibility of the Platform.

Key words: Data quality monitoring, data quality metrics, ERP information systems, problem intensity charts

1 Introduction

Computer viruses caused total loss of about 55 milliard dollars in 2003, according to the Trend Micro's study. However, yearly loss resulting from a low quality of data is estimated to 611 milliard dollars for USA companies [11]. Nevertheless, most of investments aim at the protection against outer attacks and the protection of data possessed against inner erosion is rather marginal. Data quality examination is usually carried out only when the secondary usage is attempted, for example during the construction of a corporate data warehouse [3,6]. After completing their projects only 20 per cent of companies continue regular data quality monitoring [12]. Most often the process of data quality monitoring is the introductory part of a more general process of data quality improvement [1]. It is focused on the analysis of defect occurrence in order to remove them automatically. Human verification and approval is needed to solve many problems [3], thus it is suggested to distinguish clearly both processes. At present, the definitions of good quality data focus mainly on its consumers and its use [2,9,8,11], and they often take the form of the question to what extent data satisfy the requirements of their intended use. There are some different approaches to determine metrics of the quality of data sets, e.g. local metrics [6], goal metrics [7] and generic metrics [8] and others are proposed. The construction of the Open Platform of Data Quality Monitoring presented in the paper differentiates from some solutions proposed in [4,5,6], because no specific language to define data correctness has been developed.

Please use the following format when citing this chapter:

Sieniawski, P., Trawiński, B., 2006, in IFIP International Federation for Information Processing, Volume 227, Software Engineering Techniques: Design for Quality, ed. K. Sacha, (Boston: Springer), pp. 289–299.

It has been assumed to use commonly known programming languages to detect errors in data, e.g. those included in the Microsoft .NET environment. The methodology developed incorporates the best aspects of theoretical models [6,8,9] extending them of the analyses at the strategic level. The investigation conducted by means of the Platform on six different enterprise resource planning systems made it possible to evaluate the solution proposed, to indicate significant features of different metrics and to assess some aspects influencing quality of data in the systems of this kind.

2   Features of the Monitoring Platform

The Open Platform of Data Quality Monitoring (OPDQM) has been developed to audit data gathered in any enterprise resource planning (ERP) system. It enables to obtain detailed lists of errors found in data, visualize the results in form of different graphs and to present general output calculated using several data quality metrics.

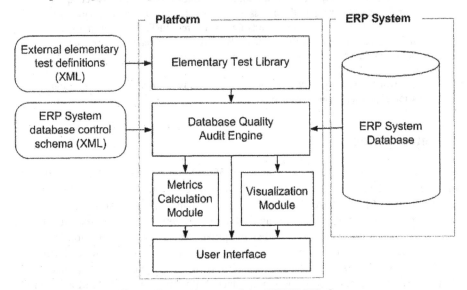

Fig. 1. The architecture of the OPDQM Platform

2.1   Architecture of the Platform.

Data quality of any database is verified using a control schema defined in XML. The database being verified can be deployed on any known database management system, only adequate ODBC or OLE DB drivers are required. Elementary test sets can be written in .NET code embedded in XML and easily incorporated into external test library. The architecture of the OPDQM platform is shown in Fig. 1. The main component of the platform is the Audit Engine, which executes elementary tests. The results of tests are passed directly to user interface in the form of list of errors found and to modules responsible for metrics calculation and visualization. The library of elementary tests can be extended by external tests in a form of source code to be compiled and incorporated as an integral part of the platform during its operation.

2.2   Uniform error messages

A unified way of error messaging has been designed in the OPDQM platform. Each elementary test can return any number of uniform data error messages. However, testing a single row or single field return usually no more than one message per one test run. Information contained in an error message is presented in Table 1.

Tab. 1. The structure of an error message

Element	Values	Description
Type	critical, warning, information, external	Determines error importance, points out also errors occurring out of the system (external)
Localization	structure pointing out a table, record or field in a database	Contains information of the nearest error occurrence place possible to be localized
Test instance name	text	Test instance name assigned in control schema.
Message	text	Error message returned by testing function
Confidence	number from the interval $[0, 1]$	Determines the probability of error occurrence
Repair cost	number	Repair cost expressed in currency, effort or other form, determined in test schema
Operator	identifier	Determines ERP system operator responsible for faultiness.
Time	datatime	Data and time of performing a test

2.3   Presentation of test results

The simplest form of presentation are tables containing all error messages obtained during test runs (Fig. 2). In order to assure effective use of the results achieved the sorting, filtering, selecting and colouring functions are provided. It is also possible to export messages in XML format. The other way of presenting quality of data are graphs showing the values of different metrics. They are calculated on the basis of error messages or received directly from a database tested.

Type ▲	Localization	Instance name	Message	Cost	Confidence
Critical	/testData/Customers...	Region_exists	Field can't be empty!	5	1
Critical	/testData/Customers...	NIP_exists	Field can't be empty!	10	1
Critical	/testData/Customers...	NIP_exists	Field can't be empty!	10	1
Critical	/testData/Customers...	NIP_numberValid	Value (126-00-29-70...	20	1
Critical	/testData/Customers...	Region_exists	Field can't be empty!	5	1

Fig. 2. Error messages in the form of a table

Very useful form of presentation are problem intensity charts which have been designed to visualize errors detected in a single table. In the problem intensity chart the x axis represents records of a table tested and the y axis its columns. A vertical bar stands for a problem detected and the intensity of colours corresponds to the number of problems occurring in a given place, i.e. in a column of a given table row. In turn, the spaces (blank places) indicate records without any error. An example of a problem intensity chart is shown in Fig. 3. The intensity of colours may alternatively denote the costs of removing errors or the severity of problems.

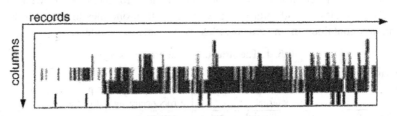

Fig. 3. An example of a problem intensity chart

3   Overview of metrics implemented in the Platform

Managers need aggregate information on quality of data gathered in an ERP system in order to be able to take a decision about repair activities. The data quality metrics seem to be the most appropriate means to provide such information. According to the rules of a good metrics [10] they are characterized using such features as readability, complexity, ability to compare different databases and mobilization of the management to undertake repair activities. So far, twelve following metrics have been implemented in the Platform. Beneath the following denotation is used: E is the set of all error messages, T is the set of all elementary test runs, R is the set of records tested, $R \leftarrow E$ is a set of all records referenced by at least one error message, F is the set of fields tested, $F \leftarrow E$ is a set of all fields referenced by at least one error message. In turn, $card(E)$, $card(T)$, $card(R)$, $card(R \leftarrow E)$, $card(F \leftarrow E)$ are the cardinalities of these sets respectively.

(1) Number of errors. It is the total number of errors detected in a database which can be expressed by the following formula:

$$DQM_E = card(E) \tag{1}$$

(2) Percentage of errors detected in tests performed. It is the ratio of the number of errors detected in a database to the number of all tests performed, expressed by the following formula:

$$DQM_{E/T} = \frac{card(E)}{card(T)} * 100\% \tag{2}$$

(3) Number of errors per 1000 records. It is equal to the number of errors detected falling on 1000 records tested and is expressed as:

$$DQM_{E/R/1000} = \frac{card(E)}{card(R)} * 1000 \tag{3}$$

(4) Number of invalid records. It is the number of records where at least one error was detected and is equal to the number of records referenced by at least one error message. It can be expressed by the following formula:

$$DQM_{R \leftarrow E} = card(R \leftarrow E) \tag{4}$$

(5) Percentage of invalid records in records tested. It is the ratio of the number of records where at least one error was detected to the number of all records tested, expressed by the following formula:

$$DQM_{R \leftarrow E/R} = \frac{card(R \leftarrow E)}{card(R)} * 100\% \tag{5}$$

(6) Number of invalid records per 1000 records. It is equal to the number of records where at least one error was detected falling on 1000 records tested, expressed as:

$$DQM_{R \leftarrow E/R/1000} = \frac{card(R \leftarrow E)}{card(R)} * 1000 \tag{6}$$

(7) Number of invalid fields. It is the number of fields where at least one error was detected and is equal to the number of fields referenced by at least one error message. It can be expressed by the following formula:

$$DQM_{F \leftarrow E} = card(F \leftarrow E) \tag{7}$$

(8) Percentage of invalid fields in fields tested. It is the ratio of the number of fields where at least one error was detected to the number of all fields tested, expressed by the following formula:

$$DQM_{F \leftarrow E/F} = \frac{card(F \leftarrow E)}{card(F)} * 100\% \tag{8}$$

(9) Number of invalid fields per 1000 records. It is equal to the number of fields where at least one error was detected falling on 1000 records tested, expressed as:

$$DQM_{F \leftarrow E/R/1000} = \frac{card(F \leftarrow E)}{card(R)} * 1000 \tag{9}$$

(10) Weighted average of percentage of errors, invalid records and invalid fields. It is the weighted average of three metrics (2), (5), (7). This hybrid metrics is expressed as follows:

$$DQM_{wav} = \frac{w_1 * DQM_{E/T} + w_2 * DQM_{R \leftarrow E/R} + w_3 * DQM_{F \leftarrow E/F}}{w_1 + w_2 + w_3} \tag{10}$$

The above weights were determined experimentally and during tests were assigned the following values: $w_1 = 0.5$, $w_2 = 0.3$ and $w_3 = 0.2$.

(11) Cost of database repair. Expressed in terms of money or effort which should be expended in order to remove all errors from the database. The value of the metrics equals to the sum of repair costs assigned to errors detected:

$$DQM_{rep} = \sum C_{rep}(e_i)$$ (11)

where $C_{rep}(e_i)$ is the cost of repair of i-th error detected.

(12) Database depreciation. It is the ratio of the cost of database repair to the total value of database, expressed by the following formula:

$$DQM_{rep} = \frac{\sum C_{rep}(e_i)}{\sum V_{rec}(r_j)} * 100\%$$ (12)

where $V_{rec}(r_j)$ is the value of j-th record in the database.

4   Data preparation for tests

The investigation has been carried out using data taken from six ERP systems exploited in medium size companies functioning on the market of the FMCGs. The systems under study ranged from single systems developed by order to the brand ones delivered by world leading producers. The characteristics of data used during tests are presented in Table 2, where the names of systems have been anonymized. In order to assure comparability of the results, a small fragment of data was chosen for tests. It was the table of clients which can be found in each system. In order to simplify the verification, only the rows containing data of companies located in Poland were taken into account.

Tab. 2. Characteristics of data used in the investigation

ERP System denotation	ERP System origin	Number of records to test	Year of data origin	ISO quality standard introduced
System 1	local	1626	2006	
System 2	local	5102	2005	+
System 3	local	6057	2005	
System 4	foreign	613	2004	
System 5	foreign	1417	2004	+
System 6	local	2228	2006	+

The list of elementary tests applied is presented in Table 3. The basic value of each record tested with correct data was assumed as equal to 100. This value could be increased by 5 when optional fields such as Phone or E-mail, were filled. For evaluation of error repair costs artificial unit of DQ$ was assumed.

5   Results of the investigation

5.1   Comparison of metrics

The results of database quality monitoring using different metrics are shown in Fig. 4. The metrics Id conform the denotation used in chapter 3. Left part of the Fig. 4 (a)

Tab. 3. Elementary test applied

Field scope	Elementary test	Error repair cost [DQ$]
Name	Check if not null	20
	Check correctness	2
	Check unique identity (min. length 6 characters)	5
	Check unique name	20
Adress	Check if not null	10
City	Check if not null	5
	Check if present in the list of 10 thousand of Polish towns and villages	5
Region	Check if not null	5
Country	Check if takes one of three values: Polska, PL, Poland	5
ZIP	Check if not null	10
	Check the mask of Polish ZIP code (xx-xxx)	10
TIN	Check if not null	10
	Check the mask of Polish tax identification number.	5
	Check if control sum conforms with Luhn's algorithm	20
Phone	Check length (min. 7 digits)	10
	Check the mask of local, intercity, international or cell number	5
E-mail	Check the conformity with e-mail address standard	5
Row/table scope	**Elementary test**	**Error repair cost [DQ$]**
Row	Check the conformity of ZIP code with town and province using external data source	5
Table	Detect duplicates using Levenshtein's distance calculated on the basis of name and tax id with threshold value of 96%	20

comprises the comparison of percentage scale metrics. All the metrics, beside the database depreciation (no. 12), range the data quality of the systems tested in the same order, what means that the system 1 contains the best data. It could be also observed that the metrics of percentage of invalid records (no. 5) is much more sensitive to error occurrence than others. It reaches values about 5 times higher than other metrics and perhaps therefore is the most frequently mentioned in the publications in the field [13]. Moreover, it is the only metrics differentiating the significance of errors detected. Further analysis of data in the system 5 revealed that its database contained considerable number of duplicates, what led to the high cost of repair. Right part of the Fig. 4 (b) comprises the results of the tests performed using the linear scale metrics. These metrics cannot serve the comparison of different databases, however they are a good starting point to the estimation of the cost or effort of database repair.

5.2 Comparison of data quality in ERP systems

There are many factors having impact on data quality in an ERP system. The most important are the quality of a system application, the history of data migration, corporate standards and regulations, organizational culture and first of all its users and administrators. Data monitoring results are given in Fig. 5. The relatively high quality of data in the system 1 is the consequence of reach prompt and control mechanisms available in the process of data input.

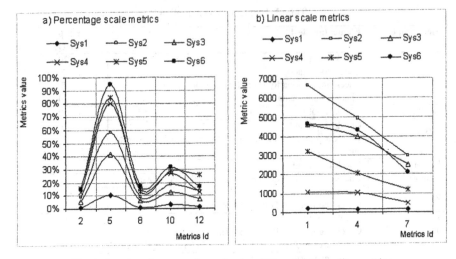

Fig. 4. Results of tests performed using different data quality metrics

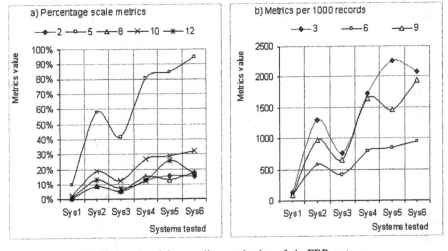

Fig. 5. Results of data quality monitoring of six ERP systems

An attempt to verify the hypothesis that the ISO quality standard introduced by the corporation influences positively the data quality is shown in Fig. 6 a). However it does not result in data quality worsening, but in practice has no effect. It turned out that the ISO quality standard does not cover the issue of the quality of corporate databases. The correlation between the ERP system origin and the data quality is presented in Fig. 6 b). The results obtained suggest that local systems, produced by Polish software companies, are equipped with more effective and better localized control tools. For example the tax identification number differs in each country in its length, format and the method of control digit calculation.

Problem intensity charts for six ERP systems are presented in Fig. 7-12. The order of records shown in charts conforms the sequence of their input into each system.

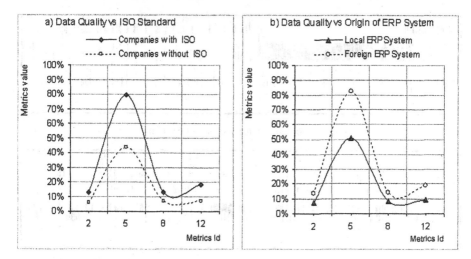

Fig. 6. The impact of external factors analysis on data quality

In the chart of the System 2 (Fig. 8) a series of records with two errors occurring simultaneously could be observed. Probably those records were imported form a previous ERP system and were not adjusted to the requirements of the new one.

In the chart for the System 4 a group of records of low quality could be observed, which significantly decrease quality of a whole database. However, there is a series of records of comparable size without any error in this system too. In the system 6 the field of Region was used inappropriately to its assumed purpose to place there different data for which there were no especially dedicated fields.

The problem intensity charts may turn out to be useful for detecting repeatable errors which can be limited at the level of ERP system applications eg. in the case of the systems 4, 5 and 6.

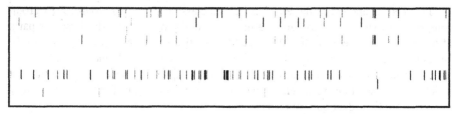

Fig. 7. Problem intensity chart for System 1

6 Conclusions and future work

The Open Platform of Data Quality Monitoring has been proved to be useful to monitor data quality of ERP systems, but it could be also used to audit other classes of information systems based on relational databases. The openness of the Platform makes it possible to use complex control techniques without the necessity to introduce a

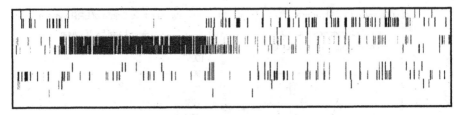

Fig. 8. Problem intensity chart for System 2

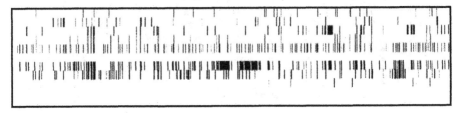

Fig. 9. Problem intensity chart for System 3

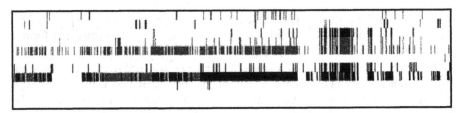

Fig. 10. Problem intensity chart for System 4

specific meta language to define data correctness. Therefore this enables to implement the Platform in fast and flexible way and achieve an acceptable level of performance.

The metrics applied in the Platform can be classified into two groups. First group comprises metrics useful to compare the data quality of different databases or parts of the same database as well as to trace the effectiveness of activities undertaken to ameliorate the quality of corporate data. These are percentage scale metrics and metrics calculated per 1000 records. In turn the second group constitute linear scale metrics which can be used to estimate effort and costs of database repair. Both groups are very important tools of data quality management.

The problem intensity charts turned out to be a usable method of visualizing the results of data monitoring. They allow to identify groups of repeatable problems occurring in data and in consequence they may contribute to the improvement of the process of collecting data.

The investigations showed also that the ERP systems developed in Poland are customized better to local regulations and standards and therefore can achieve higher quality of their databases. Moreover, the introduction of the ISO quality standard does not have practically any impact on quality of data collected by the corporation.

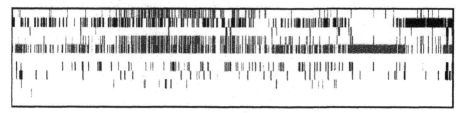

Fig. 11. Problem intensity chart for System 5

Fig. 12. Problem intensity chart for System 6

References

1. Data Monitoring: Taking Control of Your Information Assets, DataFlux Corp., (2004)
2. Defining and Measuring Traffic Data Quality, Office of Policy Federal Highway Administration, (2002)
3. English L.: Improving Data Warehouse and Business Information Quality. Wiley (1999)
4. Galhardas H., Florescu D., Shasha D., Simon E.: An Extensible Framework for Data Cleaning. ICDE 2000 poster paper, San Diego (2000)
5. Galhardas H., Florescu D., Shasha D., Simon E. and Saita C.: Declarative Data Cleaning: Language, Model and Algorithms, VLDB 2001, Rome (2001)
6. Jarke M., Jeusfeld M., Quix C.,: Design and Analysis of Quality Information for Data Warehouses. Proceedings of the 17th Internat. Conf. on Conceptual Modeling (ER'98), Singapore (1998)
7. Kovac R., Lee Y. W., Pipino L. L.: Total Data Quality Management: The Case of IRI. The 1997 Conference on Information Quality, Cambridge (1997)
8. Lee Y. W., Pipino L. L., Wang R. Y.: Data Quality Assessment. Communications of the ACM, (April 2002) 211-218
9. Lee Y. W., Strong D. M., Wang R. Y.: Data Quality In Context. Communications of the ACM, (May 1997) 103-110
10. Loshin D.: Developing Information Quality Metrics. DM Review Magazine, (May 2005)
11. Olsen J. E.: Data Quality: The Accuracy Dimension. Morgan Kaufmann Publishers, (2003)
12. Zellner G., Helfert M., Sousa C.: Data Quality Problems and Proactive Data Quality Management in Data-Warehouse-Systems. Proceedings of BITWorld, (2002)
13. Loshin D.: Developing Information Quality Metrics. DM Review Magazine, (May 2005)

Managing Data from Heterogeneous Data Sources Using Knowledge Layer

Krzysztof Goczyła, Teresa Zawadzka, Michał Zawadzki

Gdańsk University of Technology, Department of Software Engineering,
ul. Gabriela Narutowicza 11/12, 80-952 Gdańsk, Poland
{kris,tegra,michawa}@eti.pg.gda.pl

Abstract. In the process of data integration using ontologies it is important to manage data from external data sources in the same way as data stored in the *Knowledge Base*. In previous papers [1], [2] the way of inference from data stored in the Knowledge Base, using *Knowledge Cartography* idea has been presented. However, this solution requires loading all data to the Knowledge Base. The solution presented in this paper shows how the Knowledge Cartography can be used to infer from data stored in external data sources, without loading them to the Knowledge Base. The presented solution is to enrich each data source with an additional layer that allows managing data using signatures. The paper additionally describes the results of tests comparing times of inference when data are loaded to the Knowledge Base and when data are fetched on demand.

1 Introduction

Managing data from heterogeneous data sources using ontologies is a key problem that must be resolved to integrate data [3] [4] and to allow inferring from them. This problem has appeared even more important while the Internet grows larger and more popular. To achieve the aim of data integration, the Semantic Web [5] initiative has been proposed. Within this initiative the OWL [6] language has been standardized. These achievements have been a large step to data integration, however does not resolve all problems.

In the paper we propose that data coming from external data sources (e.g. from web sites) can be integrated with a Knowledge Base (KB) in such a way that logically the data sources become a integral part of the Knowledge Base. From the KB point of view, they comply with the ontology stored in the KB. In our approach, the ontology is formulated in terms of OWL-DL and managed using the Knowledge Cartography – a (presented elsewhere [1], [2]) set of algorithms for processing Description Logics ontologies.

The paper is organized as follows: Section 2 briefly recalls the idea of Knowledge Cartography and describes motivations behind our work. The rest of the paper presents the main contribution of this paper – the Knowledge Layer solution. The architecture of Knowledge Layer is described in Section 3. The next two sections: Section 4 and Section 5 describe specific solutions applied in Knowledge Layer.

Please use the following format when citing this chapter:

Goczyła, K., Zawadzka, T., Zawadzki, M., 2006, in IFIP International Federation for Information Processing, Volume 227, Software Engineering Techniques: Design for Quality, ed. K. Sacha, (Boston: Springer), pp. 301–312.

In Section 6 the results of efficiency tests comparing times of answering to the queries when data are loaded to the Knowledge Base and when data are fetched on demand from external data sources. Section 7 summarizes the paper.

2 Motivations

The idea of Knowledge Layer appears as a response for the requirement of fetching data from external data sources on demand. The solution applied in KaSeA system [1] requires inserting all data from data sources to the Knowledge Base. We can say that in the KaSeA system there are two main components. The first component – the *Inference Engine* – is responsible for inferring knowledge on the basis of information stored in the *Knowledg Base*. Two kinds of information are loaded to the Knowledge Base: terminology and assertions about individuals.

Following the idea of Knowledge Cartography, each concept has a *signature*. A signature is an array of binary digits representing a region covered by the concept in the map. A map of concepts is basically a description of interrelationships between concepts in a terminology. The map is created in the course of Knowledge Base creation. A map of concepts can be graphically represented in a form similar to a Venn diagram (see Figure 1).

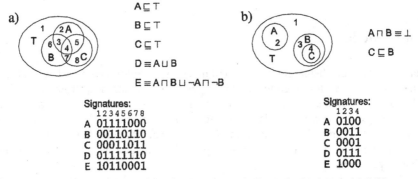

$$A \sqsubseteq T$$
$$B \sqsubseteq T$$
$$C \sqsubseteq T$$
$$D \equiv A \sqcup B$$
$$E \equiv A \sqcap B \sqcup \neg A \sqcap \neg B$$

$$A \sqcap B \equiv \perp$$
$$C \sqsubseteq B$$

Signatures:
```
   12345678
A 01111000
B 00110110
C 00011011
D 01111110
E 10110001
```

Signatures:
```
   1234
A 0100
B 0011
C 0001
D 0111
E 1000
```

Fig. 1. A map of 5 concepts (a), with two terminological axioms added (b)

Each atomic region (i.e. a region that does not contain any other region) represents a unique valid intersection of base concepts. By valid we mean an intersection that is satisfiable with respect to a given terminology. Intersections of concepts that are not allowed by terminological axioms are excluded from the map. A number of valid atomic regions n is calculated and each atomic region has assigned a subsequent integer number from the range $[1, n]$. Because any region in the map consists of some number of atomic regions it can be represented by an array of binary digits of length n with "1"s in positions mapped to contained atomic regions and "0"s elsewhere. In this way we achieve a signature and in terms of signatures we can describe any combination of complement, union and intersection of described concepts by simply mapping these operations to Boolean negation, disjunction and conjunction.

Analogically, during loading assertions about individuals, signatures for individuals are specified. The difference between the signature of a concept and the signature of an individual is the way how "1"s at specified positions of signatures are interpreted. In case of an individual, "1" means that the individual can belong to the corresponding atomic region. Also instances of roles are stored in the Knowledge Base. The process of inference is based on comparing signatures. For example, when we ask about all instances of the specified concept, the process of answering this query is reduced to the problem of finding these individuals whose which signatures are subsumed by the signature of the specified concept (signature s_1 is subsumed by the signature s_2 when each bit of signature s_1 is less than or equal to the corresponding bit in the signature s_2).

The solution applied in the KaSeA system has one indisputable advantage – all conclusions about data can be quickly retrieved. However, it has also many disadvantages:

- the process of loading data into Knowledge Base is time consuming,
- there are needed advanced techniques to update data loaded to the Knowledge Base of KaSeA system,
- KaSeA system must observe a data source to react for changes or a data source must notify KaSeA system that update must be carried out,
- the solution is not easily scalable: it is not possible to manage all data from external data sources just by loading them to the Knowledge Base.

In the case of systems which manage few data sources which are actually rarely updated the presented solution can be sufficient. However, for systems which manage numerous data sources which change very often the other way of retrieving data must be developed. The answer for this need is the Knowledge Layer.

3 Knowledge Layer Architecture

The main assumption of Knowledge Layer is the fact that the Knowledge Layer can be queried analogically as KaSeA system (e.g by DIGUT – Description Logic Interface by Gdańsk University of Technology [8]). And, what is even more important, the inference capabilities are the same as inference capabilities of KaSeA system. This is caused by the fact that both KaSeA and Knowledge Layer use Cartographic Representation of knowledge.

Within Knowledge Layer we can distinguish a set of components depicted in Figure 2. Each Knowledge Layer must logically cooperate with KaSeA system with a terminology loaded. During loading terminology all signatures for concepts are calculated. The terminology contains theses notions in terms of which the External Data Source will be queried. Another component is an XML file that contains mappings between the ontology and an external data source. We can distinguish three types of mappings: concept mappings, role mappings and attribute mappings.

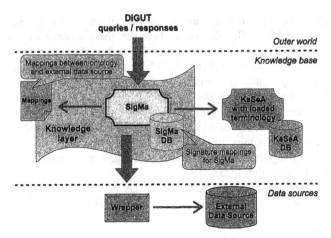

Fig. 2. The Knowledge Layer architecture

A concept mapping is a pair: concept and query allowing to retrieve all individuals belonging to this concept. By role mapping we mean a pair: role and query allowing to retrieve all pairs of individuals which are related to each other via the specified role. Analogically, by the attribute mapping we mean a pair: attribute and query allowing to retrieve values of the specified attribute for the individuals.

The key component of the Knowledge Layer is SigMa (*Signature Mapper*). SigMa is responsible for:

- transforming mappings defined in the file to the signature mappings,
- storing these mappings in the SigMa database and
- answering queries asked in terms defined in the ontology.

The first task requires obtaining information about signatures of concepts from the KaSeA system. Each pair: concept and query is transformed to another pair: signature and query. The query remains unchanged and the signature for the mapped concept (possibly complex) is calculated on the basis of signatures stored by the KaSeA. These mappings are stored in SigMa database. Answering queries asked in terms defined in the ontology requires finding the most suitable query understandable by External Data Source.

The next advantage of the Knowledge Layer is its unawareness of the variety of types of data sources (SQL, XML, CSV, XLS, MDB and so on). The only thing the Knowledge Layer must know are queries defined in the mapping file. However, the Knowledge Layer does not have to know their meanings. Another components, i.e. Wrappers, are responsible for understanding these languages. Such a situation is presented in Figure 3. In this way the process of finding by the SigMa system the most suitable query understandable by the External Data Source is independent on the type of the data source. However, such a solution puts one requirement: there must exist a query language for any, supported by the Knowledge Layer, type of data source. This language must fulfill some requirements (e.g. it must allow to formulate the union of queries returning the set being a union of results of corresponding simple queries) and in this language the queries in mapping file must be expressed. Obviously, not all previously mentioned types of data sources have such languages.

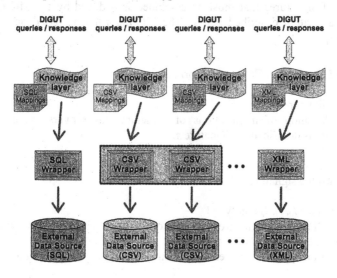

Fig. 3. Knowledge Layer for various types of External Data Sources

Thus, in the course of development of Knowledge Layer also such languages must be specified. The next part of the paper is focused on SQL Data Source because SQL allows for retrieving data and, what is even more important, most data sources are relational.

4 Maximum Coverage algorithm

The key problem in SigMa is to find the most suitable query retrieving individuals for the specified concept. The most suitable queries for mapped concepts are just the queries stored in the database. There is one very important assumption for such queries. The query corresponding to a signature always retrieves all individuals which belong to the concept with that signature. To formulate the most suitable query for concept which is not mapped, and is represented by the signature s, SigMa must create a new signature combined from some number of existing (mapped) ones that is subsumed by the signature s and which covers the maximum number of atomic regions represented by the signature s. It is important to notice that by taking the signature which covers the maximum number of atomic regions represented by the signature s we guarantee that all individuals stored in the External Data Source which certainly belong to the concept represented by the signature s will be retrieved.

However, it can be a situation when a query concerns the signature $s = 001100$ representing concept *People*, for example and in the External Data Source only a concept *Women* is mapped (in the EDS no information about men is included). Let us assume that the concept *Women* is represented by the signature 001000. In such a situation SigMa creates a signature 001000 and this signature for this specific EDS covers the maximum number of atomic regions represented by the signature 001100.

The list of signatures that must be combined is deduced by the MC (*Maximum Coverage*) algorithm described below. The MC algorithm is based on the Apriori algorithm [9].

Algorithm 1. Maximum Coverage algorithm

Input: A signature *s*.
Output: A union of intersections of signatures that covers maximal number of atomic regions described by signature *s*.

1.   If signature *s* exists:
2.   Return the signature.
3.   Else
4.   Make lists l_0, l_1, l_2 empty.
5.   Find all mapped signatures that are not disjoined with and not subsumed by *s* and append them to the list l_0.
6.   Find all mapped signatures that are subsumed by *s* and append them to the list l_1.
7.   If list l_0 is not empty:
8.   For each pair (s_i, s_j) such that $s_i, s_j \in l_0$; $s_i \neq s_j$:
9.   Calculate signature $s_t = s_i$ AND s_j (keep track of signatures used)
10.   If $s_t = s$
11.   Return a list of signatures whose intersection created signature s_t.
12.   Else If s_t is subsumed by *s* append s_t to the list l_1.
13.   Else append s_t to the list l_2.
14.   End
15.   While list l_2 is not empty:
16.   Copy list l_2 to l_3 and clear list l_2.
17.   For each pair (s_i, s_j) such that $s_i \in l_3, s_j \in l_0$:
18.   Calculate signature $s_t = s_i$ AND s_j (keep track of signatures used)
19.   If $s_t = s$
20.   Return a list of signatures whose intersection created signature s_t.
21.   Else If s_t is subsumed by *s* append s_t to the list l_1.
22.   Else append s_t to the list l_2.
23.   End
24.   End
25.   End
26.   For each $s_t \in l_1$ delete those s_t which are subsumed by any other s_t in l_1.
27.   List l_1 contains list of lists of signatures. Return this list as a union of intersections of signatures from list l_1.
28. End

5 SigMa system design

Having defined the MC algorithm it is possible to describe the solutions applied in SigMa to provide services responsible for creating signature mappings, storing these mappings in the SigMa database and answering queries asked in terms defined in the ontology. The next three subsections describe how these aims have been achieved.

5.1 Creating signature mappings

Creating signature mappings from concept, role and attribute mappings defined in the mapping file is the first task of SigMa component. Firstly, signatures for mapped concepts are calculated with the use of KaSeA system with loaded terminology. In this way it is possible to specify list of pairs consisting of a signature and a query corresponding to that signature. The pair: a signature and a query is further referred to as a signature mapping. Such a list of signature mappings is stored in the database. Secondly, signature mappings for $\neg C$ concepts, where C is a mapped concept, are created. To create a query for the signature of $\neg C$ concept, the MC algorithm is used. The last step of creating signature mappings is creating signature mappings for Top concept (using the MC algorithm) and for concepts $\exists R.C$. Having defined the query for the role R and the query for concept C (if C concept is not a mapped concept, then the query can be created using the MC algorithm) SigMa creates the query: "return all role subjects of the role R for which the role filler is an instance of the concept C". All these signature mappings are stored in the database.

5.2 SigMa Database

The schema of SigMa database is quite similar to that specified for the KaSeA system [10]. The main difference is the fact that in the SigMa database there is no information about individuals, about their names, relations between them and their signatures. However, there is an additional entity storing information about queries. The ERD diagram for the SigMa database is depicted in Figure 3.

The main entity sets presented in the logical schema are: *ConceptDefs, AttributeDefs, RoleDefs, Signatures* and *Queries. ConceptDefs, AttributeDefs* and *RoleDefs* store information about mapped concepts, attributes and roles respectively. *AttributeDefs* and *RoleDefs* are related to the entity *Queries* in that way, that for each attribute there exists a relationship to the query that returns a list of pairs of individuals and a value of the attribute, and for each role there exists a relationship to the query that returns a list of role instances. Concepts are not directly related to the queries but through their signatures. There is one more entity *RoleConcepts*. In this entity all defined in the terminology concepts of the type $\exists R.C$ are stored. This entity is related to the *Signature* entity via the two relationships. The *existsHasSignature* says what the signature is for the concept of the form $\exists R.C$. And the second relationship *conceptHasSignature* says what the signature is for the concept C. The description of the specified entities are included in Table 1.

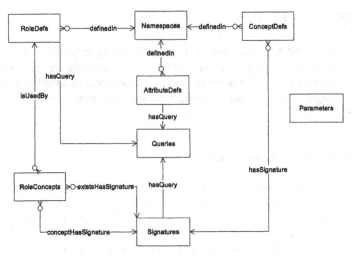

Fig. 4. ERD diagram for SigMa database

In the *Signatures* entity there are some additional attributes *hash* and *sec_i*, which have been introduced to make finding needed signatures more efficient. The application of these attributes has been described in detail in [10]. Entity *Parameters* stores the length of signatures and the entity *Namespaces* stores namespaces for the terms defined in the ontology.

Table 1. Short description of entities of SigMa database

Entities	Description	Entity Attributes
ConceptDefs	Stores information about mapped concepts	*id* – concept identifier *name* – a local name of the concept
RoleDefs	Stores information about mapped roles	*id* – role identifier *name* – a local name of the role
AttributeDefs	Stores information about mapped attributes	*id* – attribute identifier *name* – a local name of the attribute
Queries	Stores queries understandable by a wrapper of a specified type	*id* – query identifier *content* – content of the query
Signatures	Stores signatures used in signature mappings	*id* – signature identifier, *hash* – hash code for the signature, *sec_i* – no of ones in consequent n sections of the signature.
RoleConcepts	Stores concepts of the for $\exists R.C$	No attributes are defined
Namespaces	Stores namespaces	*id* – namespace identifier *uri* – uri of the namespace
Parameters	Stores parameters specific for the terminology	*name* – name of the parameter *value* – value of the parameter

5.3 Processing queries

Knowledge Layer allows processing queries about such inference problems as: instance retrieval problem, instance check problem, related individuals problem, role fillers problem and told values problems [8]. The processes of answering queries are presented below as generic algorithms which can be optimized for specific query languages and are dependent on wrappers capabilities.

Algorithm 2. Algorithm for instance retrieval problem

Input: A concept C.
Output: A set of individuals belonging to the concept C.

1. Find a signature for the concept C
2. Find a query for that signature
3. If the signature is not mapped to the query
4.   Find the most suitable query (with maximal coverage) using the MC algorithm
5. Else
6.   Fetch the query from the database
7. Execute the query
8. Return the result of the query

Algorithm 3. Algorithm for instance check problem

Input: A concept C, an individual i.
Output: *True* when i belongs to the concept C, *false* when i does not belong to the concept C and *maybe* otherwise.

1. Find a signature for the concept C
2. Find a query for that signature
3. If the signature is not mapped to the query
4.   Find the most suitable query (with maximal coverage) using MC algorithm
5. Else
6.   Fetch the query from the database
7. Execute the query
8. Check if the individual i belongs to the result of the query
9. If the individual i belongs to the result of the query
10.   Return *true*
11. Else
12.   Find a signature for the concept $\neg C$
13.   Find a query for that signature
14.   If the signature is not mapped to the query
15.   Find the most suitable query (with maximal coverage) using MC algorithm
16.   Else

17.   Fetch the query from the database
18.   Execute the query
19.   Check if the individual *i* belongs to the result of the query
20.   If the individual *i* belongs to the result of the query
21.   Return *false*
22.   Else
23.   Return *maybe*

It is worth noticing that despite the fact that External Data Sources are modeled in CWA (*Closed World Assumption*) [11], Knowledge Layer opens this world and provides answers according to OWA (*Open World Assumption*). In case of instance retrieval problem the algorithm returns only these individuals for which it is certain that they belong to the specified concept. In case of instance check problem the algorithm returns *true* when it is certain that the specified individual belongs to the specified concept, *false* when it is certain that the specified individual does not belong to the specified concept and *maybe* when it cannot be unambiguously stated whether the individual belongs to the specified concept or not.

6 Efficiency tests

The KaSeA system provides inference capabilities of various types. Firstly it allows inferring implicit knowledge both from terminology and assertions about individuals. The Knowledge Layer only allows inferring from assertions about individuals. Table 2 compares times of responses for the query about individuals belonging to the specified concept (i.e. instance retrieval problem). The test is carried out for the Drug ontology and Farmadati data source. Drug ontology has been developed by the University of Liverpool within the PIPS project. The ontology contains information about drug manufacturers, active ingredients of drugs, interactions about them and also about ATC (*Anatomical Therapeutic Chemical*) code. Farmadati data source is a relational database managed by Oracle 9i that contains information about drugs, stored in 13 tables. These tables contain 250496 rows. In a presented architecture we can treat SQL Server as a Wrapper. In case of the Knowledge Layer times of answering queries strongly depends on the efficiency of various wrappers. The tests were performed on a PC with Pentium 4, 3GHz and 1GB RAM.

Table 1 presents times of answering queries for instance retrieval problem for different concepts. The results are average times of same tests repeated 100 times.

Table 2. Times of answering queries for instance retrieval problem

	KaSeA	Knowledge Layer
Top	time to long to count	22687 ms
Drug	27407 ms	4656 ms
Drug $\int$ *DrugContainer*	35094 ms	11375 ms
$S \int U \int V$	27305 ms	18969 ms

The two first concepts are mapped explicitly; it means that the appropriate query for the signature of *Top* concept and *Drug* concept are stored in the SigMa database. For the two next concepts (*S*, *U* and *V* concepts are subconcepts of the *ATCCode* concept) the query must be formulated on the basis of the MC algorithm. The Knowledge Layer is able to cache queries previously issued. It means that when a query about the instances of concept which signature is not mapped to the appropriate query in the SigMa database is issued, then an appropriate mapping is added to the database. Then when the same query is issued again, the query is directly fetched from the database and does not have to be created anew. This feature decreases the time of executing third and fourth query for about 3000 ms.

7 Related work

The authors of this paper personally experienced the need of managing data from external data sources within PIPS project (*Personalised Information Platform for life and health Services*) [7]. PIPS is a 6th European Union Framework Programme project whose main goal is to create a Web infrastructure to support health and promote healthy life style among European communities. One of its main aims is to develop knowledge management tools covering different information sources.

In the course of the project we have developed the KaSeA (acronym for *Knowledge Signature Analyzer*) [1], [2], system, which allows efficient reasoning from data about large numbers of individuals. The KaSeA system has been developed using *Knowledge Cartography* idea. However, the KaSeA system requires all data to be loaded into the Knowledge Base. It appears that this requirement cannot be always fulfilled. Thus in the PIPS project the other solution enriching data source with *Knowledge Layer*, which allows treating data from the external data source in the same way as data stored in the Knowledge Base, has been developed.

Other known practical solutions are data integration systems like Information Manifold [13], SIMS [14] or PICSEL [15]. However, most of these systems have been developed with the use of the global view approach when the OWL language was not a W3C standard. The systems were focused on particular field of application and therefore also the type of data sources. Despite the fact they were focused on performance – they cannot fulfill the requirements put by Internet which the Knowledge Layer has been developed for.

8 Summary

The presented solution of Knowledge Layer has many advantages:

– it is independent on the format of data source – for structured data sources like XML sources, relational sources or any other sources which have a query language and the processor for this language the only thing that is needed is to define appropriate mappings in the XML file;

- it can be applied for data sources which do not have any query language defined (e.g. XLS files) – in such a situation there must be defined the way of querying a data source and must be developed a kind of wrapper;
- all changes in data source that do not affect the structure of that data source are always visible in Knowledge Layer without any updates;
- changes in the structure of a data source require changing the mappings defined in the XML file – the process of creation new signature mappings is much shorter than the process of loading data into KaSeA system, e.g. for Farmadati data source the time of loading data into KaSeA system is about 48 hours and the time of creation signature mappings is about 3 minutes;
- no advanced techniques for update of knowledge base are required.

References

1. Goczyła K., Grabowska T., Waloszek W., Zawadzki M.: *The Cartographer Algorithm for Processing and Querying Description Logics Ontologies*. LNAI 3528: Advances in Web Intelligence, Third International Atlantic Web Intelligence Conference, Springer 2005. pp. 163-169.
2. Goczyła K., Grabowska T., Waloszek W., Zawadzki M.: The Knowledge Cartography – A new approach to reasoning over Description Logics ontologies. SOFSEM 2006: Theory and Practice of Computer Science, LNCS 3831, pp. 293-302.
3. Calvanese D., Giacomo D. G., Lenzerini M.: Ontology of integration and integration of ontologies. Proceedings of the International Workshop on Description Logics, 2001.
4. Calvanese D., De Giacomo G., Lenzerini M: A Framework for Ontology Integration. Proceedings of the First Semantic Web Working Symposium, 2001, 303-316.
5. Semantic Web Initiatives, http://www.semantic-web.org/.
6. OWL Web Ontology Language Guide, W3C Recommendation 10 February 2004, http://www.w3.org/TR/owl-guide/
7. Goczyła K., Grabowska T., Waloszek W., Zawadzki M.: *Inference Mechanisms for Knowledge Management System in E-health Environment*, In: „Software Engineering: Evolution and Emerging Technologies", Eds. K. Zieliński, and T. Szmuc, IOS Press, Series: „Frontiers in Artificial Intelligence and Applications", 2005, pp. 418-423.
8. *DIGUT Interface Version 1.3*. KMG@GUT Technical Report, 2005, available at http://km.pg.gda.pl/km/digut/1.3/DIGUT_Interface_1.3.pdf.
10.Wittem I. H., Frank E.: *Data Mining. Practical Machine Learning Tools and Techniques with Java Implementations*. Morgan Kaufmann Publisher 2000.
11.Waloszek W.: *Cartographic Method of Knowledge Representation in KaSeA*, Technologie Przetwarzania Danych, Wydawnictwo Politechniki Poznańskiej, 2005, pp. 14-25 (in Polish).
12.Baader F. A., McGuiness D. L., Nardi D., Patel-Schneider P. F.: The Description Logic Handbook: Theory, implementation, and applications, Cambridge University Press, 2003.
13.Levy A. Y.: *The Information Manifold Approach to Data Integration*, IEEE Intelligent Systems, numer 13, 1998.
14.Arens Y., Knoblock C. A., Shen W.: *Query Reformulation for Dynamic Information Integration*, Journal of Intelligent Information Systems, 1996.
15.Lattes V., Rousset M.-C.: *The use of CARIN language and algorithms for Information Integration: the PICSEL project*, W: Proceedings of the ECAI-98 Workshop on Intelligent Information Integration, 1998.

Checkpoint-based resumption
in data warehouses

Marcin Gorawski and Paweł Marks

Silesian University of Technology,
Institute of Computer Science,
Akademicka 16,
44-100 Gliwice, Poland
{Marcin.Gorawski, Pawel.Marks}@polsl.pl

Abstract. In the paper we focused on the problem of efficient handling of ETL processes failures. During such a process, a data warehouse is filled with data. Because large amounts of data need to be processed, the whole process takes a lot of time. After a failure there may be no time to restart the process. In such a situation a resumption algorithm should be applied. In the paper we present a new approach to the checkpoint-based resumption method. We combine checkpointing with the Design-Resume algorithm. Such a combination is supposed to work more efficiently than the pure checkpointing. Moreover, not all the ETL application modules must implement the checkpointing. We present a basic idea of the algorithm, its requirements and necessary definitions. The proposed solution is then compared to other resumption methods and obtained results are discussed.

1 Introduction

Data warehouses collect large quantities of data. Their task is to provide the decision support applications used by managers and directors with the necessary data. The more up-to-date the warehouse is, the closer to the reality are the results of analysis performed by DSS applications, and the better decisions can be made. The data set stored in a data warehouse (DW) is usually taken from transactional systems. Not all the data are required, in business applications it is usually approximately 20% of the transactional data set. Moreover, records are usually processed before they are loaded into a destination database. A whole process of extracting and transforming the data and loading them into a destination is called ETL that is an abbreviation for *Extraction, Transformation and Loading.*

Nowadays data warehouses collect giga- or even terabytes of data. It is not a surprise that in the case of so huge data sets, an ETL process (further called simply *extraction process*) takes long hours or even days to perform a full load. Depending on a data warehouse system two kinds of DW loads may be met: full and incremental. During a full load all the data already stored in a DW are deleted, and when the warehouse is empty then a loading starts. During incremental load only the data that changed since the last load are processed. It makes the incremental load much shorter than the full load. However, it is not always possible to run the incremental load. If the

Please use the following format when citing this chapter:

Gorawski, M., Marks, P., 2006, in IFIP International Federation for Information Processing, Volume 227, Software Engineering Techniques: Design for Quality, ed. K. Sacha, (Boston: Springer), pp. 313–323.

data changes are too complex, or aggregates computation is made in a way they cannot be easily updated, we must run a full load.

During a load process, a data warehouse is not available. That is why an ETL process is usually run in a time window when the system is idle (for example in the night or during a weekend). Here a problem may appear. In order not to disrupt the managers' work, an ETL process must not exceed the fixed time window. It fits the window if the processing goes without any unpredicted events. Unfortunately such an ideal situation sometimes does not take place. Statistically every thirtieth ETL process fails due to a system or hardware failure [10].

Occurrence of a failure interrupts an ETL process. The warehouse contains partially loaded data set, which in most cases is inconsistent. Such a dataset is unusable. In such a case we have three choices:

- restart the ETL process,
- restore the warehouse from a backup copy created before starting the ETL process,
- run the resumption procedure and continue the interrupted process.

Restarting the extraction from the beginning is the easiest option but it is also the most inefficient. The second option is to use a backup copy of the warehouse content. It is better to have the old data than to have no valid data at all. The best choice is to load only the missing part of the data set. The data set will be then consistent, and the time of producing the missing tuples should be short enough to fit in the remaining time. Resuming the interrupted ETL process is called resumption process.

In this paper we focus on the algorithms for resumption of the interrupted extraction process. In section 2 we present the current state of the art, describe the most common resumption techniques, present their advantages and disadvantages. In section 3 we present our approach to the checkpoint-based resumption algorithm. The results of the performed tests are included in section 4.

2   Previous works

Most commercial tools or tools such as Ajax [3] do not consider the internal structure of transformations and the graph architecture of ETL processes. Exceptions are researches [11, 12], where the authors describe the ETL ARKTOS (ARKTOS II) tool. To optimize ETL process, there is often designed a dedicated extraction application adjusted to requirements of a particular data warehouse system. Our experience prompted the decision to build a developmental ETL environments using JavaBeans components (ETL/JB and DR/JB). In the meantime, a similar approach was proposed in paper [1].

Further speeding up of the ETL process encouraged us to abandon JavaBeans platform. Our new ETL-DR environment succeeds the previous ETL/JB (JavaBeans ETL environment) and DR/JB (ETL environment with a Design-Resume algorithm [7]). The new ETL-DR environment is a set of Java object classes, used to build extraction and resumption applications. This is analogous to JavaBeans components in the DR/JB environment. In the DR/JB we implemented a dynamic estimation mechanism detecting cases when the use of DR resumption is inefficient. Another direction of our research is combining the DR resumption with techniques such as staging and checkpointing.

Similar research was presented in [7] where the authors compared the DR algorithm to its combination with savepoints. They proved that the DR-savepoint combination performs a little better than the pure DR. Unfortunately these experiments were performed on very small TCP-D data sets. In our opinion it gives non-representative results, because in data warehousing we have to deal with much larger datasets. We tried to combine the DR algorithm with the staging. After a failure part of the data set can be restored from the disk and there is no need to process it again. We gave the name "hybrid resumption" to the obtained algorithms combination. In [5] we showed that the proper use of the staging can be a quite efficient solution. The proper selection of the nodes writing stage data to disk files is crucial to reduction of the overhead imposed on the uninterrupted extraction process. In our experiments we managed to increase the resumption efficiency whereas the normal extraction time remained almost unchanged.

3 Checkpointing

A concept of *checkpoints* or *snapshots* is in general very simple. Assuming that there is a process running for a long period of time and it is failure prone (mostly hardware failures) we can create so called checkpoints. What a checkpoint is? It is nothing more than a copy of the process state. It is saved in a way that makes it possible to revert the process to the saved state and continue the processing whenever there is such a need. There are many applications of this method: fault tolerance, process migration, job swapping [9], virtual time [2].

We decided to apply the checkpointing to increase the resistance of the data extraction process against system failures. The extraction process usually takes a lot of time and cannot be interrupted. Accidental hardware failure or blackout may lead to loss of the results of many hours of work, even if it is was very close to the end of the process.

Our previous experience with combining the Design-Resume algorithm (DR) with the staging technique prompted us to combine the DR algorithm with the checkpointing. Both the DR and checkpoints are very efficient methods. The difference between them is the overhead imposed on the normal extraction process. The DR takes no additional actions during the extraction, so it has no influence on the process duration. The checkpointing is completely different. It may lengthen the processing even a few times depending on the frequency of checkpoints creation and amount of the data stored during each save.

Increasing the frequency of checkpoints creation leads to significant drop of the processing efficiency. In our research we focus on creating checkpoints in the most efficient possible way. We want to combine the checkpoints with the DR algorithm which uses the graph-based ETL process description, so in our research we will use the graph description also.

3.1 Graph-based ETL process description

In graph representation of the ETL process, graph nodes are responsible for tuples processing and graph edges define tuple flow directions. Each node belongs to one of the three categories:

– extractors reading data from sources

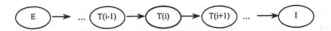

Fig. 1. Example of a simple extraction graph. E is an extractor node reading data from a source. T stands for a transformation node, such as filtration, grouping etc. I is an inserter loading data to a destination (e.g. a database table)

- transformations performing operations such as selection, projection, aggregation, etc.
- inserters loading tuples to destination places

An example graph is presented in Fig. 1. It consists of one extractor, one inserter and a few transformations. It is an example of the linear processing, it means that each graph node has at most one source node and one target node. Of course, the graph can be much more complicated: transformations can receive data from many source-nodes (joins, for example) and send results to many target-nodes.

The DR algorithm requires that the extraction graph is acyclic: during traversing the graph, there is no possibility to visit the same node twice. In our research this limitation is not a problem, it even simplifies graph analysis.

Each graph node and each node input is described by a set of boolean properties and key attributes. These properties are used by the DR algorithm to compute the place and type of additional filters used during resumption. Thanks to these properties, the algorithm can treat the nodes as black boxes and does not have to know anything more about the processing perform by them. The great advantage of the DR algorithm is no need of modifications of the existing nodes. During resumption they remain unchanged, only additional filter nodes are inserted into the graph to ensure that only the missing part of the data set will be produced.

3.2 Details of the ETL process implementation

To talk about the optimization of the checkpoints creation we have to provide some details of the ETL application implementation. The graph-based ETL process is implemented as a multi-threaded Java application. Each node works as a separate thread communicating with other nodes via shared memory and message passing.

Fig. 2 shows an example of connection between two nodes. Node 123 produces tuples and stores them in the output buffer. The buffer is a multichannel structure; it can transmit data to multiple receiver-nodes. Such a receiver in this case is node 124. It has an input parameter defined as a source node ID = 123 and output channel number = 1. Output buffer contains a packet queue in each logical channel, and each packet contains a limited number of tuples. Grouping tuples into packets increases the efficiency of communication between nodes by reducing the number of required thread synchronizations.

As can be noticed, one of the data sets that each node owns, is the output buffer containing output tuples. Moreover, there are nodes such as grouping ones, which can store in memory their temporary data structures. Depending on the kind of the processing it can be a small or quite large set of data. No matter when the checkpoint is created, all the data of each graph node must be saved. Besides the data sets, thread state has to be saved also, to enable restarting the processing from the point saved in the checkpoint.

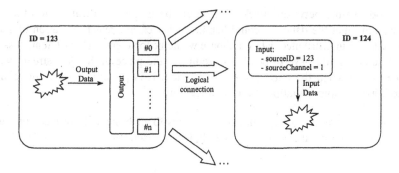

Fig. 2. Nodes interconnection on the implementation level. Data produced by node 123 are stored in a multi-channel output buffer. Source of the node 124 is defined as a node with ID = 123 and logical output channel number = 1

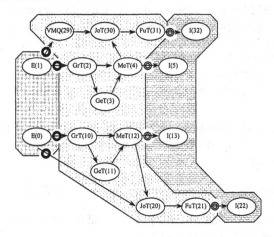

Fig. 3. Extraction graph divided into three functional blocks which are: extractors (the left most), transformations (in the middle) and inserters (the right most)

3.3 Graph analysis

We propose dual approach to the graph analysis for checkpoints. First, the graph is analysed as in the DR algorithm [7]: the nodes properties are processed. In the next step, the graph is seen as three functional blocks: extractors, transformations and inserters. Between these blocks the connections exist: many connections from extractors block to transformations block, and as many connections from transformations to inserters as many inserters there are in the graph.

Fig. 3 presents a graph split into functional blocks. Connections between the blocks are marked with circles. In the given example it would be the best to be able to save the state of all the nodes belonging to the three functional blocks. In practice it is usually impossible or it costs too much time:

- each inserter would have to make a copy of a complete database table. In data
  warehousing it means transferring even gigabytes of data which takes a very long time

- period of time between checkpoints could be treated as a transaction but even assuming that the database could handle such a case, a synchronization of such a transaction in distributed data warehouse would be too complicated (if at all possible)
- extractors would have to be able to return to the place in the data stream where they were when the checkpoint was created. It is possible to do, but requires additional implementation-level modifications

However, there are no significant difficulties to save the state of transformation nodes. This is the main assumption, the algorithm discussed below bases on.

3.4 Algorithm details

The goal of the presented algorithm is periodical saving of states of the transformation nodes and optionally extractors or inserters. The saved states should enable resumption of the interrupted ETL process. General steps of the algorithm are as follows:
1. Analysis of the graph properties to check if the algorithm can be applied
2. Periodical creation of the checkpoints
3. Assignation of filters for resumption phase
4. Insertion and initialization of resumption filters, optional switching inserters/extractors into resumption mode

Graph traversing and analysing The graph is analysed as in the DR algorithm in both topological and reversed direction. In the first step graph nodes are checked if they support checkpointing:

- a transformation should have the possibility to save and restore its state in any moment of the processing,
- an inserter should have the possibility to save and restore its state or possibility of identification of the last loaded tuple,
- an extractor should have the possibility to save and restore its state or possibility to get the part of the stream read before a failure once again,

Further in the paper we will say that if a node can save and restore its state, it holds the *checkpointable* property. Now for each graph node X, a transitive property *checkpointFeasible(X)* is computed. It is defined as follows:

Definition 1. *checkpointFeasible(X) = true, if:*

- *X is an inserter and holds checkpointable property or (it holds suffixSafe[1] and mapToOne[2] properties and can remember the last loaded tuple)*
- *X is a transformation and holds checkpointable property and all its direct target nodes holds checkpointFeasible property*
- *X is an extractor and all its direct target nodes holds checkpointFeasible property*

---

[1] $suffixSafe$[7] property is described in the definition 4
[2] $mapToOne$[7] property is held if each input tuple contributes to no more than one output tuple. All inserters hold this property

If any of the extractors does not hold the *checkpointFeasible* property, it means that the checkpointing cannot be applied to this graph, because one or more nodes do not support the method.

In the second step the graph is analysed to check the possibility of additional filters insertion. The task of an additional filter is removing from a tuple stream these tuples which were processed before creating the checkpoint (extractor filters) or tuples loaded after checkpoint creation and prior to a failure (inserter filters). Such filters can (but do not have to) be placed on connections between the three functional blocks. Here we can distinguish two cases:

- extractor does not hold *checkpointable*. The filter is inserted just behind the extractor
- inserter does not hold *checkpointable*. The filter is inserted just in front of the inserter

In the Design-Resume algorithm[7] four types of filters are used: CleanPrefix, CleanSubset, DirtyPrefix, DirtySubset. We focus only on the two first filters, which were described in details in [7].

Filters preceding inserters are inserted according to the rules known from the DR algorithm. Both CleanPrefix and CleanSubset filtration is possible. CleanPrefix filter requires the input of the inserter Y connected to the node X to hold the transitive property *sameSuffix(Y_X)*. This property denotes that on the input Y_X the suffix of the data stream will be provided in the same form as it would be provided if the processing would not have been interrupted. If this property is not held, only a CleanSubset filter can be used. The *sameSuffix* property bases on the following properties:

Definition 2. *sameSet(X) = true, if:*

- *X is an extractor and during the resumption it generates the same set of tuples as prior to a failure*
- *X is a transformation that for the same input sets always generates the same output set*

Definition 3. *setToSeq(Y_X) = true, if for any permutation of the input set received from the node X, the node Y always generates the same output sequence. It is true for sorting transformations.*

Now a *sameSuffix* property can be defined:

Definition 4. *sameSuffix(Y_X) = true, if:*

- *X is an extractor and during the resumption it generates the sequence of tuples as prior to a failure. Optionally a prefix of the sequence excluding the last prefix tuple can be removed*
- *X is a transformation that holds inDetOut[3] property and whose each input node V holds sameSuffix for each input or (it holds sameSet(V) and the X's input holds setToSeq(X_V))*

---

[3] $inDetOut$[7] property is held if for the same input sequences the node generates the same output sequence

Saving application state When a checkpoint is created, state of all nodes holding *checkpointable* is saved. These are for sure all the transformations and optionally extractors or inserters. Efficient creation of checkpoints requires a special creation procedure. Out of the discussion is the necessity of putting the nodes into the state to which they can return after restoring their states. We talk about both the temporary data and buffers and also current position in the running code. Creation of a checkpoint has been divided into three phases: stopping the nodes threads in conjunction with output queues emptying, saving nodes state, continuation of the processing.

Filter assignation Behind an extractor only a CleanPrefix filter can appear. This guarantees that only the required data stream suffix will be provided to the transformation input. Of course the input must have key attributes set, otherwise filtration will not be possible. If an extractor supports such a possibility, the built-in reextraction procedures can be used instead of filters. Known from the DR algorithm *GetSuffix* procedure replaces the CleanPrefix filter, and *GetDirtySuffix* procedure can be used instead of the DirtyPrefix filter [7]. In this case additional CleanPrefix filter is still necessary to get the same result as by use of a GetSuffix procedure. Filters placed in front of inserters are being assigned basing on the DR algorithm rules.

The filters are required only when a particular extractor or inserter does not hold a *checkpointable* property. If the extractor or inserter state can be restored from a previously created checkpoint, no filters are needed.

Resumption initialization Resumption initialization procedure is simple. After an interruption of the ETL process, the latest checkpoint must be found. Then it is loaded which means that the state of all graph nodes holding *checkpointable* property is restored. Now insertion of additional filters begins and the filters are initialized. Filters inserted behind extractors are informed what the last tuple received by the subsequent transformation is. Filters preceding the inserters are initialized with data taken from the inserters. Next inserters are switched to resumption mode. It causes that already loaded data set is not erased and new tuples are appended to the existing set.

4   Efficiency tests

4.1   Test Conditions

The base for our tests is an extraction graph containing 4 extractors reading tuples from 4 source files and 15 inserters (loading nodes) loading tuples into 15 database tables. The graph consists of three independent parts, but it is seen by the extraction application as a single ETL process.

The ETL process generates a complete data warehouse structure. It is a distributed spatial data warehouse system designed for storing and analyzing a wide range of spatial data [4]. The data is generated by media meters working in a radio-based measurement system. All the data is gathered in a telemetric server, from which it can be fetched to fill the data warehouse. The distributed system is based on a data model called the cascaded star model. The test input data set size is 500MB.

Method	Extraction time [s]	% change to the fastest method
Hybrid	1475	+8%
DR stream	1366	0%
Checkpoint	1496	+9%

Tab. 1. Measured extraction time for failureless cases

The tests were divided into three parts. In the first part we examined the resumption efficiency of the hybrid resumption algorithm (DR + staging) [5]. During this test all the join transformations worked in a buffering mode. It means that they collect all the tuples from the slave input first, then they start on-line processing of the master input. In such a mode VMQ[4] nodes are required to avoid data flow deadlocks, but on the other hand we can make use of the staging technique used by the hybrid algorithm.

In the second step we analysed the efficiency of the pure DR algorithm. This time all the join transformations worked in stream mode. In the stream mode we cannot distinguish prebuffering and on-line processing phases. Tuples from both inputs are processed simultaneously and only a small set of tuples may be buffered. In this mode the VMQ nodes are disabled.

In the third part we used the same extraction graph as in the second part, but this time we examined the efficiency of checkpointing. We focused on both: increase of the normal processing time caused by checkpoints creation and the resumption efficiency. In this test the extractors and inserters were unable to remember their states in created checkpoints, so additional filters had to be inserted into the graph.

The tests were ran on two PC machines with Pentium IV processors and 512MB of RAM. On one of them Oracle10g database was running, and on the other one the ETL application was started. Communication with the database was implemented using Oracle OCI drivers and SQL*Loader. A single uninterrupted extraction process time varied from 22 to 25 minutes.

During each loading test the extraction process was interrupted in order to simulate a failure. The resumption process was then run and the time was measured. Using collected results we prepared resumption charts showing the resumption efficiency depending on the time of a failure.

4.2 Extraction and Resumption Tests

The goal of the tests is to compare the efficiency of various extraction and resumption methods for the same extraction graph. Three aspects were analysed: influence of the chosen method on the time of the normal (uninterrupted) ETL process, resumption time and overall processing time[5].

---

[4] *VMQ* (Virtual Memory Queue) is a special node storing large amounts of data on external storage to avoid running out of memory. It is desirable not to use it because accessing external storage lowers the efficiency

[5] Overall processing time is the sum of the resumption time and the time of failure. It expresses the amount of time required to finish the ETL process in case of failures

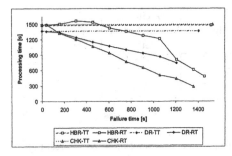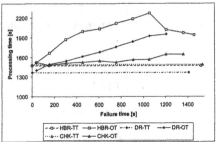

Fig. 4. Resumption (left) and overall (right) time plot. TT denotes *Total Time* of the normal processing, RT is the *Resumption time*, OT is the *Overall Time*

Table 1 compares extraction times for the three presented methods. The pure DR algorithm using stream-like joins is the fastest one. The reason why it is faster is in our opinion no VMQ nodes buffering the data. Data streams are processed on-the-fly, all the graph nodes are working all the time, none of them is idle. Unfortunately in such a case the use of staging technique makes no sense[5]. When join transformations work in a buffering mode, the data provided to the master inputs must be buffered until all the slave input tuple are read. The buffering lengthens the processing due to additional disk accesses. The third method uses the extraction graph used in the first test case, but it creates a checkpoint every 60 seconds. Creation of checkpoints lengthens the processing time also, but comparing to the hybrid method the overhead is relatively small.

Figure 4 shows the resumption times of the examined methods compared to the time of uninterrupted extraction. As we can see DR and checkpoints resumption efficiency is initially similar, but the later a failure occurs, the more efficient the checkpoint method is. For failures occurring at the end of the ETL process, the efficiency of the DR closes to the efficiency of the hybrid algorithm. The most important here is to have the resumption curve below the line denoting normal extraction time (TT). Otherwise it means that the resumption last longer than simple restarting the whole process from the beginning.

In fig. 4 overall processing times are compared also. Overall processing time is the sum of the processing time prior to a failure and the sum of the resumption time. It simply can be explained as the time between starting and finishing the ETL process assuming that after a failure the resumption process runs without any delay. Here again we can see that checkpointing is the best solution. The closer to the TT line is the resumption curve, the better. One should notice that it is impossible to have resumption curve below the TT line. If it was, it would mean that it is better to interrupt the extraction and then run the resumption.

5 Conclusions

In the paper we presented a new approach to the problem of resumption of the interrupted extraction process using checkpoints. The approach mixes two mechanisms: ETL application state saving and restoring which is typical for checkpointing, and usage of additional filters which is used in the Design-Resume[7] algorithm. We assumed that nodes such as extractors or inserters can work in a way making impossible to save and restore their states. Even if it is possible, its overhead may be too big and may lower the efficiency of the running process significantly. The proposed algorithm can work without storing the states of extractors and inserters. To make the application consistent during the resumption additional DR-like filters are inserted into the graph. The task of the filters is to remove from a tuple stream these tuples which were processed before creation of the checkpoint or were loaded by inserters. In this case data loaded after creation of the checkpoint are not lost, and additional filter ensures that they are not loaded to the warehouse again.

The proposed solution was tested in the ETL-RT extraction environment implemented in Java for research requirements. The environment supports various resumption algorithms: the Design-Resume algorithm, staging technique, hybrid algorithm (DR + staging) and the presented checkpoint-based resumption. Because all these algorithms are implemented in the same environment, the results of the tests we obtained are reliable and valuable.

The results are very encouraging and promising. The time of the normal extraction process was increased by less than 10% in comparison to the fastest tested method. In exchange for this we obtained a significant resumption efficiency growth that was presented in figure 4.

References

1. Bruckner R., List B., Schiefer J.: Striving Towards Near Real-Time Data Integration for Data Warehouses. DaWaK 2002.
2. FujiMoto R.: Parallel discrete event simulation, Communications of the ACM, 33(10), 1990
3. Galhardas H., Florescu D., Shasha D., Simon E.: Ajax: An Extensible Data Cleaning-Tool. In Proc. ACM SIGMOD Intl. Conf. On the Management of Data, Texas (2000).
4. Gorawski M., Malczok R.: Distributed Spatial Data Warehouse Indexed with Virtual Memory Aggregation Tree. 5th Workshop on Spatial-Temporal DataBase Management (STDBM_VLDB'04), Toronto, Canada 2004.
5. Gorawski M., Marks P.: High Efficiency of Hybrid Resumption in Distributed Data Warehouses. 1st Intl. Workshop on High Availability in Distributed Systems (HADIS 2005), Copenhagen, Denmark 2005.
6. Gorawski M., Chechelski R.: Spatial Telemetric Data Warehouse Balancing Algorithm in Oracle9i/Java Environment, Intelligent Information Systems, Gdansk, Poland, 2005.
7. Labio W., Wiener J., Garcia-Molina H., Gorelik V.: Efficient resumption of interrupted warehouse loads. SIGMOD Conference, 2000.
8. Labio W., Wiener J., Garcia-Molina H., Gorelik V.: Resumption algorithms. Technical report, Stanford University, 1998.
9. Plank J. S., An Overview of Checkpointing in Uniprocessor and Distributed Systems, Focusing on Implementation and Performance. Technical report, University of Tennessee. 1997
10. Sagent Technologies Inc.: Personal correspondence with customers.
11. Vassiliadis P., Simitsis A., Skiadopoulos S.: Modeling ETL Activities asGraphs. InProc. 4th Intl. Workshop on Design and Management of Data Warehouses, Canada, (2002).
12. Vassiliadis P., Simitsis A., Georgantas P., Terrovitis M.: A Framework for the Design of ETL Scenarios. CAiSE 2003.

A C++ Refactoring Browser and Method Extraction

Marian Vittek[1], Peter Borovansky[1], and Pierre-Etienne Moreau[2]

[1] FMFI, Comenius University, Mlynska dolina, 842 15 Bratislava
Slovakia
{vittek,borovan}@fmph.uniba.sk
[2] LORIA-INRIA, BP 239, 54506 Vandœuvre-lès-Nancy
France
moreau@loria.fr

Abstract. This paper presents a refactoring tool for C++. Its implementation illustrates the main difficulties of automated refactoring raising in this case from the preprocessor and from the complexity of the language. Our solution, using a back-mapping preprocessor, works in the presence of complex preprocessor constructions built upon file inclusions, macro expansions and conditional compilations. Refactorings are computed after full preprocessing and parsing of target programs, hence, they are based on the same level of program understanding as performed by compilers. The paper illustrates the main ideas of our approach on the example of *Extract Method* refactoring. [3].

1 Introduction

Maintenance of large legacy software systems is a hard task. *Refactoring* [9, 10, 15] is a promising methodology helping developers in this work. Refactoring is a software development and maintenance process where the source code is changed "in such a way that it does not alter the external behavior of the code yet improve its internal structure. It is a disciplined way to clean up code that minimizes the chances of introducing bugs" [9].

For example, renaming of a global variable *iii* to *fileIndex* on all its occurrences is a refactoring. Replacing on all its occurrences means that only occurrences of this global variable will be renamed. There may be several local variables *iii* (or many class members named *iii*) which will not be renamed because they are not *linked* to the global *iii*. In opposition to the full text replacement this is a kind of *minimal* or *required* renaming, making only necessary modifications. Such refactoring improves the quality of the code because it makes it more readable.

Refactoring browsers are software tools helping maintainers in performing refactorings. In the context of refactoring browsers, the word refactoring is used as a noun to describe a simple elementary behavior preserving source transformation. When using a refactoring tool, a human maintainer only selects the required transformation (such as *rename variable*) and its input parameters (new name for the variable) and the tool performs all necessary source modifications. The tool shall guarantee that those modifications do not change the behavior of the program and, hence, does not introduce any new bug. Use of an automatic tool allows to perform massive changes in source code

---

[3] This work was supported by Agency for Promotion Research and Development under the contract No. APVV-20-P04805.

Please use the following format when citing this chapter:

Vittek, M., Borovansky, P., Moreau, P.-E., 2006, in IFIP International Federation for Information Processing, Volume 227, Software Engineering Techniques: Design for Quality, ed. K. Sacha, (Boston: Springer), pp. 325–336.

quickly and safely. Refactoring tools usually perform a fixed set of refactorings identified by short schematic names, such as *Rename Variable, Move Field, Move Method, Encapsulate Field, Pull Up Field/Method, Push Down Field/Method, Extract Method,* etc. Among them, the *Extract Method* has a particular position from the point of view of evaluation of refactoring tools. This refactoring consists of extraction of a piece of code into a newly created method with automatically generated parameters and return value. Parameters and the return value are computed after a static analysis of the program and the quality of this analysis often indicates the quality of the whole refactoring tool. The method extraction also belongs to the most used refactorings.

In this paper, we present *Xrefactory C++*, a tool performing refactorings on C++ programs. The implementation evolved from our previous works on C language [25]. Our approach is using a back-mapping preprocessor and, while computing the refactorings, it performs full preprocessing and parsing of C++ programs. At this moment, our tool performs only a limited set of refactorings, namely all kinds of renaming, refactorings for adding, removing and moving method parameters and the method extraction. Others are in progress.

2 Related Works

The concept of refactoring has been discussed during more than a decade [9, 15, 19, 21]. In chronological order, refactoring has been investigated mainly in the context of Smalltalk and C++ programming languages without experimental implementations. Later, the Smalltalk refactoring browser [20] has been developed and was probably the world's first automated refactoring tool. The importance of refactoring was strengthen by *extreme programming* methodology [5, 14] as one of its basic rules. Independently, similar works on program transformations were held in the context of term rewriting [18, 23]. After apparition of Martin Fowler's book [9] numerous implementations of refactoring browsers for Java emerged, among them Intellij IDEA and Eclipse. Refactoring techniques heavily depend on the underlying programming language and are usually studied and implemented separately for each language. The refactoring of C/C++ has been discussed during several years [8, 19, 22]. However, problems with the language complexity and the preprocessor caused that C/C++ refactoring tools are still rare, and not widely accepted. The preprocessor is not part of the language in traditional sense. It does not enter into its grammar and it makes standard techniques very difficult to apply. Despite the practical motivations, there is only a small research activity in the area of C++ refactoring. Eclipse [1] team is working on refactoring support for the CDT module which is currently limited to a restrictive form of renaming. At the author best knowledges, the real state of the art is represented by two tools: *Visual SlickEdit* [3] and *Ref++* [2]. The first one is a self standing Integrated Development Environment (IDE) which incorporates C++ refactoring features. The second one is a plugin to MSVC++ environment. They are both approaching C++ refactoring in a practical manner implementing a large number of refactorings (between 10 and 20), however, they are both working correctly only in rather simple common circumstances. Those tools offer a usable solution while not going too deeply into the program structure and, in particular, they do not really analyze problems introduced by the combination of the language and the preprocessor. For example, at this time, none of those tools is able to perform correct refactorings at places where an #if preprocessor directive with an #else branch is present.

A deeper comparison of our approach and the mentioned two tools is difficult because both tools are commercial and there are only few informations available about their internal structure and implementation. Anyway, from the external behavior, we can see that our approach is based on deeper understanding of the source code than provided by those tools. As we will present in the paper, our tool proceeds correctly all features of the C++ language as well as all preprocessor constructions including complex combinations of #if-#else directives. On the other side, due to the complexity of the implementation, at the moment, our tool is implementing much smaller set of refactorings.

There is also a number of other related works needed to be mentioned at this place, even if they are not directly concerned by C++ refactoring. Alejandra Garrido and Ralph Johnson work on a C refactoring browser at University of Illinois at Urbana-Champaign [11–13]. Their approach is focused on correct handling of all preprocessor constructions, including very complex conditional directives, however, few syntactical restrictions on the usage of those directives are applied. Their tool is relied to the C language and the solution is not directly extensible to C++. In Berkeley, Bill McCloskey and Eric Brewer [17] work on a C-like language, where preprocessor directives will be defined at the language level instead of being purely textual. They suppose that each C program can be translated into this language and then easily refactored. Several other projects are dealing with preprocessor while not focused on refactoring. Semantic Designs is working on a set of source understanding and transformation tools for variety of languages including C and C++ [4]. An interesting tool focused on porting C++ programs from one platform to another is developed by D. Waddington and B. Yao from Lucent Technologies [7]. Those projects are, in general, incorporating preprocessor constructions in the Abstract Syntax Tree (AST), or they are incorporating them directly into the grammar of the language. Last but not least, a number of practical problems connected to the preprocessor has been seriously examined in independent works focused on source understanding tools [6, 24].

3 C++ Refactoring and the Preprocessor

The C++ language evolved from C by accepting wide range of extensions, including object oriented classes, (multiple) inheritance, overloaded methods and operators, virtual methods, namespaces, exceptions, templates, etc. An unwanted side effect of those generous extensions is the difficulty of parsing, understanding and refactoring C++ programs. Moreover, a usual C++ program is not written in C++. It contains *preprocessor directives* which are not part of C++ grammar.

Preprocessor is a serious obstacle in development of a refactoring tool. One possible approach how to deal with preprocessor directives is their incorporation into the grammar and the AST and development of a parser working with those extensions. Unfortunately, the C++ parser itself is very complex and its development is on the limits of many companies, a direct combination with the preprocessor and development of a parser for such mixed language seems unrealistic for us. For this reason, we are using a different approach in our implementation. We are using a standard preprocessor, parser and AST. Similarly to [6], our preprocessor is extended to generate an additional back-mapping information allowing to trace each character of the code. Beyond the usual preprocessed code, the preprocessor generates a table determining for each character of preprocessed code, from which place of the original source code it comes. Refactorings are then computed on the preprocessed AST and the necessary source transformations are backmapped to the original code. This approach is solving majority of problems related to the parsing of C++, because we can use a standard parser developed for compilers. With a small effort, it also solves problems related to macro expansions and file inclusions. The real problem is the presence of #if-#else directives. This directive is basically used to trigger different fragments of code in or out of the compilation depending on an external configuration. Different configurations are represented by different initial setting of predefined macros. In order to be able to correctly understand the whole program (i.e. both positive and negative branches of #if directives), we have decided to parse the source code several times during a single refactoring. Each parsing is performed with different initial macro settings. The considered initial macro settings are entered by the user and are supposed to cover all possible compilations of the project. The refactoring is computed after having performed all parsings. The way, how the resulting refactoring is combined from the parsings is specific for each particular refactoring. For example, in the case of symbol renaming and parameter manipulations, the resulting refactoring is basically a union of all required modifications (renaming) from all passes. The situation is more difficult in the case of method extraction.

In the rest of the paper, we will illustrate our implementation by describing in details the implementation of the method extraction. We prefer to explain our approach by introducing this single refactoring instead of describing the whole tool. We feel that in this way, we will illustrate better the main ideas on which the tool is built as well as the overall complexity of the implementation.

4   Simple Code Extraction

Extraction of a method is a simple and intuitive program transformation, a kind of intelligent 'cut and paste'. For example, lets take the following program computing the n-th Fibonacci number for a given parameter:

```
ln  1: int main(int argc, char **argv) −
ln  2:    int i,n,x,y,t;
ln  3:    sscanf(argv[1], "%d", &n);
ln  4:    x=0; y=1;
ln  5:    for(i=0; i¡n; i++) −
ln  6:       t=x+y; x=y; y=t;
ln  7:    ˝
ln  8:    printf("%d-th fib == %d˝n", n, x);
ln  9:    return(0);
ln 10: ˝
```

When a refactoring tool is asked to extract the code between lines 4 and 7 into a method (say fib), it replaces the original code by:

```
ln  1: static int fib(int n) −
```

```
ln  2:    int t, y, x, i;
ln  3:    x=0; y=1;
ln  4:    for(i=0; i¡n; i++) –
ln  5:        t=x+y; x=y; y=t;
ln  6:    ˮ
ln  7:    return(x);
ln  8: ˮ
ln  9:
ln 10: int main(int argc, char **argv) –
ln 11:    int i,n,x,y,t;
ln 12:    sscanf(argv[1], "%d", &n);
ln 13:    x = fib(n);
ln 14:    printf("%d-th fib == %d"n", n, x);
ln 15:    return(0);
ln 16: ˮ
```

Determining which variable should be a parameter of the new method is made automatically. From the implementation point of view, it requires static analysis of the method, in particular of its local variables. The analysis classifies each local variable into one of five categories: *none, local, in, out, in-out* saying that it is respectively not concerned by the extraction, will become a local variable of the new method, will become an input parameter (passed by value), output parameter, or input/output parameter (passed by address). Later, if there is only one output variable, (and it has a base type), it may be reclassified to *return value*.

The analysis of local variables is similar to variable lifetime analysis performed by compilers. For each variable, the method is transformed into a control flow diagram. The diagram is examined and all usages of each variable are watched. The tool is especially examining whether a value assigned outside the extracted block is used inside the block, and vice-versa. If such a control flow is discovered, the corresponding flag is set. After examination of all possible control flows, resulting flags are evaluated and the variable is classified to one of the above five categories. There is one more problem needed to be considered. Let's take the following simple function writing numbers from 0 to 9 and let us suppose that we are going to extract the single line 5 into a new method.

```
ln  1: void fun() –
ln  2:    int i=0;
ln  3:    for(int j=0; j¡10; j++) –
ln  4:        /* block begin */
ln  5:        cout ¡¡ i++;
ln  6:        /* block end */
ln  7:    ˮ
ln  8: ˮ
```

In this case, the above analysis indicates that there is a value of the variable i assigned outside the block which is used inside and there is no value of the variable i assigned inside the block which is used outside. Logically, this would give a classification for i as being an *input* variable. However, due to the loop re-entrance, this variable has to be classified as *input/output*. At the time, this benchmark has caused problems to many professional refactoring browsers. In our implementation, we have solved this problem by introducing a new flag, indicating whether, in the given control flow, a value has been passed outside the block and reentered into the block and then reused inside. The presence of address parameters is a particularity of C++ compared to Java and C. Their presence in a method requires another small refinement. When watching an address parameter, all leaving points of the method has to be considered as places where it is (potentially) used. This is because it may carry out resulting values.

After having classified all variables, the actual extraction of the code is just a question of text editing. The tool performs moving of the extracted text, generates the header and the footer of the method and its invocation at the place from where it was extracted. When a method is a class member and its body is not inside the class, a declaration of the method into the corresponding class definition has to be generated too.

So far, we did not consider the preprocessor. Possible presence of preprocessor directives complicates nearly all parts of the implementation. In the following text we will discuss the complications and the solutions, we have adopted, for each of preprocessor directives separately.

5   Macros

Macros are defined with the #define preprocessor directive. They allow to textually replace *macro usages* into *macro bodies*, which are usually pieces of code. During the method extraction, a question arises whether to perform extraction after the macro expansion or before. In Xrefactory, we are using in fact a combination of both. It is obvious that the analysis and classification of local variables has to be done after macro expansion. Otherwise the analysis may be wrong. For example, if we take a fragment:

```
#define ASSIGN(x,v) −x=v;˜
...
   int i;
   ASSIGN(i,5);
```

without the macro expansion, we do not know that the variable i is used as an l-value in the fragment.

On the other side, the new extracted method must be unpreprocessed. It corresponds to the intuition that the code written in a file is not preprocessed and the new method should be written in the same manner as it was written by the original developer. We have solved those two points in a direct ad-hoc way, the variable analysis is performed after the full preprocessing of the source code, while the actual text extraction is performed on the original unpreprocessed code. Xrefactory actually implements a real textual cut and paste of the original code moving the method body as text. This solution protects original formatting and unpreprocessed structure. It means also that macro usages are not expanded in the extracted method (even if they were during the variable analysis).

A similar situation occurs during the generation of the *header* and the *footer* of the new method. In our terminology, the header is the beginning of the new method defining parameters and those local variables carried from outer environment. In the introductory example, that were the lines 1 and 2 of the method fib. The footer is the piece of code assigning the return value (if any). In our introductory example, that were the lines 7 and 8. The header and the footer are pieces of code entirely generated by Xrefactory, it may seem, that they will be generated from an internal program representation. However, it may happen that, for example, definitions of variables present in the header used macros. The typical situation is definition of arrays using macros in their dimensions. Let's take a code containing an array a and let us suppose that the array is classified as a *local* variable for the extracted method. So, the situation in the original code is:

```
#define MAX`VALUES 1000
...
    int i, j, a[MAX`VALUES];
...
```

It is logical that the generated header should be:

```
void extracted() –
  int a[MAX`VALUES];
```

instead of:

```
void extracted() –
  int a[1000];
```

In other words, when the original definition of the variable contains macros, it is expected that the definition in the generated header will contain macros too. For this reason, Xrefactory composes also definitions of all parameters by a copy-pasting of corresponding pieces of the original text. From the implementation point of view, it requires that the parser remembers source positions of corresponding syntactic categories, such as *declaration specifiers* and *declarator* of the parsed text. Moreover, because the parser acts on the preprocessed code, those positions has to be back-mapped to positions in the unpreprocessed code and corresponding pieces of code are taken from there.

6 File Inclusion

The include directive allows to insert an entire file into a particular place of source code. In a usual case, this directive does not represent a particular complication for method extraction. Inclusion is, in its nature, a very similar operation to macro expansion. One can imagine that the whole included file is just a body of a long macro which is expanded at the given place. Effects of the file inclusion are then handled by the same techniques as macro expansions, i.e. by the back-mapping preprocessor. Note also, that the include directive rarely occurs in the body of a method, hence, it only rarely interfere with extraction.

7 Conditional Compilation

The C/C++ preprocessor allows to include or exclude some part of source code depending on a condition evaluated in compile time. The mechanism is implemented via #if directive and looks like a usual if statement. Conditional compilation is the main difficulty introduced by the preprocessor to refactoring tools. The difficulty comes from usages where the #if directive is used in combination with platform or compiler specific features. Let's take, for example, the code:

```
ln  1: #if defined(``WIN32)
ln  2: #include ¡windows.h¿
ln  3: #define PMACRO(x) Jbox(x++)
ln  4: #else
ln  5: #define PMACRO(f,x) printf(f,x)
ln  6: #endif

ln  8: ...
ln  9: #if defined(``WIN32)
ln 10:     PMACRO(i);
ln 11: #else
ln 12:     PMACRO("%d", i);
ln 13: #endif
ln 14: ...
```

This example is a bit artificial, however it perfectly illustrates two problems related to conditionals. The first problem is that there may be several dependent conditionals and the program may be unparsable if they are not processed in the same way. The second problem is that when extracting lines $9 - 13$, then two analysis on two different platforms lead to different classifications of the parameter i. On Windows platform, it will be classified as *input/output* parameter and on other platforms as *input* parameter. The problem is: in which way to pass this variable to the extracted method so that it works under both systems?

In our implementation, we have solved both problems by performing multiple passes over the source code. The number of passes as well as the initial configurations are fully specified by the user. The user has to specify all combinations of initial macro definitions which occur in various compilations of the project. For each such combination (for each preprocessor pass), the source is preprocessed, parsed and the static analysis of variables is performed. Variables are classified (to be *input, output, etc.* parameters) as described in the previous section. After all passes, those informations are combined into a final resulting classification. The computation of the final classification is quite intuitive, it is implemented by a binary operation $reclassify$ starting from the initial classification and merging it with all following passes. The table 1 shows all possibilities of variable reclassification. After all passes a variable obtains its final classification (which is the most general of all passes) and the corresponding header of the new method is generated upon this resulting classification. So, finishing our example, the variable i would be classified as being an *input/output* parameter after both passes.

This solution works well when the variable occurs in all passes. However, a variable can be missing in some passes. For example, let us take the situation:

```
ln  1: void drawCircle(Point c, int d
ln  2: #if defined(USE`COLORS)
ln  3:                 , Color color
```

	n	l	i	o	io
n	n	l	i	o	io
l	l	l	i	o	io
i	i	i	i	io	io
o	o	o	io	o	io
io	io	io	io	io	io

Tab. 1. Reclassification of variables after two preprocessor passes. The figure shows the resulting classification of a variable depending on its classifications in the first and the second pass. Abbreviations for classifications are: n=*none*, l=*local*, i=*input*, o=*output*, io=*input/output*.

```
ln  4: #endif
ln  5:              ) –
ln  6: ...
ln  7: #if defined(USE'COLORS)
ln  8:     setColor(color);
ln  9: #endif
ln 10: ...
ln 11: ˝
```

In this example if we are extracting a block containing only one line, namely the line 8 with setColor invocation, there will be (at least) two preprocessor passes. A pass where USE'COLORS is defined and another where it is not. In the first pass, (when USE'COLORS is defined) there is a variable color, which is classified as an *input* parameter. When USE'COLORS is not defined, the variable does not exist at all, so the above reclassification is not possible. In our implementation, we have considered two solutions for merging both passes in such situation. The first possibility is to classify the variable according to the existing pass and to ignore another pass. The second solution is to note that the variable exists only in some passes and to generate additional #if directive around its definition. Those approaches would lead respectively to following extractions, the first approach would generate:

```
void extracted(Color color) –
    setColor(color);
˝

...
#if defined(USE'COLORS)
  extracted(color);
#endif
```

and the second approach:

```
void extracted(
#if defined(USE'COLORS)
            Color color
#endif
            ) –
    setColor(color);
```

```
~

...
#if defined(USE`COLORS)
 extracted(
#if defined(USE`COLORS)
        color
#endif
        );
#endif
```

In the last example, a more careful evaluation of guarding #if directives may remove the nested conditional. It seems to us that the first approach generates a more appropriate extraction for human maintainers. Its risky point is that the definition of the variable may be unparsable in some circumstances. For example, if the type Color is defined only in passes when USE`COLORS was predefined. The situation may be even worse, in the following example. Let's consider that we extract also the guarding #if directives, i.e. we extract a block of lines 7 − 9 instead of the single line 9. To compare both approaches in this case, we will get the following extraction for the first approach:

```
void extracted(Color color) −
#if defined(USE`COLORS)
  setColor(color);
#endif
~

...
 extracted(color);
```

and for the second:

```
void extracted(
#if defined(USE`COLORS)
         Color color
#endif
         ) −
#if defined(USE`COLORS)
  setColor(color);
#endif
~

...
 extracted(
#if defined(USE`COLORS)
       color
#endif
       );
```

In the first approach, the invocation of the extracted method is clearly unparsable, because the variable color is not defined at the point of invocation of the new method. On the other hand, in the second approach, the additional generated #if directives can not be removed at all. The decision which of the two approaches should be implemented in our tool was rather a question of taste. The second solution is safe, however, we do not like it, because of explosion of new generated #if conditionals. Possible reduction of new conditionals would be a hard task, taking into account how difficult the static analysis of cpp conditionals is [16]. Moreover, in majority of practical cases, user can always get sufficiently good extraction with the first approach. In cases when the first approach fails it is producing syntax error and, hence, there is no danger of introducing an unwanted bug to the runtime. For all those reasons, we have adopted the first approach in our implementation. Xrefactory generates non-guarded declarations of variables and it warns the user in cases when a variable does not occur in all preprocessor passes.

8 Conclusion

In this paper we have presented an implementation of a C++ refactoring browser. In order to deal with preprocessor, it computes refactorings in terms of source editing commands instead of AST transformations. Those editing commands are backmapped from preprocessed code to original unpreprocessed code and then applied. Conditionals are handled by multiple preprocessor passes and multiple parsings of source code. The final refactoring is combined from all parsings. This ad-hoc approach works well even in very complex circumstances and it allows to use a standard C++ parser taken from a compiler. In our implementation, we are using a professional compiler front-end produced by EDG company. The whole implementation consists of around 50 000 lines of code plus around 350 000 lines in the C++ parser. The implementation is available for download at the address *http://www.xref-tech.com/xrefactory*.

References

1. Eclipse. *http://www.eclipse.org*.
2. Ref++. *http://www.refpp.com*.
3. Visual slickedit. *http://www.slickedit.com*.
4. Ira D. Baxter and Michael Mehlich. Preprocessor conditional removal by simple partial evaluation. In *Proceedings of WCRE 2001: Working Conference on Reverse Engineering*, Stuttgart, Germany, 2001. IEEE Computer Society Press.
5. Kent Beck. *Extreme Programming explained*. Reading, MA, Addison Wesley Longman, Inc., 107108., 2000.
6. Anthony Cox and Charles Clarke. Relocating xml elements from preprocessed to unprocessed code. In *Proceedings of IWPC 2002: International Workshop on Program Comprehension*, Paris, France, 2002.
7. D.G.Waddington and B.Yao. High fidelity c++ code transformation. In *Proceedings of the 5th workshop on Language Descriptions, Tools and Applications (LDTA 2005), Edinburgh University, UK*, 2005.
8. R. Fanta and V. Rajlich. Reengineering an object oriented code. In *Procceedings of IEEE International Conference On Software Maintenance*, pages 238–246, 1999.
9. Martin Fowler, (with contributions by K. Beck, J. Brant, W. Opdyke, and D. Roberts). *Refactoring: Improving the Design of Existing Code*. Addison-Wesley, 1999.
10. E. Gamma, R. Helm, R. Johnson, and J. Vlissides. *Design Patterns: Elements of Reusable Object-Oriented Software*. Addison-Wesley, 1994.

11. A. Garrido and R. Johnson. Analyzing multiple configurations of a c program. In *Procceedings of IEEE International Conference On Software Maintenance, Budapest, Hungary*, 2005.
12. Alejandra Garrido. *Program Refactoring in the Presence of Preprocessor Directives*. PhD thesis, University of Illinois, Urbana-Champaign, IL, USA, 2005.
13. Alejandra Garrido and Ralph Johnson. Refactoring c with conditional compilation. In *18th IEEE International Conference on Automated Software Engineering*, Montreal, Canada, 2003.
14. Richard Garzaniti, Jim Huangs, and Chet Hendrickson. Everything i need to know i learned from the chrysler payroll project. In *Conference Addendum to the Proceedings of OOPSLA'97*, 1997.
15. Ralph E. Johnson and Brian Foote. Designing reusable classes. *Journal of Object-Oriented Programming*, 1(2):22–25, July 1988.
16. M. Latendresse. Fast symbolic evaluation of c/c++ preprocessing using conditional values. In *Procceedings of the seventh European Conference on Software Maintenance and Reengineering, Benevento, Italy*, pages 170–182, 2003.
17. Bill McCloskey and Eric Brewer. Astec: A new approach to c refactoring. *ACM SIGSOFT Software Engineering Notes*, 30(5), Sep 2005.
18. P. E. Moreau, C. Ringeissen, and M. Vittek. A pattern matching compiler for multiple target languages. In *International Conference on Compiler Construction, Varsovie, Pologne*, volume 2622 of *Lecture Notes in Computer Science*, pages 61–76, 2003.
19. William F. Opdyke. *Refactoring Object-Oriented Frameworks*. PhD thesis, University of Illinois, Urbana-Champaign, IL, USA, 1992.
20. Don Roberts, John Brant, and Ralph Johnson. A refactoring tool for smalltalk. *Theory and Practice of Object Systems*, 3(4), 1997.
21. Don Bradley Roberts. *Practical Analysis for Refactoring*. PhD thesis, University of Illinois, Urbana-Champaign, IL, USA, 1999.
22. L. Tokuda and D. Batory. Evolving object-oriented architectures with refactorings. In *Conf. on Automated Software Engineering, Orlando, Florida*, 1999.
23. Mark van den Brand, Paul Klint, and Chris Verhoef. Re-engineering needs generic programming language technology. *ACM SIGPLAN Notices*, 2(32):54–61, February 1997.
24. Laszlo Vidacs, Arpad Beszedes, and Rudolf Ferenc. Columbus schema for c/c++ preprocessing. In *8th European Conference on Software Maintenance and Reengineering, Tampere, Finland*, pages 75–84. IEEE Computer Society, 2004.
25. Marian Vittek. A refactoring browser with preprocessor. In *Procceedings of the seventh European Conference on Software Maintenance and Reengineering, Benevento, Italy*, pages 101–111. IEEE Computer Society Press, 2003.

ESC/Java2 as a Tool to Ensure Security in the Source Code of Java Applications*

Aleksy Schubert[1,2] and Jacek Chrząszcz[1]

[1]Institute of Informatics
Warsaw University, Poland
[2]SoS Group NIII
Faculty of Science
University of Nijmegen, Netherlands

Abstract. The paper shows how extended static checking tools like ESC/Java2 can be used to ensure source code security properties of Java applications. It is demonstrated in a case study on a simple personal password manager. In case of such an application the ensuring of security is one of the most important goals. We present the possible threats connected with the current state of the code and its possible future extensions. This investigation is further accompanied by a presentation on how these threats can be controlled by JML specifications and ESC/Java2.

1 Introduction

Security sensitive applications require a thorough analysis of their security properties. In order to assure the high degree of security of an application, the software industry uses the techniques such as careful design and testing.

Another way to ensure the high quality of the source code is to use some tool supported way of ensuring additional properties of the code. It is usually based on the static examination of the code structure and interdependencies. These techniques require different amounts of additional human labour. The least costly ones are those based on finding error prone coding patterns (PREfix [1], FindBugs [2]) and can be used to enforce certain coding guidelines. The more laborious techniques like static typing (Splint [3], JFlow [4] etc.), extended static checking (ESC/Java [5] and its successor ESC/Java2) and model checking (Bandera [6]) require more human effort. They rely on the source code annotation that instructs tools how to conduct the verification. The conformance of the source code to the annotations is subsequently automatically proved. The additional work allows to discover less obvious bugs and provide additional documentation which allows to better express and enforce the design decisions done by the designers of the systems. The most laborious techniques are the ones which involve the full formal verification of systems (Jack [7], Loop [8] etc.). They require both additional annotations with detailed specifications and construction of a proof that the code matches the specifications. The latter task is the most time consuming one.

* This work was partly supported by KBN grant 3 T11C 002 27 and Sixth Framework Programme MEIF-CT-2005-024306 SOJOURN.

Please use the following format when citing this chapter:

Schubert, A., Chrząszcz, J., 2006, in IFIP International Federation for Information Processing, Volume 227, Software Engineering Techniques: Design for Quality, ed. K. Sacha, (Boston: Springer), pp. 337–348.

In this paper, we focus on the application of the extended static checking. This method is one of the static verification methods that presents certain trade-off between no annotation effort techniques like FindBugs and full functional verification systems like Jack or Loop. The extended static checking relies on additional annotations in the source code and offers automatically generated proofs that the source code conforms to them. This allows to express more complicated properties of the code, however the strength of this method is limited by the abilities of the provers employed.

The annotations used in this work are expressed in the Java Modelling Language (JML [9]). JML is a specification language which is supported by several, actively developed tools [10]. It is grounded on solid foundation of numerous scientific papers that discuss its design [11] and specific constructs e.g. [12, 13]. It is based on the standard notions such as pre-, post-conditions, invariants etc. in the style of Design by Contract [14] (see Section 4 for more details).

The JML annotations allow to smoothly scale the development process of the Java source code from lightweight specification annotations, that for instance specify simple properties like non-nullness of references, up to full-fledged functional specification. In the case study, JML served to describe additional requirements for the source code which should diminish the chances that uncontrolled exceptions are thrown (it is impossible to prevent JVM errors using these techniques) and that the sensitive data, like passwords or relations between passwords and computers, will leak in an uncontrolled way.

In order to enforce the properties expressed in JML, an extended static checking tool ESC/Java2 was used [15]. ESC/Java2 is the successor of ESC/Java developed in Compaq [5]. This tool takes JML annotated Java source code and reports inconsistencies between the specifications and the code. This is done by constructing verification conditions which are subsequently checked against a mathematical model of the Java source code. The verification process is done by a first-order logic prover Simplify [16]. The model is an approximation of the real program so certain kinds of errors are not captured (for instance the checker does not take into account integer overflows). Still, it allows to discover many inconsistencies in the program design.

It is worth mentioning that the C# platform has an specification language Spec# [17] analogous to JML and a verification tool Boogie [18]. In this light, the general conclusions from the paper may be also applied also to these tools.

The specification and verification techniques based on JML were applied in the context of JavaCard applications [19]. The aim of this research is to show the applicability of these tools and methods to ensure the high quality of the resulting source code in applications beyond the context of JavaCard. We present here a small security sensitive Java application Passwords (Section 2) and the analysis of possible threats for the application (Section 3). After that we demonstrate the annotation techniques used to prevent the threats (Section 4), and then the discovered inconsistencies in the source code (Section 5). We sum up the paper with a description of encountered difficulties in using of the tools (Section 6) and general conclusions (Section 7).

2 The Passwords application

Functionality The application is a simple password manager similar to the ones used in web browsers. Its GUI has two tabs. The first one allows to add new password entities to the application, the second allows to associate passwords with computers. It is impossible to delete the entries. The access to the whole application is protected by a single master password. The user is allowed to see directly the connections between computers and the numerical identifiers of passwords (see Fig. 1) He can also temporarily see the actual password by clicking the right mouse button on its numerical identifier. As soon as the button is released, the password disappears.

Fig. 1. The two tabs of the Passwords application. The first one presents the interface for adding passwords, the second one presented the interface for adding computers and relations between computers and passwords.

The internal structure The application is a typical three-layer application (see Fig. 2). The first layer is a user interface which allows to add information on computers and passwords. The second layer is a communication layer with the permanent storage that keeps the information. The third layer is the storage. The current implementation uses a standard file as the storage. This can be changed by reimplementation of one class.

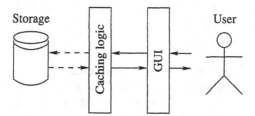

Fig. 2. The basic structure of the Passwords application. It consists of three layers: the GUI that interacts with the user, the logic that provides the interface between the GUI and the data storage and the data storage.

The most important classes and interfaces of the application are:

– MainWindow which implements the GUI layer of the application,

- PasswordsLogicIntf which is the interface that abstracts the connection between the GUI and the layer of the logic,
- PasswordsFileLogic which is an implementation of PasswordsLogicIntf that works on files,
- Password and Computer are the classes that package the sensitive information concerning passwords, computers and relations between them; in particular the Computer class contains the collection of passwords associated with it.

Other informations on the programme The whole application was developed in Java 1.4 with detailed JavaDoc documentation. It consists of 23 classes. The overall code size of the application is 4433 lines of source code, including all the comments and JML specifications. The JML specifications constitute 482 lines of the comments. The number of physical source code lines, as generated using David A. Wheeler's 'SLOCCount' is 1650.

Additionally, this software development was supplemented with extension of the specifications for the Java standard library classes. The specifications are necessary when the verification with ESC/Java2 is conducted. This exertion resulted in additional 36 specification files and modification of 10 existing specification files. We added 133 lines of JML specifications to the existing specification files. The 36 specification files that were added amounted to 9838 lines, 97% of which was automatically generated by the JML Eclipse plug-in. The code of the application together with the specifications is available from http://www.mimuw.edu.pl/~alx/Passwords.tgz

3   Threat analysis

Extent of the analysis In this work, we focus on the source code security. Therefore we omit all the considerations connected with the security of the particular data representation that is used in the file and all possible threats connected with the social security attacks. We are aware that the solution used presents certain trade-off between security and both the usability and the applicability. The application gives a controlled access to a single asset, namely password.

Ways to acquire or destroy the asset The basic threats in the application is that somebody who is not allowed will compromise the confidentiality, integrity or availability of the password data.

1. Confidentiality
   a) the assets can be sent to an uncontrolled channel:
      i. the password may be frozen in GUI on the screen (due to a hardware failure, due to a dead-lock in the operating system kernel etc.)
      ii. the assets can be printed out clear-text on a console device,
         A. the asset can be printed out as a part of an exception message or a stack trace,
         B. the asset can be printed out as a result of a debugging message,
         C. the asset can be printed out as a result of wrong aliasing in the application,
         D. the asset can be printed out as a result of public access to some fields.

        iii. the assets can be sent out clear-text using an Internet connection, (the ways to gain the asset in this case and in the subsequent ones are similar to the ones in the point 1.(a))ii),

        iv. the assets can be sent out clear-text to another application using the operating system communication facilities such as shared memory,

        v. the assets can be stored clear-text in a file out of control,

        vi. the assets can be sent to another application using memory allocation or swapping;

    b) the information on assets can be leaked to an uncontrolled channel:

        i. the assets can be revealed as a result of differences in behaviour (e.g. longer waiting time for longer passwords),

        ii. a result of a computation (e.g. all letters of the password XOR-ed with "a") can be sent to an uncontrolled channel;

    c) the information on assets can be revealed by a side channel (e.g. the sound of the cooling fan on the processor);

    d) the assets can be acquired by a person who has access to the system administrator privileges.

2. Integrity

    a) the password can be overwritten by a malicious extension of the application;

    b) the relation between computer and can be changed by such an extension.

3. Availability

    a) the password file can be destroyed by a malicious extension of the application;

    b) the password can be destroyed by a malicious extension;

    c) the application can be hung by a malicious extension.

In this research we focused on the ways to prevent attacks that exploit bugs in the software. That is why we look mainly at the leaking of passwords from the application which can be prevented by the way the source code is written. We limit our further considerations to cases (1.(a))ii)-(1.(a))v), (b)), (2.), and (3.).

4 Employed formal techniques

4.1 JML constructs used in the case-study

We present here the most important features of JML which are used in the case study to prevent the coding errors that might lead to the cases of information compromise described at the end of Section 3.

JML assertions are written in the source code comments of a special form. The comments which can span several lines have the form /*@ ... @*/ while one-line specifications follow //@.

Ghost fields enable a thorough analysis of the information flow and type properties. Variables of this kind are auxiliary fields which are not used by the implementation, but occur in specifications. We can declare in the Object class a field which allows to mark objects as confidential or non-confidential:

```
//@ ghost public boolean isConfidential = false;
```

Similarly, the container classes can have a ghost field which indicates the type of the elements gathered in it:

```
//@ instance ghost public "TYPE elementType;
```

Another example of the use of the ghost field is the variable which keeps track of the aliasing of objects. We can declare owner of each object

```
//@ ghost public Object owner;
```

and delegate to the owner the right to modify the state.

The mere declaration of the fields does not ensure that particular code property is maintained. We need additional mechanisms which are described hereafter.

Object Invariants express properties which should hold at the entry and exit to each method. The invariants serve as a device to describe the meaning of the consistency of the object data. They can express for instance that certain variables are set to certain values, e.g.

```
//@ invariant passwords.isConfidential == true;
```

Object invariants allow to specify that the contents of the passwords container class Computer is confidential. They also allow us to specify that collections contain particular kinds of objects (e.g. that the collection of passwords contains objects of the class Password; Java 1.4 does not guarantee this in its type system) as well as that certain data was initialised during the lifetime of an object, and that certain data is not shared between different objects. These specifications allowed us to diminish chances that the data from the confidential container would leak, that uncontrolled exceptions would occur, and that certain data would be shared in an uncontrolled way.

Pre- and postconditions Each method in Java code is supposed to be called in certain context i.e. it assumes that certain fields of its object are appropriately set, that the parameters come from specific ranges (e.g. between 0 and 10), that a particular parameter has a particular type, and in general that certain relations hold between the input data and/or the fields of the object. Here is an example of such a precondition

```
/*@      requires !mstring.isConfidential && mstring.owner == this ...
  @*/
private ... String decrypt(..., String mstring, ...)
```

In this case we specify that the method decrypt requires the parameter mstring to be not confidential (for instance we may impose the policy that we decrypt only data which is publicly available).

Similarly, it is usually the case that a method guarantees that certain fields are set or that a certain relation between the object state, result and the input data holds. This is done by means of postconditions. We can for instance specify that the result of the decrypt method is confidential and should be protected from exposure in the code of the application.

```
/*@  ... ensures "result.isConfidential && "fresh("result) ...
  @*/
private ... String decrypt(..., String mstring, ...)
```

In this case we specify that the method decrypt requires the parameter mstring to be not confidential (we impose the policy that we decrypt only data which is anyway public). Additionally, we require the result to be fresh i.e. that the resulting object is created inside the decrypt method. This solution is one of the way to prevent from uncontrolled aliasing of the confidential data.

Control over exceptions The exception mechanism used in Java is sometimes insufficient. It is permitted to omit runtime exceptions in throws declarations. ESC/Java2 signals when the runtime exception thrown is not declared in the throws clause. Additionally, the JML specifications allow to describe exactly the conditions which are guaranteed to hold after an exception is raised.

```
/*@ ... signals (EncryptionImpossibleException e1)
  @                          mstring.length() % 2 == 1 ——
  @                          mstring.length() ¡2;
  @*/
private ... String decrypt(... String mstring, ...)
```

In this example, when the EncryptionImpossibleException is raised, the decrypted string has improper format. Here, this means that either the string is too short or has odd length.

JML allows also for other means to control the occurrence of exceptions. In particular, it allows to supplement a variable declaration with an information on whether the variable is allowed to be null. This enables fine-grained control over the occurrence of the NullPointerException. This feature is visible for instance in the way the decrypt method is annotated:

```
private /*@ non'null @*/ ... String decrypt(
                /*@ non'null @*/ String mstring,
                /*@ non'null @*/ String passwordsPassword2)
```

In this case, we allow the decrypt method to be called with non-null parameters only. This method also can only return non-null values. ESC/Java2 checks that whenever the method is called, the actual parameters are non-null. It can also exploit the information that the result is non-null.

We also decided to protect the application against the type-cast errors. The main problem occurs when the collections are used as the operations that return elements of collections usually return objects of the class Object which should have to be subsequently cast to actual types. In JML, this behaviour can be modelled by a property of the collection which contains the elements:

```
/*@ invariant passwds.elementType == "type(Password) && ...
```

In this case, we enforce that the type of elements in the passwds collection is always equal to the type Password.

Specifications of the standard library One more crucial JML feature is its ability to separate the specification from the actual implementation. In this way, we can describe the behaviour of the classes in the standard Java API without modification (or even access) to the actual source code. In this case study, we had to specify the behaviour of the methods in the standard library with regard to the newly added ghost field isConfidential. We also had to add general specifications for some classes which have not been specified yet in the original specification bundle shipped with ESC/Java2.

4.2 The use of ESC/Java2 in the case-study

In order to verify the conformance of the source code to the specifications, we used the extended static checking tool ESC/Java2. This tool translates the JML specifications together with the source code to formulae in the first-order logic and feeds them into the Simplify theorem prover. This prover verifies if there are logical inconsistencies in the formulae, in particular it is able to discover counterexamples to the specified specifications.

The light-weight approach to apply this kind of tool is just to provide some specifications to the source code depending on the development needs (for instance one may decide to introduce non'null annotations only during the development of the application and then afterwards to introduce more thorough annotations whenever a bug is encountered) and after an initial analysis, treat the output of the tool as a false positives list. This list is archived and whenever new features are introduced or bugs fixed the developers can focus on the difference between the original report and the newly generated one.

In this case study, we took another approach. We wanted to get rid of all the warnings to gather as many information on bugs or on inconsistencies in the code as possible.

5 Discovered code inconsistencies

We started the work on the application without significant knowledge of the JML and JML tools like ESC. Both authors of the source code give programming courses, especially Java programming courses so one may assume that the quality of the initial code was at least at the level of an average graduate.

In the course of the code annotation and analysis we discovered the following code flaws:

• We discovered that certain standard library methods we used throw the runtime exception HeadlessException which is not reported in the throws clauses. In order to make sure that the messages in these exceptions do not compromise any sensitive data, we introduced an explicit reporting on exceptions of this kind throughout the code of the application.

• We introduced new exceptions to the application to handle erroneous situations which were omitted during the initial development of the source code.

• We found that a printing of confidential data for debugging purposes had been left in the code.

• We discovered numerous lacking null checks.

• We discovered a few lacking sanity range checks for the data used.

• It turned out several times that we expected the standard GUI library Swing to return non-null results whereas in fact they do not. This was especially appealing as in order to discover that it was really the case that we had to analyse a few subsequent internal calls in the Java standard library.

• We removed methods which leaked references to the content of internal security sensitive information. This was a flaw of the initial design. We decided to remove the methods as they were not used in the solution, but could be exploited in attacker code to compromise integrity and/or availability of the passwords.

• We also gave up one design solution which was connected with the use of interfaces. We used in one class a field of an interface type. The problem with the interface types is that one can extend an existing class to be an implementation of the interface. In this situation, one can obtain very troubling aliasing possibilities which were suggested by the tool. As our focus was on security, we decided to sacrifice the ease of extendability with regard to the issue for a more secure solution when the possibility of the future aliasing is diminished.

• The application contains a graphical user interface. The GUI library is a very big and complicated piece of code. In the course of the case study, it turned out that we made many assumptions on the data exchange between the application and the GUI library during the development stage. Thanks to the tool support we were able to introduce all the necessary checks concerning the data that comes from the GUI library to prevent uncontrolled break down of the application due to bugs or unknown features of the GUI code. It turns out that these additional checks are especially important since the Swing library works partly by means of registering objects for callbacks. As some asynchronous event may trigger such a callback in the middle of the construction process for a bigger object, such a sanity checks may be critical for the secure execution of the resulting application.

6 Encountered problems and deficiencies of the tools

Additional annotation support ESC/Java2 is a tool that checks the conformance of the specifications with the existing source code at compile time. The tool enforces that the process of annotating is local — the specifications that describe the intent for the current piece of code are in its close vicinity. This feature imposes that specifications serve as the documentation for the code. However, some design decisions in one place dictate some solution in a distant place. For instance, requiring non-nullness for certain field may require or imply some other fields to be non-null. What is more, such conscious design decisions may be contradictory. The process of co-ordination for non-null annotations is very tedious and it is sometimes difficult to figure out which real design decisions led to particular contradictions. This process, however, could be automated using known information flow techniques similar to JFlow [4]. A similar remark can be made for the confidentiality annotations that we proposed.

Annotation overhead The annotation process is quite labour intensive. It resembles to some degree providing another implementation of the existing functionality. Still, the descriptions contribute to fewer lines than the real code. In fact, they do not describe the same functionality of the code, but only some of its additional aspects.

Specifications of the standard library Another deficiency of ESC/Java2 is that the standard Java library is not completely covered with specifications. The most basic classes in java.lang or java.util have already been specified in great detail, but there are no specifications for GUI API. We had to provide our own specifications there. This deficiency, however, has one advantage. In order to specify them, we had to analyse the code of the methods which were interesting for us. This revealed that in many cases the specifications provided in the Sun JavaDocs are not sufficient for security purposes.

Human error in specifications There is no guarantee, that the specifications that are written in the application are 100% correct. The process of writing the specs is as error prone as the usual source coding. Still, the double description of the programme behaviour increases the chances that a particular behaviour is the result of a conscious, well founded decision of a programmer or designer.

Bugs and incompleteness of the tools Similarly, there is no guarantee that the tool we used is bug free. Actually, during the course of the case-study a few bugs in ESC/Java2 were discovered. These bugs increased the time needed to develop the whole project. Moreover, the documentation of ESC/Java2 says explicitly that the tool is not sound with regard to the Java semantics. In particular, it does not handle the integer overflow and all memory management problems connected with the execution of a Java programmes. Still, the work with the tool allows to increase the confidence that the application has fewer bugs. The actual application of the tool in the industrial context should be coupled with the common testing techniques.

Problems with modelling in JML The proposed solution to trace the information flow of the confidential data has one deficiency. It allows to trace the flow of objects only and is incapable of tracing the information flow of data encoded as primitive values. We found a workaround for that. We generated a list of method calls in the application and whenever a method with primitive types in parameters was called we inspected the code by hand. This however is not satisfactory and in order to avoid that we face an strong design constraint — the security sensitive applications which are to be checked with tools like ESC/Java2 should wrap the primitive types with objects like Integer or Float.

Another deficiency is difficulty in describing the content of the current stack in JML. This is important when one describes the result of the message printed out after an exception is thrown. It is possible to model this in the current version of JML, but it incurs a high specification overhead.

7 Conclusions

The techniques employed in this case study are still very time consuming and additional tool support to avoid manual annotation of all the information flow paths would be of great value here. However, they are capable of pinpointing certain bugs and source code deficiencies. Assuming that the specification process is similar to the programming and that the verification process using ESC/Java2 is similar to debugging, we can estimate the time needed to develop the annotations that match the source code to be 24 days (assuming typical programming efficiency 20 lines per day).

Although the methods do not give the guarantee of full security, they provide a certain standardised level of assurance that the source code is well written with regard to the assumed threat analysis. They can be used in areas where the high cost of their applicability can be matched with the high cost of possible design or implementation flaws. Moreover, it is usually the case that the reading of the specifications is easier than the reading of the actual source code, as they provide certain abstraction of the functionality. They also give a stable representation of the expected functionality while the implementation is free to change. In this way, these techniques can also contribute to more stable maintainability of the source code.

References

1. Bush, W., Pincus, J., Sielaff, D.: A static analyzer for finding dynamic programming errors. Softw. Pract. Exper. **30**(7) (2000) 775–802
2. Hovemeyer, D., Pugh, W.: Finding bugs is easy. In: OOPSLA'04 Companion, ACM Press (2004) 132–136
3. Evans, D., Larochelle, D.: Improving Security Using Extensible Lightweight Static Analysis. IEEE Softw. **19**(1) (2002) 42–51
4. Myers, A.: JFlow: Practical Mostly-Static Information Flow Control. In: POPL. (1999) 228–241
5. Flanagan, C., Leino, K.R.M., Lillibridge, M., Nelson, G., Saxe, J.B., Stata, R.: Extended static checking for Java. In: PLDI '02: Proceedings of the ACM SIGPLAN 2002 Conference on Programming language design and implementation, New York, NY, USA, ACM Press (2002) 234–245
6. Corbett, J.C., Dwyer, M.B., Hatcliff, J., Roby: Bandera: a source-level interface for model checking Java programs. In: ICSE '00, ACM Press (2000) 762–765
7. Burdy, L., Requet, A.: Jack: Java Applet Correctness Kit. In: Gemplus Developer Conference 2002, Singapore (2002)
8. van den Berg, J., Jacobs, B.: The LOOP Compiler for Java and JML. In: TACAS 2001: Proceedings of the 7th International Conference on Tools and Algorithms for the Construction and Analysis of Systems, London, UK, Springer-Verlag (2001) 299–312
9. Leavens, G.T., Baker, A.L., Ruby, C.: JML: A Notation for Detailed Design. In: Behavioral Specifications of Businesses and Systems. Kluwer (1999) 175–188
10. Burdy, L., Cheon, Y., Cok, D., Ernst, M.D., Kiniry, J., Leavens, G.T., Leino, K.R.M., Poll, E.: An overview of JML tools and applications. Software Tools for Technology Transfer **7**(3) (2005) 212–232
11. Leavens, G.T., Baker, A.L.: Enhancing the Pre- and Postcondition Technique for More Expressive Specifications. In: FM '99: Proceedings of the Wold Congress on Formal Methods in the Development of Computing Systems-Volume II, London, UK, Springer-Verlag (1999) 1087–1106
12. Ruby, C.D.: Safely creating correct subclasses without seeing superclass code. In: OOPSLA '00: Addendum to the 2000 proceedings of the conference on Object-oriented programming, systems, languages, and applications (Addendum), New York, NY, USA, ACM Press (2000) 155–156
13. Chalin, P.: Improving JML: For a Safer and More Effective Language. In Araki, K., Gnesi, S., Mandrioli, D., eds.: FME 2003: Formal Methods, International Symposium of Formal Methods Europe. Volume 2805 of LNCS., Springer (2003) 440–461
14. Meyer, B.: Object Oriented Software Construction, Second Edition. Prentice Hall (1997)
15. Cok, D.R., Kiniry, J.R.: Esc/Java2: Uniting ESC/Java and JML: Progress and issues in building and using ESC/Java2 and a report on a case study involving the use of ESC/Java2 to verify portions of an Internet voting tally system. In Barthe, G., Burdy, L., Huisman, M., Lanet, J.L., Muntean, T., eds.: Construction and Analysis of Safe, Secure, and Interoperable Smart Devices: International Workshop, CASSIS 2004. Number 3362 in LNCS, Marseille, France, Springer (2004)
16. Detlefs, D., Nelson, G., Saxe, J.B.: Simplify: a theorem prover for program checking. J. ACM **52**(3) (2005) 365–473
17. Barnett, M., Leino, K.R.M., Schulte, W.: The Spec# programming system: An overview. In: Construction and Analysis of Safe, Secure and Interoperable Smart devices (CASSIS). Number 3362 in LNCS, Springer (2004) 49–69

18. Barnett, M., Chang, B.Y.E., DeLine, R., Jacobs, B., Leino, K.R.M.: Boogie: A modular reusable verifier for object-oriented programs. In: Fourth International Symposium on Formal Methods for Components and Objects (FMCO'05), Post-Proceedings. LNCS (2006) to be published.
19. Breunesse, C., Cataño, N., Huisman, M., Jacobs, B.: Formal methods for smart cards: an experience report. Science of Computer Programming **55** (2005) 53–80

Formalizing Software Refactoring in the Distributed Environment by aedNLC Graph Grammar

Leszek Kotulski, Adrian Nowak

Institute of Computer Science, Jagiellonian University
Nawojki 11, 30-072 Kraków, Poland
kotulski@agh.edu.pl, nowaka@ii.uj.edu.pl

Abstract. Being a commonly used technique to enrich the software structure, refactoring – as well as any software changes performed every day – still lacks a good formal definition. Especially in the distributed environment there is a great need for a better mechanism allowing to avoid conflicts and properly merge the changes introduced by different developers. In this paper we continue our project of a core of distributed environment based on graph repository, which helped us to defeat and significantly decrease problems of refactoring conflicts. We focus on technical aspects of the environment and present precise description of the refactorings with the help of aedNLC graph grammar and graph transformation mechanisms. We also discuss some other properties of the graph repository including its abilities to store dynamic software description. Presented approach is based on UML notation, however it could be easily extended for any object-oriented language. The graph repository concept alone could lead to a model of a modern integrated software development environment.

1 Introduction

Modifying and maintaining existing software has become an important part of the job of software developers. Any changes made to the software (code or model) should contribute to this software evolution and maturity. Some operations might change the behavior of the software while others just modify the structure. These changes which improve object-oriented software while preserving its behavior are well known as refactorings [1, 2]. When applied properly, refactorings help in many ways to improve not only the software itself [1] but also the whole process of software development and maintenance.

Nowadays there exists a number of tools to support such operations for many different programming languages, e.g. Refactoring Browser [3] for Smalltalk or Eclipse [4] for Java. A great deal of research in this area was conducted, but not much focused on formalizing the refactoring and its properties. Furthermore, the distributed environment, used naturally in case of any application developed by a team, was not taken into account. We try to deal with both these issues in the paper – formalize refactoring in the distributed environment – since it is essential to take into account all the factors which may have any influence on the refactoring operation.

Please use the following format when citing this chapter:

Kotulski, L., Nowak, A., 2006, in IFIP International Federation for Information Processing, Volume 227, Software Engineering Techniques: Design for Quality, ed. K. Sacha, (Boston: Springer), pp. 349–360.

As pointed in [5, 6, 7] many problems appear when two developers decide to make refactorings, in a parallel way, on the same software. As a very simple example, even an Encapsulate Variable and a Move Variable refactorings applied to the same variable by different developers cause a structural conflict, due to lost of the variable identification in the system [7].

As a formal framework, we use graph-based representation, utilizing Mens's notation [8]. However we extend the approach by introduction of the graph repository concept [7] and online graph transformations controlled by aedNLC graph grammar [9]. We compose refactorings from simple grammar productions, and provide atomicity by a special execution environment. This formalism allows us to describe and synchronize refactoring operations and also – under some conditions – exclude many conflicts.

In the next section of the paper we present a concept of graph representation of the software structures, where refactorings are represented as graph transformations. Section 3 overviews appearance of refactoring conflicts in a collaborative environment and some other common refactoring problems specific for team software development. Section 4 introduces formal definitions. Section 5 describes details of representing refactorings as aedNLC grammar productions. Section 6 shows how the refactoring conflicts can be automatically excluded using this approach. Some other properties of the repository are also discussed. Finally, section 7 concludes our work and proposes some future research.

2   Software as a graph

An idea of representing software as a graph is very reasonable and quite natural, hence commonly used in research [8, 10] and tools [4]. Compared with tree based representations it does not only allow to represent static relations between program elements but also dynamic relations such as method call, variable access and late polymorphism binding.

2.1   Metamodel

A graph representation of all allowed connections between potential software components as well as all necessary attributes is known as a metamodel. Formally it is also called a type graph [11, 8]. An example of a simplified metamodel for object-oriented programming language (or UML class diagram) was presented in [7] and is now extended to distinguish method definitions – following Mens [8] – see figure 1.

Graph nodes are labeled by: "Class" for nodes representing classes (or types), "MethodDef" for method definitions, "Method" for method signatures, "VariableDef" for variable definitions, "Variable" for variable signatures and "Parameter" for method parameters. The separation between the definition and the method or variable itself is crucial as we have to provide a possibility to introduce many definitions of a single component within a hierarchy (due to late binding and polymorphism). We use the UML notation, relying on the composition (depicted as filled rhombi) as the most suitable for representing strong inclusion between main and part components – further

called a <<member>> relation. Other relations are represented by attributed references. Multiplicities of the relations are written along edges as number, range, or an *
(asterisk) in case of being not strictly defined. We do not interfere with methods bodies (as [8] by introducing an expression component) – this is another hierarchy level
(after package and class levels) in hierarchical graph which we normally use as a full
metamodel – not essential to present in this paper. The OCL[12] in turns allows us to
express constraints to exclude illegal components and relations in the instance graph,
that is for example exclude two methods or two variables with the same signature
within a class.

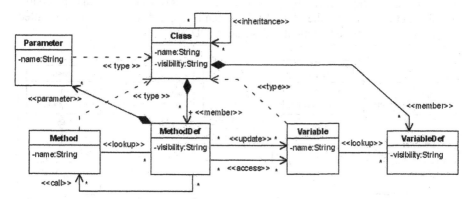

Fig. 1. Simple metamodel.

For better understanding of the metamodel let us take a look at its sample instance
(Figure 2). Now we operate on particular components instances with given names and
attribute values.

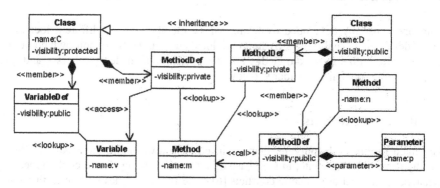

Fig. 2. Example of the metamodel instance.

The relations "m is a member method of class C" or "v is a member variable of the
C" or "m calls n" can be expressed by a suitable node interconnection, presented appropriately by compositions and associations. A real example of Local Area Network
with program code and method definitions was presented in [8].

2.2 Refactorings

We assume that any changes made to the software will have one-to-one mapping inside the software instance graph. The result of such changes might be very simple, like a single attribute change, but can be also quite complicated like change to thousands of expressions appearing throughout the project.

An example of a Move Variable refactoring representation is depicted in figure 3. There are two graphs describing the software fragment – before and right after the transformation (as a result of applying a single grammar production or a whole set of productions). Usually refactorings can be processed only when particular preconditions are met [2, 10] (here the Move Variable can be applied when the variable called "v" is not already defined within the class named "D").

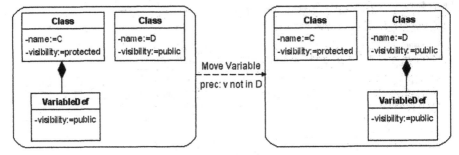

Fig. 3. Move Variable refactoring and its precondition - *v is not in D*.

3 Distributed environment

Software is usually developed by teams, which members are in different locations. These developers usually work in their own local environments on their own copies of the software, without any knowledge about modifications made by others – and this may cause the problems considered below.

3.1 Refactoring conflicts

The main problem of applying changes in collaborative environment are conflicts, usually detectable quite late, in the phase of software merging. These could appear as syntactic, structural or semantic conflicts [6] – the first two types will be further considered in the paper.

Let us get back to the example mentioned in the introduction. Suppose two developers decide to make changes involving the same variable from the same class. One of them performs the Encapsulate Variable refactoring (changing visibility and adding setter and getter methods) while another performs the Move Variable refactoring (from the class named "C" to another named "D"). When, probably after a sequence of other modifications, developers finally decide to share new versions with the rest of the team, the second developer should encounter a problem - conflicts will appear in all places where the variable was accessed or updated. The issue is that when using any of currently existing commercial tools (e.g. the Eclipse [4] with external version control system like CVS) the source codes of all classes are sent as text. This way we are able to detect only very basic conflicts, and often there is no possibility to avoid them. If we just try to automate the merging, we may lose the result of one refactoring or get two similar variables [7]. In consequence, quite frequently a developer has to realize what was really modified and decide which operation should be accepted. In many cases it might be even necessary to redo some operations. Moreover, sometimes such decisions must be discussed with the rest of the developer team.

3.2 Graph repository

Number of conflict possibilities arise together with the number of changes being applied. If we are able to imagine a sequence of refactoring operations on the same piece of code or a group of such sequences, then it is easy to imagine that conflicts number might increase dramatically[1].

Further, when concerning large refactorings performed step by step even through few days (and so interacting with many other changes, no matter how carefully planed), it is easy to notice that a kind of long term control mechanism is necessary.

The mentioned mechanism should also support ordinary developers work, that is provide possibilities such as undo the changes (including refactorings) or history and version management.

Refactoring tools already utilize a full code description but currently all analysis is done in complete separation from the rest of the distributed environment. We suggest to utilize a graph repository, introduced by us in [7]. The internal graph describing current state of the maintained software will be modified by a graph transformation system [13] according to software changes. The term "graph repository" is used on purpose, to put the emphasis on concurrent access to the graph. We assume that the graph should give us a possibility of unique components identification. It is an instance of the metamodel and additionally may hold some technical attributes for better description and analysis of refactoring preconditions as well as performance issues.

4 Formal definitions

The solution presented in the paper is supported by an aedNLC graph grammar [9, 13, 14, 15], so the basic properties of this grammar should be outlined.

---

[1] Important issue here, not only applicable when considering distributed environment, is providing a possibility of operation grouping in order to get better performance e.g. by gathering preconditions or finding context once.

4.1 EDG Graph

The graph generated by grammar consists of nodes and directed edges; both nodes and edges are labeled (its general properties are established e.g. a can node represent class or method) and attributed (the individual components properties are defined e.g. class name).

An attributed directed node- and edge-labeled graph, EDG graph, over Σ and Γ is a quintuple H = (V, D, Σ, Γ, δ), where:

V   – is a finite, non-empty set of nodes, to which unique indices are
             ascribed, defining the order within the set

Σ – is a set of attributed node labels

Γ – is a set of attributed edge labels

D   – is a set of edges in the form of (v,μ,w) where w, v $\in$ V and $\mu \in \Gamma$

δ: V$\rightarrow\Sigma$ – is a function, which labels the nodes.

For the metamodel presented in the section 2.1 we should have:

Σ = {"Class", "Method", "MethodDef", "Variable", "VariableDef", "Parameter"}

Γ = {<inheritance>, <member>, <type>, <parameter>, <call>, <access>, <update>, <lookup>}

4.2 Graph transformation

Any graph grammar production P is represented by a left-hand (L) and a right-hand side (R) graphs and an embedding transformation E, thus P=(L, R, E). Modification of the graph H, describing a current state of the system, is made by applying graph grammar production. First, a subgraph of the H, that is homomorphic (by a homo-morfism h) to L is localized (so the subgraph is equal to h(L)), next h(L) is removed from H and the right-hand side graph R is placed instead; the embedding transformation E specifies a way in which the nodes of the graphs R and H-h(L) should be associated by edges. The left-hand and right-hand sides of productions could be easy presented graphically, but the embedding transformation is rather described using a special notation.

The equation E(γ, in, v) = {(Q, (X, π), μ, in)} is interpreted as follows: every edge labeled by "γ" and coming into (thus "in" or "out" will be used to show a direction) the node h(v) within the graph H should be replaced by an edge connecting a node (w) labeled by "Q" from the right–hand side graph R with a node labeled by "X" from the rest of the graph (H-h(L)) on condition that the formula π is fulfilled (for the nodes belonging to this edge). Newly introduced edge will be labeled by "μ" and will come into the node w. In order to simplify the notation, we assume that the dangling edges (not described by E) will be connected to a node (inside right-hand side graph R) with the nodes designated as follows:

- if the removed node (u$\in$L) appears in the right-hand side of production (i.e. exist node with the same index as u) the edge will be connected to this node
- otherwise the edge will be connected to the least node inside R with the same label as u.

The above rule we will call COPY_REST embedding transformation rule.

The homomorphism used have to be unambiguously defined, so when the left-hand-side graph of the considered production consists with a single node v_L then we assume the homomorphism is defined as a unique homomorphism from the node v_L to the node for which the production is applied that is v. Note that, in such a case the embedding transformation is equivalent to the one introduced in [9, 16].

Application of productions should be done in context of the repository graph H by a special Derivation Control Environment (DCE). The proposition of DCE usage is based on previous solutions that were utilized to control the software allocation process in a distributed system [14] and to describe a behavior of the mobile agent systems [13].

The DCE services developers and system requests; when a request appears either a waiting control thread is activated or a new thread of control is created for starting point.

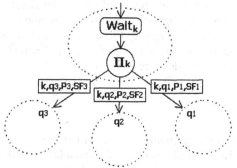

Fig. 4. Derivation control environment.

The DCE can be interpreted as a diagram (see Figure 4) connecting control points (the dotted circles) inside which a synchronizing functions $Wait_k$ (if exist) and a selector Π_k are sequentially evaluated. The synchronizing function $Wait_k$ is evaluated basing on the current graph value and the queue of requests (that have to be sent to the DCE). If this evaluation fails then the control point activity will be delayed until the environment changes (i.e. a new request appears), otherwise the selector Π_k is evaluated (also basing on the same elements) and designates the proper transition. The transition not only moves the activity to the next control point but also both a semantic function and the graph grammar production (pointed out as edge attributes – SF_i and P_i) are performed. The semantics function (associated with the transition):

- adds new request to the order queue (requesting some actions from refactoring system),
- removes the request, which is serviced from the queue,
- evaluates parameters of the right-hand side graph of the production.

When the production P is applied to the current graph H a new graph H' is created in a way defined by the transformation rules of the graph grammar associated with this derivation control diagram.

Introduction of the concurrent threads of control simplifies the DCE description, however to assure proper data modifications we have to introduce a general synchronization rule: each thread of control has exclusive access to the data representing graph H and to the requests queue in the period beginning from $Wait_k$ evaluation to the moment when a new graph H' is created.

5 Refactorings as aedNLC grammar productions

As described in the section 2.2 any refactoring corresponds to the graph repository transformation. To introduce such transformation we need to be able to apply an adequate grammar production. However, due to restrictions on the graph, graph grammar and performance issues, we will usually need several productions to define a single refactoring. For this we will further utilize the derivation control mechanism described in the previous section. In order to easily describe refactorings we will use parameterized productions – to locate nodes of the left-hand side L of production by graph indices and to avoid ambiguous definition of the homomorphism h. For simplicity, due to one-one mapping, we will also incorporate all information from "VariableDef" and "MethodDef" nodes into "Variable" and "Method" accordingly. Let us introduce productions for considered refactorings.

5.1 Move Variable

The MoveVariable refactoring should take effect not only in origin (C) and destination (D) classes but also in all places where the variable was updated or accessed (e.g. in Java by adding new imports or class prefixes). Fortunately this information is associated with VariableDef node, so embedding transformation consist only of the COPY_REST rule.

An adequate part of the derivation control diagram is presented in Figure 5. The condition Π_1 corresponds to the MoveVariable refactoring precondition that is "*v is not in D*". The Move variable production P_{mv} is the same as the transformation shown previously in Figure 3.

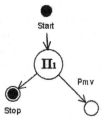

Fig. 5. A part of the appropriate DCE for MoveVariable(v, C, D).

5.2 Encapsulate Variable

The EncapsulateVariable should make the considered variable v a private, add get() and set() methods as well as introduce calls to these methods in all places where the variable was accessed or updated. We can provide three separated productions – two for introducing the methods (Figure 6a, 6b) and one for changing the variable attribute (Figure 6c) – the sequence is controlled by dedicated DCE fragment (Figure 6d). The embedding transformations are, accordingly:

$$E_1(<access>, in, 2)) = \{(Method, (Method, true), <call>, out)\}$$

$$E_2(<update>, in, 2)) = \{(Method, (Method, true), <call>, out)\}$$

$$E_3 \Leftrightarrow COPY\_REST$$

The condition Π_1 is checking whether the methods set() and get() already exist in class "D", Π_2 is always true and Π_3 checks if the variable is public (in case it is not no production is applied).

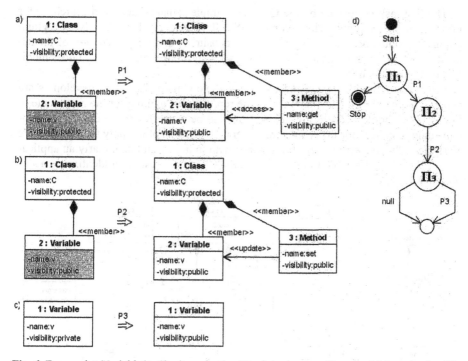

Fig. 6. EncapsulateVariable(v, C). a) production P1 - introduces get() method, b) production P2 - introduces set() method, c) production P3 - changes the variable visibility to private, d) DCE used to control application of these productions.

6 Graph repository idea revisited

Our approach supporting global refactoring consists of Graph Management System[7] (GMS) and a few Local Refactoring Environments (LRE). The GMS maintains the graph repository. Each of LRE performs the sequence of the following tasks:

- asking the GMS for searching a part of the graph associated with the refactoring operation (and possibly, synchronize it with the others) – find_context request
- performing the refactoring operation basing on the code,
- informing the GMS that the refactoring operation has to be performed – Move_variable, Encapsulate_variable requests
- updating the code maintained by LRE on GMS demands.

The first task performed by the GMS is a simple semantic action of searching for information in the graph. The second GMS task is associated with applying a graph grammar production (modifying the graph repository) and with execution of the semantic action (which requests all LREs to update the code maintained by nodes modified by this production).

Let us trace the above schema on the example (Figure 7a). Both developers are choosing some components to modify – the repository is looking for the right context. For unique identification of the components and better performance the GMS maintains unique indices for every node in the graph. An attempt to apply the Encapsulate Variable to "v" results on identifying nodes with indices 1 and 2,similarly an application of the Move Variable to move "v" from "C" to "D" results in identifying nodes with indices 1, 2 and 3.

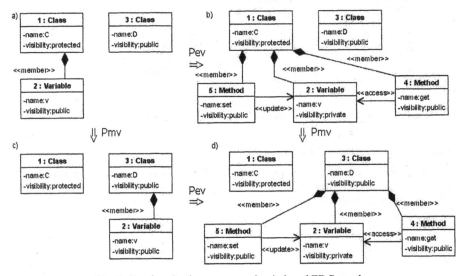

Fig. 7. Synchronization process using indexed EDG graphs.

After the context of these operations has been established we can read and share this part of graph in a parallel way. The Move variable and Encapsulate variable requests on the nodes can be serviced by DCE. However sometimes the request can not be served or can be only served partially with respect to preserving some of preconditions associated with the request. Let us note the important role of the semantic actions, that are tracing the graph modification (associated with the embedded transformation) and creating the refactoring orders for all LREs maintaining the source code associated with this graph modification.

Finally, in cooperation, both LREs and the GMS update the graphs to new instances. It is easy to notice that the order in which the developers make synchronization does not matter (Figure 7d). The key assumption for this method is that both productions have to preserve nodes indices.

It is easy to find out that the following conflicts pointed by [5] can be excluded in the same way:

- Rename Variable and Move Variable applied to the same variable,
- Rename Variable and Variable Encapsulate applied to the same variable,
- Rename Variable and Pull Up Variable applied to the same variable,
- Rename Method and Pull Up Method applied to the same method,
- Rename Method applied twice (separately by two developers) to the method within the same class,
- Rename Variable applied twice to a variable within the same class.

While dealing with other conflicts, when adding new components or deleting existing ones, the proposed method is not useful. To avoid such conflicts we have to exclude concurrent execution of the conflicted refactoring operations. This is a simple task from synchronization point of view (some operations can be delayed until global predicates, based on attributes, are fulfilled). This solution is still difficult to approve by developer teams. One of the developers should wait, however now the time of waiting is considerably decreased (only one refactoring operation should be completed instead of a full sequence). Moreover, introduction of the graph repository causes that developers are informed about conflict just in the time when it appears, while earlier they were informed after finishing of sharing a new software version.

7 Conclusions

In the paper we propose a solution dealing with refactoring conflicts based on [5] classification. Introduced graph repository concept, properly transformed (under control of graph grammars) is completely enough to defeat the kind of conflicts where the key problem was losing method or variable identification while merging the changes. The introduced environment allows us to solve these conflicts automatically.

In order to prove the theoretical value of the method the centralized service of the graph repository is sufficient, but in the practical solution it seems that the repository should be distributed (together with system source code). Fortunately, for the aedNLC graph grammar semi-parallel derivation mechanism over the distributed graph has been introduced [13]. Moreover, the parser of aedNLC graph grammar is based on

ETPL(k) graph grammar with O(n2) computational complexity [16] and the effectiveness is the most important issue in the system working online. Graph parsing will be useful when describing and allocating the nested distributed system [6], we can utilize it to exchange whole subgraphs in case of complex refactorings.

The graph repository could be further utilized by holding additional attributes of the software, also including dynamic parameters suitable to calculate metrics and using these to perform automate refactorings. Derivation control diagram is able to manage refactoring compositions to introduce patterns and should be extended to manage plans of large refactorings (under interactive control of a developer).

References

1. Fowler, M.: Refactoring: Improving the Design of Existing Programs. Addison-Wesley (1999)
2. Opdyke, W.F.: Refactoring: A Program Restructuring Aid in Designing Object-Oriented Application Frameworks, Ph.D. thesis, University of Illinois at Urbana-Champaign (1992)
3. Roberts, D., Brant, J., Johnson, R.: A Refactoring Tool for Smalltalk, Theory and Practice of Object systems (1997) 253-263
4. Eclipse Foundation, http://www.eclipse.org/eclipse/, The Eclipse Project (2005)
5. Mens, T., Taentzer, G., Runge, O.: Detecting Structural Refactoring Conflicts Using Critical Pair Analysis. Electronic Notes in Theoretical Computer Science, Vol. 127(3) (2005) 113-128
6. Mens, T.: A state-of-the-art survey on software merging, IEEE Transactions on Software Engineering 28(5) (2002) 449-462
7. Kotulski, L., Nowak, A.: Graph Repository As a Core of Environment for Distributed Software Restructuring and Refactoring, 24th IASTED International Conference on Applied Informatics, Insbruck (2006)
8. Mens, T., Eetvelde, N., Janssens, D., Demeyer, S.: Formalising Refactoring with Graph Transformations, Journal of Software Maintenance and Evolution (2004) 1001-1025
9. Flasiński, M., Kotulski, L.: On the Use of Graph Grammars for the Control of a Distributed Software Allocation, The Computer Journal, 35(1) (1992) 167-175
10. Roberts, D.: Practical Analysis for Refactoring, Ph.D. thesis, University of Illinois at Urbana-Champaign (1999)
11. Engels, G., Schurr, A.: Encapsulated Hierarchical Graphs, Graph Types and Meta Types, Electronic Notes in Theoretical Computer Science (1995) 2
12. Warmer, J., Kleppe, A.: The Object Constraint Language: Precise Modeling with UML, Addison-Weslay (1998)
13. Kotulski, L.: Parallel Allocation of the Distributed Software Using Node Label Controlled Graph Grammars, Krakow, Poland, Jagiellonian University, Inst. of Comp. Science (2003)
14. Kotulski, L.: Model systemu wspomagania generacji oprogramowania współbieżnego w środowisku rozproszonym za pomocą gramatyk grafowych (in Polish), Krakow, Poland, Jagiellonian University Press (2000)
15. Kotulski, L.: Graph representation of the nested software structure, Proc. 5th International Conference on Computational Science, Atlanta, GA (2005) 1008-1011
16. Flasiński M.: Power Properties of NLC Graph Grammars with a Polynomial Membership Problem, Theoretical Computer Science, 201(2) (1998) 189-231

Minik: A Tool for Maintaining Proper Java Code Structure[*]

Jacek Chrząszcz[2], Tomasz Stachowicz[1],
Andrzej Gąsienica-Samek[1], and Aleksy Schubert[2,3]

[1] Comarch SA, Warsaw, Poland
[2] Institute of Informatics
Warsaw University, Poland
[3] SoS Group NIII,
Faculty of Science, University of Nijmegen, Netherlands

Abstract. Maintaining discipline of code in an evolving software project is known to be difficult. We present Minik, an automatic tool written in Java and for Java, that assists technical managers to enforce high and medium level design decisions on programmers. The tool supports hierarchical encapsulation of software components and helps to maintain order in dependencies between parts of the project's source code and to control calls to external libraries.

Minik was created to support the development of Ocean GenRap Report Generator, a complex Java project of over 350KLOC, developed in Comarch Research Center. With time, it became an invaluable help for technical managers as well as for new programmers who could quickly learn the structure of the code base.

1 Introduction

Development of large software projects often escapes traditional waterfall software creation methodology. This concerns in particular systems of big complexity, such as compilers, database engines or modern spreadsheets. Agile approach to software creation process seems much better suited to this kind of software, which is by nature in constant development, improving (hopefully) with each release in terms of enhanced functionality and stability. However, this kind of iterative development style may easily lead to overly complicated code, where almost every part of code depends on every other. Such structure is very difficult to maintain and develop [21], so it is crucial to create methodologies and tools supporting project managers in their task of limiting the code complexity without precluding integration of new features and improvements.

Mainstream programming languages, such as Java, offer some support for hierarchical code organization, but the support is limited. While encapsulation on the level of one file (class) or one directory (package) is supported by the language, higher level encapsulation is left to the programmer. In particular, even if files are placed in a hierarchical directory structure, from the Java programming language point of view the package structure is flat. As far as e.g. method visibility is concerned, two classes

---

[*] This work was partly supported by KBN grant 3 T11C 002 27 and Sixth Framework Programme MEIF-CT-2005-024306 SOJOURN.

---

may either be from the same package or from different ones, regardless if they are just in sibling directories or far away apart in the directory structure. Consequently, a modification of a method annotated as *public*, may potentially require the knowledge needed to modify any part of the program.

Moreover, the flexibility of these design standards and programming language grouping constructs like packages make it easy to introduce circular dependencies. The experience in software development shows that circular dependencies cause problems [9, 17, 23, 26] so the acyclic coding pattern occurs often in project design guidelines [7, 16, 18]. Cyclic dependencies are regarded as a strong factor in measures of code complexity [27] especially when maintainability of code is of the main interest [15]. Moreover, the presentation of code dependencies in form of a DAG (directed acyclic graph) has already been used in the context of support for maintainability [2] and easy extensibility [19].

In this paper we present Minik, the code management tool, primarily created to support orderly development of the Ocean GenRap Report Generator [10] by the Comarch Research Center. Minik supports a true hierarchical encapsulation and enforces a transparent and simple acyclic dependency structure. In a project managed using Minik, dependencies on distant packages are declared in a separate .minik management file of each component. The tool makes sure that all dependencies are declared and that they form an acyclic structure. Programmers are required to run Minik at every build, so the dependency descriptions are always up-to-date. Moreover, a modification of the .minik file, requires the consent of the technical manager. Experience shows that these changes tend to happen less and less frequently. Minik is also useful in enforcing certain design patterns, e.g. Facade or Bridge [11], which can be recorded in the .minik files and hence become harder to break by programmers.

Another important aspect of Minik is the possibility to constrain the usage of external dependencies inside the project. Minik can immediately enforce the manager's decisions that e.g. JDBC classes can only be used in the DAO implementation or that the class java.lang.Thread can only be used in the main package of the application and not inside components. Any programmer trying to break this policy, either by haste or unawareness, will immediately be warned by Minik and forced to correct the mistake.

The adoption of Minik by GenRap programmers turned out to be very smooth. After an initial reluctance, a natural people's reaction to any limitation, the programmers started treating the Minik discipline as part of the limitations of the programming environment, like e.g. Java type system. Moreover, since .minik files constitute only a fraction of the whole code (less than 1%), they proved to form a very good guide for programmers which were new to the GenRap project.

Minik implements the core functionality of the Kotek methodology. The latter, presented in [12], is an advanced module system combined with a build tool, that extends Minik with precise inter-component contract specifications, parametrisation of large code fragments with respect to some interface (e.g. widget library) and conditional compilation, depending e.g. on a hardware platform.

The present paper is organized as follows. In the next section we describe basic features of Minik and limitations that it puts on the project structure in order to maintain clarity. In the presentation we use a simple example of a toy project MiniEdit, whose structure is a (substantial) simplification of the structure of GenRap. Then we present and explain the syntax of the .minik files and describe the impact of Minik on the development of the GenRap project.

2 The structure of software projects

The complexity of contemporary software structure has led to several approaches aiming to conceptually simplify dependency diagrams of software. Most approaches rely on providing the developers means to present the code interdependencies and coupling them with source code quality metrics. Examples of systems in this category are [5,6,13,22,24]. The systems give guidance to good source code structure, but do not enforce or enforce in a weak manner the structural rules which are appropriate for the project at hand.

Another approach is represented by MJ [3], a rich system of modules for Java. In this case, the software modules are the grouping entities which forbid accesses which are not explicitly declared in module descriptions. This mechanism, however, does not impose any structural restrictions on the way the dependencies are organized.

Yet another approach to structuring the source code consists in the use of a type system which controls the read or write access to particular pieces of the code. In this case, a separation between different code pieces is governed by local annotations in the source code (or in the comments in the source code) that specify which classes are intended to be used as a single module. Examples of systems in this group are [4,8,28]. These systems allow to describe detailed data dependencies up to the level of fields in objects.

2.1 Software project structure enforced by Minik

We describe here the structure of projects that is enforced by our tool and methodology. We focus on greater units of source code, called modules or components. Conceptually, the basic ones should contain several classes or packages, the complex ones consist of several sub-components (and possibly a few additional classes). To introduce the notions addressed by Minik, we use a simple example of a hypothetical editor MiniEdit, whose structure is a considerable simplification of the structure of the GenRap project.

The strength of Minik results from the structure of possible interdependencies between components that describe the way the source code is organised. We consider two perspectives of code organisation. The first one, vertical, corresponds to the hierarchical division of the project into components, components into sub-components and so forth. The second one, horizontal, describes functional dependencies between fragments of code. Other Java module systems did not consider explicitly these code organisation facets [1,3,14].

2.2 Vertical structure

The hierarchical structure of the project that is enforced by Minik corresponds well to good organisational patterns in which hierarchical connections allow to avoid communication blow-up between different organisational units. This kind of code

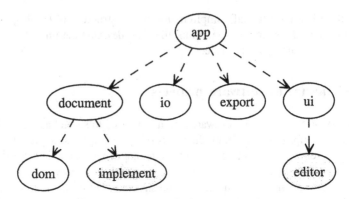

Fig. 1. The vertical structure of the MiniEdit project.

management support is often present in programming languages. The Java package system, in which packages correspond literally to the directory tree of the development site, is the most notable example of it. In our example (Fig. 1) the MiniEdit application (represented by the topmost component app) is divided into four components of which two have sub-components. Minik strengthens the Java package system by enforcing a true hierarchical encapsulation: it is forbidden to refer to the insides of a component without its permission. We discuss it further at the end of the next section.

2.3   Horizontal structure

By horizontal structure of the project we mean functional dependencies between components of our project. We say that an entity (class/package/component) M depends on another entity N when the source code in M refers a class, a method or a value in N. Figure 2 presents the graph of dependencies between main components of the MiniEdit application. In order to obtain a system with low maintenance cost, we impose several restrictions on the structure of possible references between components.

The first restriction is based on the assumption that functional dependencies between components should form a DAG. The experience in software development shows that circular dependencies cause problems, especially when maintainability of the code is of the main interest.

Of course, cyclic dependencies are not problematic when they occur in a fragment of code whose size is small enough to be easily grasped by a programmer. Therefore Minik does not prevent dependency cycles between classes belonging to one component, but only the *big* cycles, i.e. involving classes in several components.

Dependencies and encapsulation The second restriction concerns the vertical structure that we introduced earlier. It is based on a natural principle that one should not manipulate the internals of another component, unless explicitly authorised. In our example the document.minik file declares the dom sub-component as exported (see Fig. 5 and its description in Sect. 3), but not the implement sub-component (marked gray in Fig. 1). Consequently, the code in e.g. ui may use the (public) classes defined in app.document.dom, but not those defined in app.document.implement.

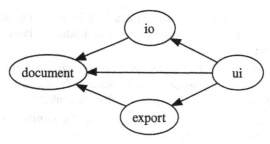

Fig. 2. The horizontal structure of the middle layer of MiniEdit.

3   Syntax and example

The usage of Minik is directed by .minik files, which are placed in most directories of the project source tree. The syntax of those files is very straightforward (see Fig. 3). We explain it here, using our MiniEdit example, whose structure is depicted in Fig. 1 and 2.

The contents of a .minik file consists of four parts. The first one, starting with the keyword **use**, specifies the dependencies of the the given component. In Fig. 4, one can see the contents of the main .minik file of the MiniEdit application, app.minik, so its first line specifies external dependencies of the whole project: the Java standard library and an (imaginary) library to produce PDF documents. For internal components, such as ui (Fig. 6), one specifies dependencies on (parts of) external components of the whole projects (like java_lang, java_ui) and other components of the project (document, io, export).

The second section contains definitions of restricted components. They are used to control which parts of external dependencies are used where in the project source. In general, from the dependency control point of view, a component is simply a name attached to a list of class names. Consequently, a definition of a restricted component consists just in creating a new name for the list of classes obtained by restricting the list attached to the original component. One can use the following optional restriction operations:

- positive restriction – keyword **allow** – from the list of class names of the original component, we select only those which match at least one of the given class patterns,
- negative restriction – keyword **deny** – from the list of class names, we subtract those which match one of the given class patterns.

Of course if both restrictions are omitted the new component is just a renaming of the original one.

In case of app.minik, we name various parts of standard library and the PDF writer in order to precisely say, in the next section of app.minik, which classes can be used in which components. The third section describes how sub-components of the given component depend on one another, on external components and on restricted components. For example, it is easy to see that the ui component depends on all other sub-components of app and that it is the only one allowed to manipulate reflection, threads and other java_lang classes not included in java_core. Besides, only export can access classes of pdfwriter, and only those defined in the topmost package, not internal ones. A special name **this** can be used as the target of the last build clause (see e.g. Fig 5) to indicate what dependencies are allowed in classes from the current directory.

Since the name of a sub-component c_1 can only be used as a dependency of the another sub-component c_2 after the corresponding **build** c_1 clause, the structure of dependencies cannot contain cycles.

The last part of the .minik file lists the names of the sub-components to be exported. This is where hierarchical encapsulation is implemented: other components can only refer to those parts of the current component which it explicitly lists as exported.

In case of the topmost .minik file of the application, the **return** clause only indicates the component containing the class with the main method.

<minik>	::=	*<use><define>* .. *<define><build>* .. *<build><return>*
<use>	::=	**use** *<ident>* .. *<ident>*
<define>	::=	**define** *<ident>* = *<ident>* [**allow** {*<package>*, .., *<package>*}]
		[**deny** {*<package>*, .., *<package>*}]
<package>	::=	*<ident>*.*<package>* | *<ident>* | * | **
<build>	::=	**build** *<thident>* : *<ident>* .. *<ident>*
<return>	::=	**return** *<thident>* .. *<thident>*
<thident>	::=	**this** | *<ident>*

Fig. 3. Syntax of .minik *files.*

use *java pdfwriter*

define *java_core* =
  java **allow** { *java.lang.* }
      deny { *java.lang.Class, java.lang.ClassLoader, java.lang.Compiler,*
          java.lang.Process, java.lang.Runtime, java.lang.Thread }
define *java_lang* = *java* **allow** { *java.lang.* }
define *java_io* = *java* **allow** { *java.io.*, java.nio.** }
define *java_xml* = *java* **allow** { *javax.xml.**, org.xml.**, org.w3c.dom.** }
define *java_ui* = *java* **allow** { *java.awt.**, javax.swing.**, javax.print.** }

define *pdf* = *pdfwriter* **allow** { *com.pdfwriter.* }

build *document* : *java_core*
build *io* : *document java_core java_io java_xml*
build *export* : *document pdf java_core java_io*
build *ui* : *document io export java_lang java_ui*

return *ui*

Fig. 4. The file app.minik *of MiniEdit.*

use *java_core*

build *dom* : *java_core*
build *implement* : *dom java_core*
build this : *dom implement java_core*

return *dom* **this**

Fig. 5. The file document.minik *of MiniEdit.*

Every directory of the project can have its own .minik file. If it is missing, all classes in the directory and its subdirectories are treated as one basic component.

use *document io export java_lang java_ui*

build *editor* : *document java_lang java_ui*
build this : *editor document io export java_lang java_ui*

return this

Fig. 6. *The file* ui.minik *of MiniEdit.*

Its exported classes are those declared as public. In MiniEdit the document and ui components have their own .minik files. The document.minik file is given in Fig. 5. It specifies the Facade design pattern: the dom sub-component defines the interface, i.e. the data object model together with the names of the operations that can be performed on the document. Next, the implement sub-component contains the actual implementation of the data structure representing the edited document. It may use the dom sub-component, for example to say that some classes of implement are instances of interfaces defined in dom. The classes in the document directory relate the specification and implementation, for example by providing factory functions returning an object created by a class from implement, satisfying an interface specified in dom. The last line says that only the classes exported by the dom component and classes in the document directory can be used outside document.

The file ui.minik, presented in Fig 6 is similar to document.minik, but the interface part is not placed in a separate sub-component.

It is worth noting how the use of the external component pdfwriter can be traced in the project using the .minik files. Indeed, app.minik tells us to look only in the export component and nowhere else.

How Minik *works.* The most important part of Minik is the recursive function *minik_fun* operating on an environment which maps component names to sets of Java class names.

The initial environment describes the external dependencies of the project and is created from the arguments supplied by the user in the invocation of Minik. One of the arguments is the directory containing .jar files of the dependencies. By default, for each dependency M, the file M.jar should be placed in this directory, apart from the java component, which is found in the standard location of the Java installation. For our example, the only external dependency file is pdfwriter.jar.

The initial environment passed to the first invocation of minik_fun is created by scanning the .jar files of dependencies.

The function *minik_fun* takes an environment E and a directory name D, and returns the set of names of classes exported by the component located in the directory D.

If the .minik file is missing in the directory D, the function just checks the legality of the dependencies of all classes in D and its sub-directories: it is verified that all referenced class names are in the range of the environment E. The returned set of classes includes all public classes of D and its sub-directories.

If .minik is present in D, minik_fun operates in four steps, corresponding to sections of .minik. The first step consists in checking that dependency names listed in the **use** clause are valid, i.e. they are in the domain of the environment. In the second step the **define** clauses are processed: the environment E is extended with restricted components. In the third step, for each clause **build** $c : d_1 \ldots d_n$, the function *minik_fun* is called recursively with the environment $E|_{d_1 \ldots d_n}$ (i.e. E restricted to the dependencies allowed for the sub-component c) and directory name D/c, which checks correctness of the dependency structure of the sub-component c and returns the set of classes C_c exported by c. The mapping $c \mapsto C_c$ is then added to E for the processing of subsequent sub-components. If the last build clause is of the form **build this** : $d_1 \ldots d_m$, the legality of dependencies of classes in D is checked: all referenced class names must be members of the components $d_1 \ldots d_m$. The last step is the processing of the **return** $c_1 \ldots c_k$ clause. It is checked that $c_1 \ldots c_k$ are components built in step 3 (and not external or restricted components) and the set of all classes exported by components $c_1 \ldots c_k$ is returned as the result of *minik_fun*.

4   GenRap: The Minik experience

Ocean GenRap [10] is a complex application of over 350 thousand lines of code, written mostly in Java. It is a report generator for database applications, allowing for intuitive and easy edition of reports with constant data view, enabling data analysis directly in the edited document. It has a graphical user interface, similar to modern text editors or spreadsheets, and a novel live context association mechanism, allowing the user to move fragments of reports between documents. GenRap has the possibility to connect to a number of database engines and export the generated report to popular formats, including pdf and html. It is available as part of the CDN OPT!MA system [20] since mid 2005 and as a standalone application since January 2006.

The development of GenRap started in 2003. Since then, it has been actively developed by a dozen of enthusiastic programmers, following an agile development methodology. There is no precise long term development plan, only the product vision from which the detailed plan for a following couple of months is derived. The vision itself is modified as new features are implemented and users give their feedback. Such cycles usually take two to three months. During that time two processes are done in parallel: implementation of new features and maintenance, consisting in bug-fixing and code refactoring.

From the historical perspective, the need for a tool helping to manage the code became clear after a few months of intensive coding, when the code reached 40 thousand lines. In order to be maintainable the project needed a strict regime in encapsulating and separating components. A simple bash script to separately compile components in restricted environments was used at first. If the code contained a disallowed dependency the compilation just stopped with an error.

Later, it was decided that this policy was too strict. For productivity reasons, a developer should be able to build the project with bad dependencies, but a patch supplied to the central repository should always ensure a correct dependency structure.

Minik was implemented with this idea in mind. The tool automatically checks the structure of the code without completely preventing defective builds. Apart from that, other correctness tests were incorporated to Minik, which are beyond the scope of this paper.

As experience shows, the .minik files constitute between 0.5% and 1% of the whole code (see Fig. 7). It turns out that they are modified more-less in one out of 10

Month	Patches				Source Code					
	P	PM	PM/P	PLOC	NM	LM	NJ	LJ	NM/NJ	LM/LJ
2004-10	67	2	2.98%	5 970	65	1065	1106	124 283	5.87%	0.85%
2004-11	136	15	11.02%	35 871	66	1158	1120	146 076	5.89%	0.79%
2004-12	78	8	10.25%	57 856	70	1216	1219	159 238	5.74%	0.76%
2005-01	53	14	26.41%	70 518	75	1282	1246	178 340	6.01%	0.71%
2005-02	65	17	26.15%	73 442	79	1388	1330	187 130	5.93%	0.74%
2005-03	89	13	14.60%	38 898	100	1734	1372	199 035	7.28%	0.87%
2005-04	33	6	18.18%	15 013	106	1871	1459	220 518	7.26%	0.84%
2005-05	66	13	19.69%	43 454	113	1960	1512	227 104	7.47%	0.86%
2005-06	105	12	11.42%	22 368	125	2200	1612	244 235	7.75%	0.90%
2005-07	85	5	5.88%	89 641	126	2245	1638	249 815	7.69%	0.89%
2005-08	114	5	4.38%	10 940	127	2260	1653	251 459	7.68%	0.89%
2005-09	89	1	1.12%	7 699	129	2292	1662	254 513	7.76%	0.90%
2005-10	130	10	7.69%	51 236	129	2292	1676	257 662	7.69%	0.88%
2005-11	191	19	9.94%	42 754	137	2431	1746	278 380	7.84%	0.87%
2005-12	190	12	6.31%	44 669	158	2683	1864	311 194	8.47%	0.86%
2006-01	130	2	1.53%	14 965	164	2758	1921	327 098	8.53%	0.84%
2006-02	119	9	7.56%	44 640	164	2761	1939	332 677	8.45%	0.82%
2006-03	115	12	10.43%	49 366	164	2768	1923	326 754	8.52%	0.84%
2006-04	20	4	20.00%	38 420	168	2864	2002	345 471	8.39%	0.82%
Total	1875	179	9.54%	757 720						

P = Total no of patches   PM = No of patches touching .minik
PLOC = Total no of lines of code patched
NM = No of .minik files   LM = LOC of .minik
NJ = No of .java files   LJ = LOC of .java

Fig. 7. GenRap development statistics.

commits. Thanks to the good structure, the project enjoys a stable growth in lines of code per month and the project managers are not afraid to improve any of its components. Indeed, since it is easy to see what depends on a given fragment of code, it is possible to foresee the impact of a planned refactoring on the rest of the code base.

Currently the GenRap code is divided into around 170 hierarchic components, described by as little as 2800 lines of .minik files. Almost all of these files are smaller than 50 lines, the average being about 17. Their structure is also very simple so they are very easy to understand.

Using Minik in the project has also a positive psychological impact on the programming team's integrity. The programmers do not feel intimidated by a manager pointing out their structure errors. Instead, they just treat limitations imposed by Minik as part of the limitations of the working environment: the language, the compiler, design patterns and Minik.

The tool itself is written in Java, it has about 3000 lines and uses a custom class file parser. To increase its integration with the working environment an Eclipse plugin for Minik has been developed. It is rather basic, but nevertheless it is possible to automatically start the verification process and easily access the files with bad dependencies.

5   Conclusions

The need to synchronize architecture documents with the actual source code is a very important aspect of modeling. Many tools supporting UML technology, e.g IBM Rational Software Architect [25] or Microsoft Visual Studio [29], have included utilities to synchronize source code changes with the evolution of the visual model, which is called round-trip engineering. However, the tools based on UML emphasise early project development stages. In particular, they provide clustering and encapsulation mechanisms in the design stage of software production but these architectural decisions are weakly enforced in the coding and maintenance stages. Moreover, they do not encourage comprehensive arrangement of construction blocks and so complicated diagrams are commonly encountered.

In this paper, we have presented Minik, a light-weight tool to maintain proper structure of Java projects, realized in Comarch Research Center as a development utility for the Ocean GenRap Report Generator. Minik supports the technical managers in enforcing acyclic structure of inter-component dependencies and helps programmers understand and maintain the structure of the project. It supports true hierarchical encapsulation of software components, helps tracking where external dependencies are used in the code and permits to foresee the impact of planned refactoring.

Thanks to Minik and its consistent use in project management, the development pace of GenRap is steady for over two years without increasing the programmers team. It turns out that the structure of the code grows as fast as its size and therefore the development does not lead to bloated code which is often a nightmare in large software projects.

References

1. Davide Ancona and Elena Zucca. True Modules for Java-like Languages. In *ECOOP '01: Proceedings of the 15th European Conference on Object-Oriented Programming*, pages 354–380, London, UK, 2001. Springer-Verlag.
2. Liz Burd and Stephen Rank. Using Automated Source Code Analysis for Software Evolution. In *1st IEEE International Workshop on Source Code Analysis and Manipulation (SCAM 2001), 10 November 2001, Florence, Italy*, pages 206–212, 2001.
3. John Corwin, David F. Bacon, David Grove, and Chet Murthy. MJ: A Rational Module System for Java and its Applications. In *Object-Oriented Programming, Systems, Langauges & Applications*, 2003.
4. Dave Clarke and Sophia Drossopoulou. Ownership, encapsulation and the disjointness of type and effect. In *OOPSLA '02: Proceedings of the 17th ACM SIGPLAN conference on Object-oriented programming, systems, languages, and applications*, pages 292–310, New York, NY, USA, 2002. ACM Press.
5. Mike Clark. Jdepend. http://www.clarkware.com/software/JDepend.html.
6. Compuware. JavaCentral. http://frontline.compuware.com/javacentral/tools/26222.asp.
7. Compuware. Optimaladvisor supersedes the Package Structure Analysis Tool. Technical report, JavaCentral, 2005.
8. W. Dietl and P. Müller. Universes: Lightweight ownership for JML. *Journal of Object Technology (JOT)*, 4(8):5–32, October 2005.
9. Martin Fowler. Reducing Coupling. *IEEE Software*, July/August 2001.
10. Ocean GenRap report generator. Comarch Research Center. http://ocean.comarch.pl/genrap/.

11. Erich Gamma, Richard Helm, Ralph Johnson, and John Vlissides. *Design Patterns: Elements od Reusable Object-Oriented Software*. Addison-Wesley Professional Computing Series. Addison-Wesley, New York, NY, 1995.
12. Andrzej Gąsienica-Samek, Tomasz Stachowicz, Jacek Chrząszcz, and Aleksy Schubert. KOTEK: Clustering of The Enterprise Code. In Krzysztof Zieliński and Tomasz Szmuc, editors, *Software Engineering: Evolution and Emerging Technologies*, volume 130, pages 412–417. IOS Press, 2005.
13. Alex Iskold, Daniel Kogan, and Goran Begic.   Structural analysis for java. http://www.alphaworks.ibm.com/tech/sa4j.
14. Yuuji Ichisugi and Akira Tanaka. Difference-Based Modules: A Class-Independent Module Mechanism. In *ECOOP '02: Proceedings of the 16th European Conference on Object-Oriented Programming*, pages 62–88, London, UK, 2002. Springer-Verlag.
15. Stefan Jungmayr. Testability Measurment and Software Dependencies. In *Software Measurement and Estimation, Proceedings of the 12th International Workshop on Software Measurement (IWSM2002)*. Shaker Verlag, 2002. ISBN 3-8322-0765-1.
16. Kirk Knoernschild. Acyclic Dependencies Principle. Technical report, Object Mentor, Inc., 2001.
17. J. Lakos. *Large-scale C++ software design*. Addison-Wesley, 1996.
18. Robert C. Martin. *Agile Software Development, Principles, Patterns, and Practices*. Prentice Hall, 2002.
19. D. Notkin and W. G. Griswold. Extension and software development. In *ICSE '88: Proceedings of the 10th international conference on Software engineering*, pages 274–283, Los Alamitos, CA, USA, 1988. IEEE Computer Society Press.
20. CDN OPT!MA. Comarch. http://www.comarch.pl/cdn/Products/.
21. A. Podgurski and L. A. Clarke. A Formal Model of Program Dependencies and Its Implications for Software Testing, Debugging, and Maintenance. *IEEE Transactions on Software Engineering*, 16(9):965–979, 1990.
22. Neeraj Sangal, Ev Jordan, Vineet Sinha, and Daniel Jackson. Using dependency models to manage complex software architecture. In *OOPSLA '05: Proceedings of the 20th ACM SIGPLAN conference on Object-oriented programming, systems, languages, and applications*, pages 167–176, New York, NY, USA, 2005. ACM Press.
23. Barry Searle and Ellen McKay. Circular Project Dependencies in WebSphere Studio. *developerWorks, IBM*, 2003.
24. Chris Smith. Japan. http://japan.sourceforge.net/.
25. Ibm Rational Software Architect. http://www-306.ibm.com/software/awdtools/architect/swarchitect/.
26. J. Soukup. *Taming C++*. Addison-Wesley, 1994.
27. Lassi A. Tuura and Lucas Taylor. Ignominy: a tool for software dependency and metricanalysis with examples from large HEP packages. In *Proceedings of Computing in High Energy and Nuclear Physics, 2001*, 2001.
28. Jan Vitek and Boris Bokowski. Confined types. In *OOPSLA '99: Proceedings of the 14th ACM SIGPLAN conference on Object-oriented programming, systems, languages, and applications*, pages 82–96, New York, NY, USA, 1999. ACM Press.
29. Microsoft Visual Studio 2005. http://msdn.microsoft.com/vstudio/.

Multidimensional Legacy Aspects of Modernizing Web Based Systems

Henryk Krawczyk[1], Konrad Dusza[1], Łukasz Budnik[1], Łukasz Byczkowski[1]

[1] Gdansk University of Technology,
Faculty of Electronics, Telecommunications and Informatics
ul. Gabriela Narutowicza 11/12, 80-952 Gdańsk, Poland

Abstract. The paper presents basic legacy transition techniques used in software lifecycle either on system or component levels. It discusses a user case of the Endoscopy Recommender System. It also considers an impact of requirements, programming platforms, software development strategies and software standards on legacy status of web applications.

1 Introduction

With web technologies developing at a growing pace and IT systems being adopted into business models, there occur situations where increasing number of companies face the urging need for serious changes in their IT systems [1]. Legacy Information Systems can be defined as "any IT system that significantly resists modification and evolution" [2] that most often are the IT backbone of a company [3]. In general, the topic of Legacy Information Systems has been thoroughly examined and the common problems are well identified [3][4][5]. Even though, case studies show that no miracle cure for "migration migraine" has been developed. However, there are three main concepts regarding coping with Legacy Information Systems. These are [3] (from the most lightweight, to the most revolutionary one) as follows:

Wrapping – accomplished by developing a small software component that connects a legacy component with a new component. A wrapper serves as a translator in communication between these components.

Migration – a much more complex approach, used when both wrapping and re-development cannot be afforded either in terms of risk level or when transition between components must be transparent.

Re-development – means developing a component from scratch, usually re-implementing a component in a different programming language.

All these strategies can be deployed on both the system level and on the component level. For instance, we could wrap the business tier, re-develop presentation tier and migrate data tier in a web application.

The next section discusses attributes that describe legacy characteristics of web-based legacy IT systems. Section 3 describes a solution for legacy problems supported by a real-world case study. It concerns modernizing Endoscopy Recommender

Please use the following format when citing this chapter:

Krawczyk, H., Dusza, K., Budnik, Ł., Byczkowski, Ł., 2006, in IFIP International Federation for Information Processing, Volume 227, Software Engineering Techniques: Design for Quality, ed. K. Sacha, (Boston: Springer), pp. 373–378.

System working at the Medical University of Gdańsk. Besides, it provides a general methodology of developing legacy transition strategies in web based IT systems. The concluding section presents general suggestions relating to inclusion of legacy factors into software life-cycles.

2 Legacy Attributes of Web Applications

One can define a typical web-based legacy information application as a system which functions are crucial for supporting business in the company of which upgrade involves a high degree of risk. One example is an e-shop based on Apache 1.3, Perl CGI-scripts and MySQL 3.2 DBMS in which business logic and presentation layer are intertwined. The main questions concerning legacy issues are: When does a system become a legacy one? When a transition cannot be avoided? A legacy system is a system that still fulfills software requirements imposed by the contract under which the system has been developed.

Below is the analysis of engineering-related external factors that are the catalysts of changes in the system. They can be divided into four main categories: extra functional requirements and expectations, technological platform changes, software architecture modifications, standards and interoperability support. These categories of changes are illustrated in Fig.1 – Fig. 4.

The most common reason for serious improvements in an information system are changes in software requirements. Apart from functional ones, there are groups of other requirements that are often not fulfilled in the first version of a system. The increasing importance of different kinds of requirements in time is suggested in Fig.1.

Fig. 1. Distribution of requirements importance in web based systems.

Today, there is a plethora of technologies that support web application development (see Fig.2). Decision on rewriting a web application to a different technological platform can be taken to: achieve better scalability, efficiency and maintainability; show customers that the company uses the newest technologies; merge with other systems written in other technologies. Some migrations are easy to conduct from that point of view, eg. from PHP3 to PHP5, others require quite an effort (eg. PHP to J2EE). In most cases, change of technological platform by itself should not be the only reason to conduct migration.

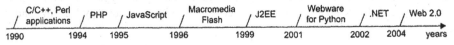

Fig. 2. Utilization of technological progress in web application development.

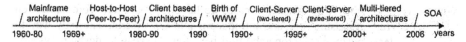

Fig. 3. Trends in distributed software architecture development.

Switching between different technological platforms is often accompanied by a decision to improve system's architecture during migration (see Fig.3).

Software architecture evolves towards multi-tiered applications and SOA [7], which are meant to be the tools for achieving business flexibility in on-demand solutions. However, real-world web-based legacy systems often have data, business and presentation intertwined, which is often a result of inappropriate development process and setting aside the principles of software design for the sake of approaching deadlines.

During migration process, we might want to use a different software engineering methodology than the one used during development of a legacy system. The will to reconstruct the system in a different way is rarely the sole reason to migrate. Similar situation arises with quality management. Migrations are often occasions to introduce quality management into the software development process. In general quality management can contribute to the fact that the system will not be considered as a legacy one for a long time.

Web application environments also include a numerous group of quickly evolving standards that the application should comply with (see Fig.4). Introducing new functionalities into application often involves conforming to a certain web standard, eg. news headlines in RSS. When some web standards supersede others a web application that does not conform to new standards is often considered legacy. However, in most cases, wrappers should be a sufficient solution for such problems.

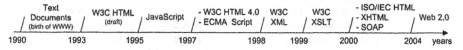

Fig. 4. Evolution of standards for web applications.

When determining the legacy status of an application, we should firstly determine its current position on each of these timelines. The distance between the present date and the latest date corresponding to the desired state of the system is a measure for the system's legacy level, which will help to determine the need for software development. If a difference can be seen only in one or two aspects, then perhaps a simple transition should be reconsidered. If not, developing a complex, component-level transition strategy is recommended, with carefully planned use of wrapping, migration and re-development techniques.

Another legacy aspect is system interoperability, meaning, that if maintenance phase changes distort system's communication with other systems, then the other systems become legacy ones. Such situation is usually unacceptable for most of primary system's users. For example, our e-shop cooperates with another e-shop, which was forced to change technology platform from ASP.NET to J2EE. Previously, we used .NET remoting to access another shop's data, now we have to switch to either

Web Services or Java RMI. In such a case, we have to create new communication module or wrap an existing one and introduce it into our system. The only way to avoid or at least postpone interoperability-driven transitions is to develop systems with high flexibility and extendibility. However, it is a very difficult task in practice.

3   A Solution for Legacy Problems with ERS Example

Transformation types discussed in Section 2, were applied in ERS development as shown in Table 1. The first implementation of the Endoscopy Recommender System (ERS) was deployed in 1997 as a standalone application, without using web technologies. The next generations of the system were introduced in 2001 and 2005 respectively. Table 1 presents a detailed history of the system along with technologies employed in each generation of the system and theirs key features.

Table 1. History of ERS development.

Version, release date	Features	Used tech-nologies	Legacy transformation approach
ERS 1, 1997	Database of patients and examination data. Reports and statistics generation.	MS-DOS, Clipper	none (first ERS version)
ERS 2, 2001	MST standardization of examination descriptions, client-server architecture, replication of medical data for reliability improvement.	Windows and Linux, PHP4, MySQL 3.23, Java 1.2, Apache 1.2	re-development (transition to web based platform)
ERS 3, 2005	New, three-tiered architecture, DVD medical data analysis, security, safety and data integrity assurance. Addition of new reports and other functions requested by client.	Windows and Linux, PHP5, MySQL 5, Apache 2, XML, XSLT, SOAP	DBMS communication wrapping, inner-system data-flow migration to XML, presentation and business tier re-development

As shown in Table 1, the system became legacy two times, in 2001 and 2005. The reasons for transitions were as follows:

1. System requirements were defined incrementally because of extra needs of system users – physicians.
2. Personnel rotation in system development team of successive versions (always students of our faculty, each time with better knowledge of new software technology)
3. Emergence of new web technologies provided means for achieving better implementations of functionalities and higher quality.

Below, we focus on transition from ERS 2001 to ERS 2005. Among different approaches we have decided to use the following one:

1. Begin with architectural changes.

2. Switch to a new technology (writing new source code).
3. Implement new functionalities.

This approach allows us to transform the system into a three-tiered application in natural way. Medical environment is very volatile, which urged ERS to be highly flexible and adaptive. Its component architecture was developed mainly to fulfill that need. Development of a new, properly tiered architecture enabled designing a system engine based on XML and XSLT processing. Transition to the latest PHP, MySQL and Apache versions available made it possible to implement a broader set of requirements.

The ERS database engine was migrated from MySQL3 to the newest MySQL5 and took full advantage of its new DBMS features (see Table 1). All broken interrelations were copied into separate database. Medical data collected by many years should never be deleted or discarded. Instead, they should be stored in safe and secure archives – this data is a great source of information. Foreign key constraints were added – responsibility for foreign key checks was transferred from programmers to DBMS and is processed automatically without any interference. New ERS uses also trigger mechanism for consistency checks during e.g. delete operations. Data storage engine was moved from MyISAM to InnoDB. Transaction support was implemented in the target system and the new ERS now works in fully transactional mode.

To cope with intertwined business logic tier, our team created a template of the ERS business logic, which proved very useful in further development. Previously, business logic of the system was highly integrated with other tiers, which forced programmers to carefully analyze this aspect and separate respective business functions. As a result, an XML file was created, which contained data describing division of business functionalities into modules and structure of entire system. Later we used the XML business logic files to automatically generate directory tree, database queries and even code templates for the system, which was achieved by building different sets of XSL transformation sheets. XML business logic files also helped developers to keep references between parts being re-developed and corresponding functionalities in the legacy version of ERS. We found this feature particularly useful when assuring that the new version meets all functional requirements that the old system met.

Although the ERS interface turned to be proper for managing functionalities offered by the system, and it did not need updating itself, a new system architecture forced developers to isolate presentation logic from the rest of a system, which was highly interspersed with business and data tier's code in the previous ERS generation.

Knowledge collected during earlier stages of ERS development helped to decide, which parts of the system can be transformed and how. Analyses of risk, costs and benefits have shown that the structure of legacy data in the system should remain unchanged. What could have been done was the creation of wrappers enabling accessing previous, legacy-structured data-tier in order to migrate to new MySQL5 DBMS with all the latest transaction techniques. The rest of the system was re-developed in correlation with new ERS system architecture. It guaranteed easy modifications and expansion, which is highly valued in system user's environment.

Our experience gained during the development of ERS 2005 shows that a methodology to create transition strategy can be developed and included in a software lifecycle development. A system becomes legacy one during maintenance phase, when system's current features no longer satisfy the needs of users and its environment. Moreover, the legacy state is periodic, and should be expected in every life-cycle regardless of software engineering techniques and technological frameworks used. Web applications are even more endangered to legacy issues as the technologies used in this area of IT are not mature and evolve faster than in other areas.

4   Conclusions

Software life-cycles foresee the needs for smaller changes of software and its requirements during different phases and at the same time neglect the legacy issue caused by both user requirements changes and technological progress. The legacy boundary is often flexible and the legacy state is proclaimed arbitrarily by business-related managers regardless of the life-cycle.

In order to conduct a transition from a legacy system to a newly developed one, one of the three approaches can be adopted both on system and a component level. These approaches are wrapping, migration and re-development. They differ in terms of software re-use that can be applied and the effort that has to be committed to the transition process.

Our work on ERS has shown that further legacy transitions of information systems are inevitable. However, the integration of the legacy state into our software life-cycle should reduce the cost of future legacy transition, due to greater flexibility of a system architecture and design. In this case, previous transition took 18 months, and the present one – 15 months, measuring from the decision to initiate legacy transition to deployment of the final product.

References

1. Flawn D, The Legacy Systems Dilemma Fujitsu, Legacy Migration, http://www2.cio.com/consultant/report2337.html
2. Brodie M., Stonebraker M., Migrating Legacy Systems: Gateways, Interfaces and the Incremental Approach, Morgan Kaufmann Publishers, Inc. USA, 1995
3. Bisbal J., Lawless D., Wu B., Grimson J., Legacy Information System Migration: A Brief Review of Problems, Solutions and Research Issues, Computer Science Department, Trinity College, Dublin, Ireland 1999
4. Hassan A. E., Holt R. C. A Lightweight Approach for Migrating Web Frameworks, Software Architecture Group (SWAG), Department of Computer Science University of Waterloo, Waterloo, Canada 2004
5. Hassan A. E., Holt R. C. A Visual Architectural Approach to Maintaining Web Applications, Software Architecture Group (SWAG), Department of Computer Science University of Waterloo, Waterloo, Canada 2002
6. Krawczyk H., Knopa R., Kruk S., Mazurkiewicz A., Zieliński J., Predictive-incremental strategy of application development, KKIO 2001, Otwock, Poland
7. OASIS, Reference Model for Service Oriented Architecture, http:// www.oasis-open.org/committees/download.php/16628/wd-soa-rm-pr1.pdf